Shojo Beat

From Me to You

Vol. 27

Story & Art by
Karuho Shiina

Volume 27

Contents

Story Thus Far

Sawako Kuronuma has always been a loner. Though not by choice, this optimistic 16-year-old girl can't seem to make any friends. Stuck with the unfortunate nickname "Sadako" after the haunting movie character, rumors about her summoning spirits have been greatly exaggerated. With her shy personality and scary looks, most of her classmates will barely talk to her, much less look into her eyes for more than three seconds lest they be cursed. Thanks to Kazehaya, who always treats her nicely, Sawako makes her first friends at school, Ayane and Chizu. Eventually, Sawako finds the courage to date Kazehaya.

Sawako can't decide whether to go to a local university with Kazehaya or attend an educational university in Sapporo once she graduates. This momentous decision is the cause of their first big fight, but when they open up about what they really want, their relationship deepens. When their schoolmate Kurumi stays over at Sawako's house for a study date, she apologizes about the way she acted in the past and asks Sawako to attend the educational university with her. Meanwhile, Sawako's friend Ayane is totally preoccupied by her crush on her tutor, Pin—and then she randomly runs into him at the train station! It's becoming harder and harder for her to hide the way she feels about him...

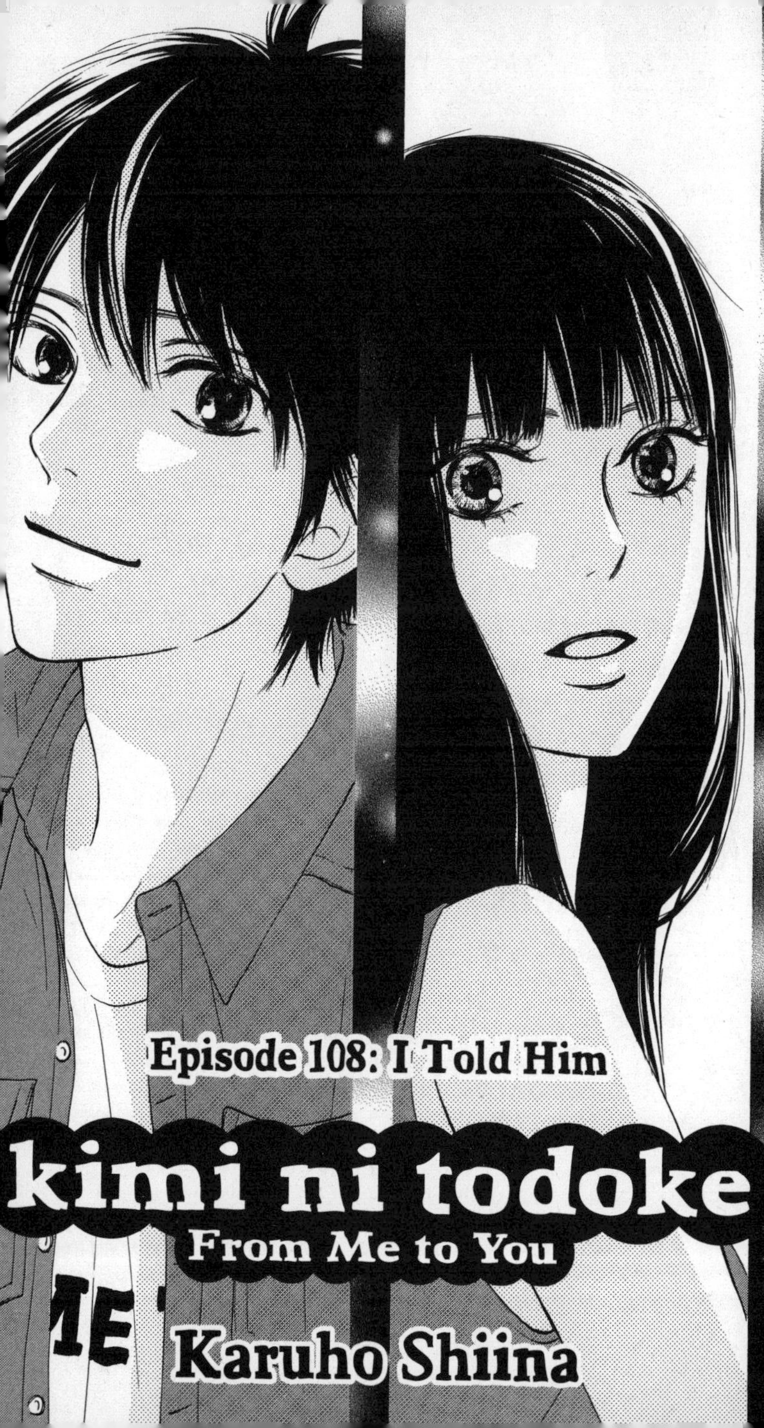
Episode 108: I Told Him
kimi ni todoke
From Me to You
Karuho Shiina

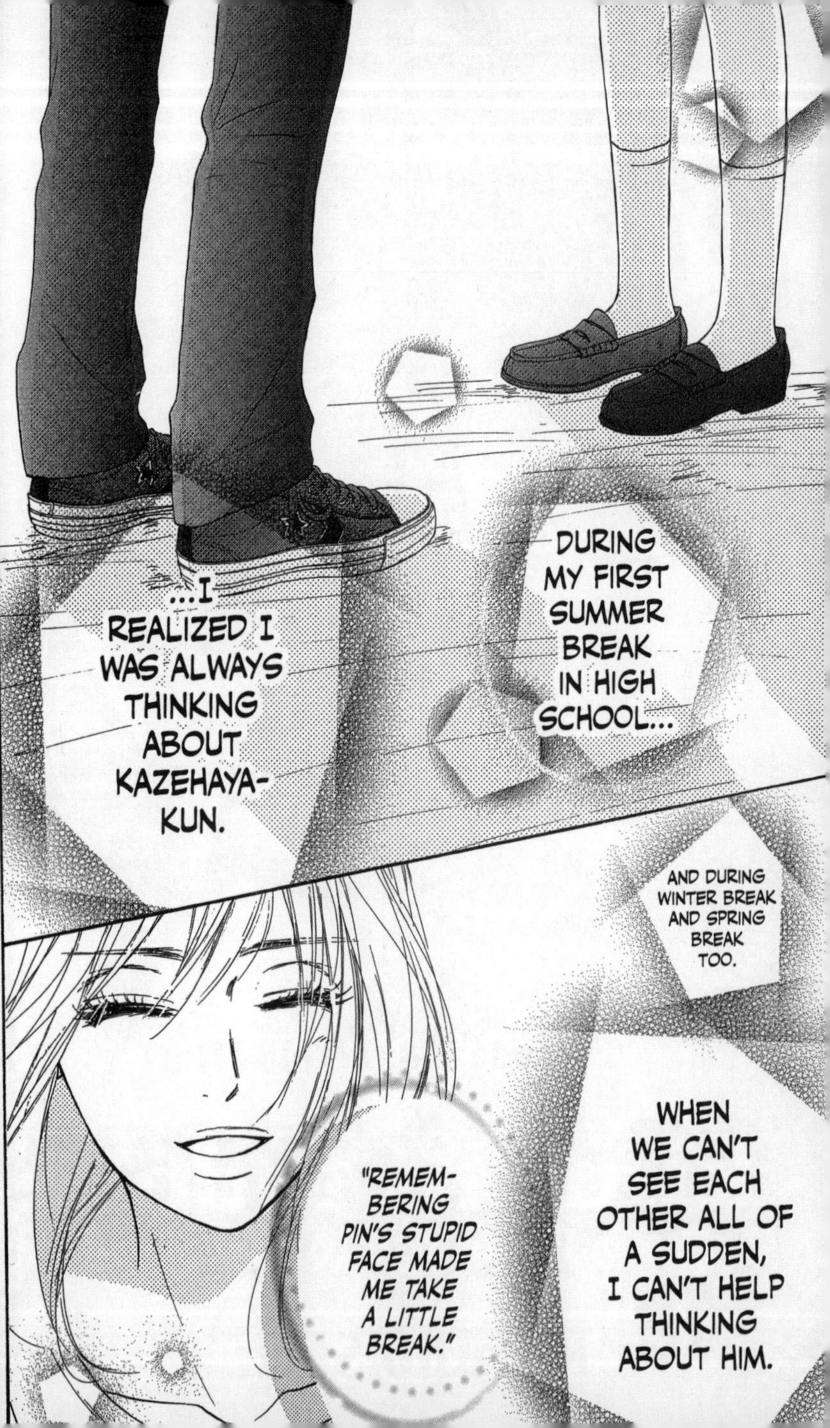
DURING MY FIRST SUMMER BREAK IN HIGH SCHOOL...
...I REALIZED I WAS ALWAYS THINKING ABOUT KAZEHAYA-KUN.
AND DURING WINTER BREAK AND SPRING BREAK TOO.
WHEN WE CAN'T SEE EACH OTHER ALL OF A SUDDEN, I CAN'T HELP THINKING ABOUT HIM.
"REMEM-BERING PIN'S STUPID FACE MADE ME TAKE A LITTLE BREAK."

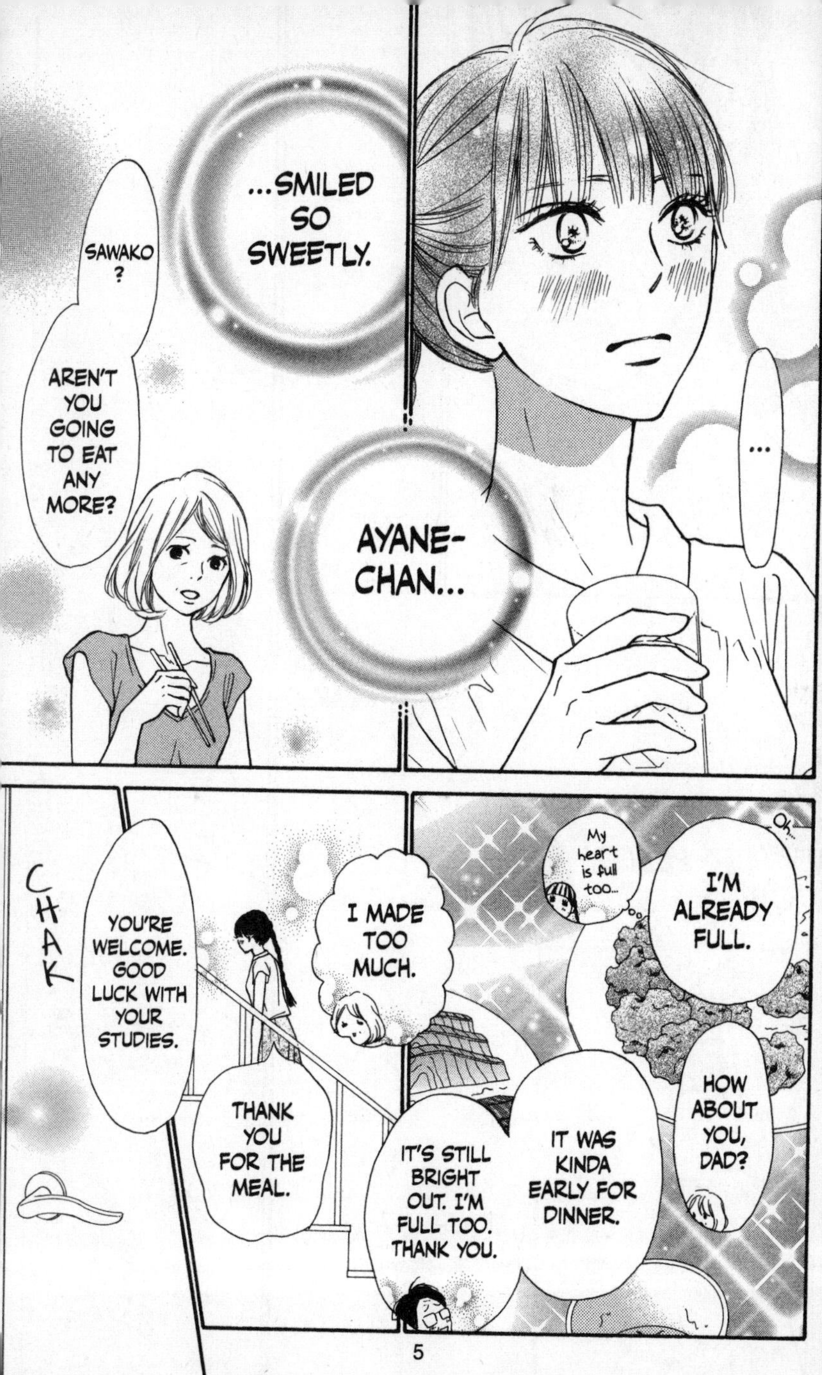
...SMILED SO SWEETLY.
AYANE-CHAN...
...
SAWAKO?
AREN'T YOU GOING TO EAT ANY MORE?
Oh...
I'M ALREADY FULL.
My heart is full too...
HOW ABOUT YOU, DAD?
IT WAS KINDA EARLY FOR DINNER.
IT'S STILL BRIGHT OUT. I'M FULL TOO. THANK YOU.
I MADE TOO MUCH.
THANK YOU FOR THE MEAL.
YOU'RE WELCOME. GOOD LUCK WITH YOUR STUDIES.
CHAK

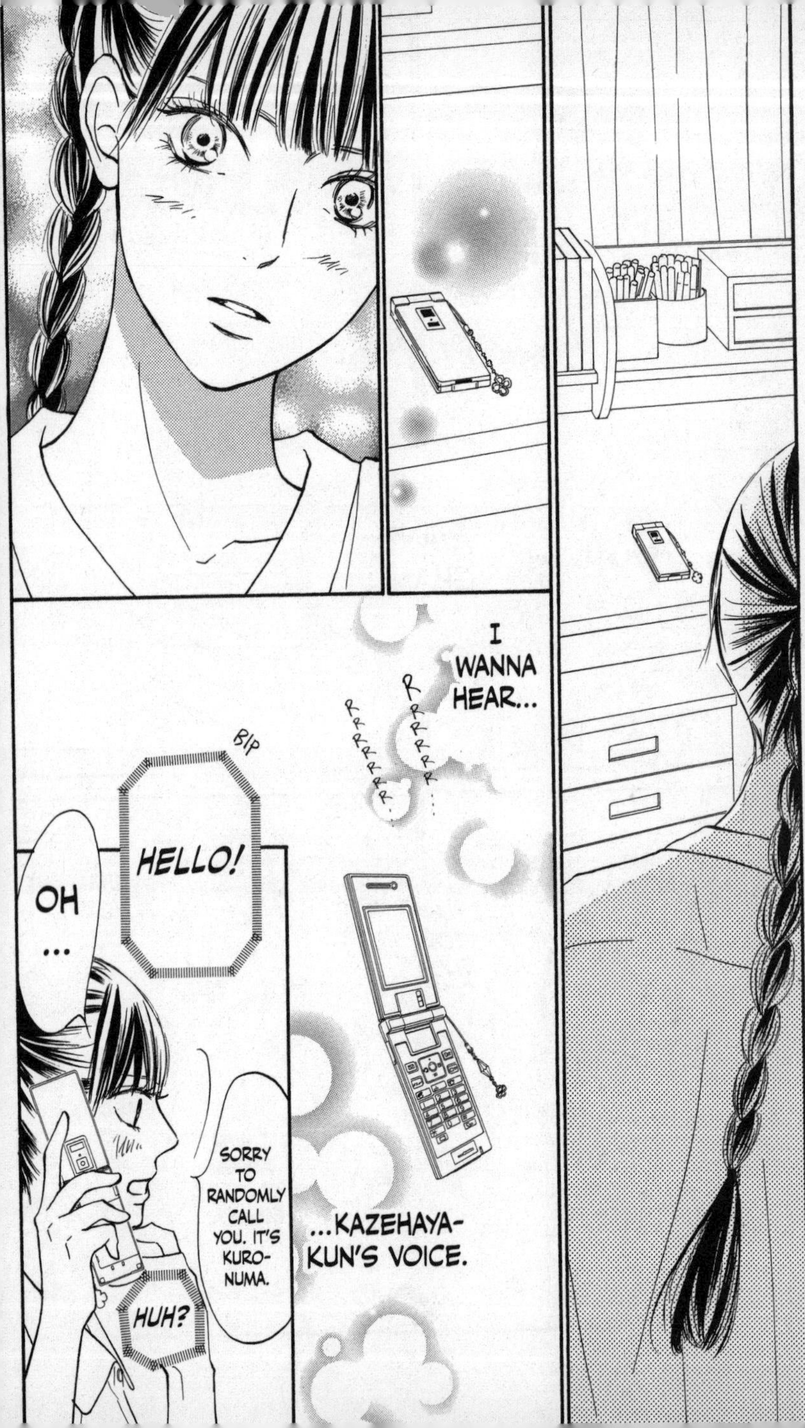
I WANNA HEAR...
RRRRRR...
RRRRRRR...
...KAZEHAYA-KUN'S VOICE.
BIP
HELLO!
OH ...
SORRY TO RANDOMLY CALL YOU. IT'S KURO-NUMA.
HUH?

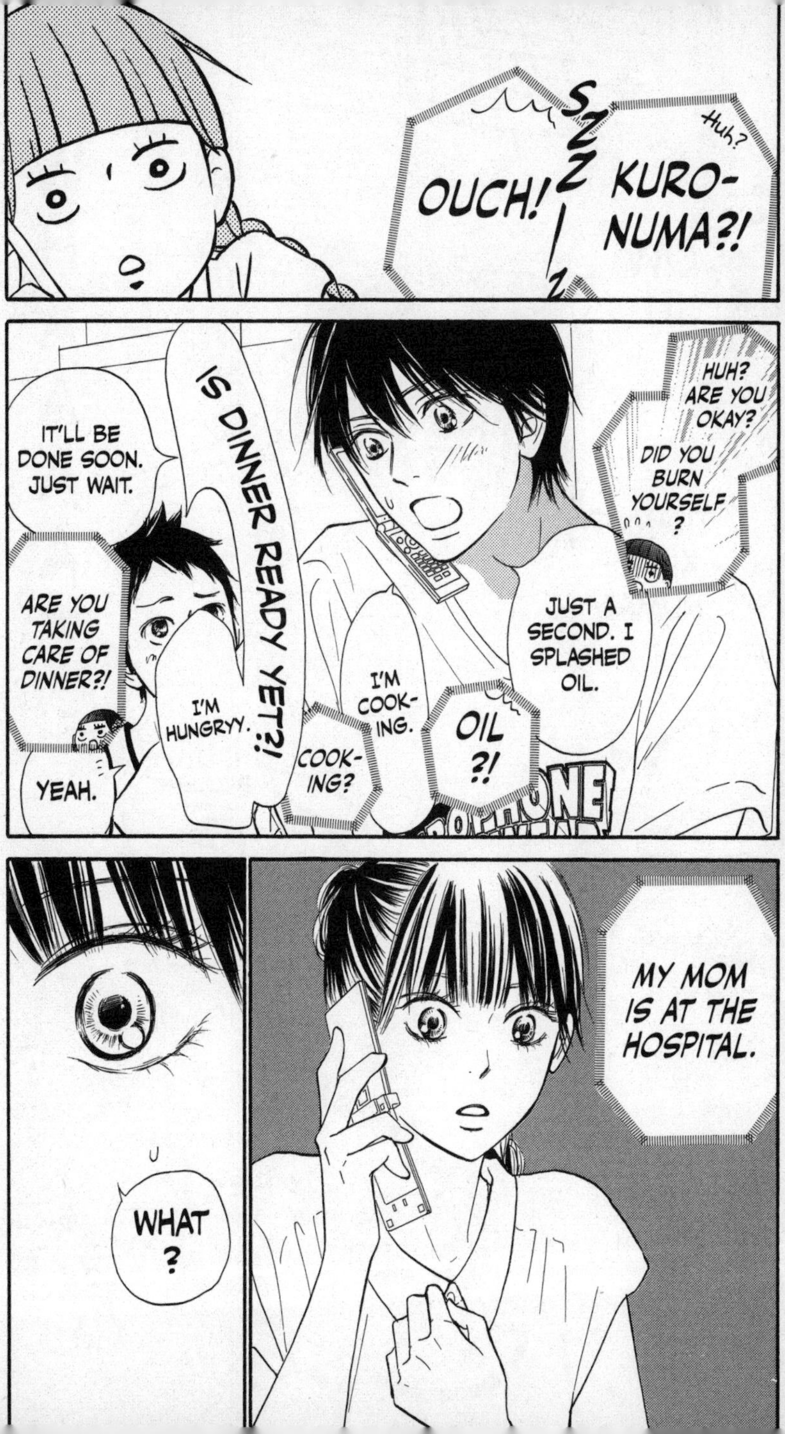
Huh?
KURO-NUMA?!
SZZ
OUCH!
HUH? ARE YOU OKAY?
DID YOU BURN YOURSELF?
JUST A SECOND. I SPLASHED OIL.
OIL?!
I'M COOK-ING.
COOK-ING?
IS DINNER READY YET?!
I'M HUNGRYY.
IT'LL BE DONE SOON. JUST WAIT.
ARE YOU TAKING CARE OF DINNER?!
YEAH.
MY MOM IS AT THE HOSPITAL.
WHAT?

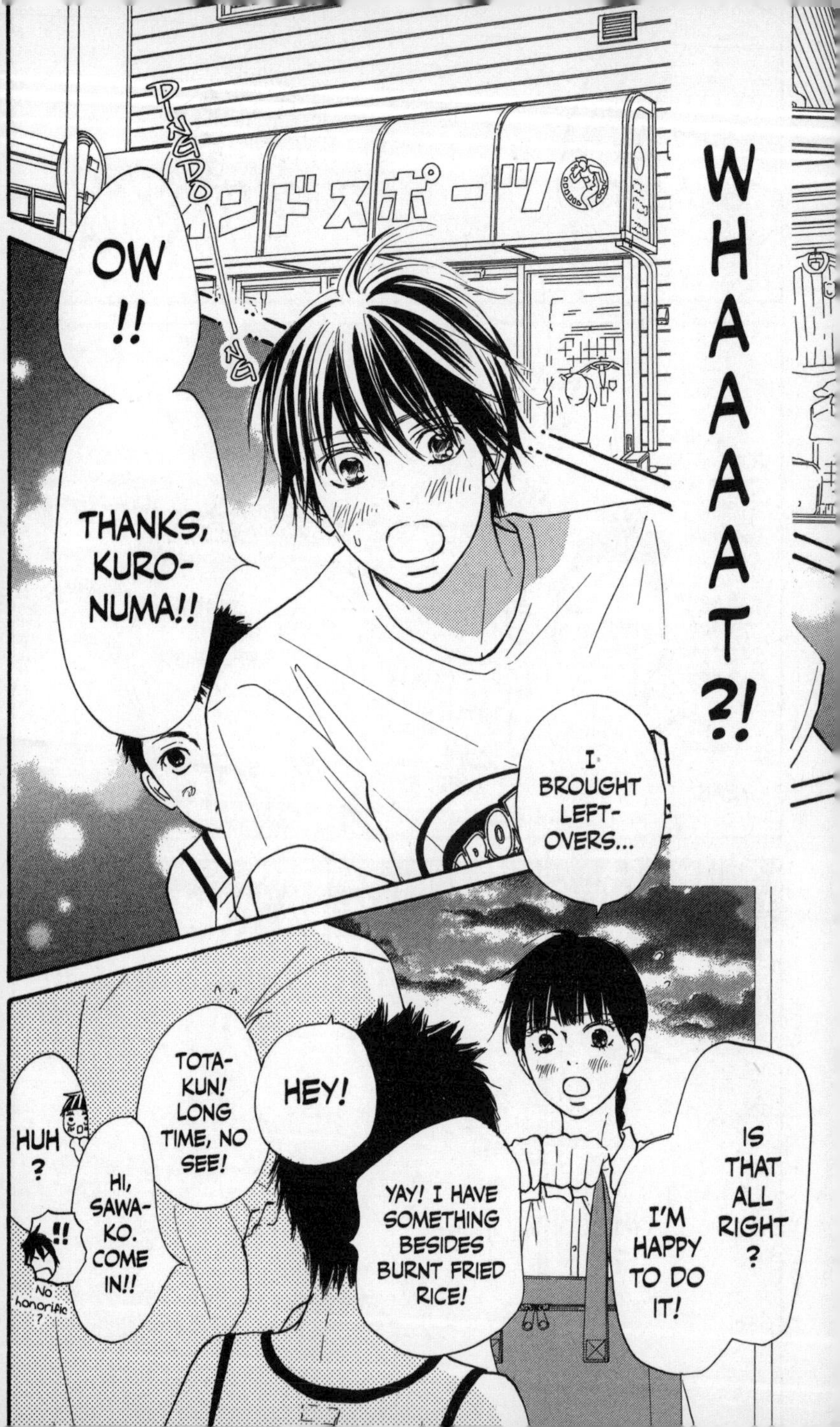
ンドスポーツ
DINGDONG
I BROUGHT LEFT-OVERS...
OW!! THANKS, KURO-NUMA!!
WHAAAAT?!
IS THAT ALL RIGHT?
I'M HAPPY TO DO IT!
YAY! I HAVE SOMETHING BESIDES BURNT FRIED RICE!
HEY!
TOTA-KUN! LONG TIME, NO SEE!
HI, SAWAKO. COME IN!!
HUH?
!!
No honorific?

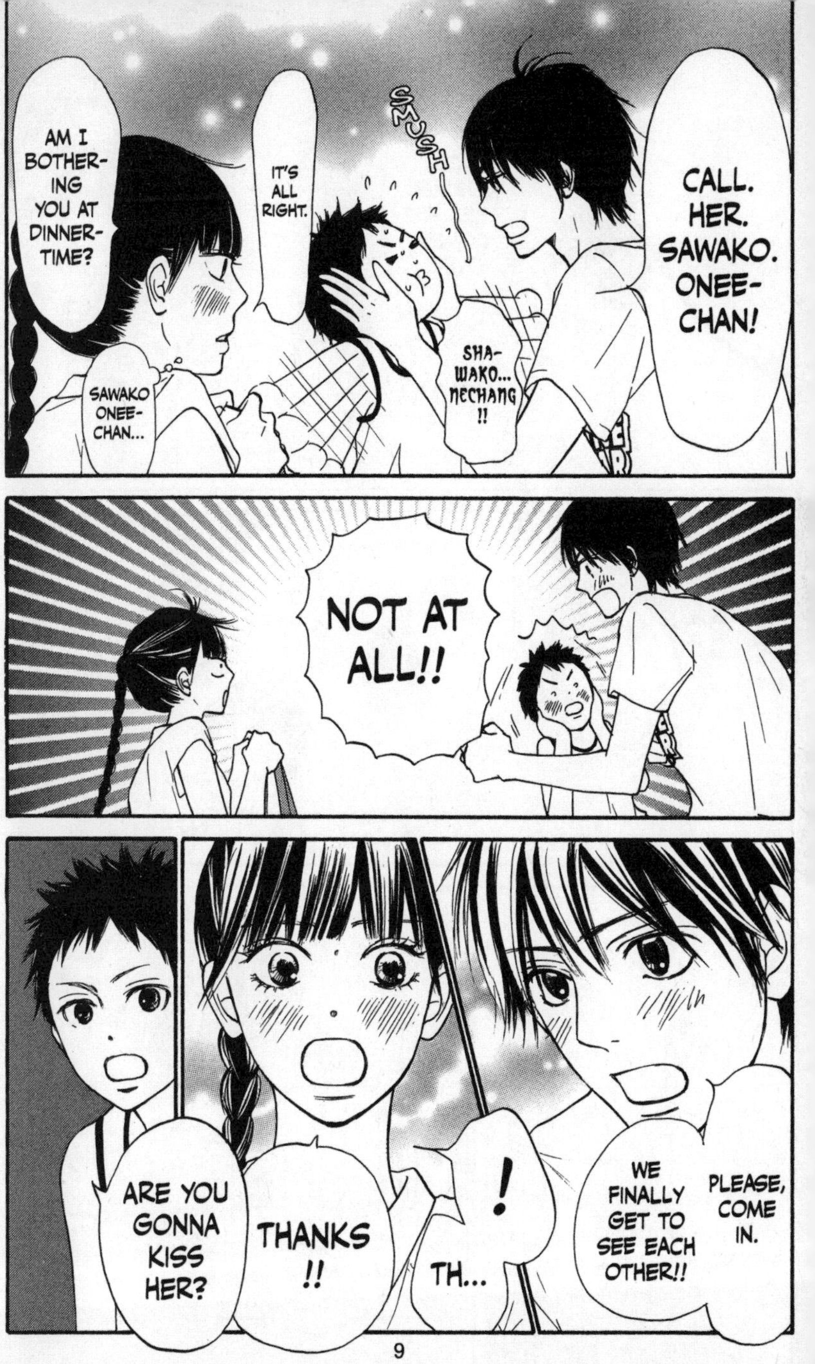
CALL. HER. SAWAKO. ONEE-CHAN!
SMUSH
IT'S ALL RIGHT.
AM I BOTHER-ING YOU AT DINNER-TIME?
SHA-WAKO... NECHANG !!
SAWAKO ONEE-CHAN...
NOT AT ALL!!
PLEASE, COME IN.
WE FINALLY GET TO SEE EACH OTHER!!
!
TH...
THANKS !!
ARE YOU GONNA KISS HER?

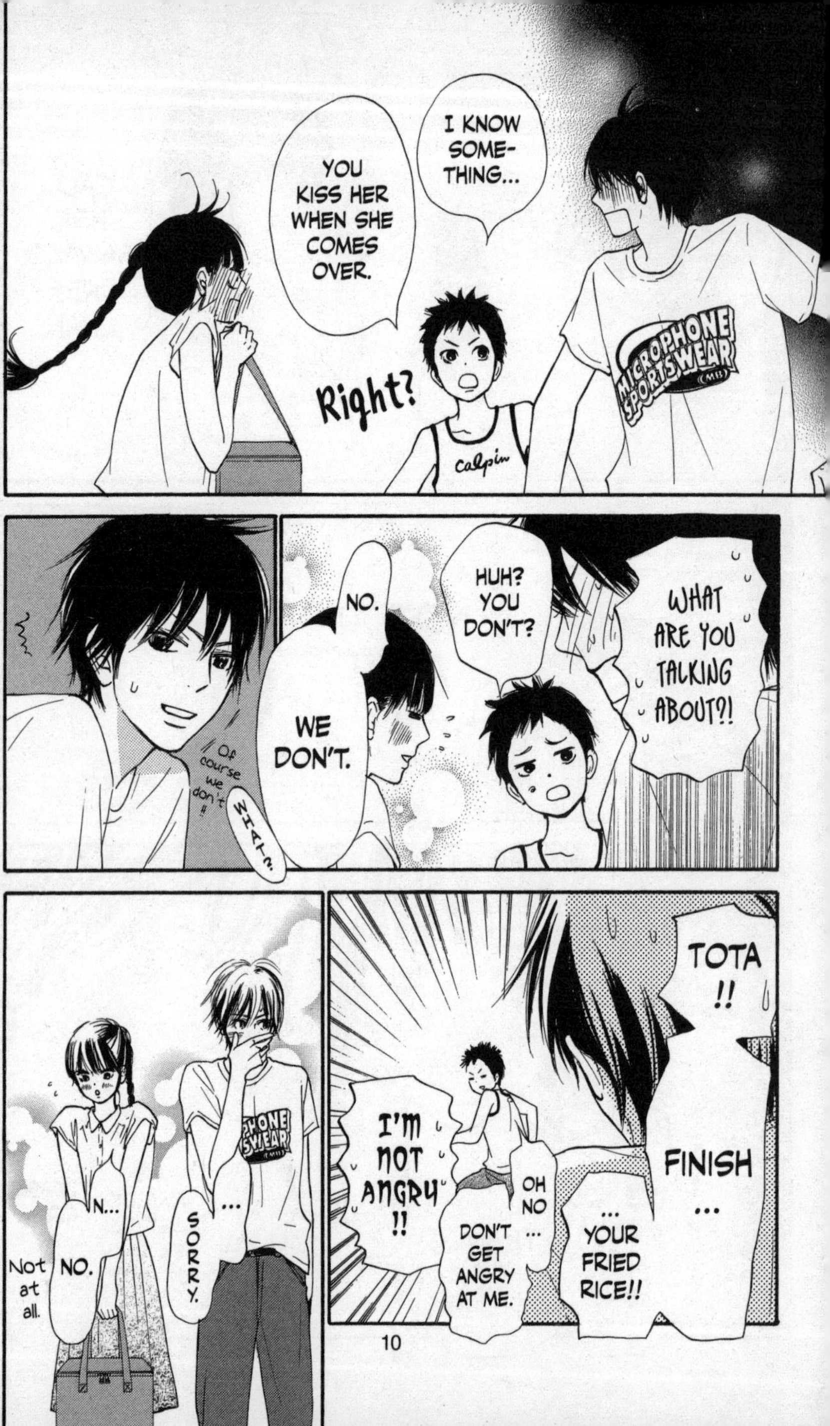
I KNOW SOME-THING...
YOU KISS HER WHEN SHE COMES OVER.
Right?
WHAT ARE YOU TALKING ABOUT?!
HUH? YOU DON'T?
NO.
WE DON'T.
WHAT?
Of course we don't!
TOTA!!
FINISH... ...YOUR FRIED RICE!!
OH NO... DON'T GET ANGRY AT ME.
I'M NOT ANGRY!!
...
SORRY.
N...
NO.
Not at all.

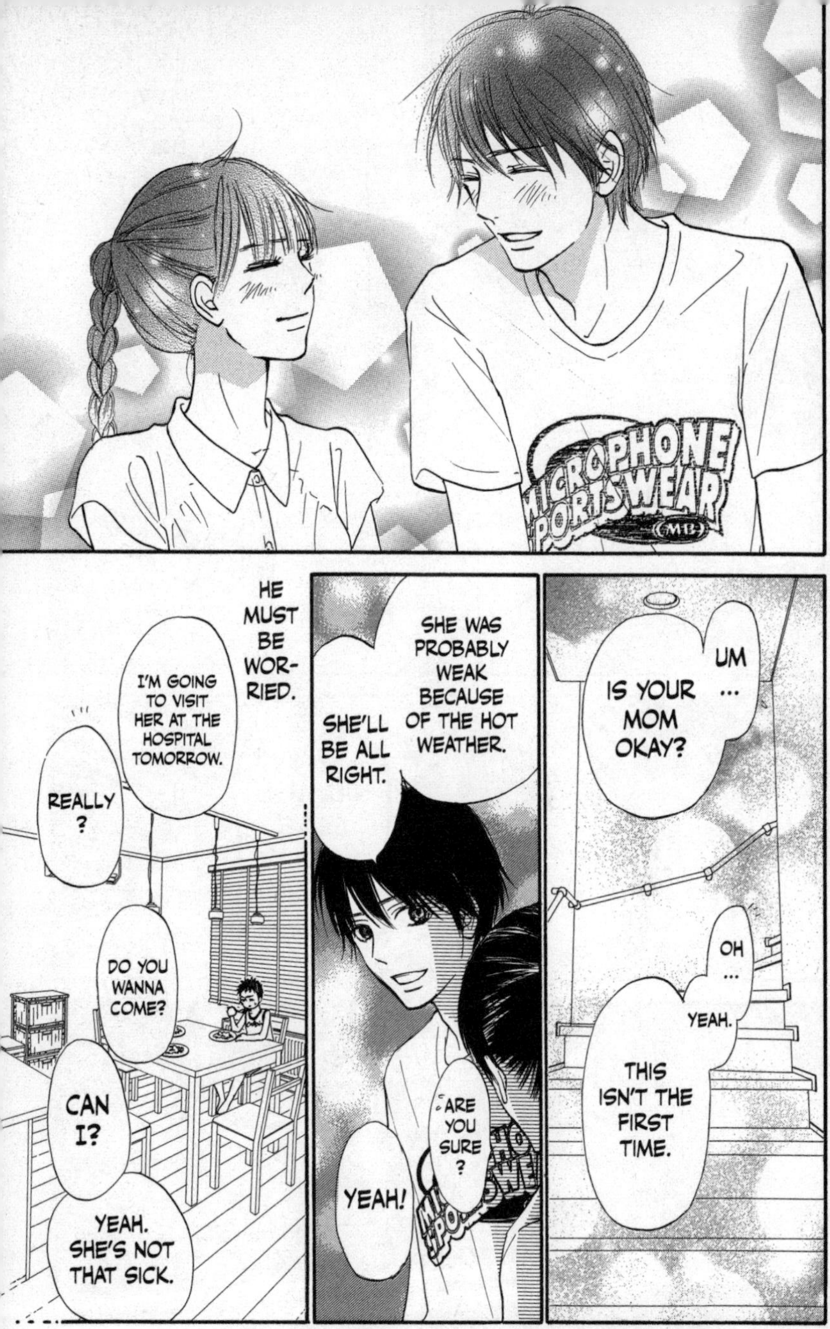
MICROPHONE SPORTSWEAR
MB
UM ...
IS YOUR MOM OKAY?
OH ... YEAH.
THIS ISN'T THE FIRST TIME.
SHE WAS PROBABLY WEAK BECAUSE OF THE HOT WEATHER.
SHE'LL BE ALL RIGHT.
ARE YOU SURE?
YEAH!
HE MUST BE WOR-RIED.
I'M GOING TO VISIT HER AT THE HOSPITAL TOMORROW.
REALLY?
DO YOU WANNA COME?
CAN I?
YEAH. SHE'S NOT THAT SICK.

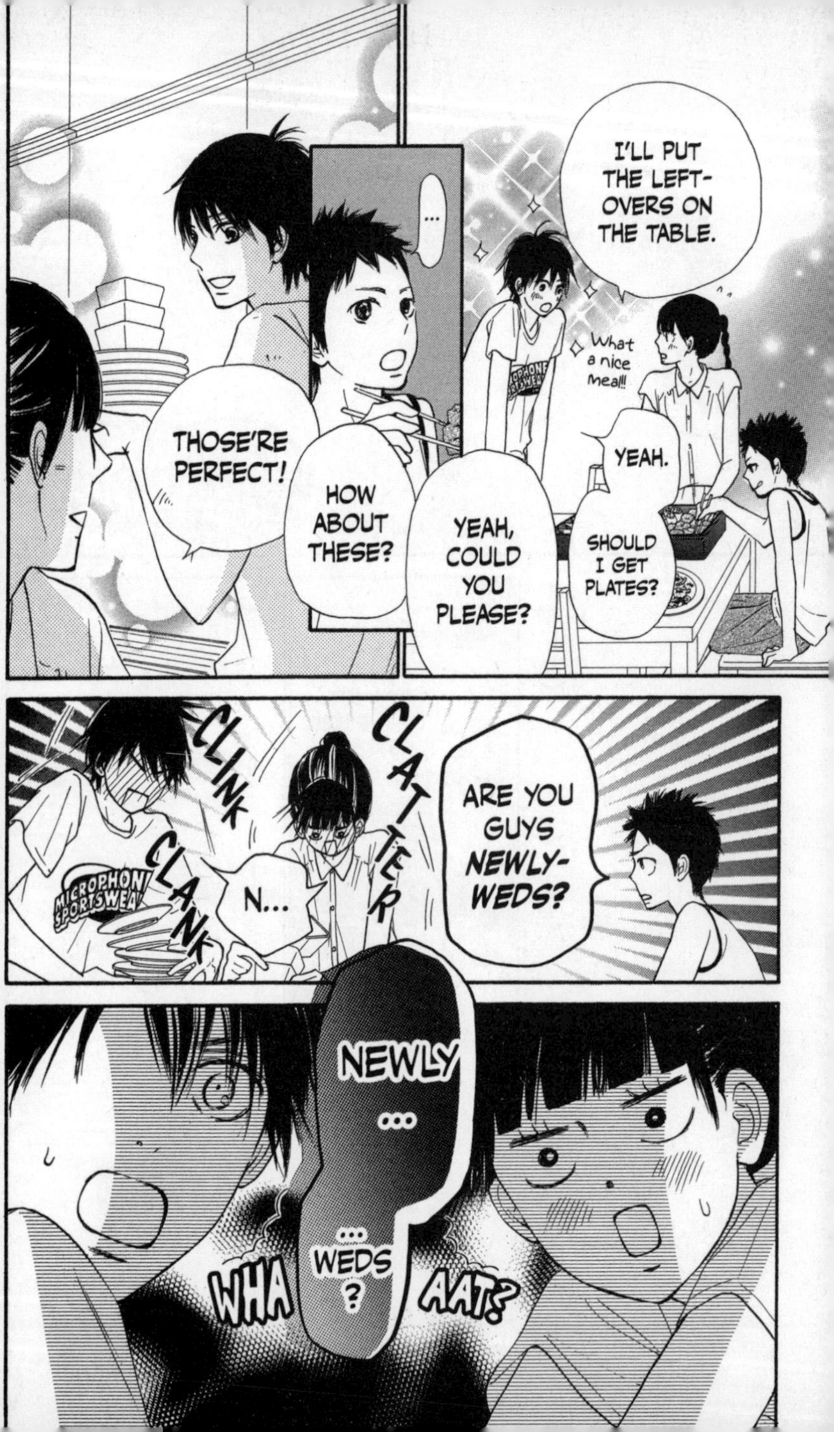
I'LL PUT THE LEFT-OVERS ON THE TABLE.
What a nice meal!!
YEAH.
SHOULD I GET PLATES?
YEAH, COULD YOU PLEASE?
...
HOW ABOUT THESE?
THOSE'RE PERFECT!
ARE YOU GUYS NEWLY-WEDS?
CLATTER
N...
CLINK
CLANK
MICROPHON SPORTSWEA
NEWLY
...
...WEDS
?
WHA
AAT?

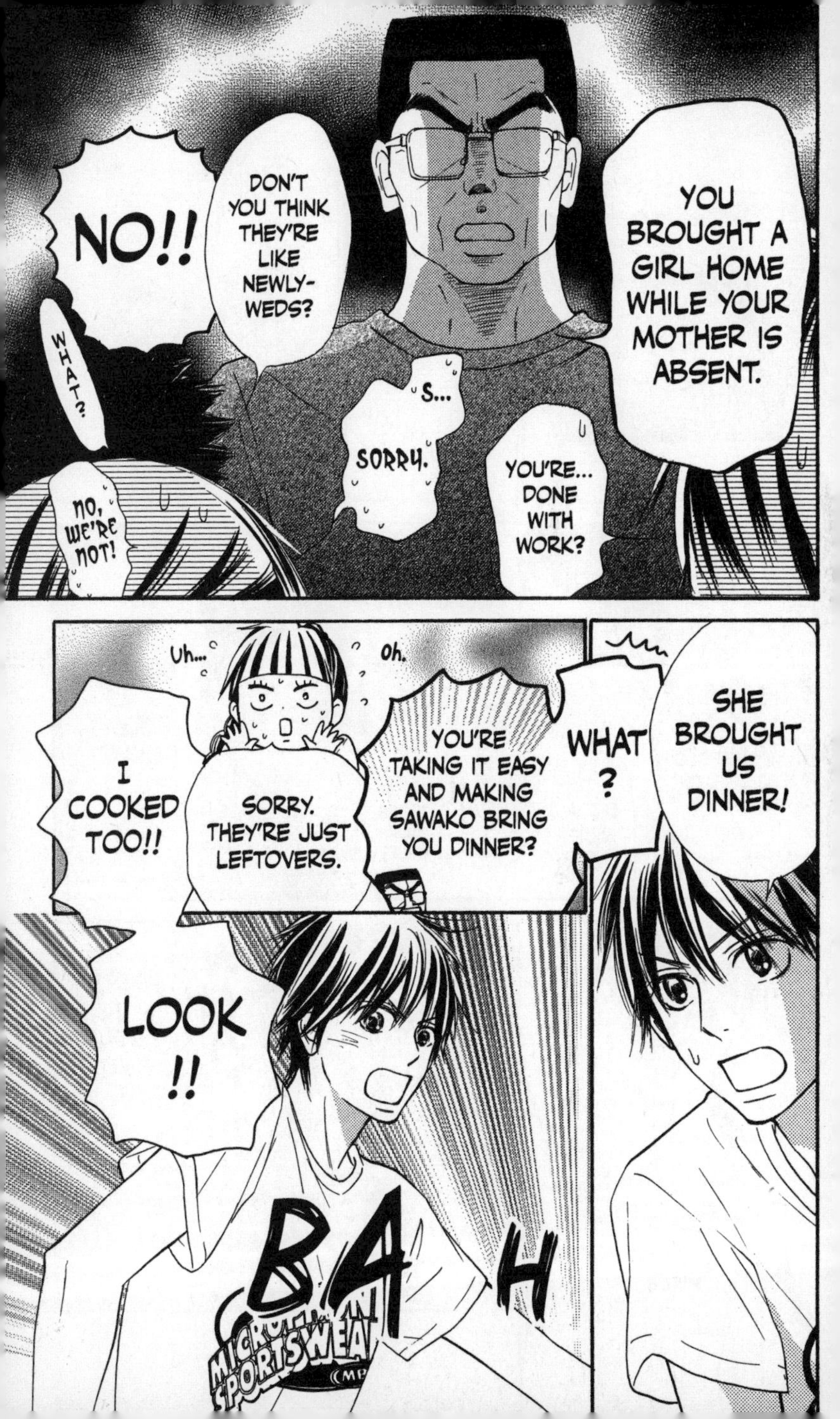
YOU BROUGHT A GIRL HOME WHILE YOUR MOTHER IS ABSENT.
YOU'RE... DONE WITH WORK?
S...
SORRY.
DON'T YOU THINK THEY'RE LIKE NEWLY-WEDS?
NO!!
WHAT?
no, we're not!
SHE BROUGHT US DINNER!
WHAT?
YOU'RE TAKING IT EASY AND MAKING SAWAKO BRING YOU DINNER?
Oh.
Uh...
SORRY. THEY'RE JUST LEFTOVERS.
I COOKED TOO!!
LOOK!!
BAH

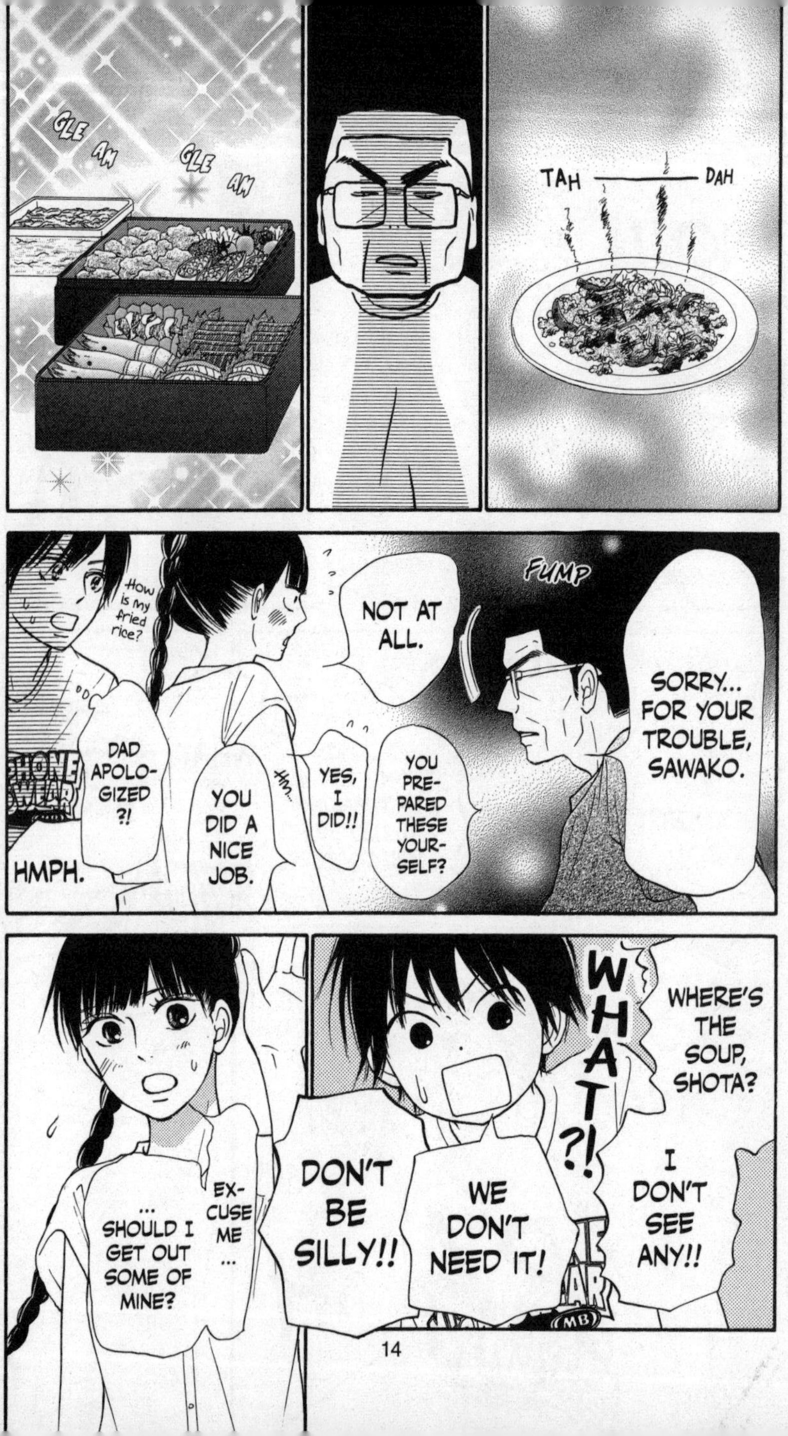
TAH — DAH
GLE AM
GLE AM
FUMP
SORRY... FOR YOUR TROUBLE, SAWAKO.
NOT AT ALL.
YOU PRE-PARED THESE YOUR-SELF?
YES, I DID!!
YOU DID A NICE JOB.
How is my fried rice?
DAD APOLO-GIZED?!
HMPH.
WHERE'S THE SOUP, SHOTA?
WHAT?!
I DON'T SEE ANY!!
WE DON'T NEED IT!
DON'T BE SILLY!!
EX-CUSE ME ...
... SHOULD I GET OUT SOME OF MINE?

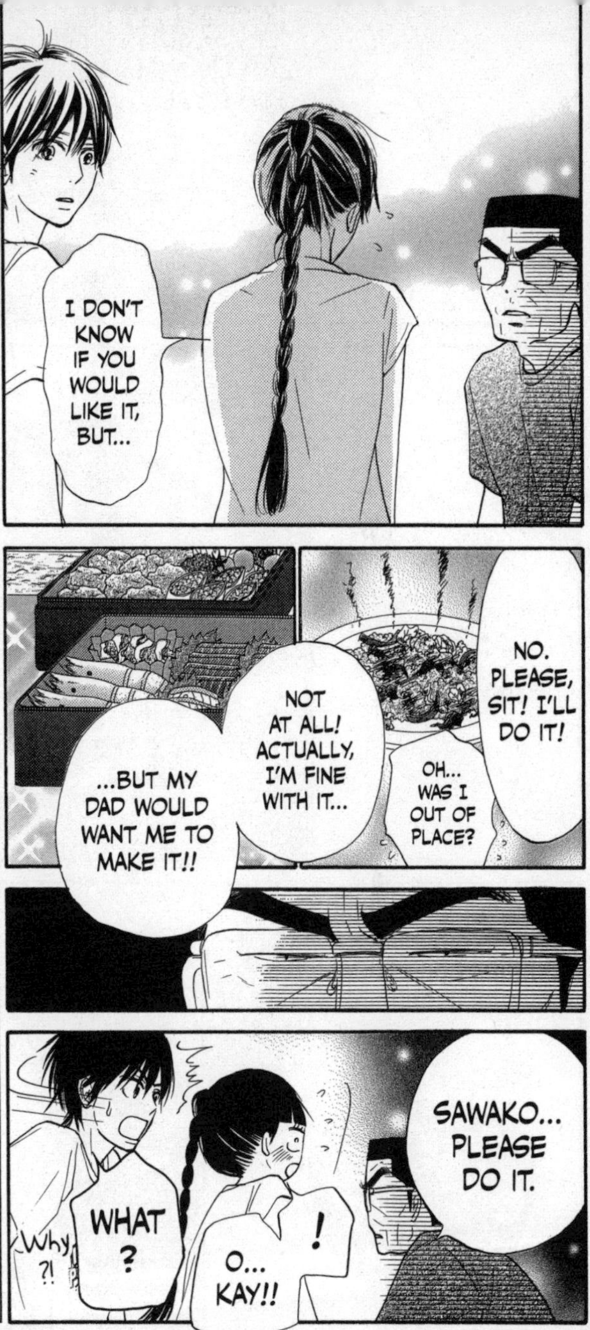
I DON'T KNOW IF YOU WOULD LIKE IT, BUT...
NO. PLEASE, SIT! I'LL DO IT!
OH... WAS I OUT OF PLACE?
NOT AT ALL! ACTUALLY, I'M FINE WITH IT...
...BUT MY DAD WOULD WANT ME TO MAKE IT!!
SAWAKO... PLEASE DO IT.
!
O... KAY!!
WHAT?
Why?!

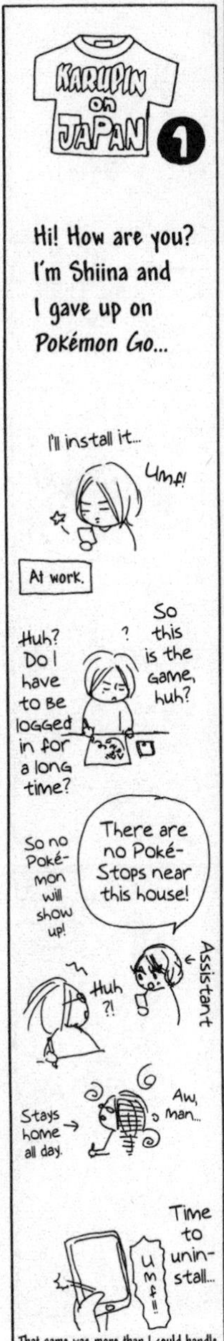
KARUPIN on JAPAN
1
Hi! How are you? I'm Shiina and I gave up on Pokémon Go...
I'll install it...
Umf!
At work.
So this is the game, huh?
?
Huh? Do I have to be logged in for a long time?
There are no Poké-Stops near this house!
So no Pokémon will show up!
Assistant
Huh?!
Aw, man...
Stays home all day.
Time to uninstall...
Umf!!
That game was more than I could handle.
Because I don't go out...

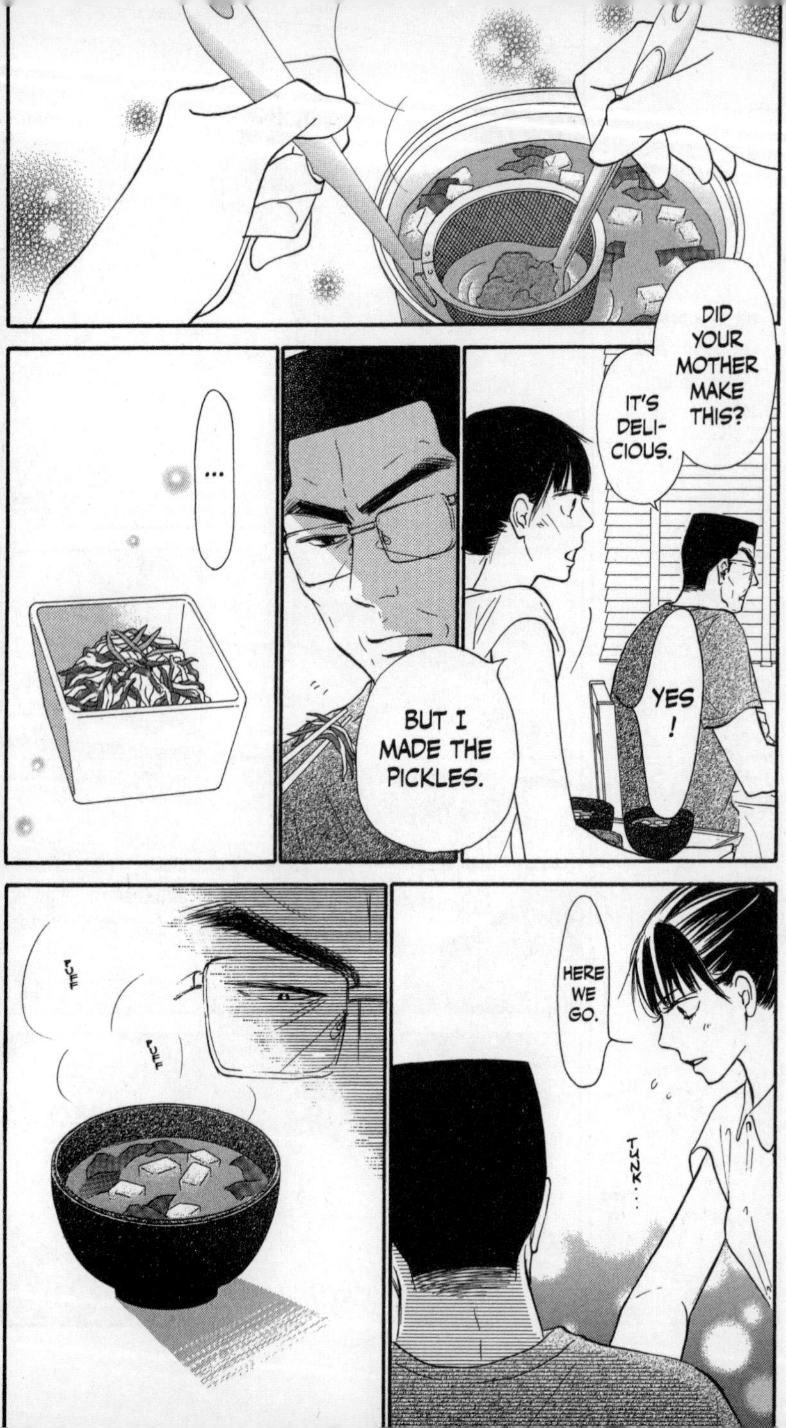
DID YOUR MOTHER MAKE THIS?
IT'S DELICIOUS.
YES!
BUT I MADE THE PICKLES.
...
HERE WE GO.
TUNK...
PUFF
PUFF

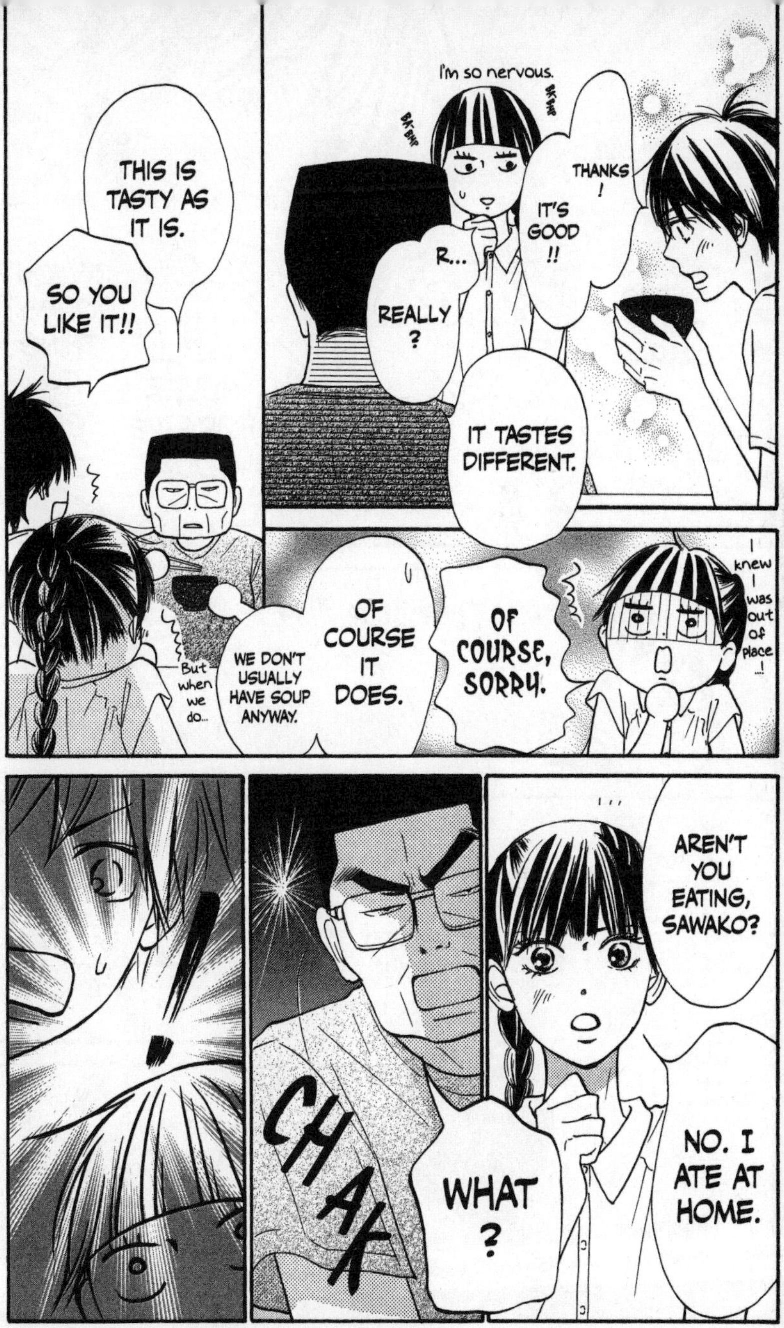
I'm so nervous.
THANKS! IT'S GOOD!!
R... REALLY?
IT TASTES DIFFERENT.
I knew I was out of place...!
OF COURSE, SORRY.
OF COURSE IT DOES.
WE DON'T USUALLY HAVE SOUP ANYWAY.
But when we do...
THIS IS TASTY AS IT IS.
SO YOU LIKE IT!!
...
AREN'T YOU EATING, SAWAKO?
NO. I ATE AT HOME.
WHAT?
CHAK

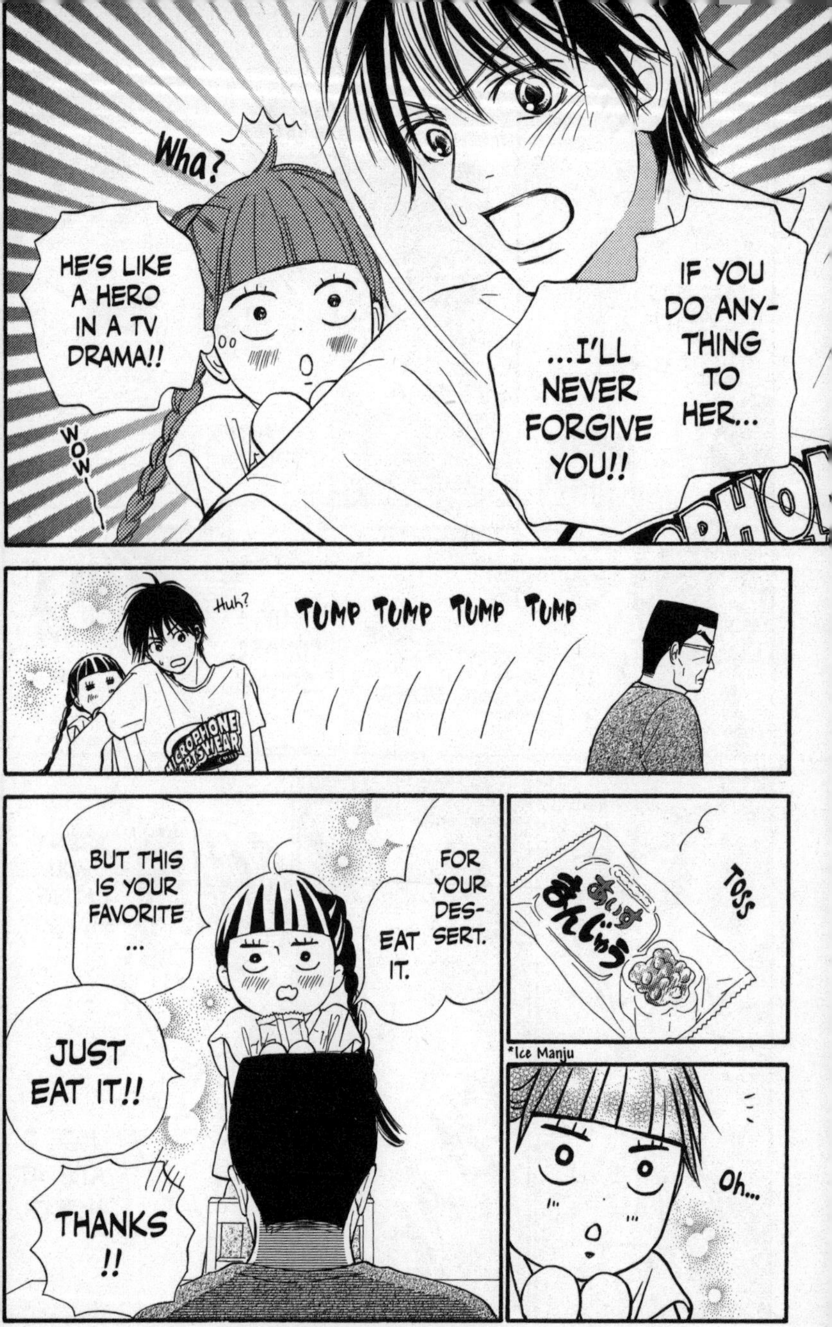
IF YOU DO ANY-THING TO HER...
...I'LL NEVER FORGIVE YOU!!
Wha?
HE'S LIKE A HERO IN A TV DRAMA!!
WOW
TUMP TUMP TUMP TUMP
Huh?
TOSS
あいす まんじゅう
*Ice Manju
Oh...
FOR YOUR DES-SERT.
EAT IT.
BUT THIS IS YOUR FAVORITE ...
JUST EAT IT!!
THANKS !!

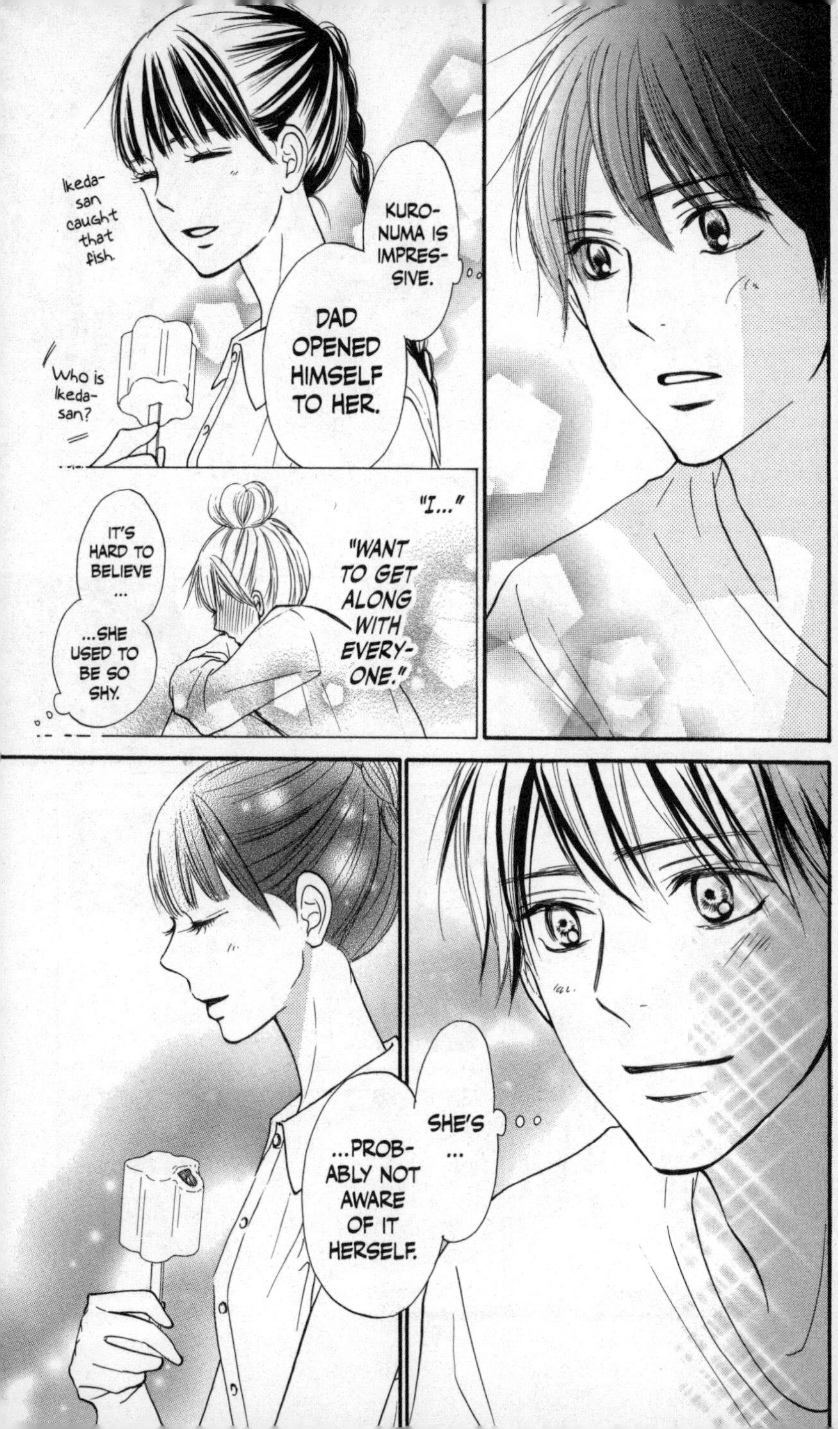
KURO-NUMA IS IMPRESSIVE.
DAD OPENED HIMSELF TO HER.
Ikeda-san caught that fish.
Who is Ikeda-san?
"I..."
"WANT TO GET ALONG WITH EVERY-ONE."
IT'S HARD TO BELIEVE...
...SHE USED TO BE SO SHY.
SHE'S...
...PROB-ABLY NOT AWARE OF IT HERSELF.

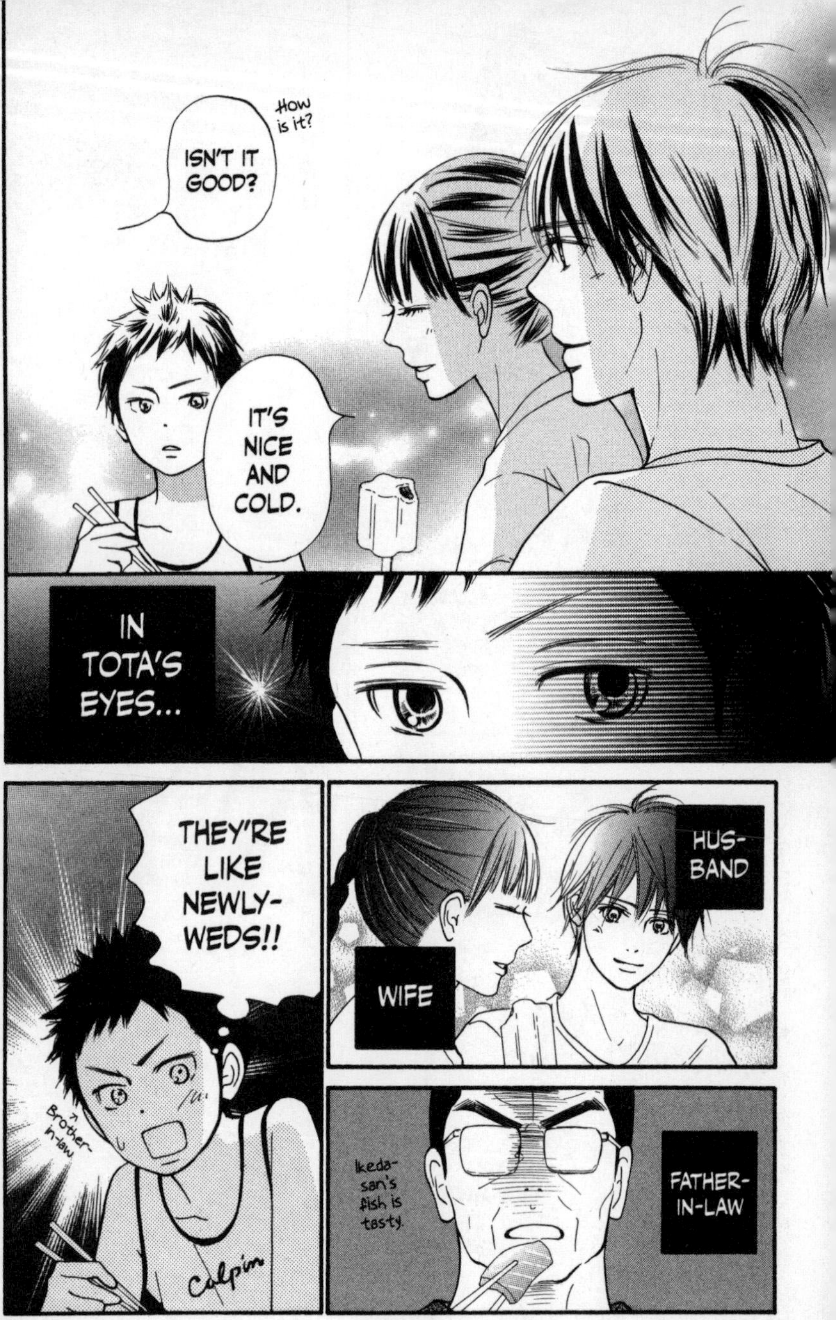
How is it?
ISN'T IT GOOD?
IT'S NICE AND COLD.
IN TOTA'S EYES...
HUS-BAND
WIFE
FATHER-IN-LAW
Ikeda-san's fish is tasty.
THEY'RE LIKE NEWLY-WEDS!!
Brother-in-law
Calpis

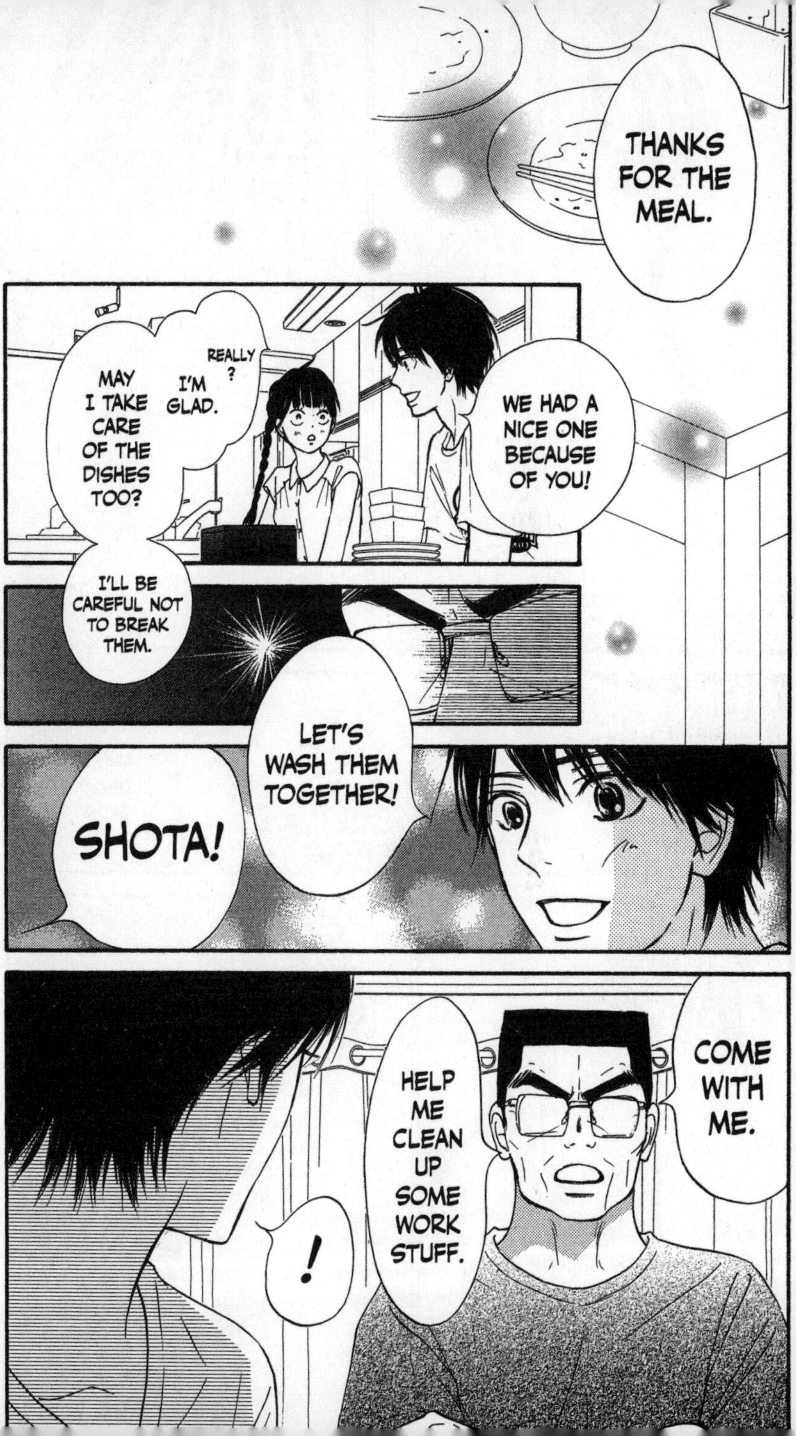
THANKS FOR THE MEAL.
WE HAD A NICE ONE BECAUSE OF YOU!
REALLY?
I'M GLAD.
MAY I TAKE CARE OF THE DISHES TOO?
I'LL BE CAREFUL NOT TO BREAK THEM.
LET'S WASH THEM TOGETHER!
SHOTA!
COME WITH ME.
HELP ME CLEAN UP SOME WORK STUFF.
!

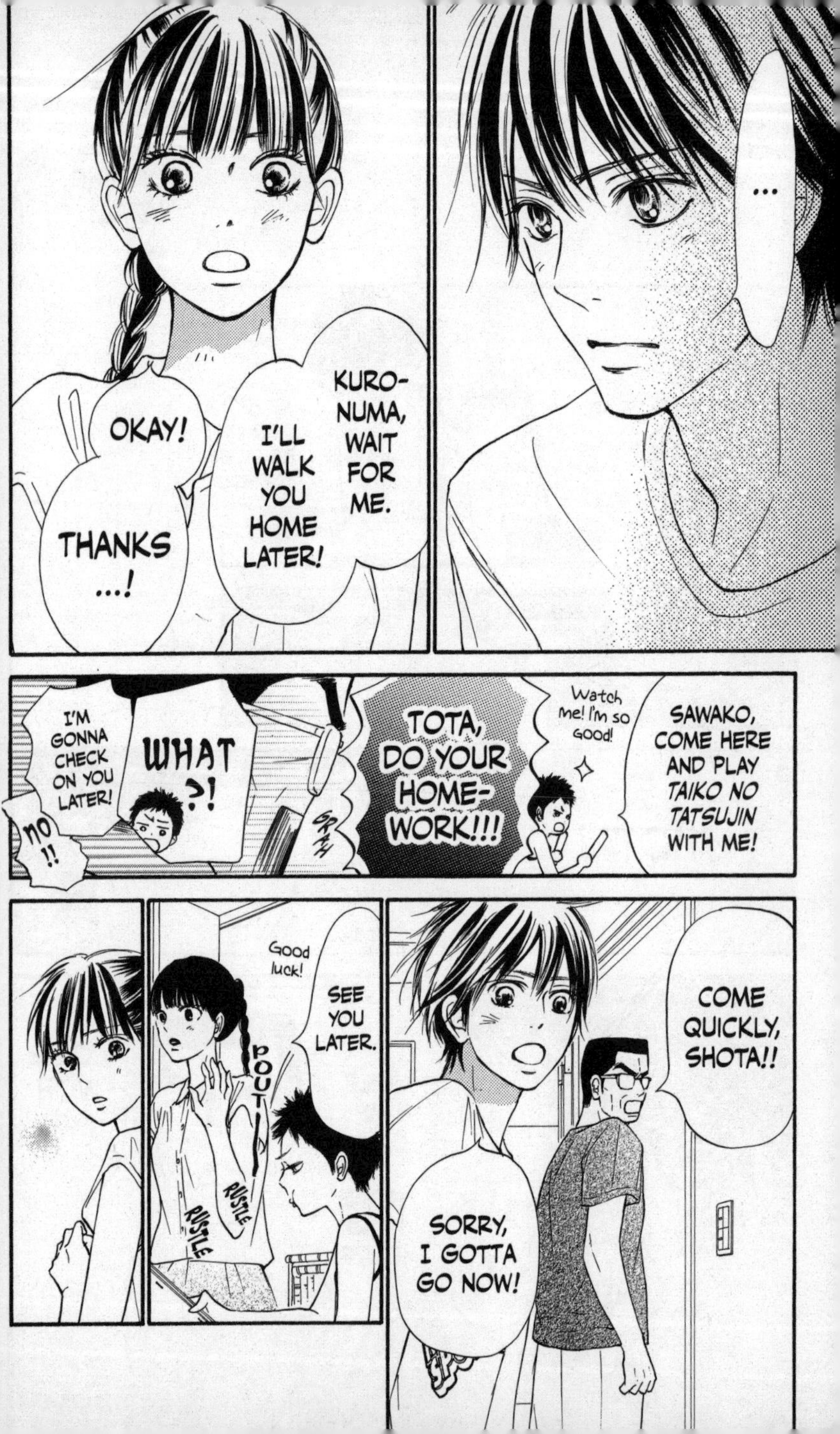
...
KURO-NUMA, WAIT FOR ME.
I'LL WALK YOU HOME LATER!
OKAY!
THANKS ...!
SAWAKO, COME HERE AND PLAY TAIKO NO TATSUJIN WITH ME!
Watch me! I'm so good!
TOTA, DO YOUR HOME-WORK!!!
GRAH
WHAT ?!
I'M GONNA CHECK ON YOU LATER!
no !!
COME QUICKLY, SHOTA!!
SORRY, I GOTTA GO NOW!
SEE YOU LATER.
Good luck!
POUT
RUSTLE
RUSTLE

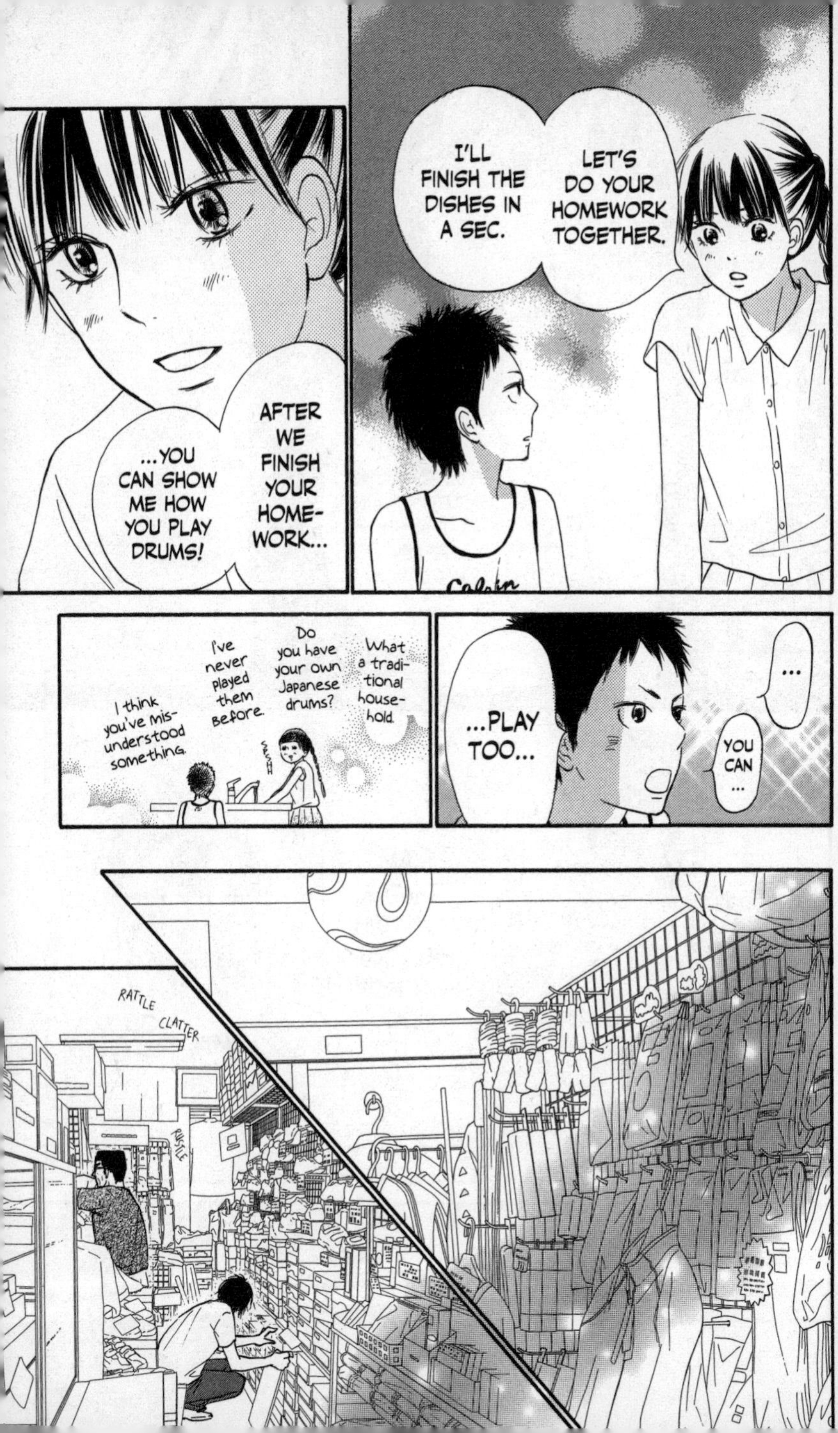
LET'S DO YOUR HOMEWORK TOGETHER.
I'LL FINISH THE DISHES IN A SEC.
AFTER WE FINISH YOUR HOMEWORK...
...YOU CAN SHOW ME HOW YOU PLAY DRUMS!
...
YOU CAN ...
...PLAY TOO...
What a traditional household.
Do you have your own Japanese drums?
I've never played them before.
I think you've misunderstood something.
RATTLE
CLATTER
RUSTLE

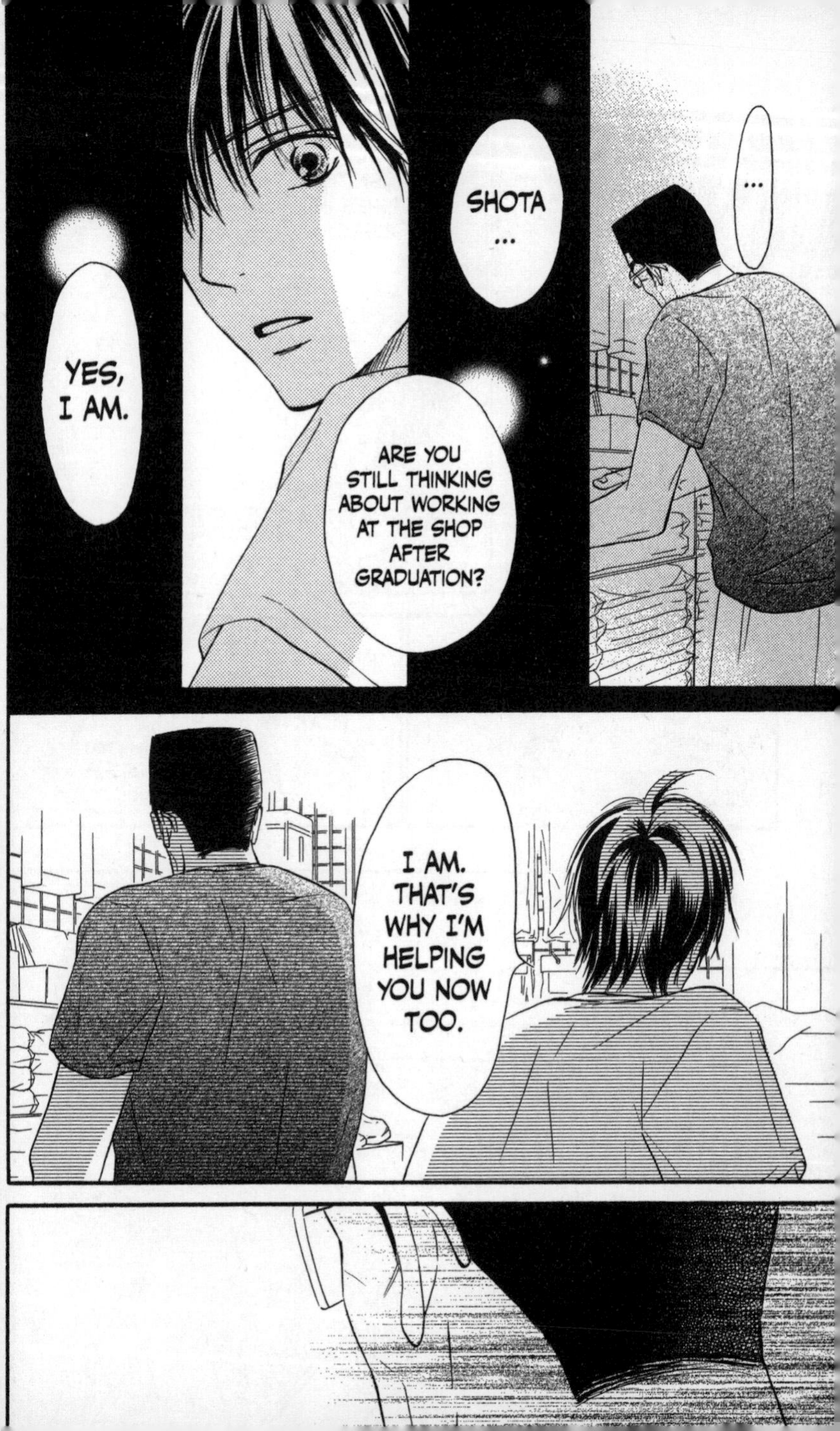
...
SHOTA ...
ARE YOU STILL THINKING ABOUT WORKING AT THE SHOP AFTER GRADUATION?
YES, I AM.
I AM. THAT'S WHY I'M HELPING YOU NOW TOO.

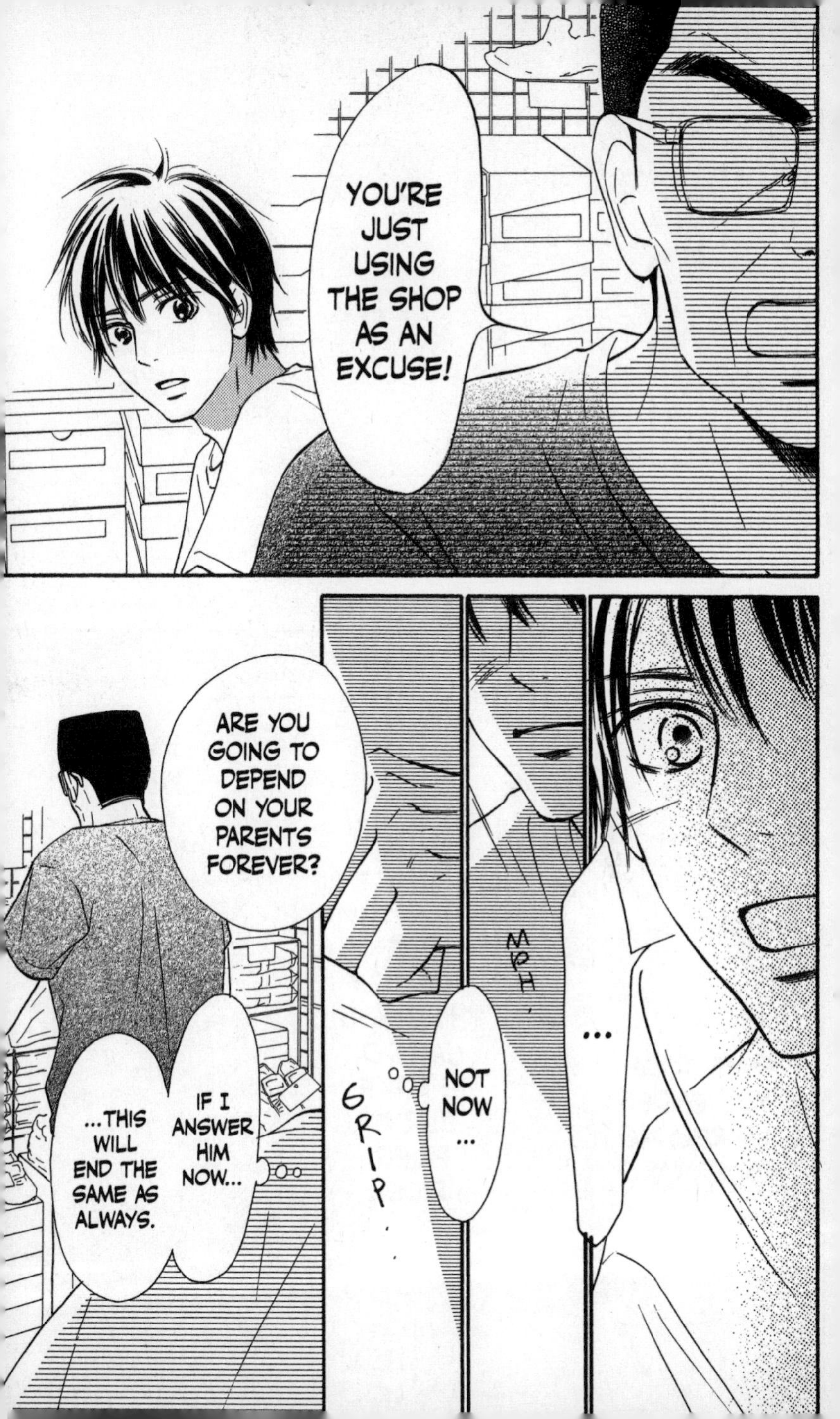
YOU'RE JUST USING THE SHOP AS AN EXCUSE!
...
MPH
NOT NOW ...
GRIP
ARE YOU GOING TO DEPEND ON YOUR PARENTS FOREVER?
IF I ANSWER HIM NOW...
...THIS WILL END THE SAME AS ALWAYS.

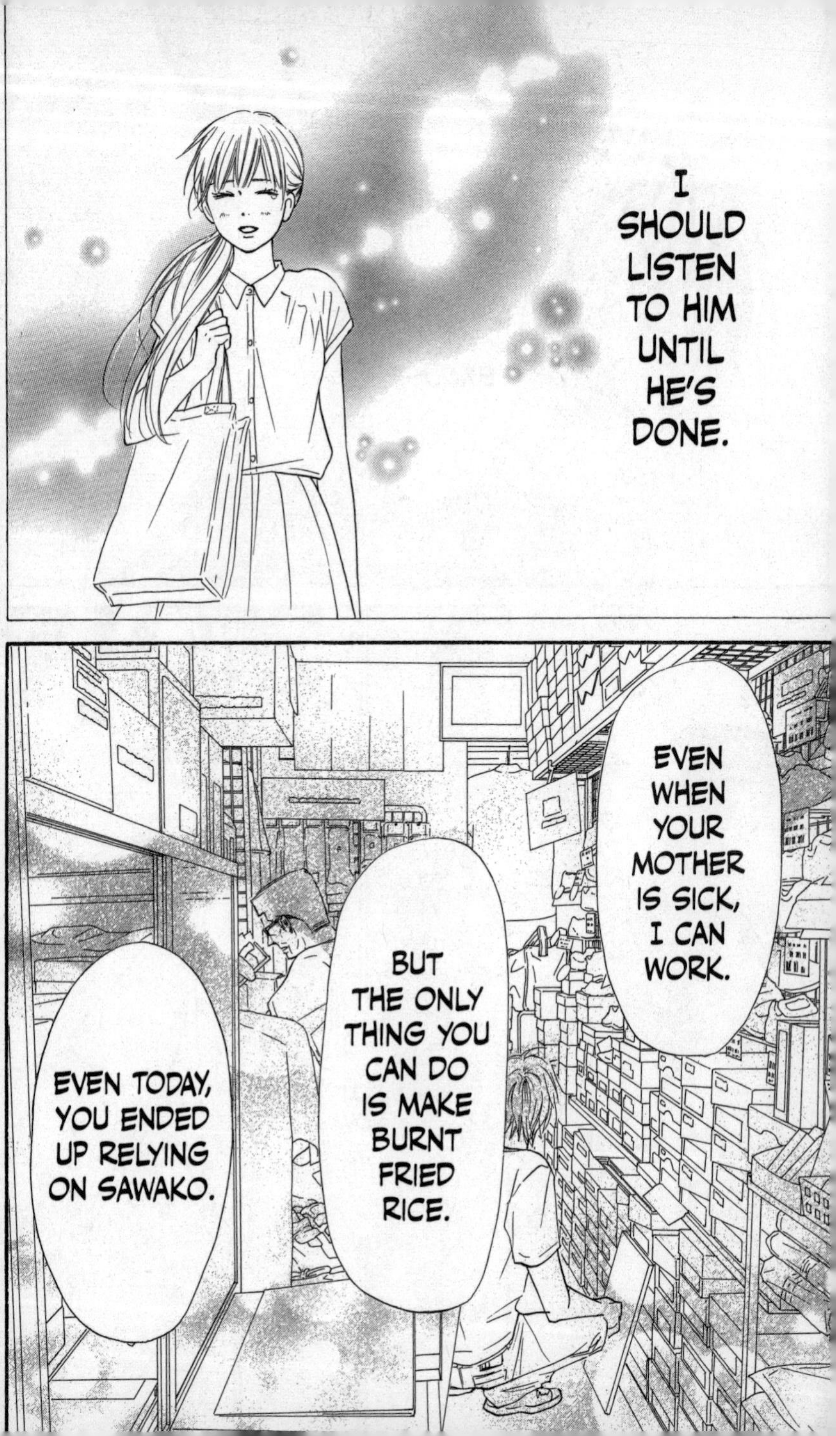
I SHOULD LISTEN TO HIM UNTIL HE'S DONE.
EVEN WHEN YOUR MOTHER IS SICK, I CAN WORK.
BUT THE ONLY THING YOU CAN DO IS MAKE BURNT FRIED RICE.
EVEN TODAY, YOU ENDED UP RELYING ON SAWAKO.

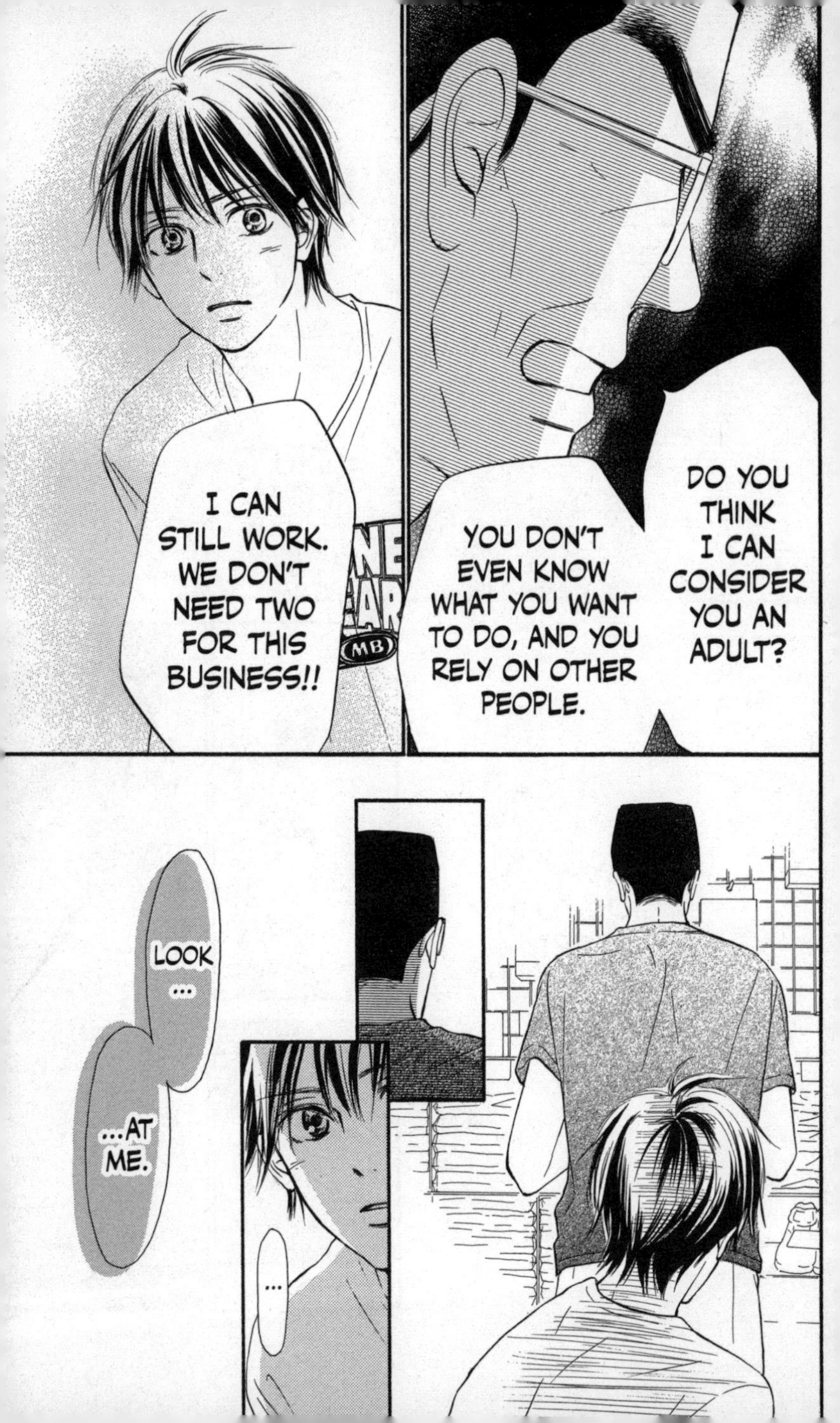
DO YOU THINK I CAN CONSIDER YOU AN ADULT?
YOU DON'T EVEN KNOW WHAT YOU WANT TO DO, AND YOU RELY ON OTHER PEOPLE.
I CAN STILL WORK. WE DON'T NEED TWO FOR THIS BUSINESS!!
...
LOOK ...
...AT ME.

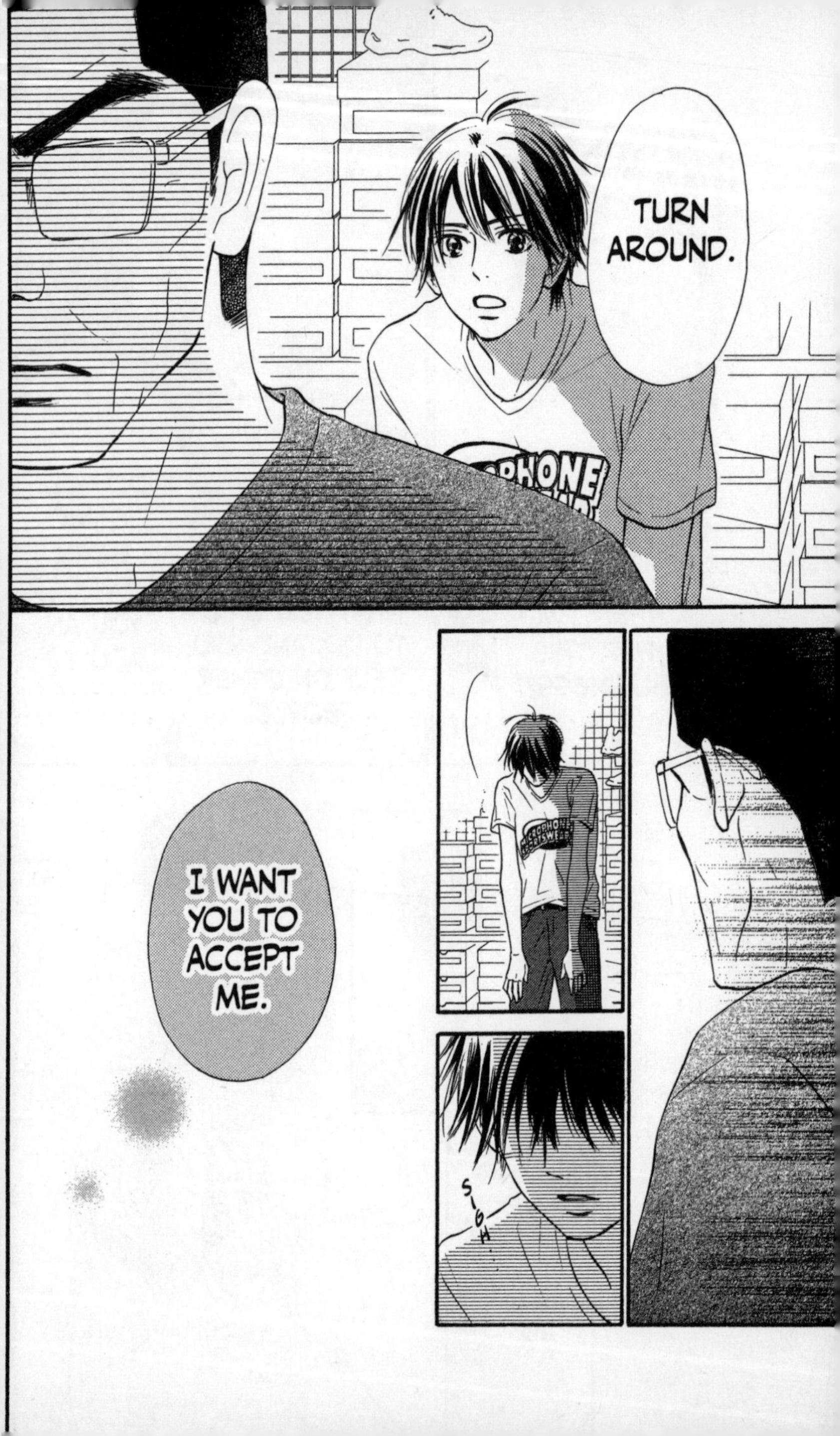
TURN AROUND.
SIGH
I WANT YOU TO ACCEPT ME.

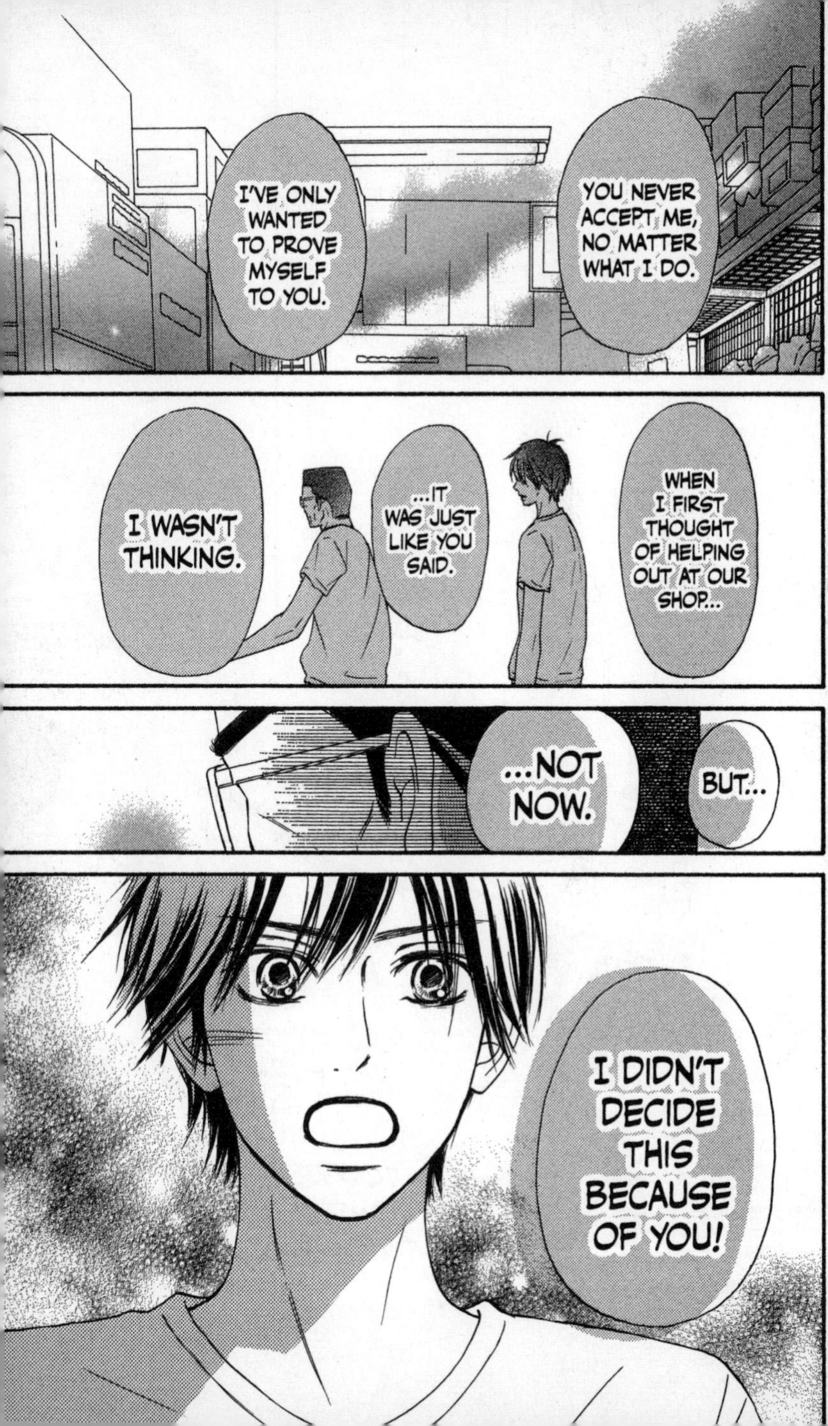
YOU NEVER ACCEPT ME, NO MATTER WHAT I DO.
I'VE ONLY WANTED TO PROVE MYSELF TO YOU.
WHEN I FIRST THOUGHT OF HELPING OUT AT OUR SHOP...
...IT WAS JUST LIKE YOU SAID.
I WASN'T THINKING.
BUT...
...NOT NOW.
I DIDN'T DECIDE THIS BECAUSE OF YOU!

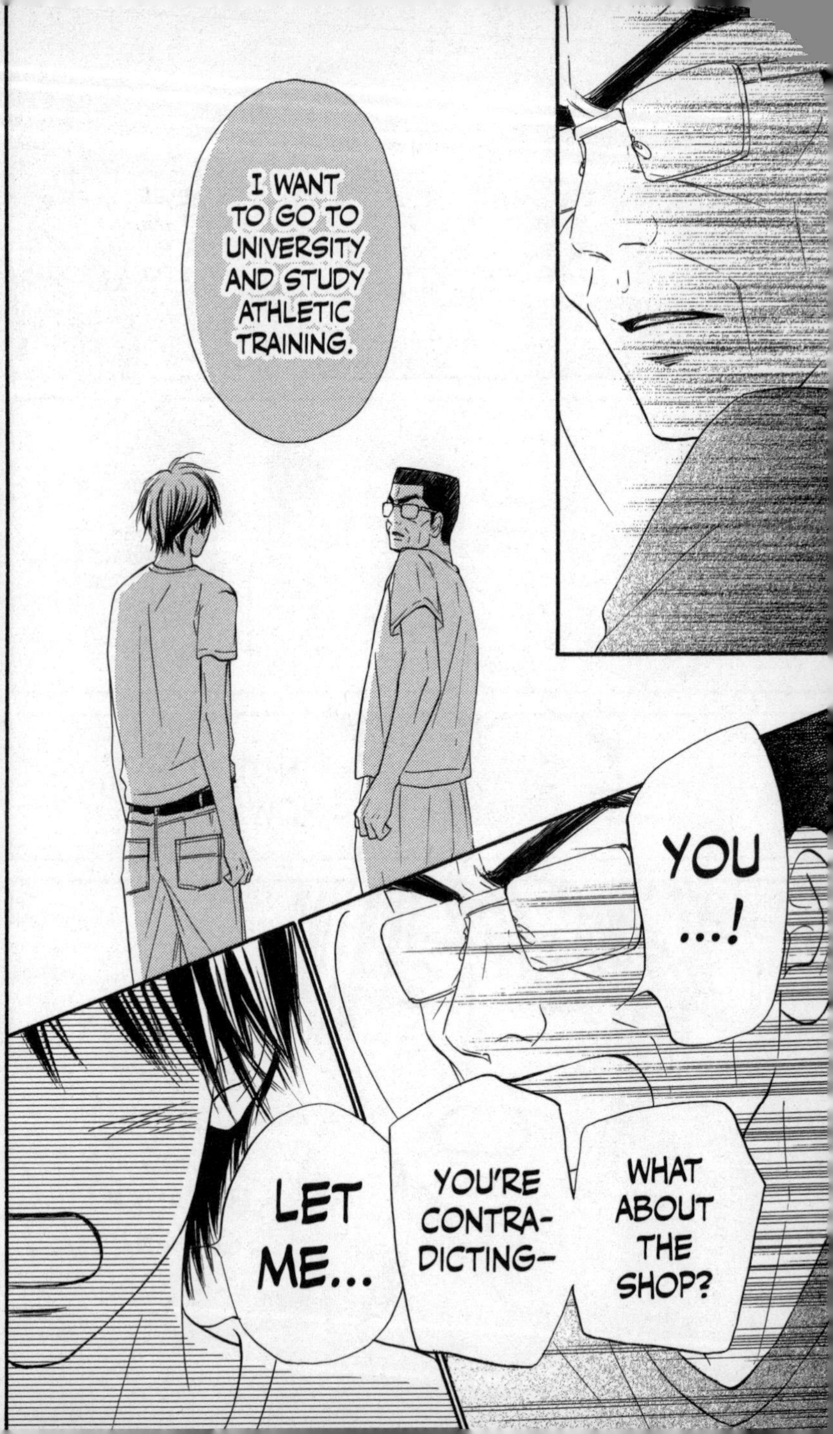
I WANT TO GO TO UNIVERSITY AND STUDY ATHLETIC TRAINING.
YOU ...!
WHAT ABOUT THE SHOP?
YOU'RE CONTRA-DICTING-
LET ME...

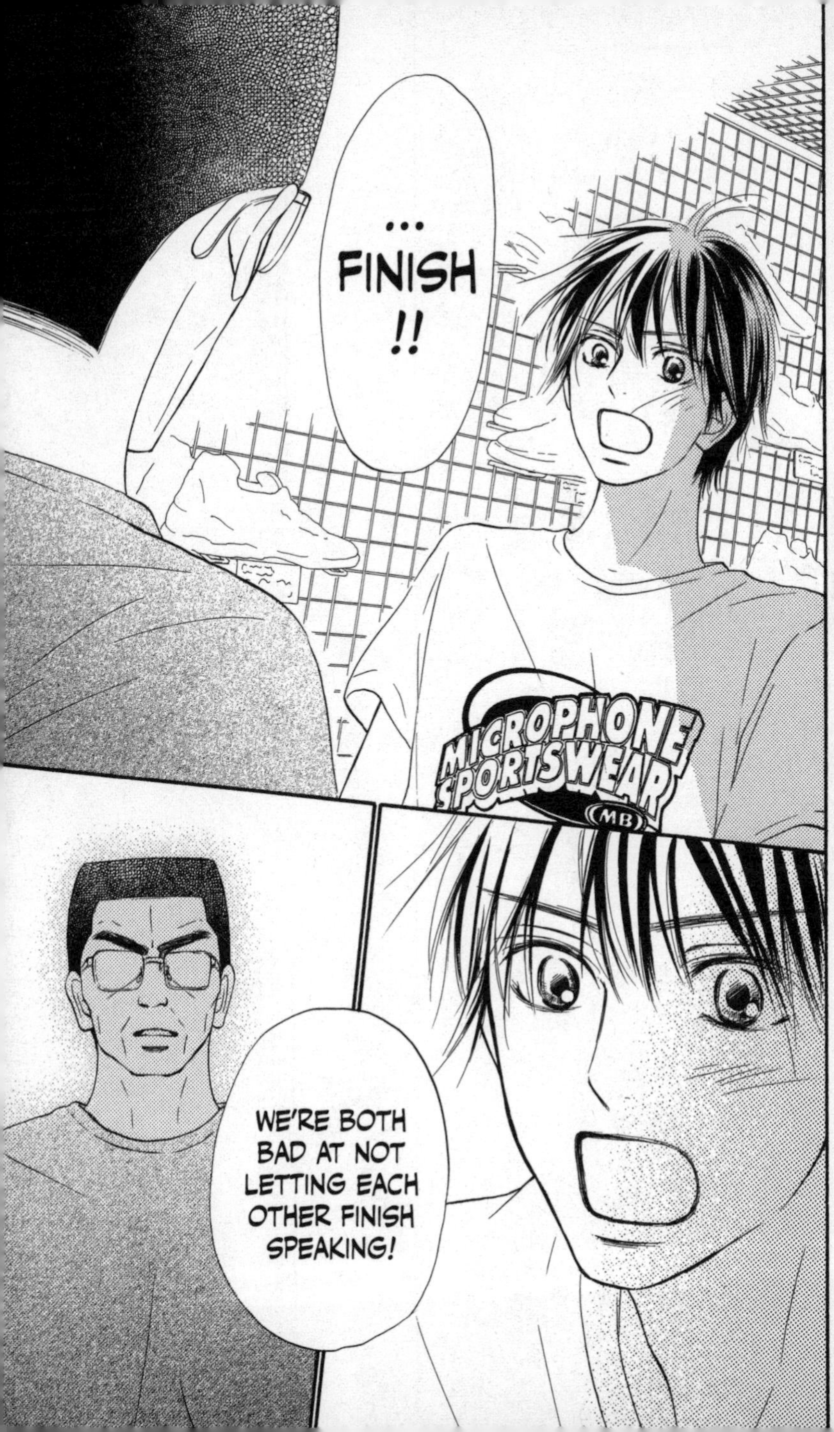
...FINISH!!
MICROPHONE SPORTSWEAR MB
WE'RE BOTH BAD AT NOT LETTING EACH OTHER FINISH SPEAKING!

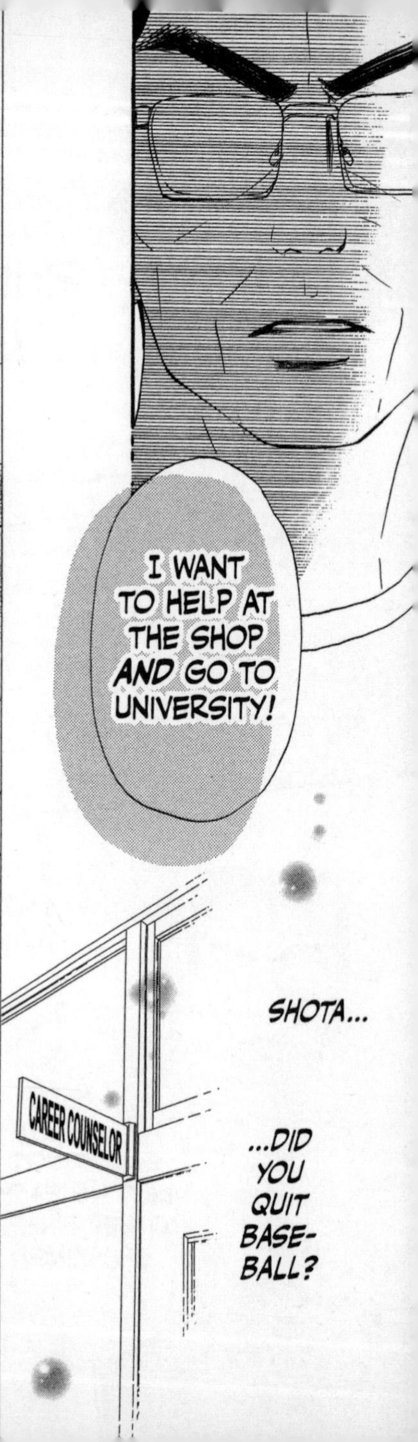
I WANT TO HELP AT THE SHOP AND GO TO UNIVERSITY!
SHOTA...
...DID YOU QUIT BASEBALL?
CAREER COUNSELOR
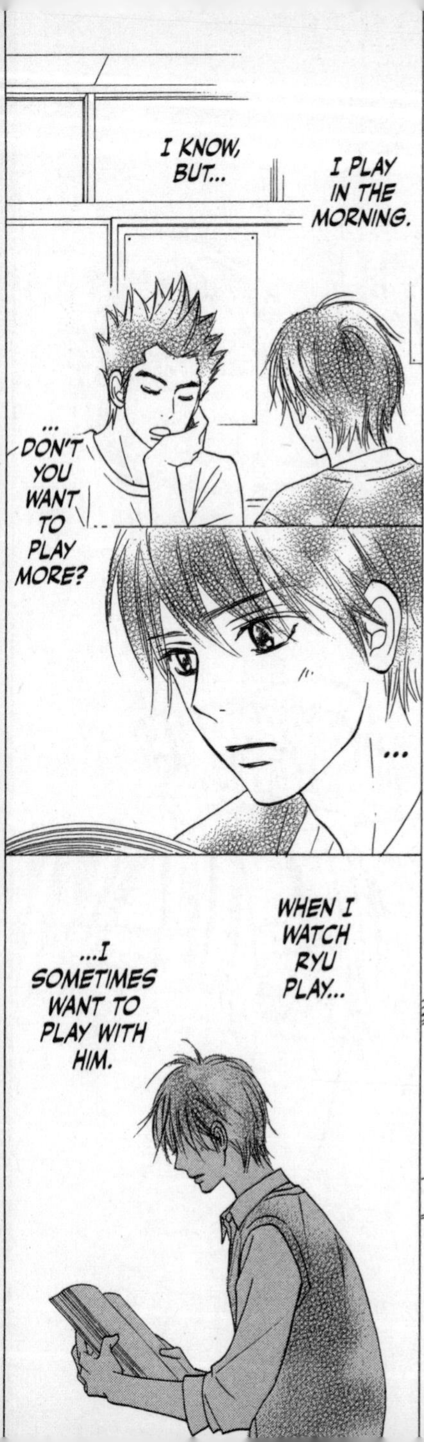
I PLAY IN THE MORNING.
I KNOW, BUT...
...DON'T YOU WANT TO PLAY MORE?
...
WHEN I WATCH RYU PLAY...
...I SOMETIMES WANT TO PLAY WITH HIM.

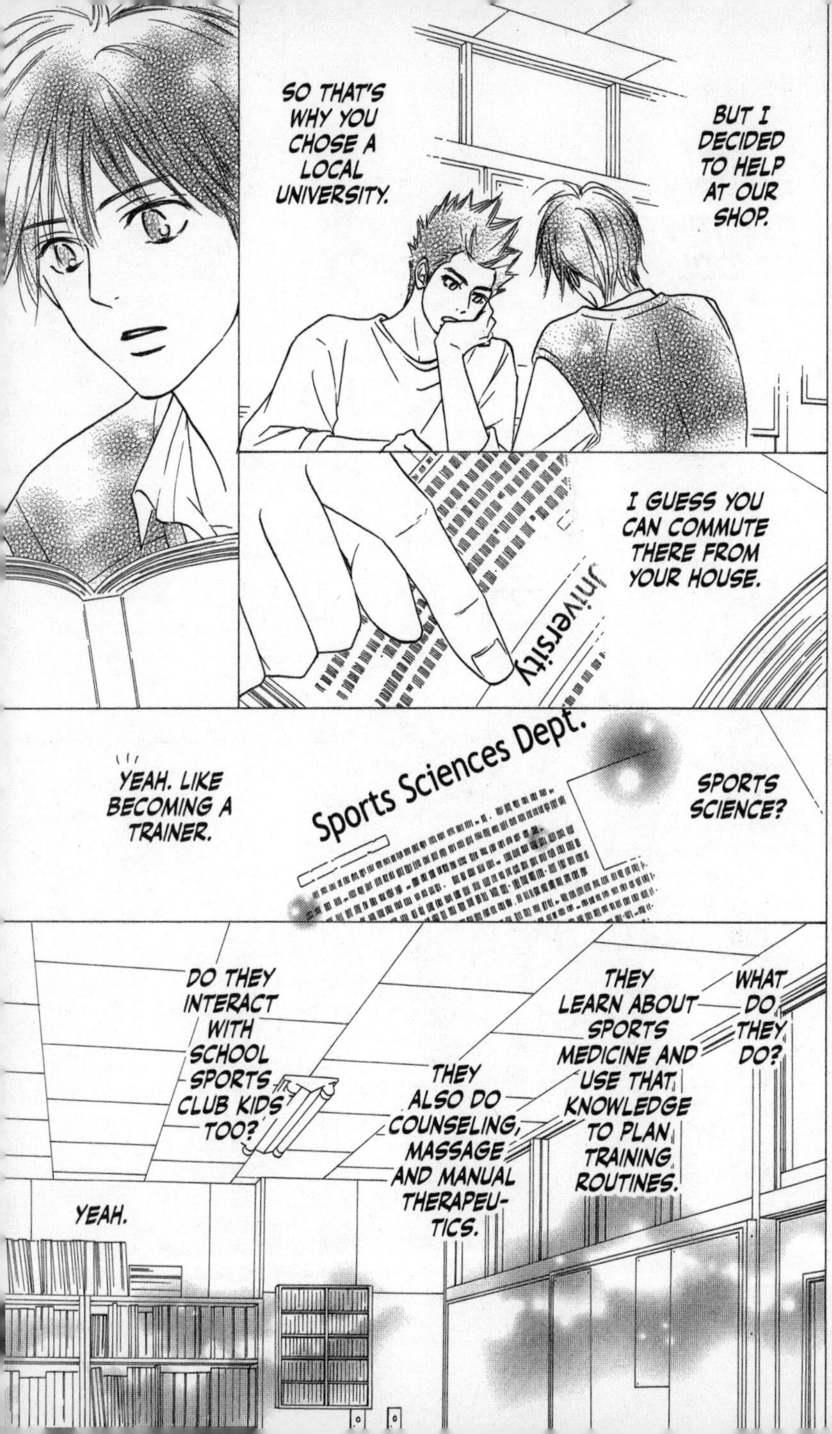
BUT I DECIDED TO HELP AT OUR SHOP.
SO THAT'S WHY YOU CHOSE A LOCAL UNIVERSITY.
I GUESS YOU CAN COMMUTE THERE FROM YOUR HOUSE.
University
SPORTS SCIENCE?
Sports Sciences Dept.
YEAH. LIKE BECOMING A TRAINER.
WHAT DO THEY DO?
THEY LEARN ABOUT SPORTS MEDICINE AND USE THAT KNOWLEDGE TO PLAN TRAINING ROUTINES.
THEY ALSO DO COUNSELING, MASSAGE AND MANUAL THERAPEU-TICS.
DO THEY INTERACT WITH SCHOOL SPORTS CLUB KIDS TOO?
YEAH.

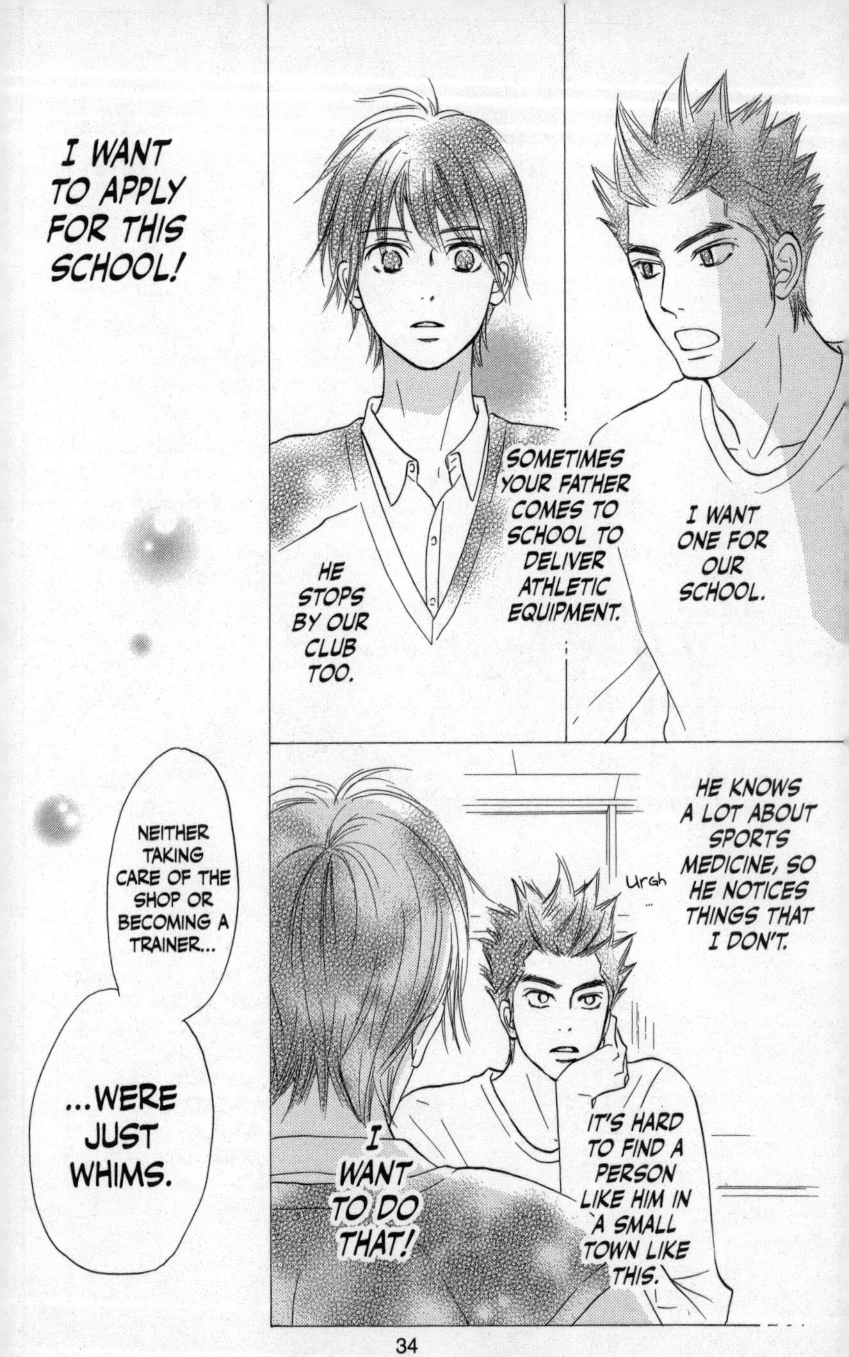

I WANT ONE FOR OUR SCHOOL.
SOMETIMES YOUR FATHER COMES TO SCHOOL TO DELIVER ATHLETIC EQUIPMENT.
HE STOPS BY OUR CLUB TOO.
HE KNOWS A LOT ABOUT SPORTS MEDICINE, SO HE NOTICES THINGS THAT I DON'T.
Urgh ...
IT'S HARD TO FIND A PERSON LIKE HIM IN A SMALL TOWN LIKE THIS.
I WANT TO DO THAT!
I WANT TO APPLY FOR THIS SCHOOL!
NEITHER TAKING CARE OF THE SHOP OR BECOMING A TRAINER...
...WERE JUST WHIMS.

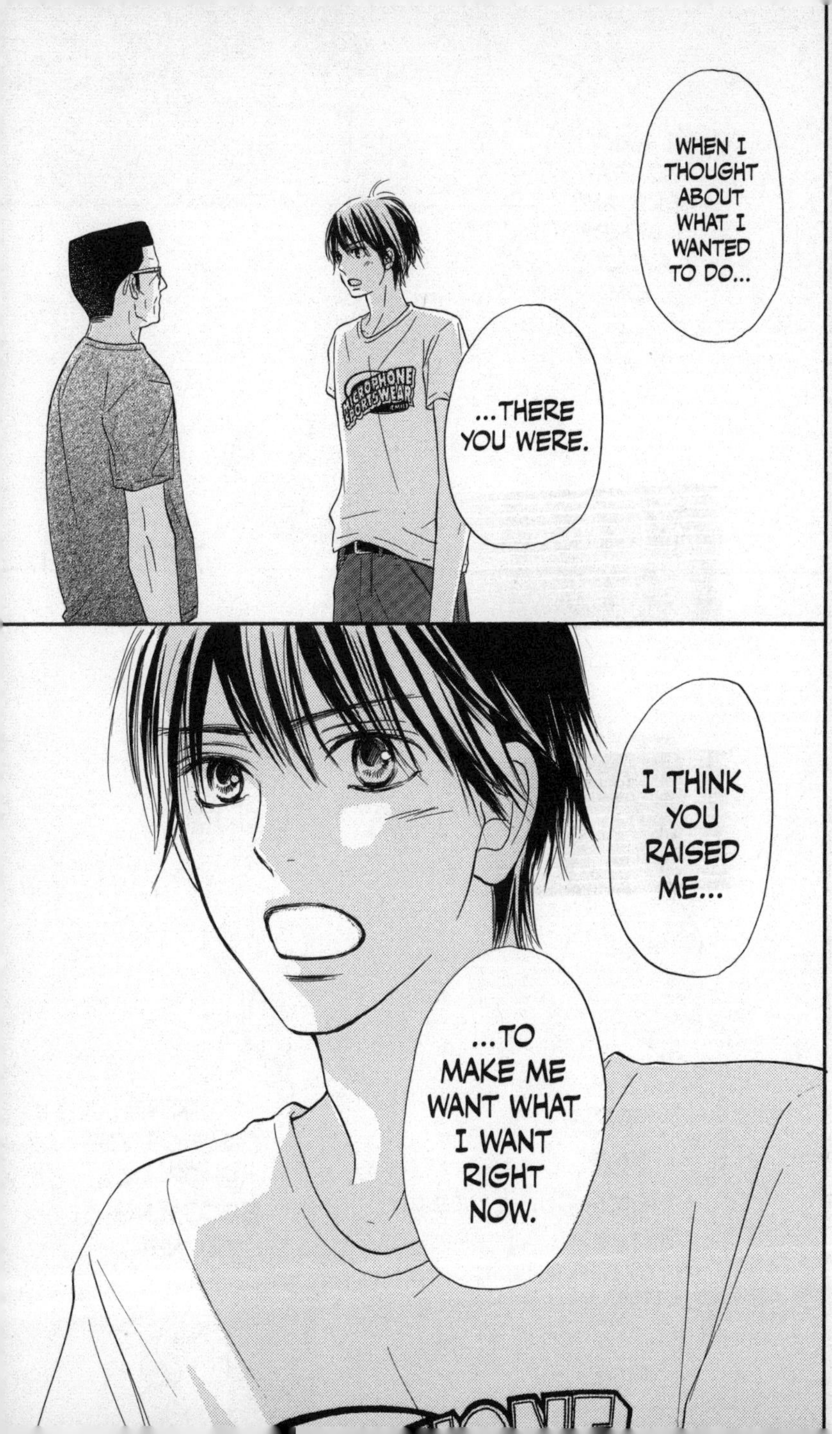

WHEN I THOUGHT ABOUT WHAT I WANTED TO DO...
...THERE YOU WERE.
MICROPHONE SPORTSWEAR
I THINK YOU RAISED ME...
...TO MAKE ME WANT WHAT I WANT RIGHT NOW.

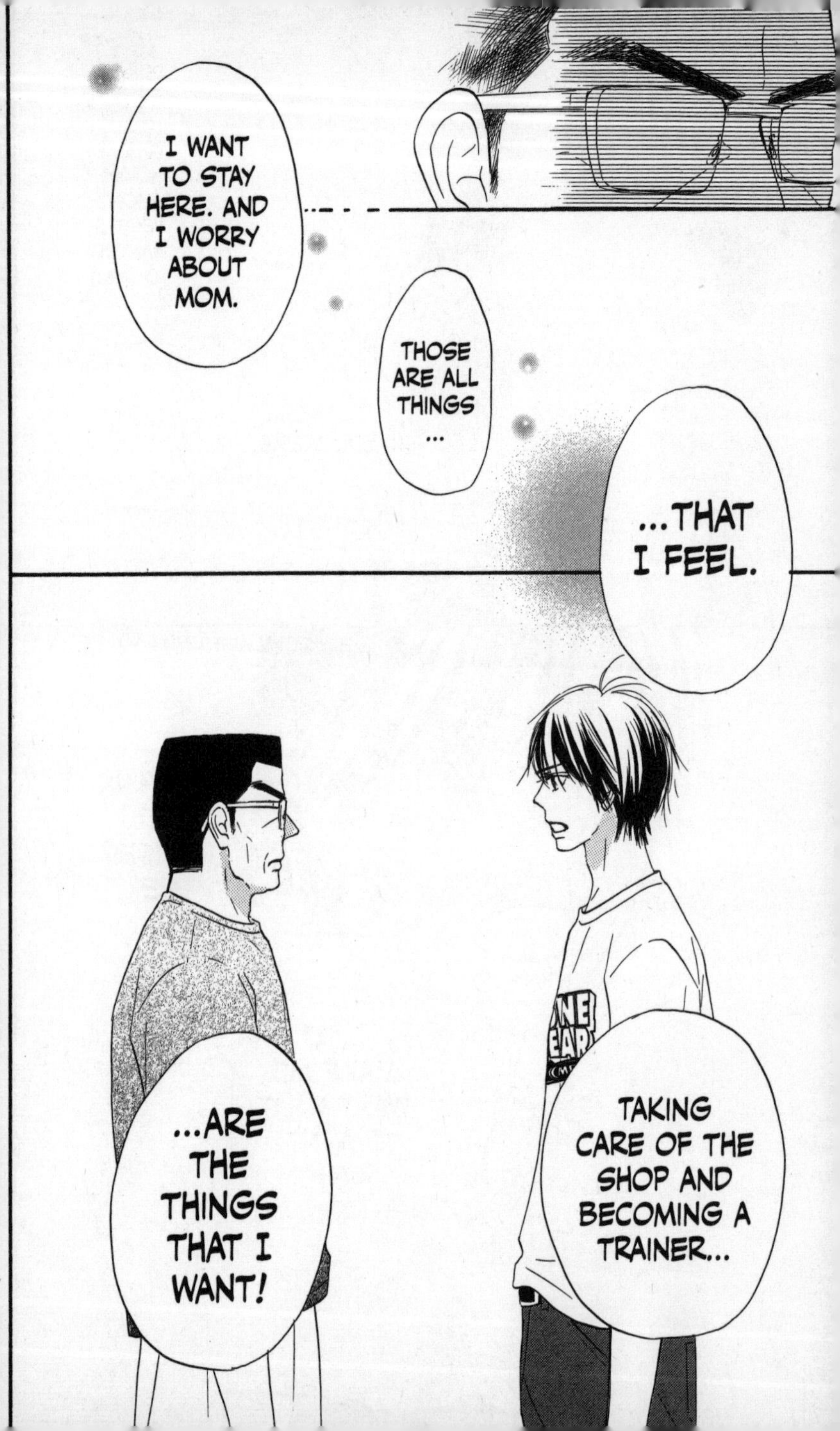
I WANT TO STAY HERE. AND I WORRY ABOUT MOM.
THOSE ARE ALL THINGS ...
...THAT I FEEL.
TAKING CARE OF THE SHOP AND BECOMING A TRAINER...
...ARE THE THINGS THAT I WANT!

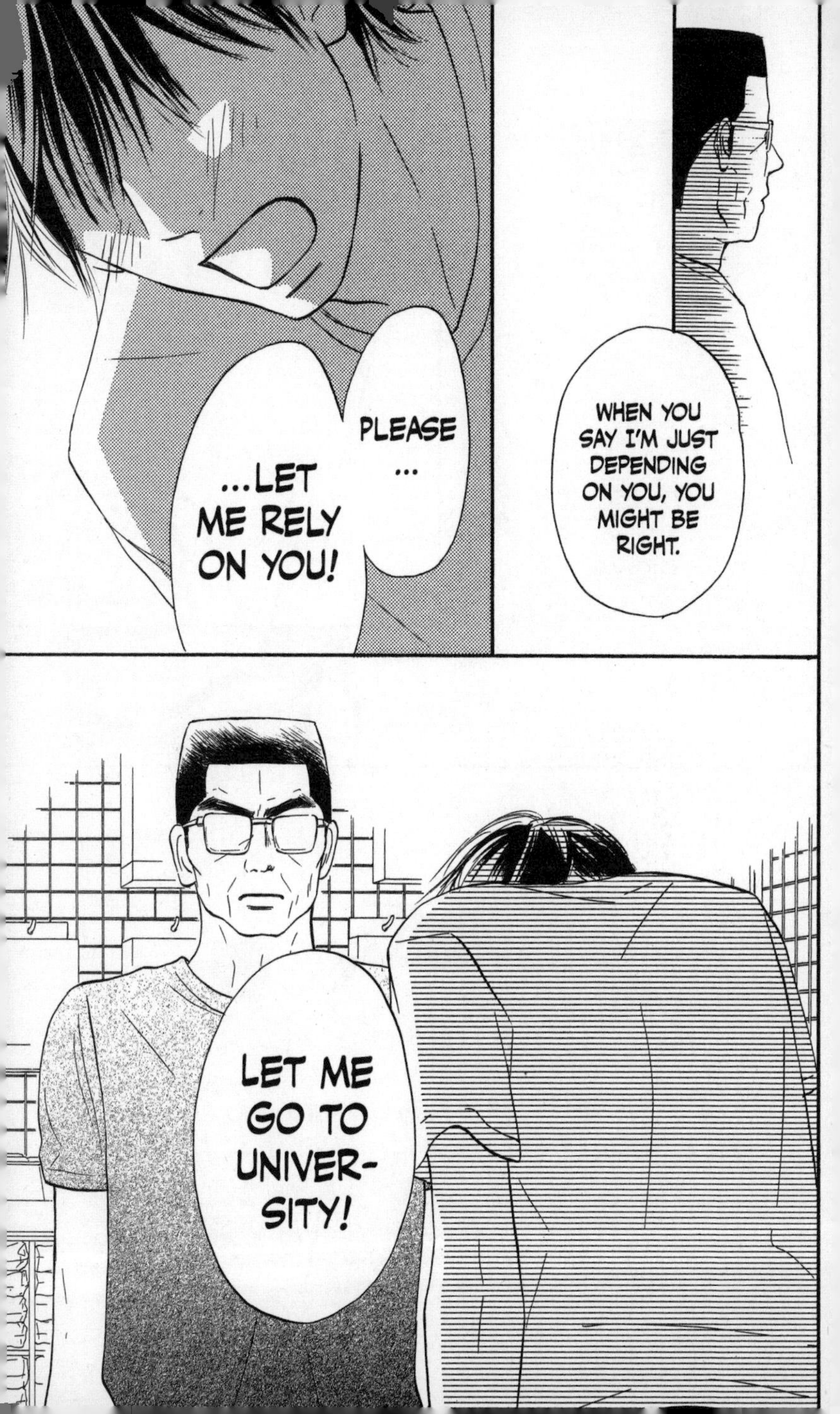
WHEN YOU SAY I'M JUST DEPENDING ON YOU, YOU MIGHT BE RIGHT.
PLEASE ...
...LET ME RELY ON YOU!
LET ME GO TO UNIVER-SITY!

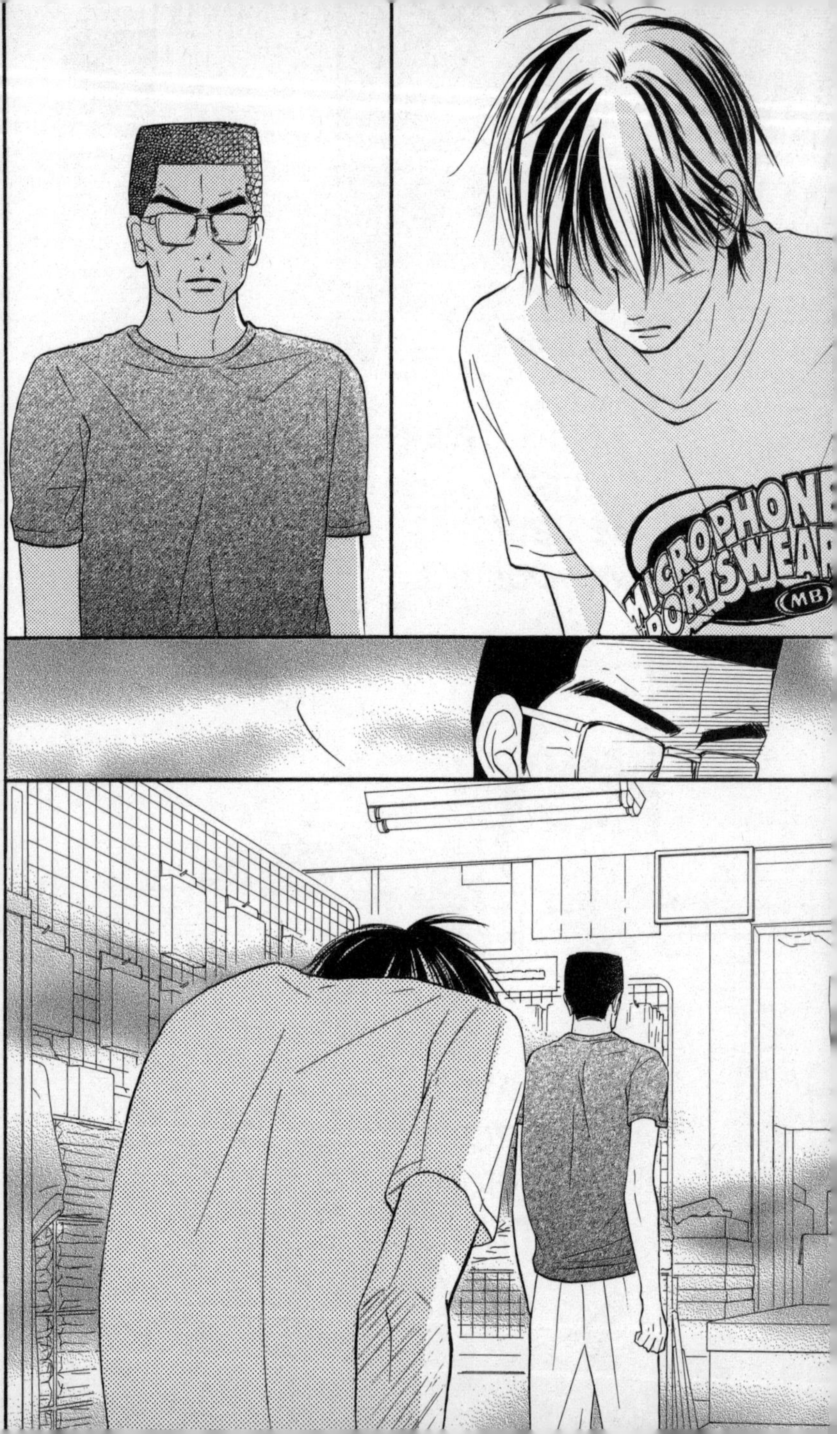
MICROPHONE
MB

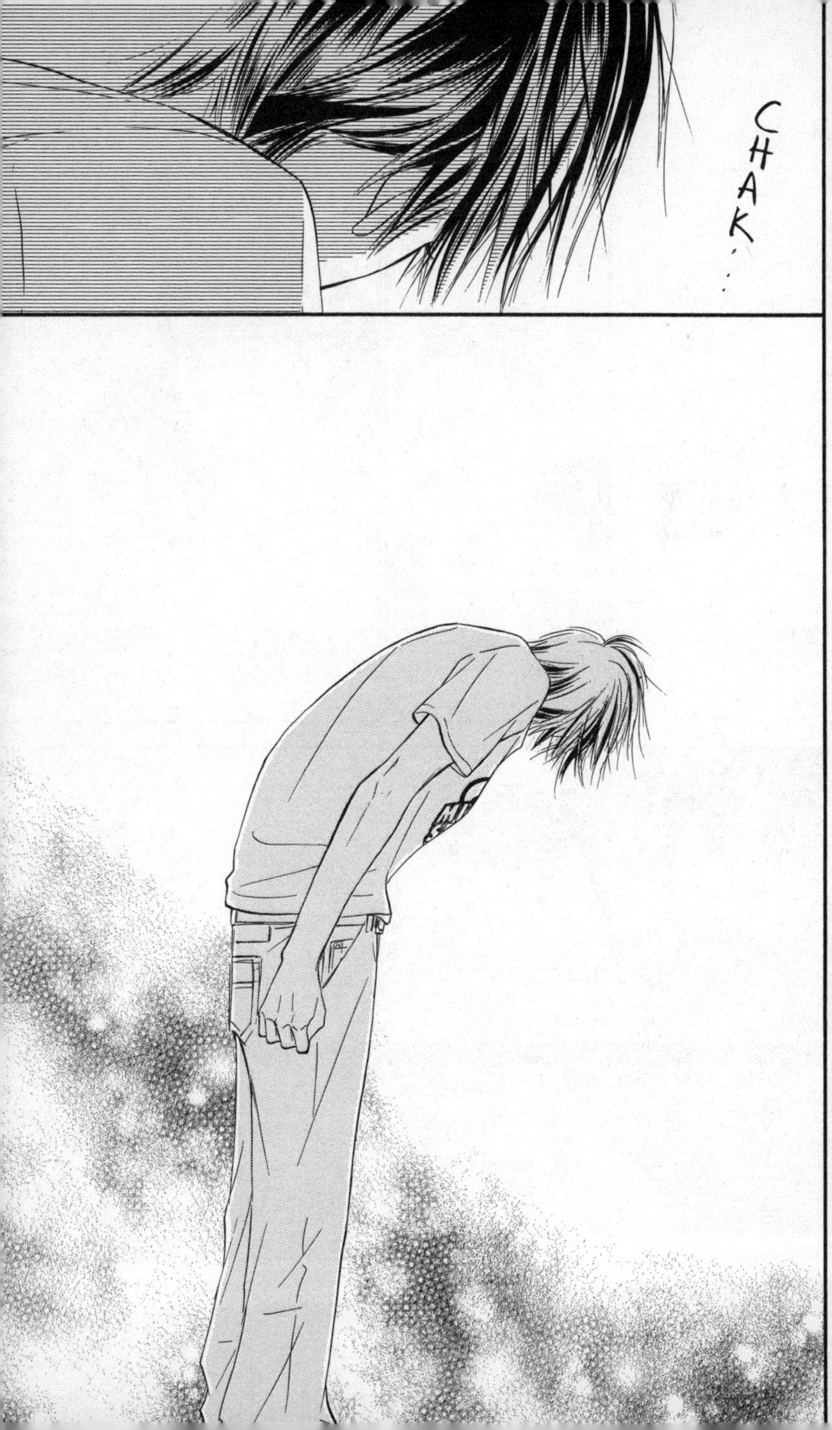
CHAK...

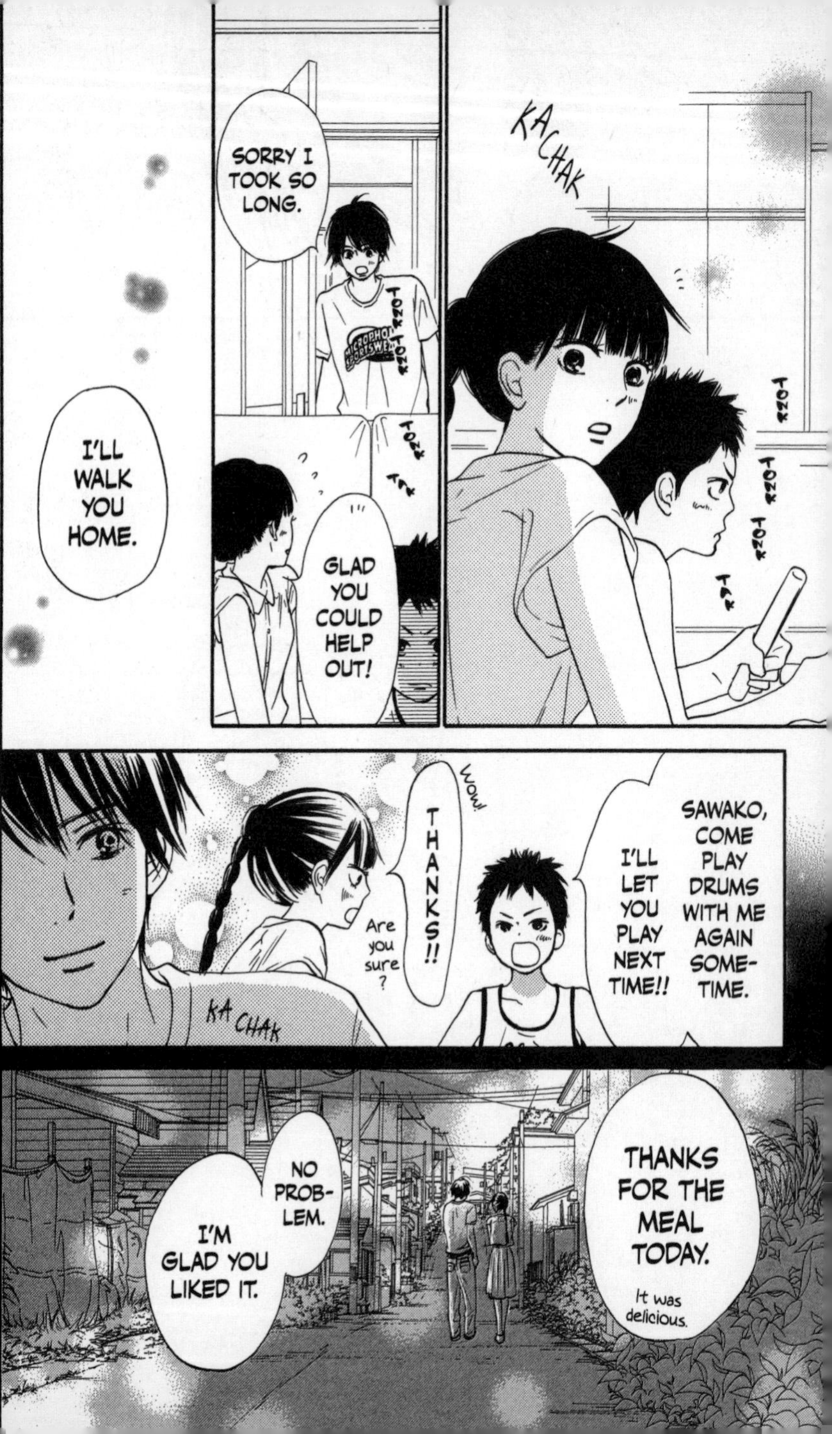
KACHAK
TONK
TONK
TONK
TAK
SORRY I TOOK SO LONG.
TONK TONK TONK
TONK
TAK
GLAD YOU COULD HELP OUT!
I'LL WALK YOU HOME.
SAWAKO, COME PLAY DRUMS WITH ME AGAIN SOMETIME.
I'LL LET YOU PLAY NEXT TIME!!
Wow!
THANKS!!
Are you sure?
KA CHAK
THANKS FOR THE MEAL TODAY.
It was delicious.
NO PROBLEM.
I'M GLAD YOU LIKED IT.

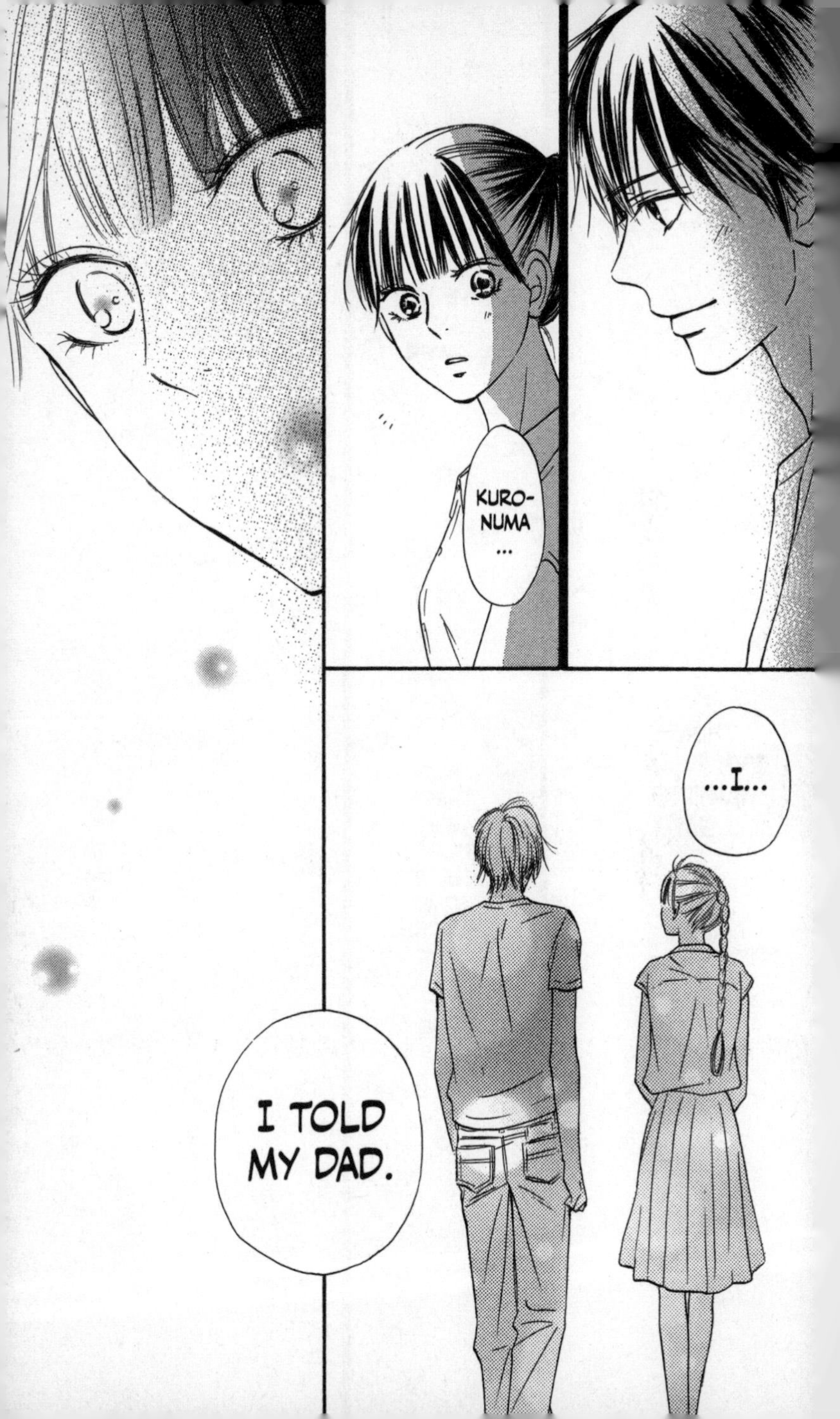
KURO-NUMA ...
...I...
I TOLD MY DAD.

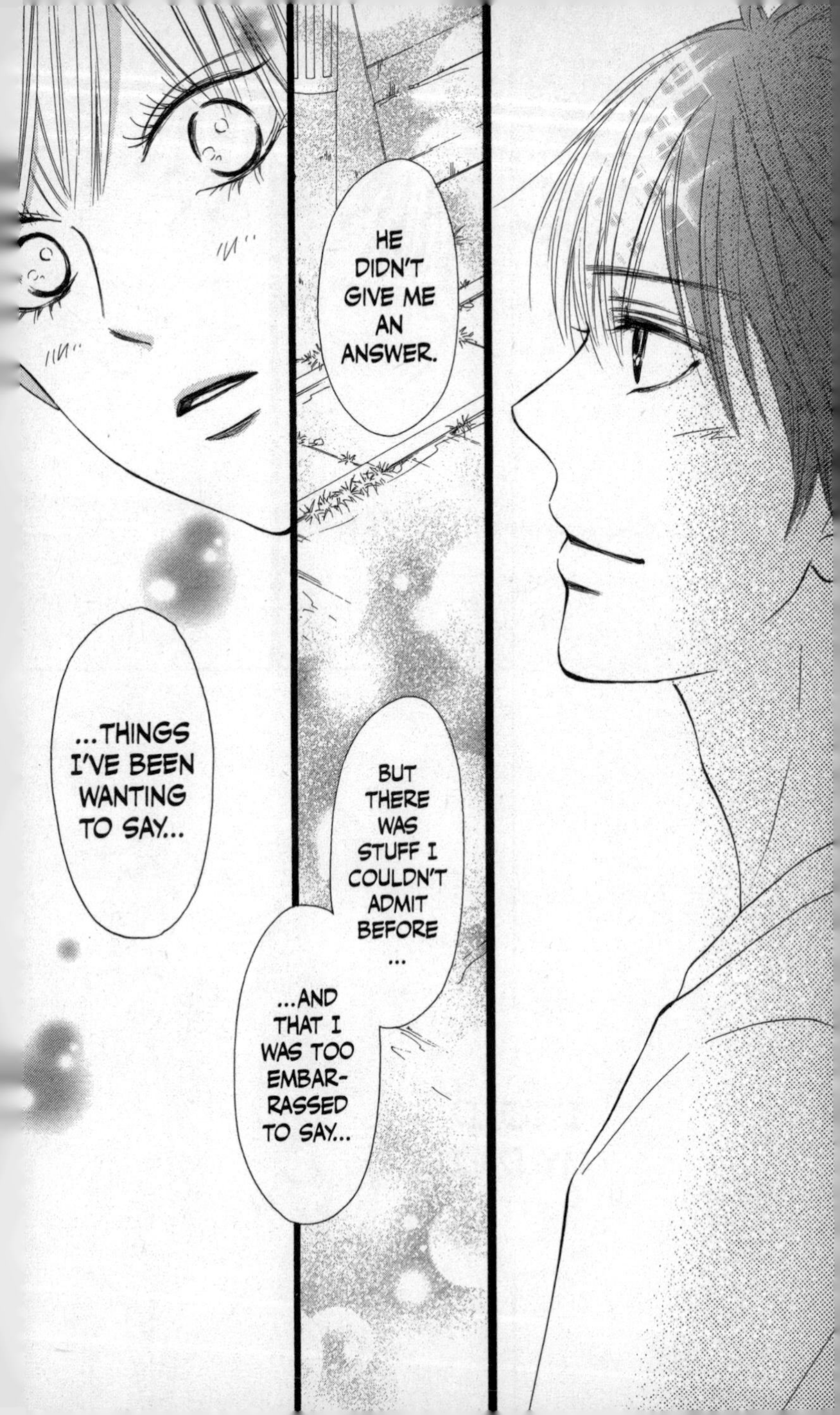
HE DIDN'T GIVE ME AN ANSWER.
BUT THERE WAS STUFF I COULDN'T ADMIT BEFORE ...
...AND THAT I WAS TOO EMBAR-RASSED TO SAY...
...THINGS I'VE BEEN WANTING TO SAY...

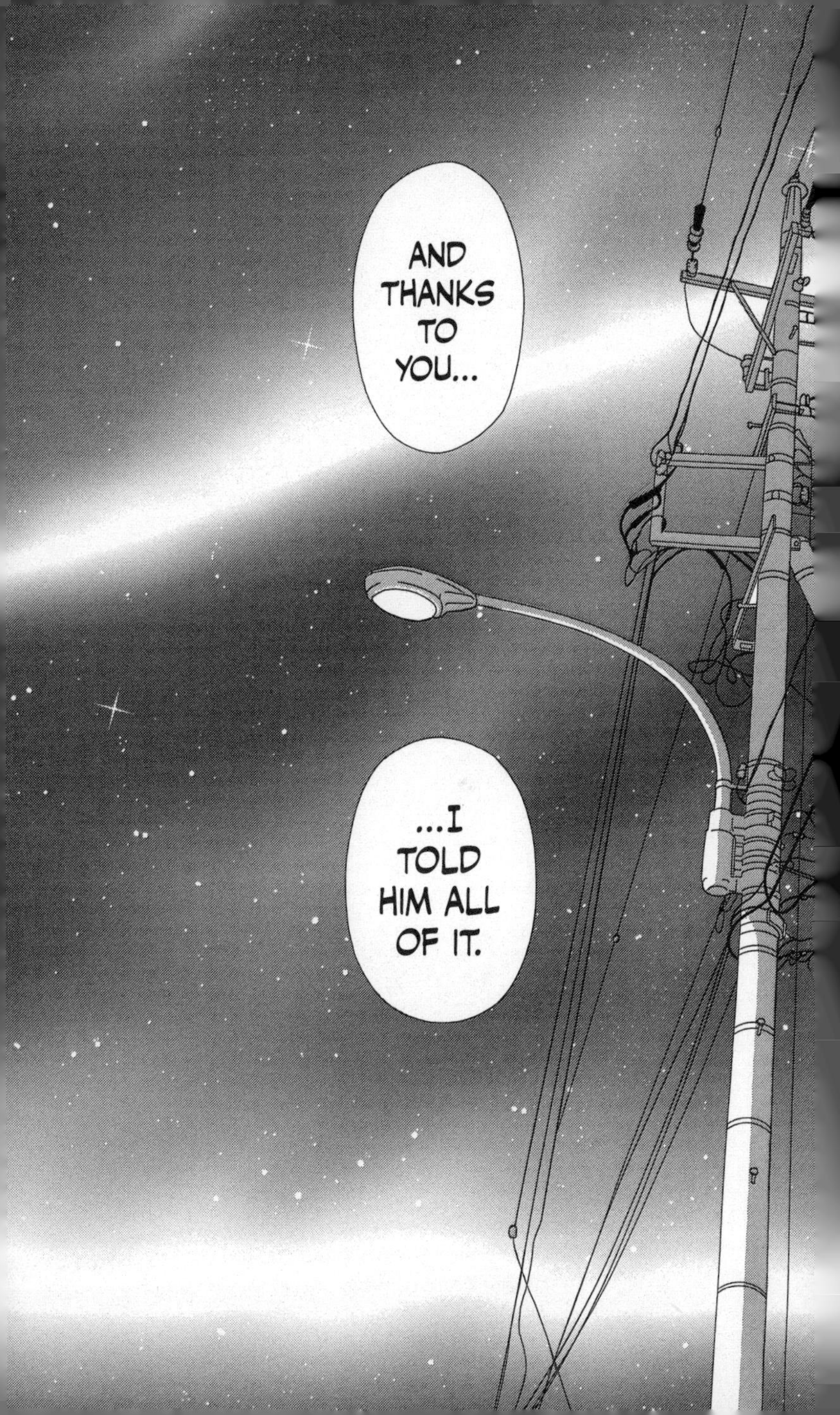
AND THANKS TO YOU...
...I TOLD HIM ALL OF IT.

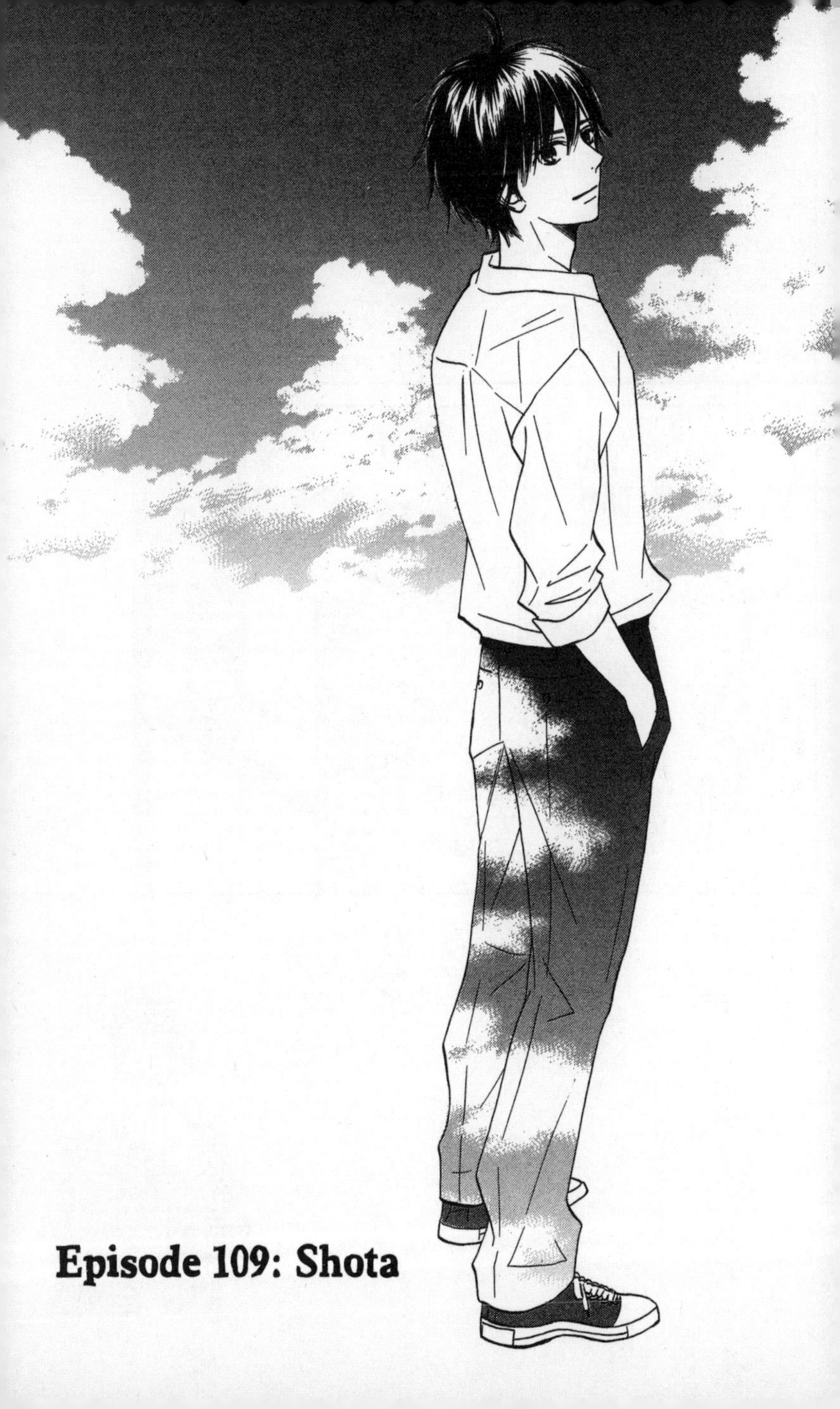

Episode 109: Shota

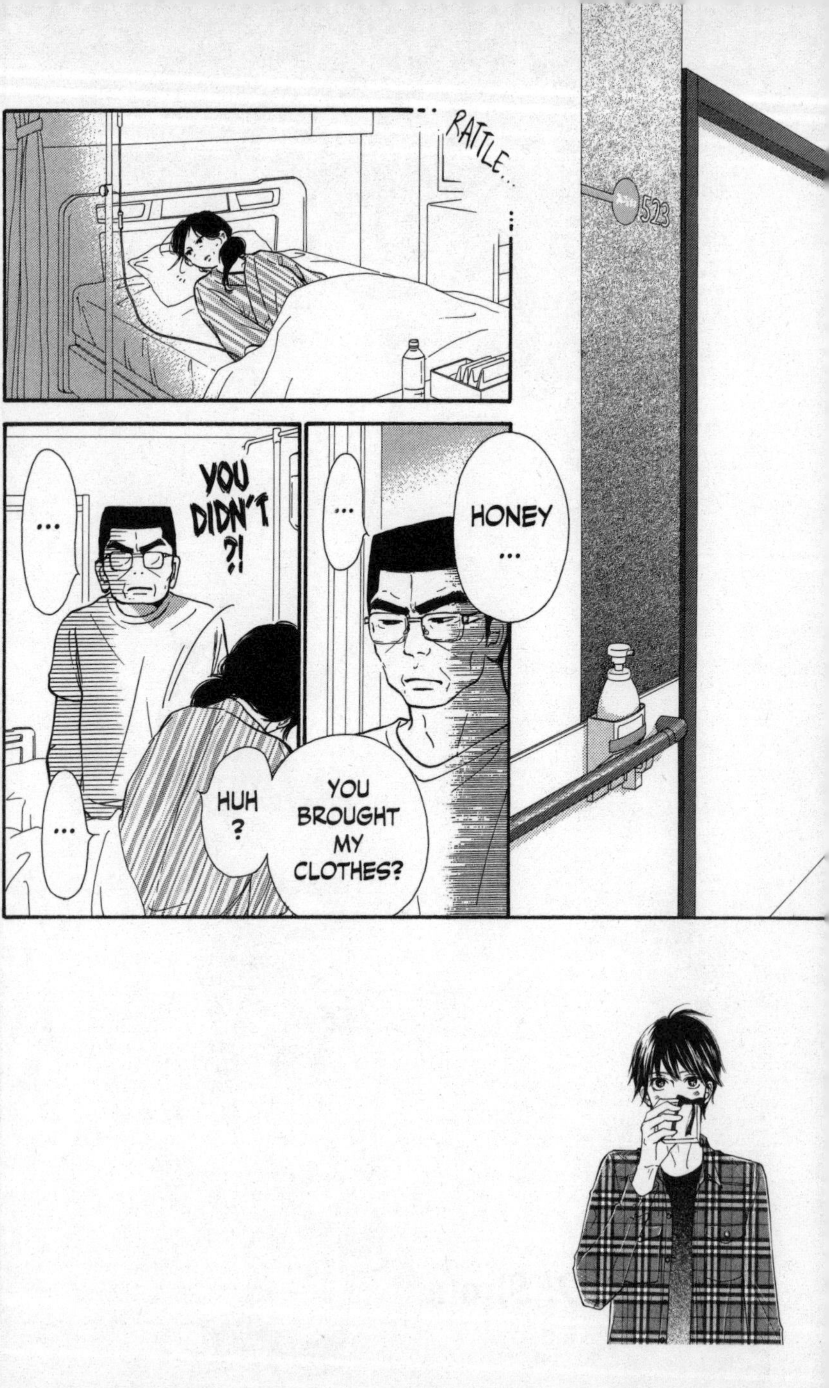
RATTLE...
523
HONEY ...
...
YOU BROUGHT MY CLOTHES?
HUH ?
YOU DIDN'T ?!
...
...

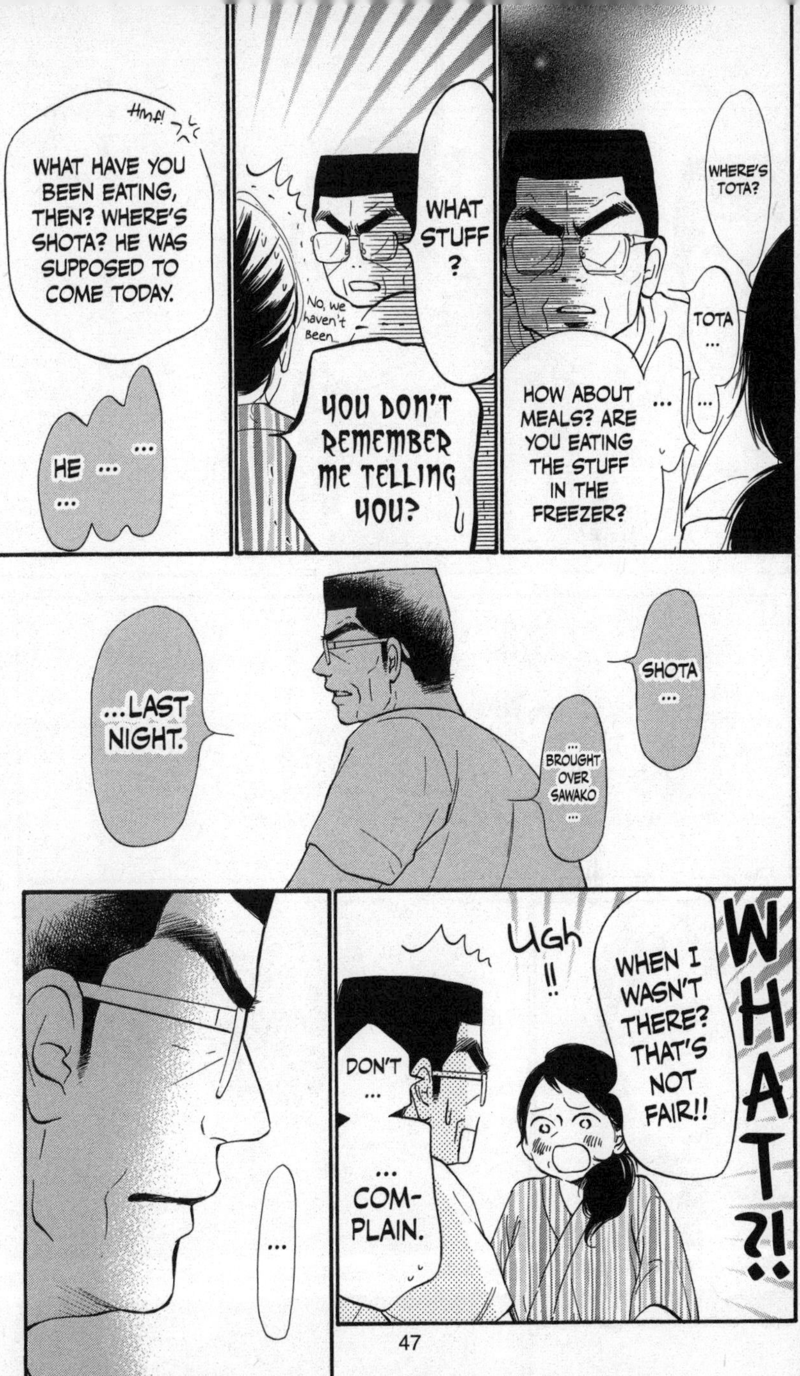
WHERE'S TOTA?
TOTA ...
...
...
HOW ABOUT MEALS? ARE YOU EATING THE STUFF IN THE FREEZER?
WHAT STUFF ?
No, we haven't Been...
YOU DON'T REMEMBER ME TELLING YOU?
Hmf!
WHAT HAVE YOU BEEN EATING, THEN? WHERE'S SHOTA? HE WAS SUPPOSED TO COME TODAY.
HE ... ...
SHOTA ...
... BROUGHT OVER SAWAKO ...
...LAST NIGHT.
WHAT?!
WHEN I WASN'T THERE? THAT'S NOT FAIR!!
Ugh !!
DON'T ... ... COM-PLAIN.
...

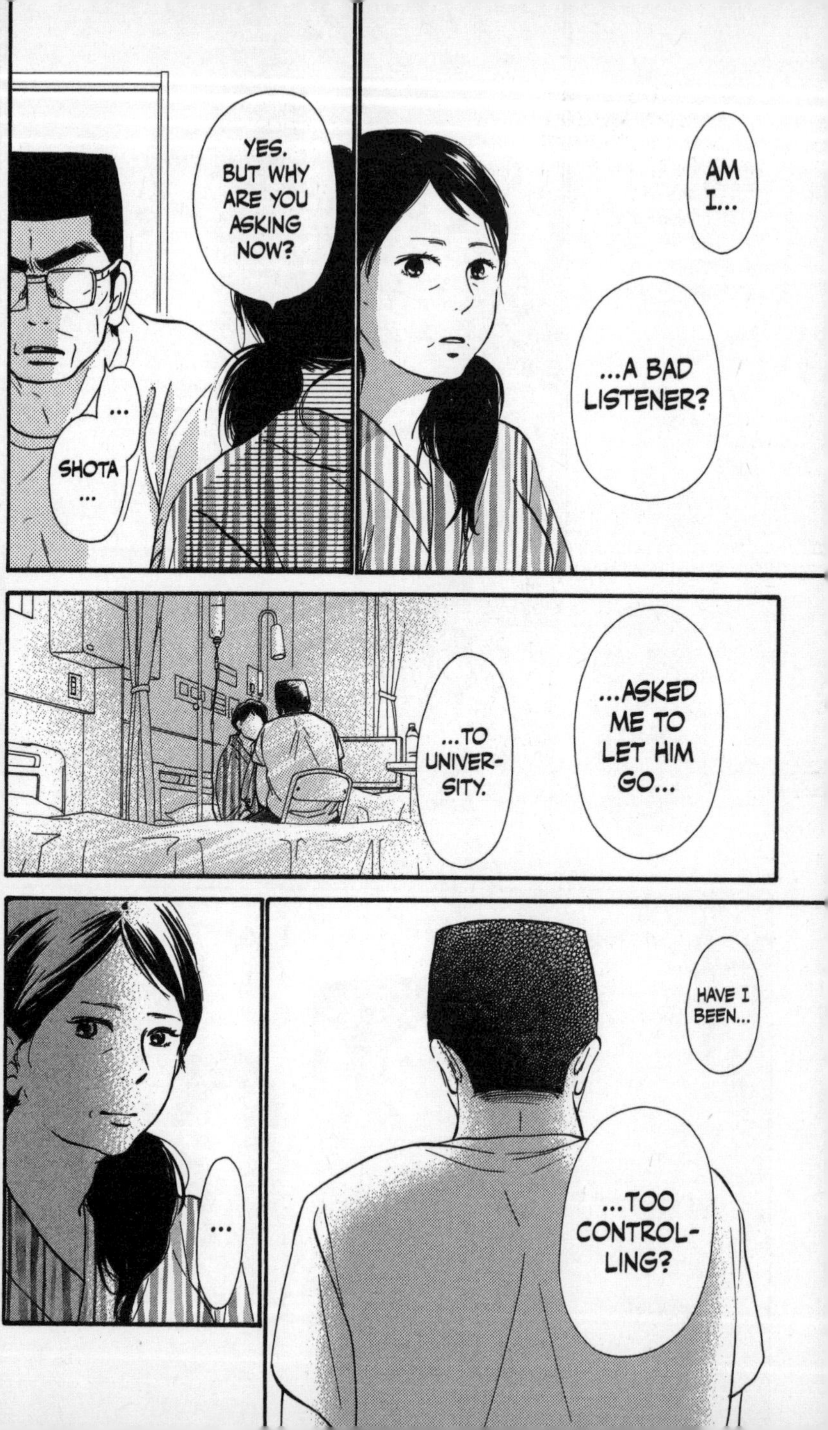
AM I...
...A BAD LISTENER?
YES. BUT WHY ARE YOU ASKING NOW?
...
SHOTA...
...ASKED ME TO LET HIM GO...
...TO UNIVERSITY.
HAVE I BEEN...
...TOO CONTROLLING?
...

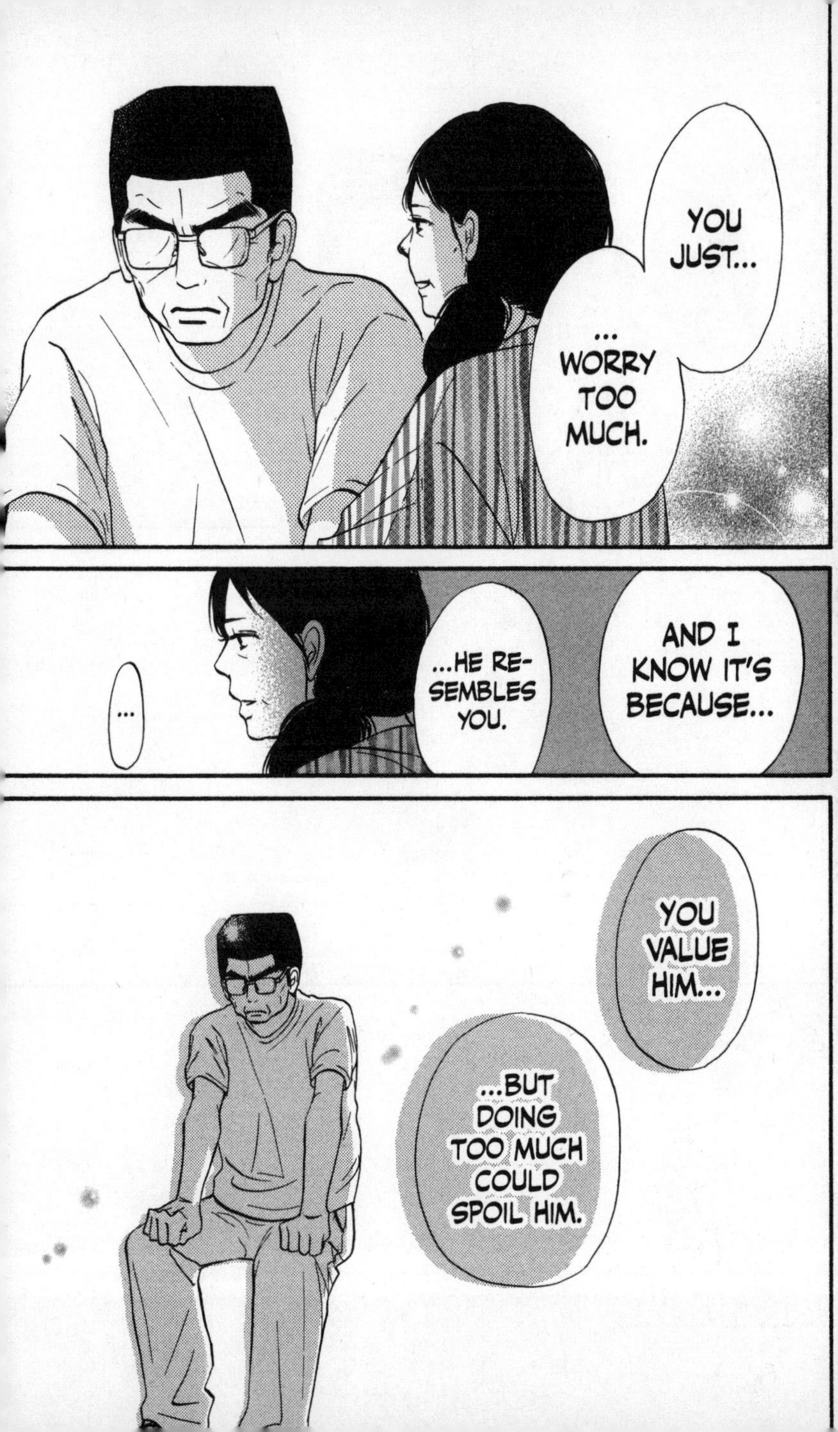
YOU JUST...
...WORRY TOO MUCH.
AND I KNOW IT'S BECAUSE...
...HE RE-SEMBLES YOU.
...
YOU VALUE HIM...
...BUT DOING TOO MUCH COULD SPOIL HIM.

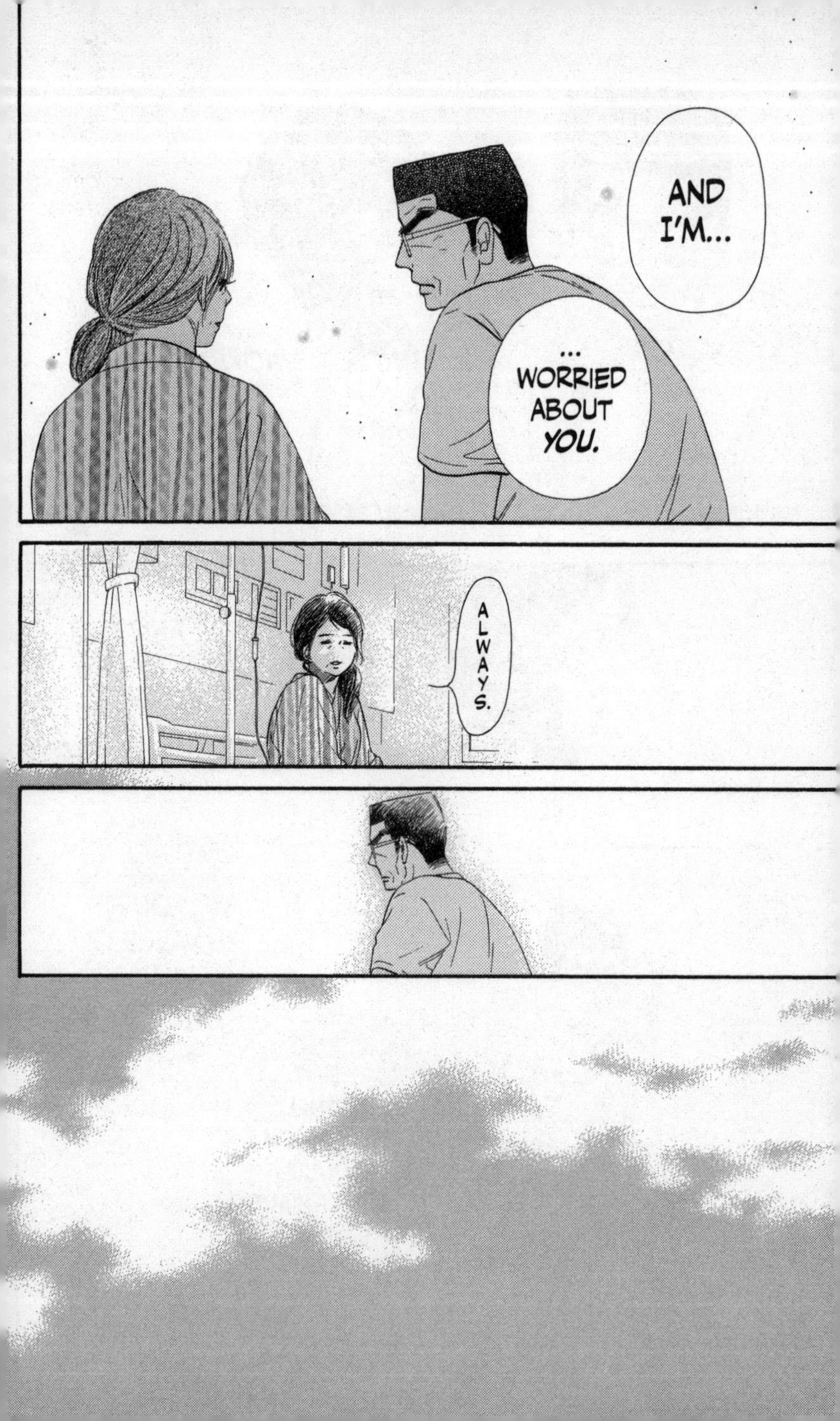
AND I'M...
... WORRIED ABOUT YOU.
ALWAYS.

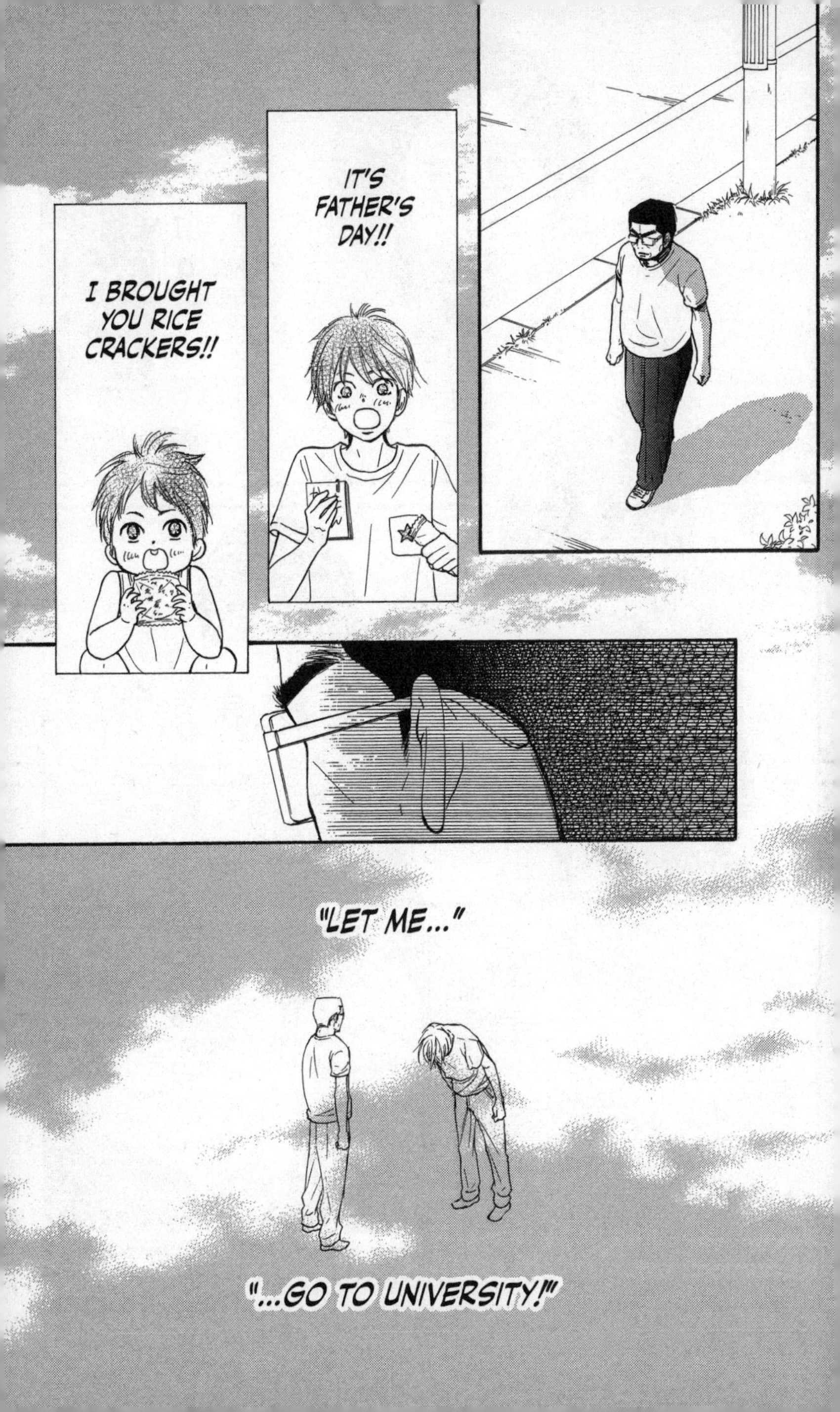
IT'S FATHER'S DAY!!
I BROUGHT YOU RICE CRACKERS!!
"LET ME..."
"...GO TO UNIVERSITY!"

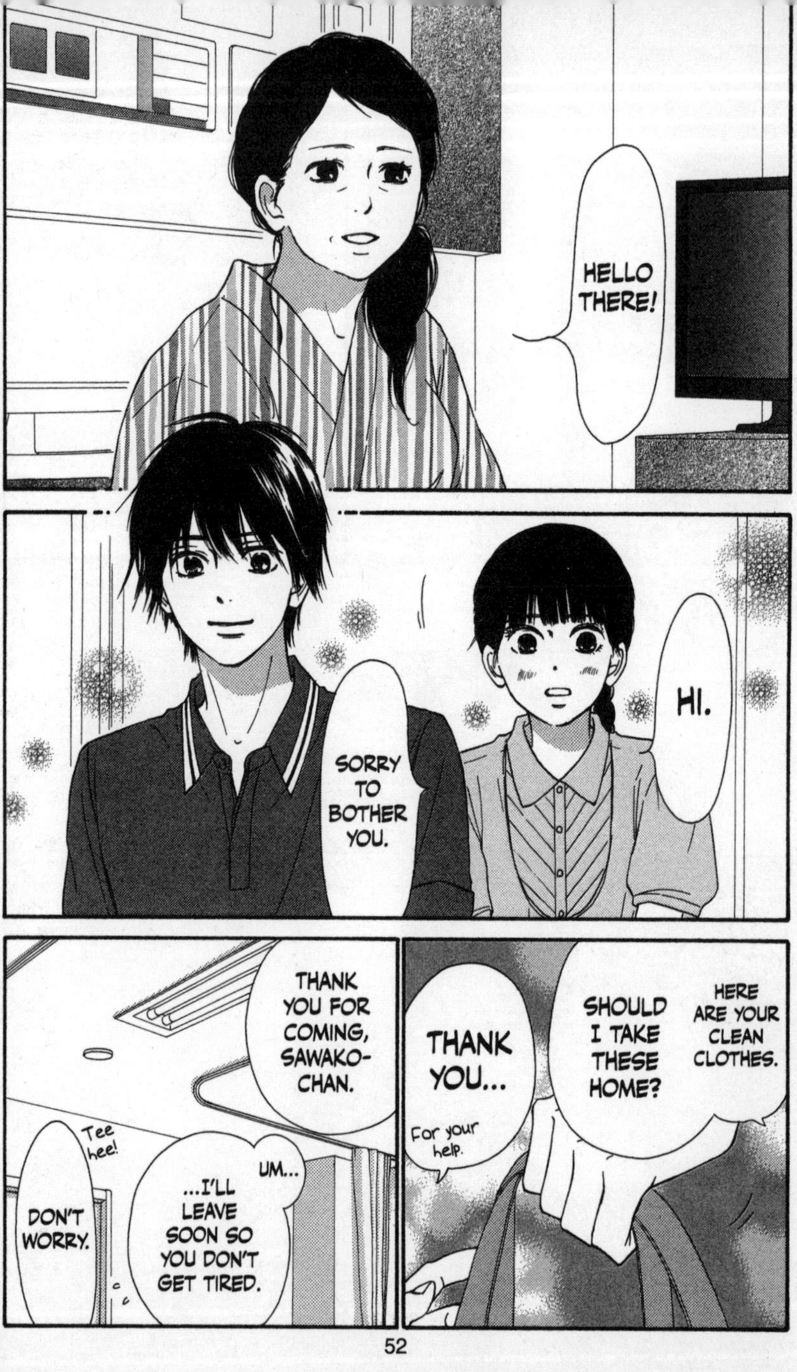
HELLO THERE!
HI.
SORRY TO BOTHER YOU.
HERE ARE YOUR CLEAN CLOTHES.
SHOULD I TAKE THESE HOME?
THANK YOU...
For your help.
THANK YOU FOR COMING, SAWAKO-CHAN.
UM...
...I'LL LEAVE SOON SO YOU DON'T GET TIRED.
Tee hee!
DON'T WORRY.

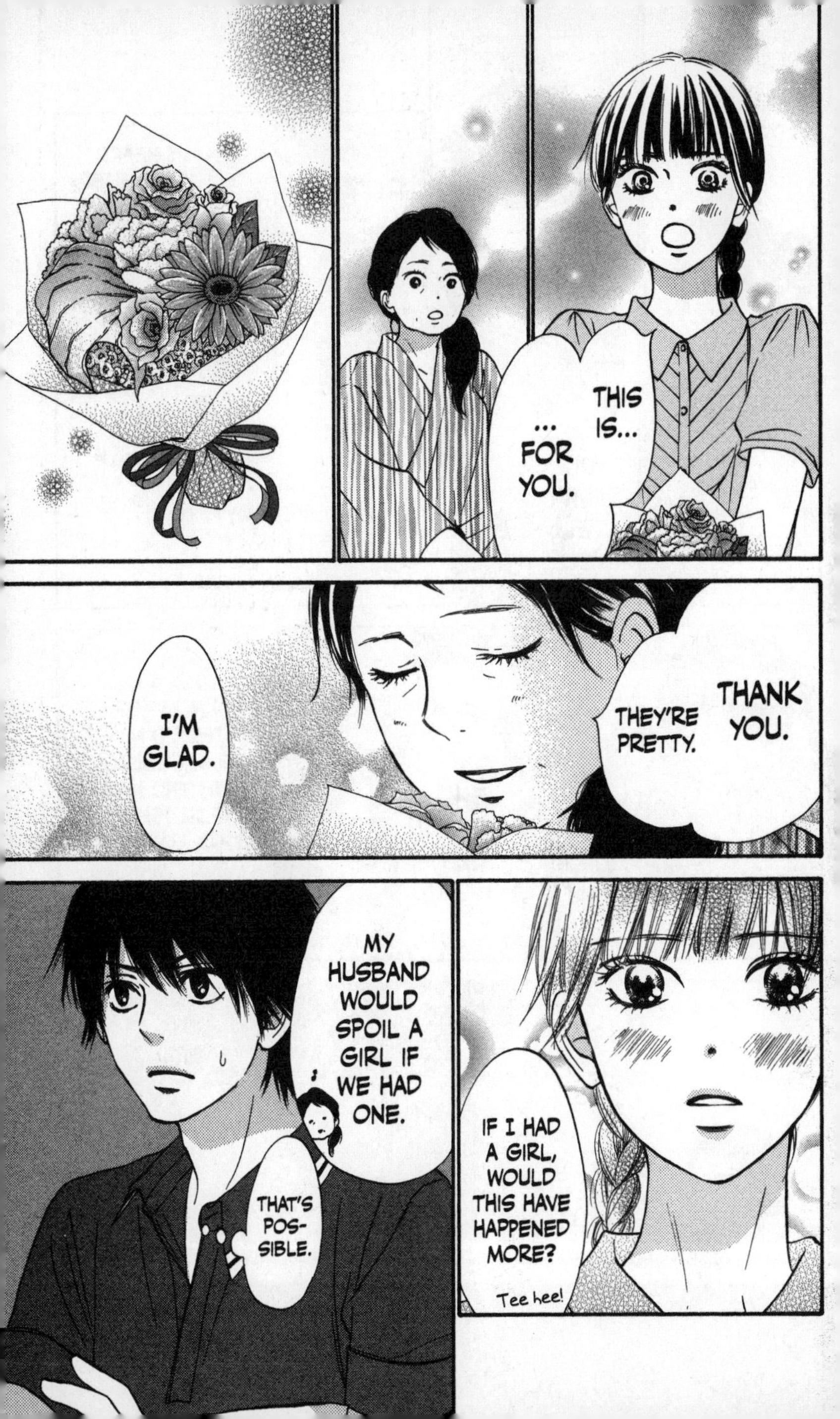
THIS IS... ...FOR YOU.
THANK YOU. THEY'RE PRETTY.
I'M GLAD.
IF I HAD A GIRL, WOULD THIS HAVE HAPPENED MORE?
Tee hee!
MY HUSBAND WOULD SPOIL A GIRL IF WE HAD ONE.
THAT'S POS-SIBLE.

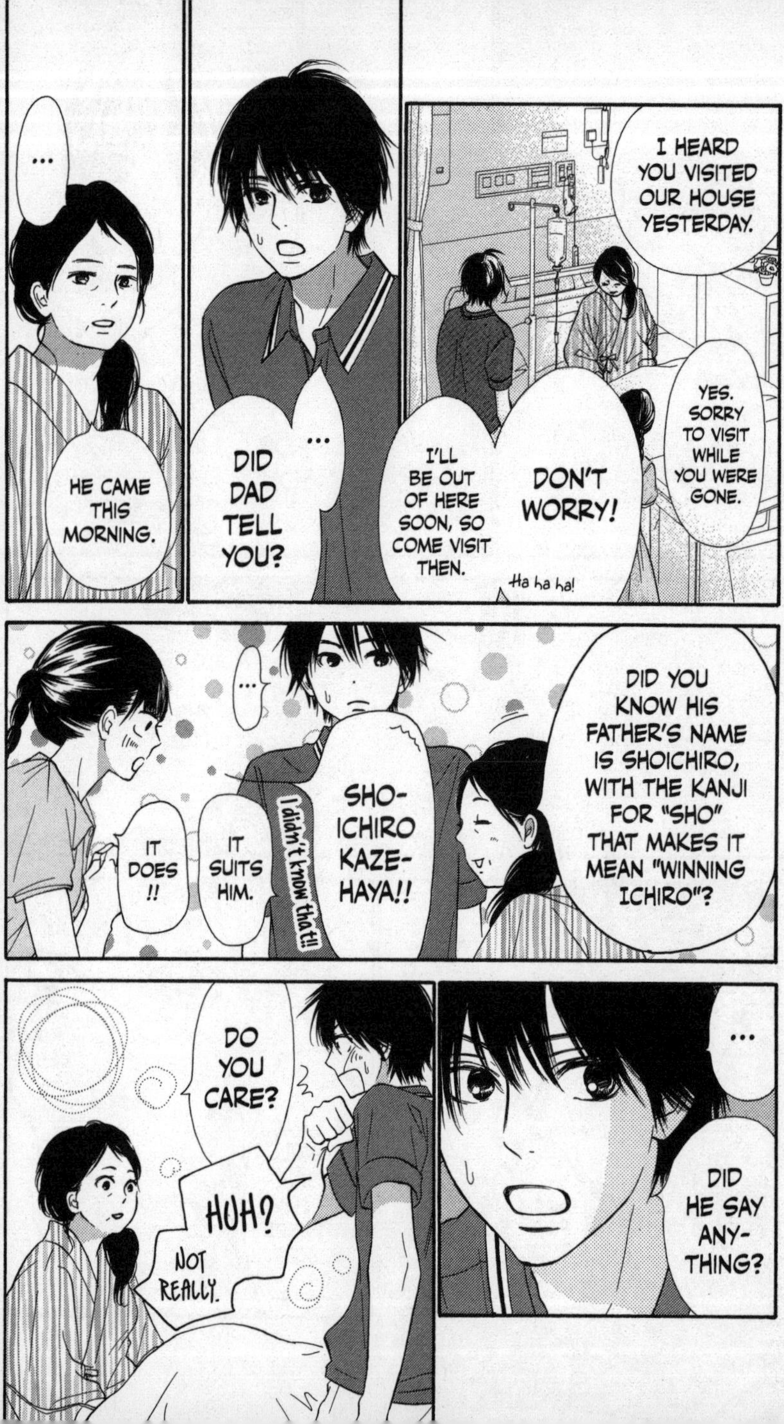
I HEARD YOU VISITED OUR HOUSE YESTERDAY.
YES. SORRY TO VISIT WHILE YOU WERE GONE.
DON'T WORRY!
I'LL BE OUT OF HERE SOON, SO COME VISIT THEN.
Ha ha ha!
...
DID DAD TELL YOU?
...
HE CAME THIS MORNING.
DID YOU KNOW HIS FATHER'S NAME IS SHOICHIRO, WITH THE KANJI FOR "SHO" THAT MAKES IT MEAN "WINNING ICHIRO"?
SHO-ICHIRO KAZE-HAYA!!
I didn't know that!!
...
IT SUITS HIM.
IT DOES!!
...
DID HE SAY ANY-THING?
DO YOU CARE?
HUH?
NOT REALLY.

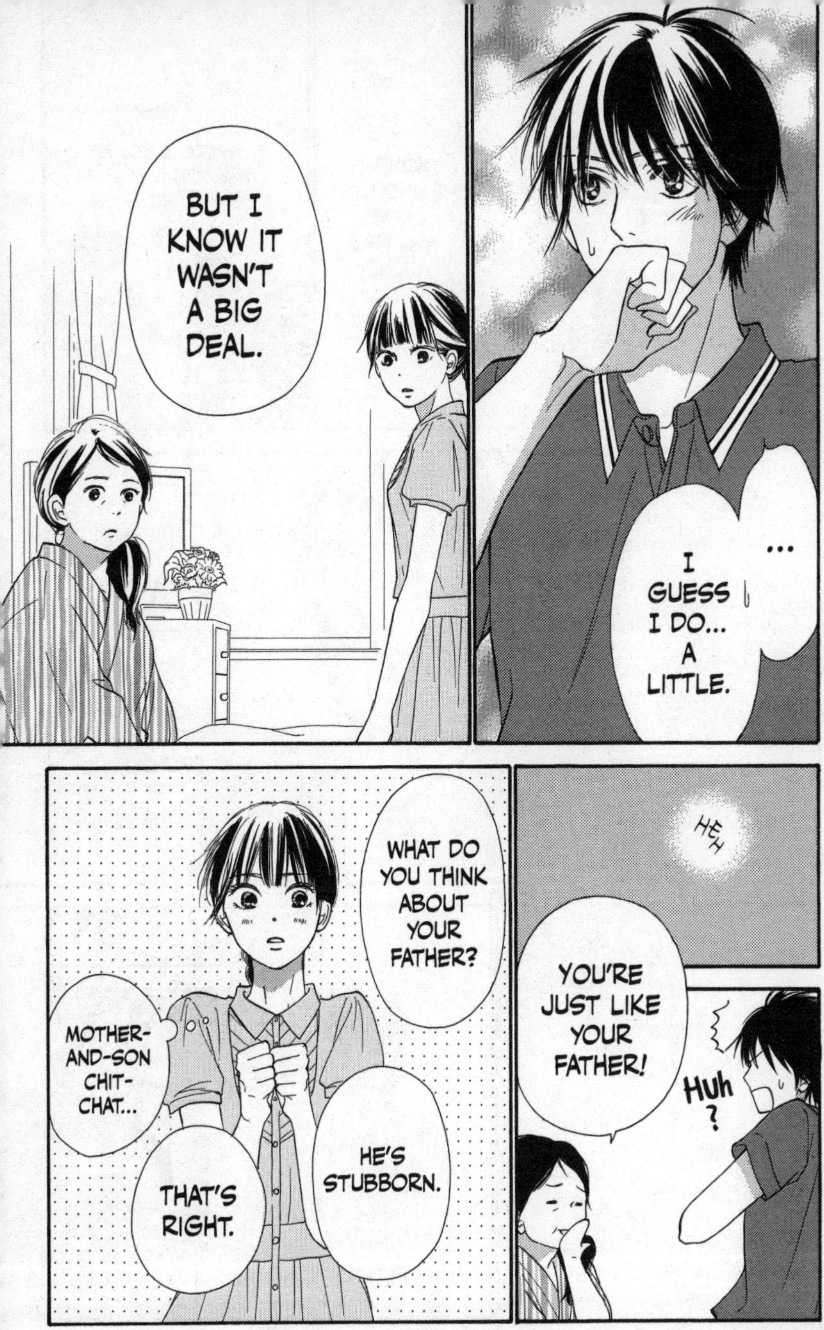
...
I GUESS I DO... A LITTLE.
BUT I KNOW IT WASN'T A BIG DEAL.
HEH
YOU'RE JUST LIKE YOUR FATHER!
Huh?
WHAT DO YOU THINK ABOUT YOUR FATHER?
HE'S STUBBORN.
MOTHER-AND-SON CHIT-CHAT...
THAT'S RIGHT.

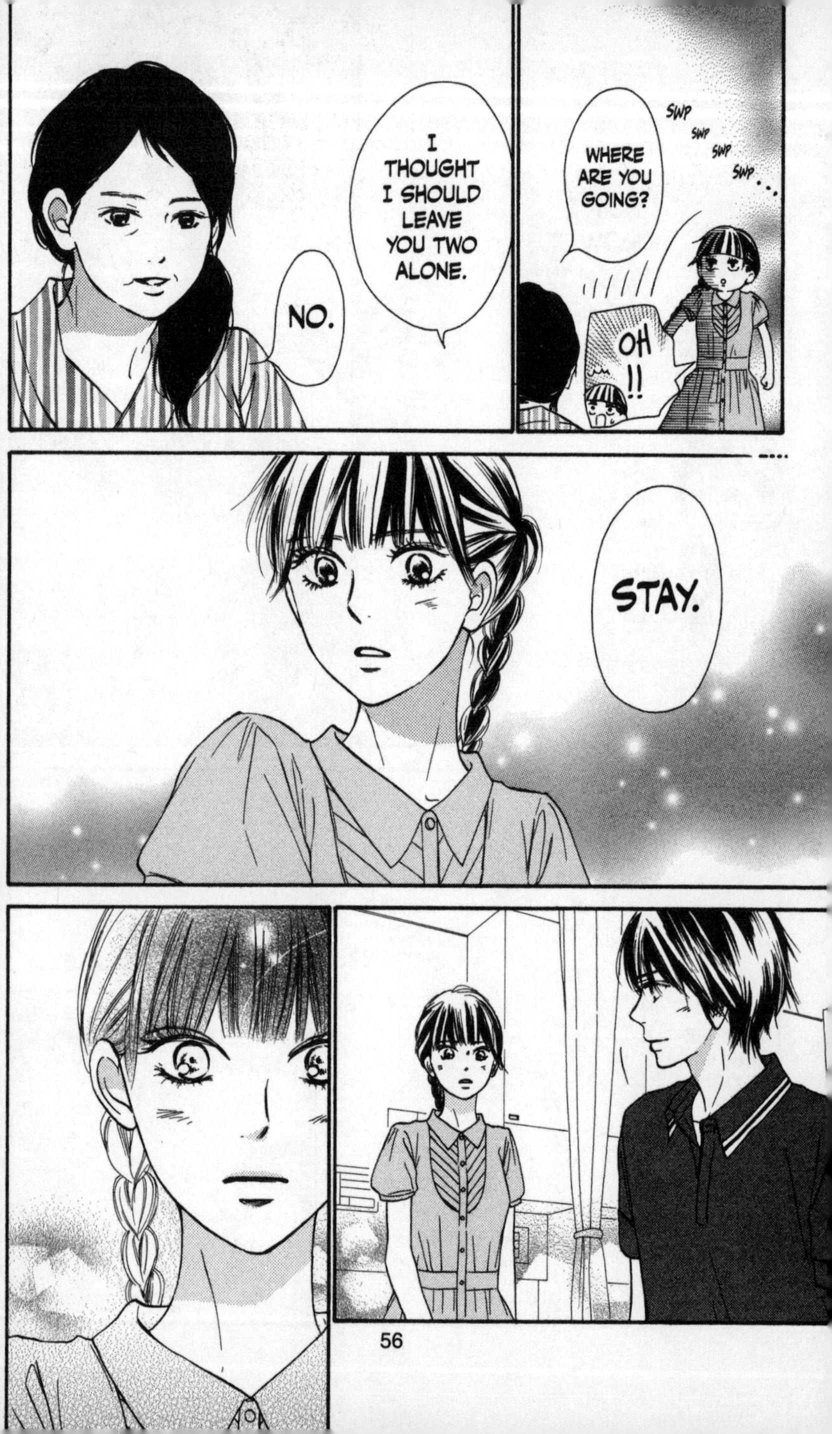
WHERE ARE YOU GOING?
SWP SWP SWP SWP...
OH!!
I THOUGHT I SHOULD LEAVE YOU TWO ALONE.
NO.
STAY.

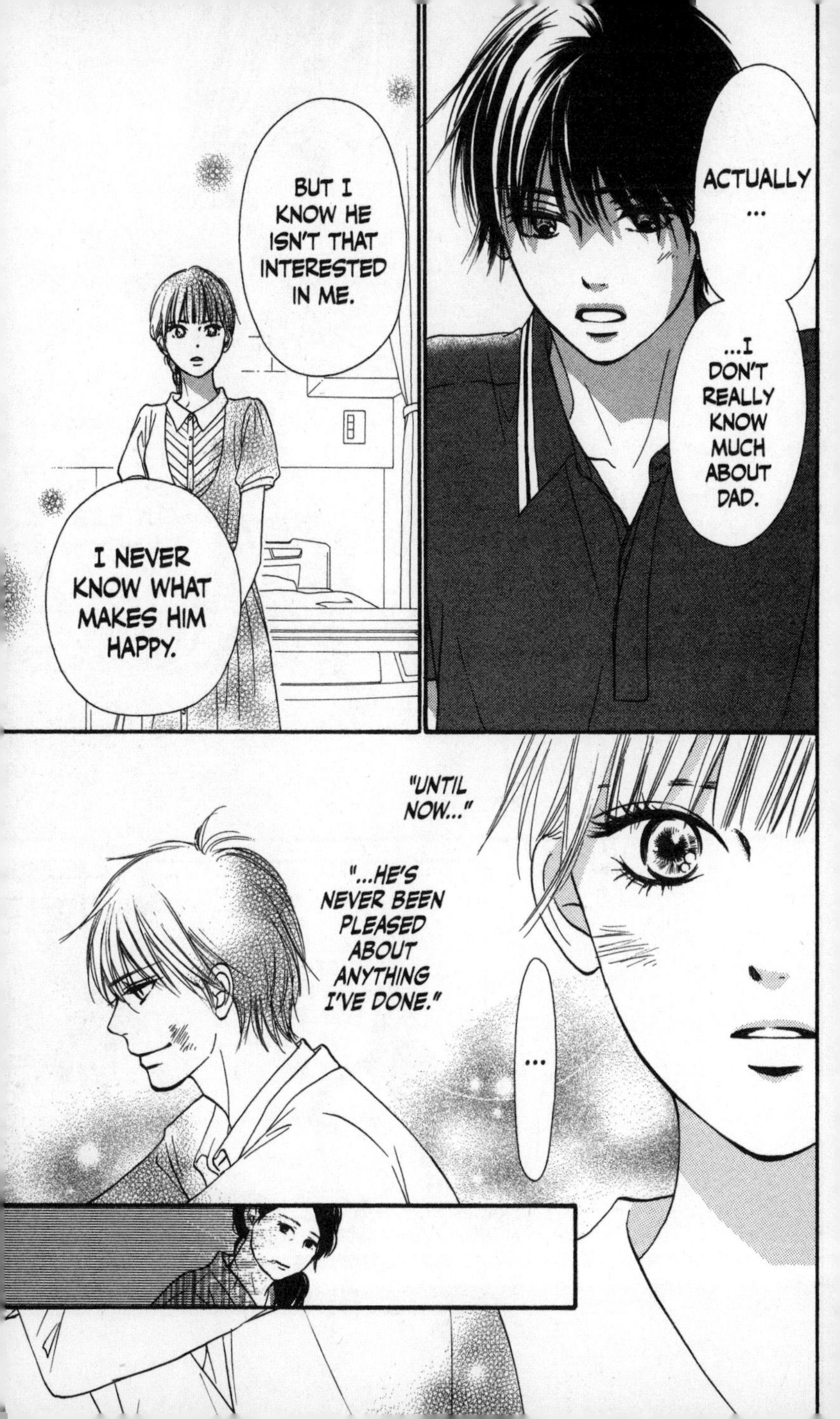
ACTUALLY ...
...I DON'T REALLY KNOW MUCH ABOUT DAD.
BUT I KNOW HE ISN'T THAT INTERESTED IN ME.
I NEVER KNOW WHAT MAKES HIM HAPPY.
"UNTIL NOW..."
"...HE'S NEVER BEEN PLEASED ABOUT ANYTHING I'VE DONE."
...

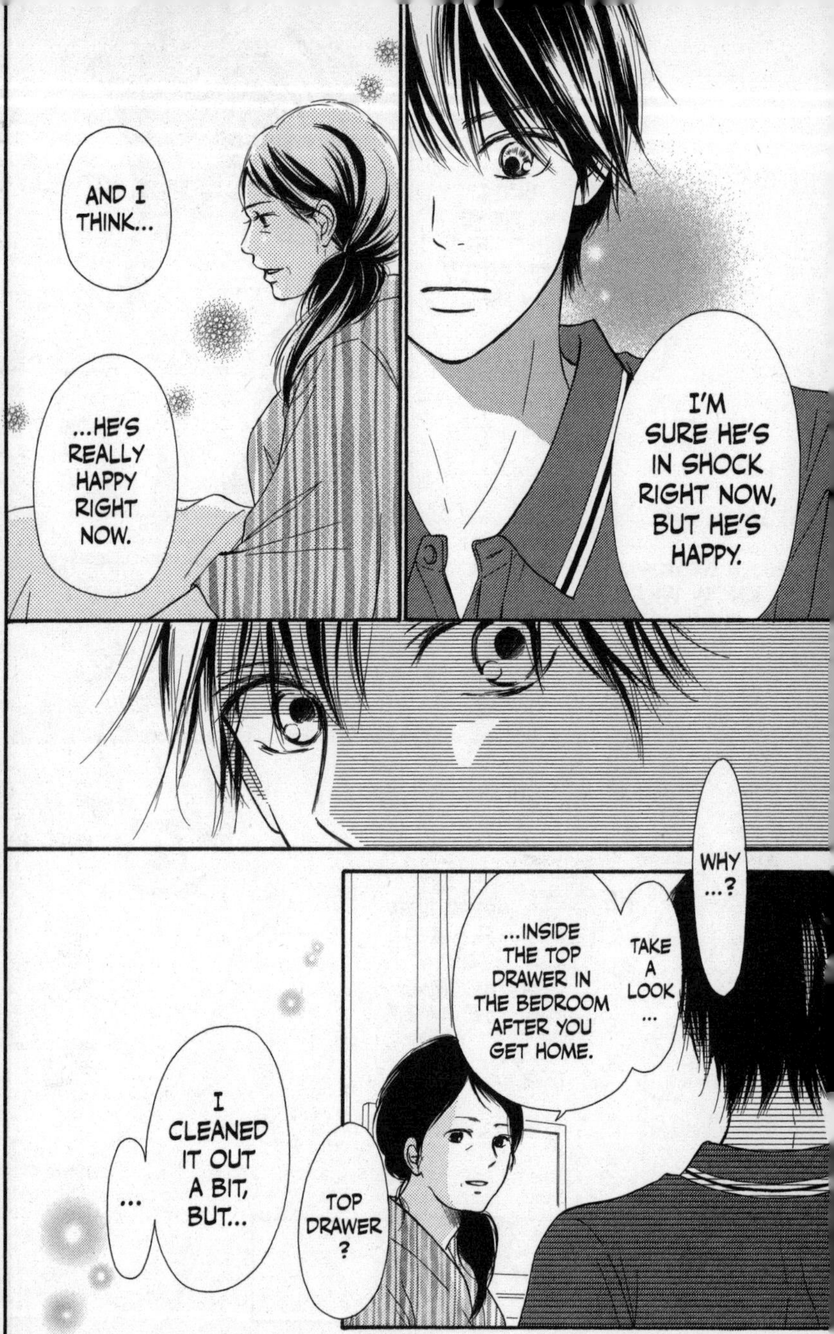
I'M SURE HE'S IN SHOCK RIGHT NOW, BUT HE'S HAPPY.
AND I THINK...
...HE'S REALLY HAPPY RIGHT NOW.
WHY ...?
TAKE A LOOK ...
...INSIDE THE TOP DRAWER IN THE BEDROOM AFTER YOU GET HOME.
TOP DRAWER ?
I CLEANED IT OUT A BIT, BUT...
...

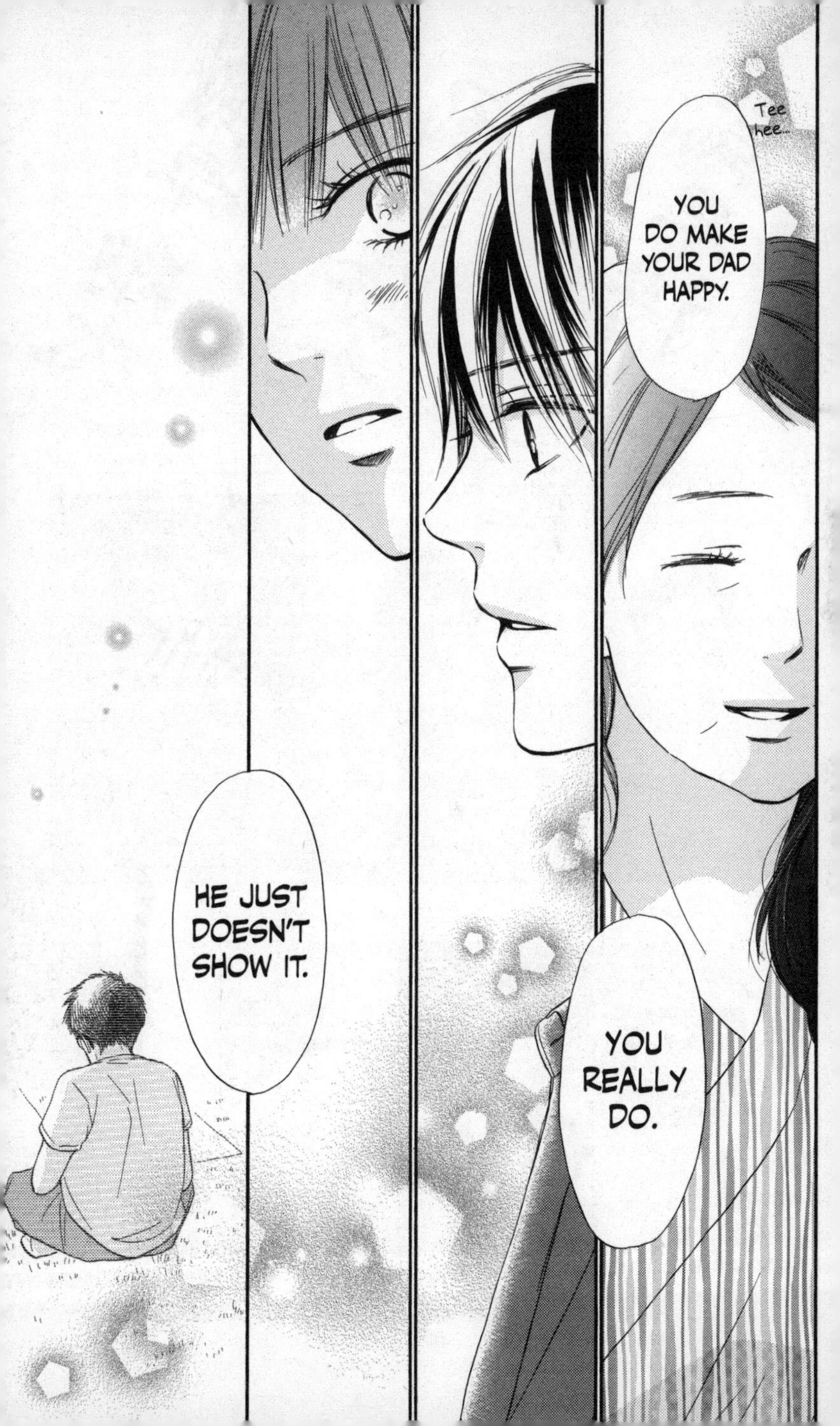
Tee hee...
YOU DO MAKE YOUR DAD HAPPY.
YOU REALLY DO.
HE JUST DOESN'T SHOW IT.

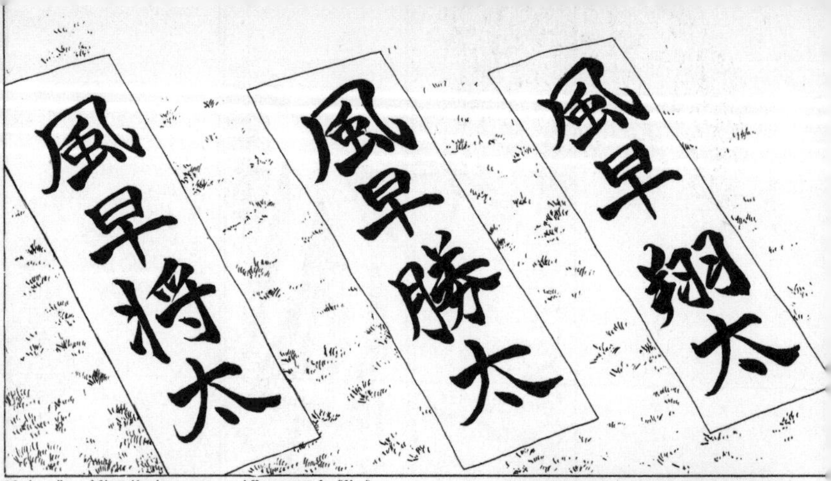
風早翔太
風早勝太
風早将太

*Each spelling of Shota Kazehaya contains a different kanji for "Sho."

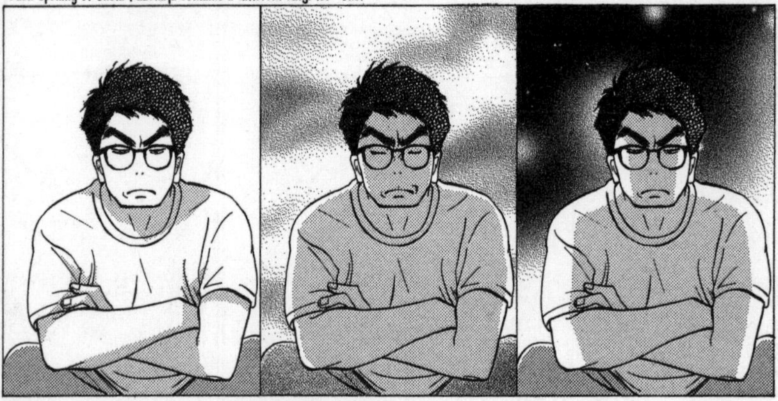

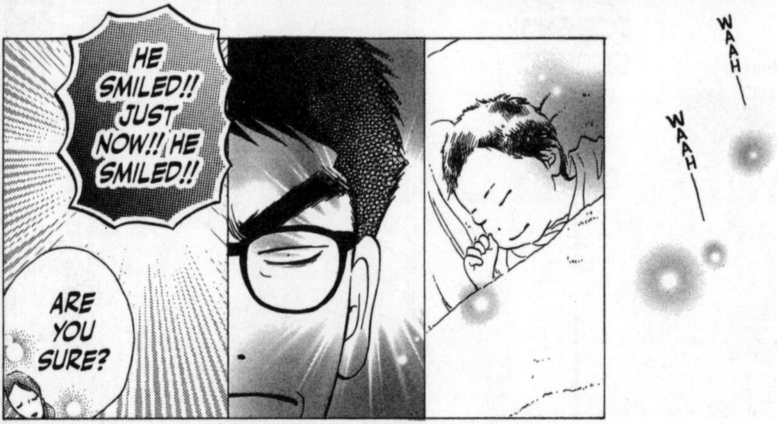
WAAH
WAAH
HE SMILED!! JUST NOW!! HE SMILED!!
ARE YOU SURE?

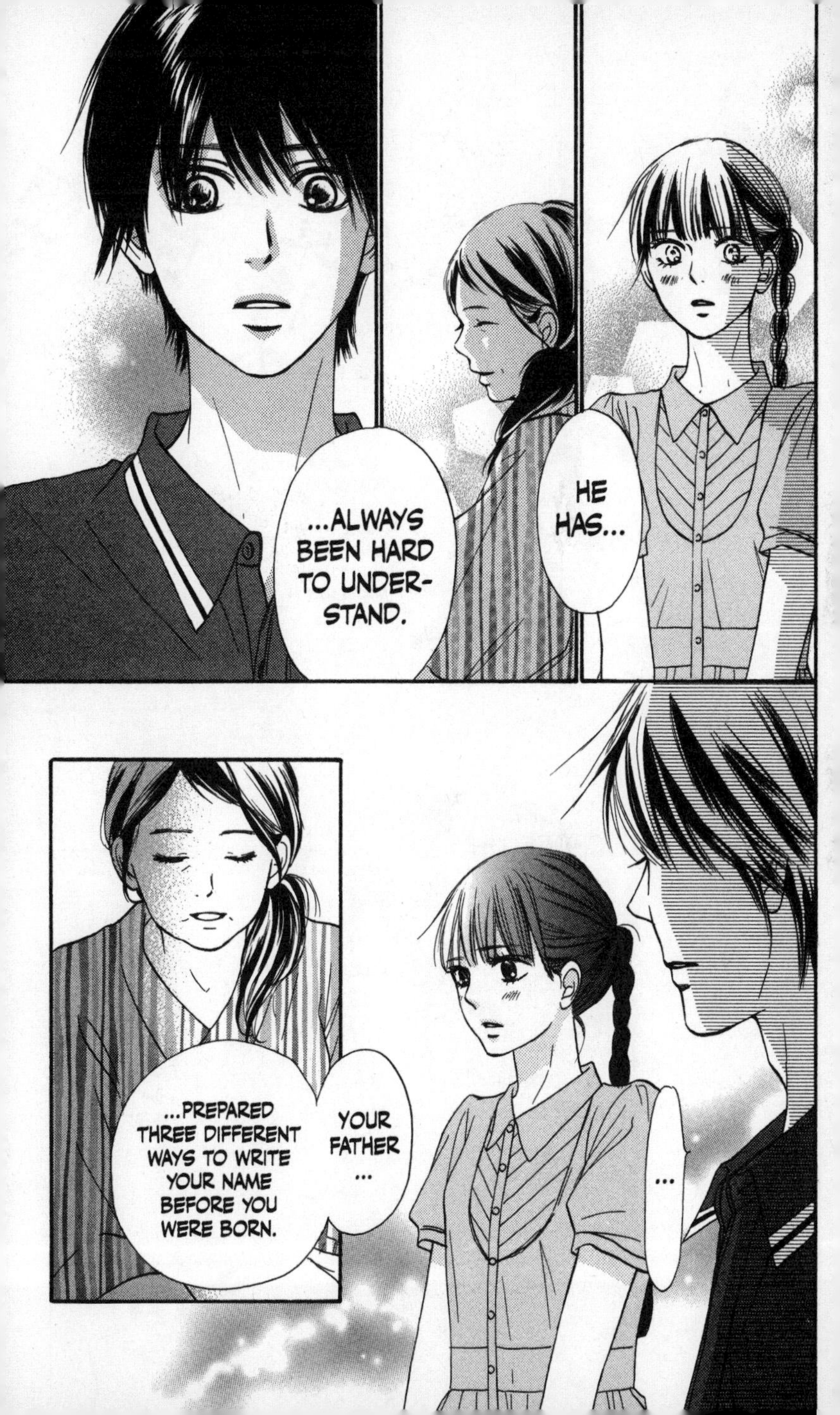
HE HAS...
...ALWAYS BEEN HARD TO UNDER-STAND.
...
YOUR FATHER ...
...PREPARED THREE DIFFERENT WAYS TO WRITE YOUR NAME BEFORE YOU WERE BORN.

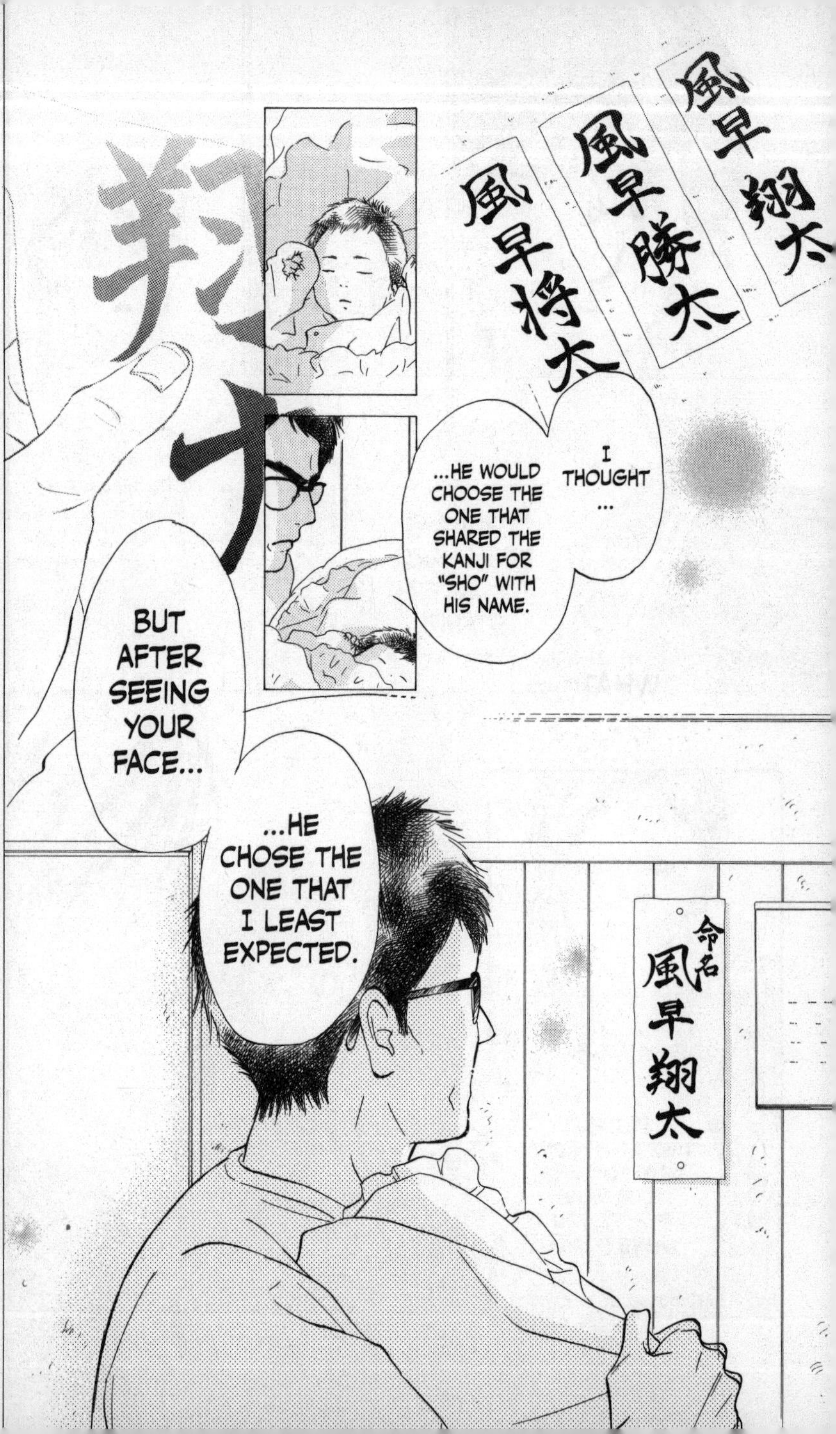
風早翔太
風早勝太
風早将太
I THOUGHT...
...HE WOULD CHOOSE THE ONE THAT SHARED THE KANJI FOR "SHO" WITH HIS NAME.
BUT AFTER SEEING YOUR FACE...
...HE CHOSE THE ONE THAT I LEAST EXPECTED.
命名 風早翔太

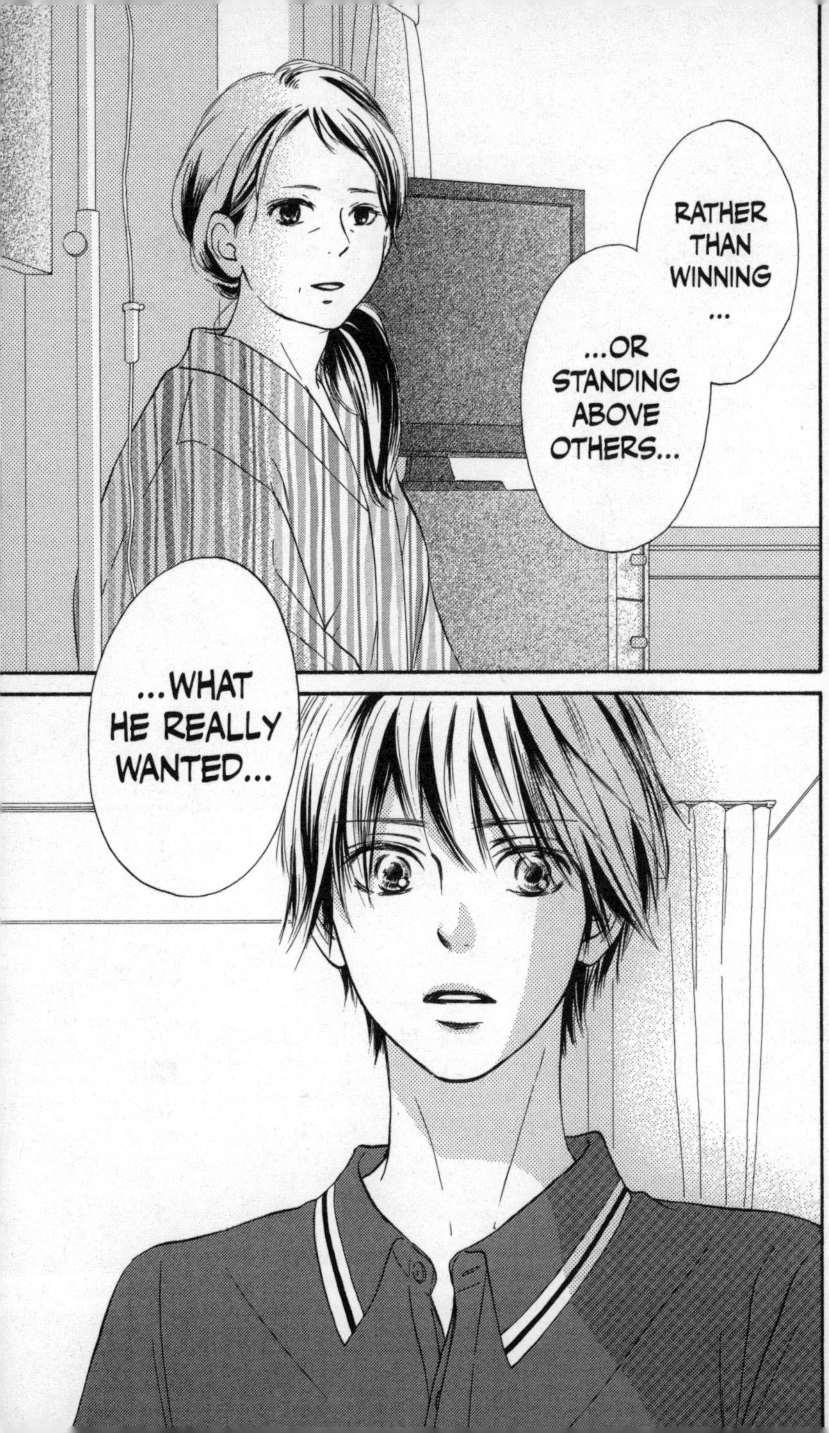
RATHER THAN WINNING ...
...OR STANDING ABOVE OTHERS...
...WHAT HE REALLY WANTED...

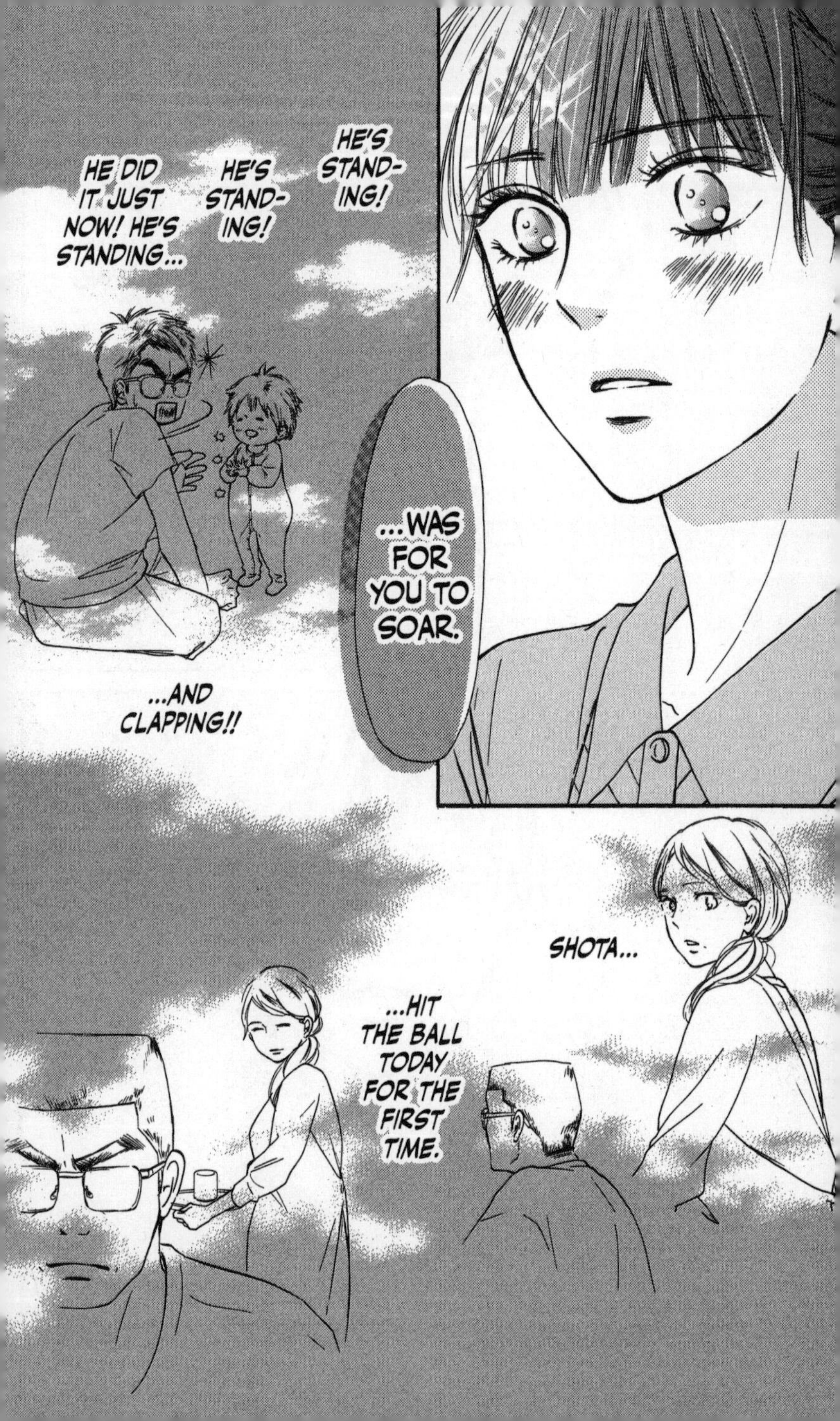
...WAS FOR YOU TO SOAR.
HE'S STANDING!
HE'S STANDING!
HE DID IT JUST NOW! HE'S STANDING...
...AND CLAPPING!!
SHOTA...
...HIT THE BALL TODAY FOR THE FIRST TIME.

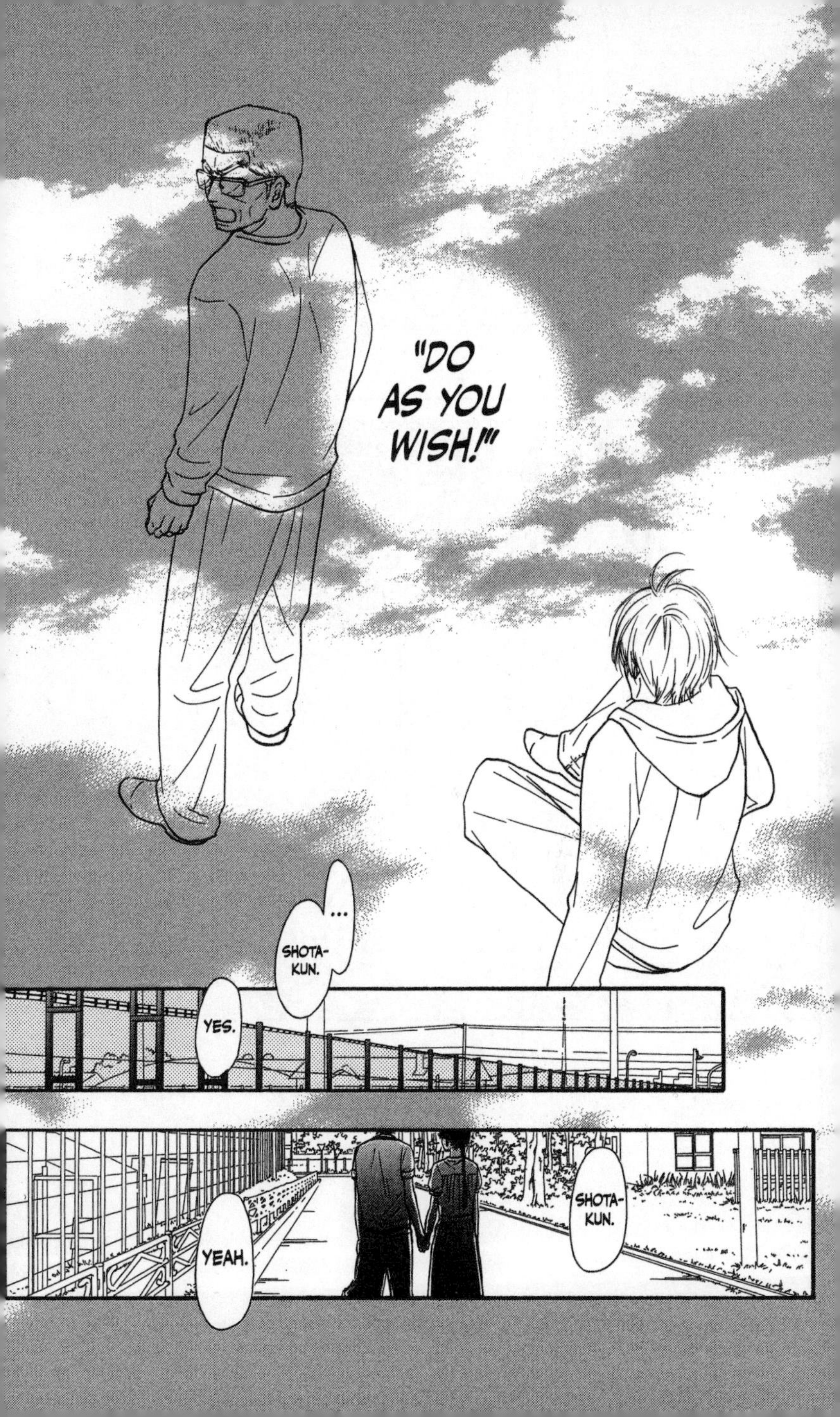
"DO AS YOU WISH!"
... SHOTA-KUN.
YES.
SHOTA-KUN.
YEAH.

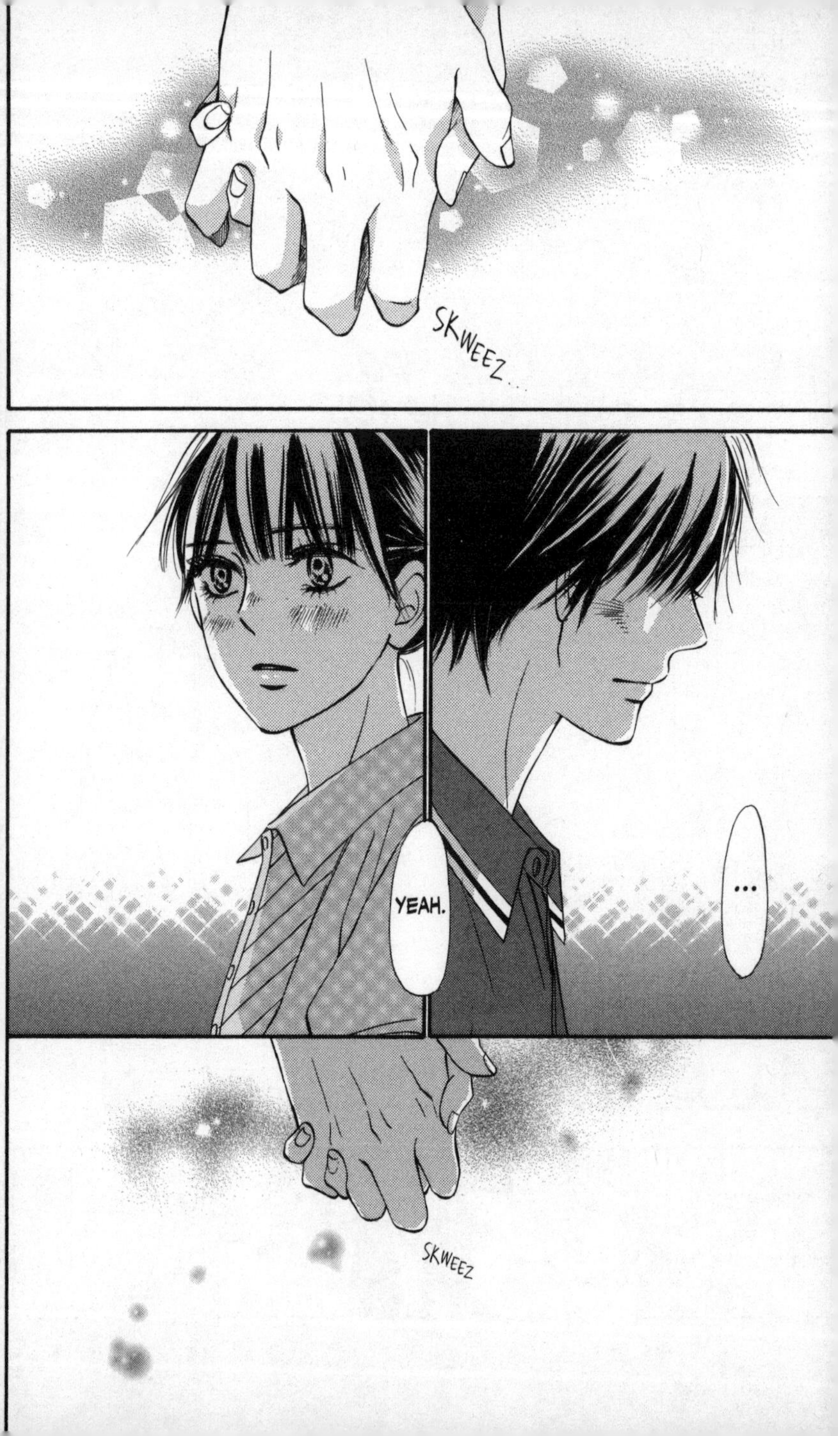
SKWEEZ...
...
YEAH.
SKWEEZ

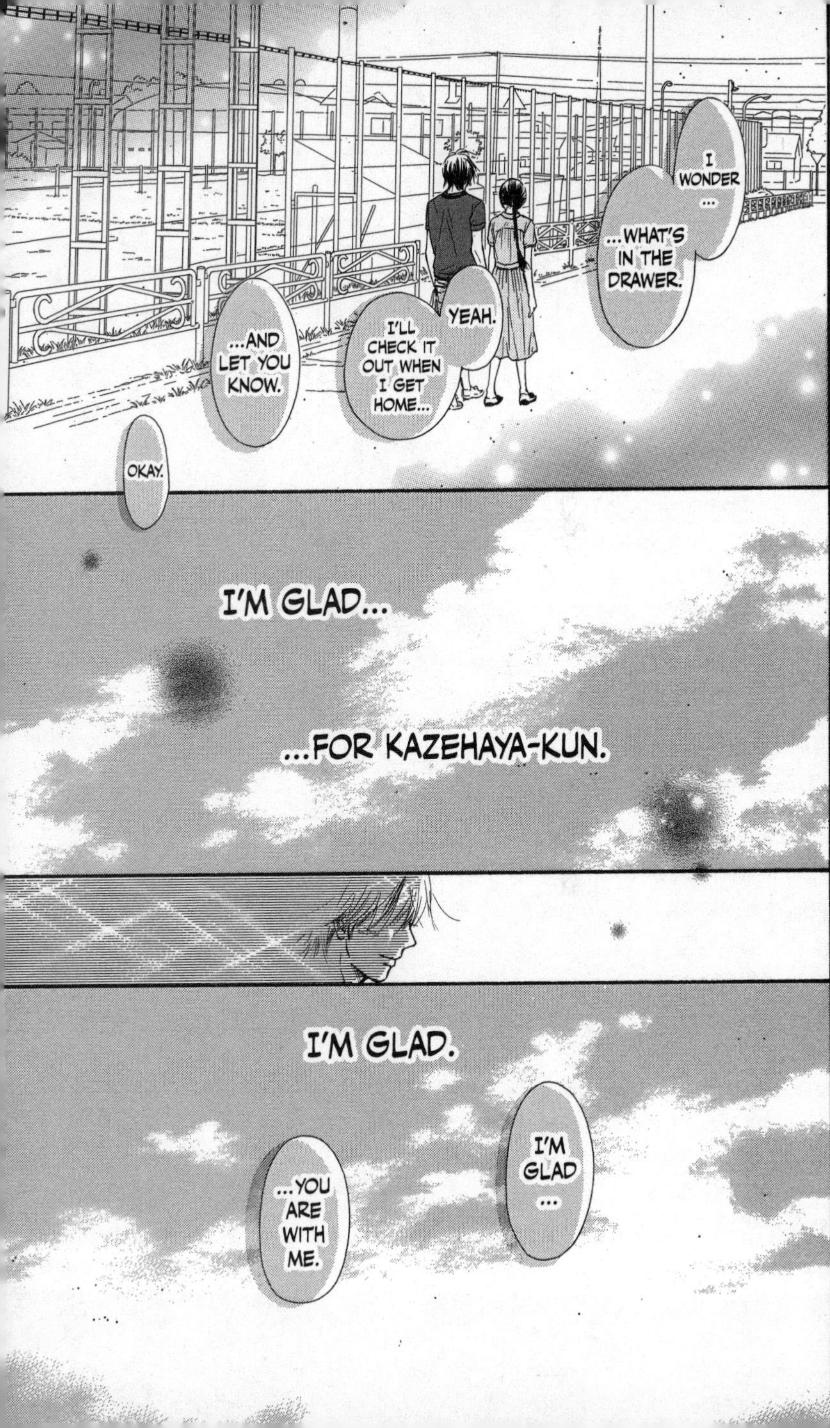
I WONDER ...
...WHAT'S IN THE DRAWER.
YEAH.
I'LL CHECK IT OUT WHEN I GET HOME...
...AND LET YOU KNOW.
OKAY.
I'M GLAD...
...FOR KAZEHAYA-KUN.
I'M GLAD.
I'M GLAD ...
...YOU ARE WITH ME.

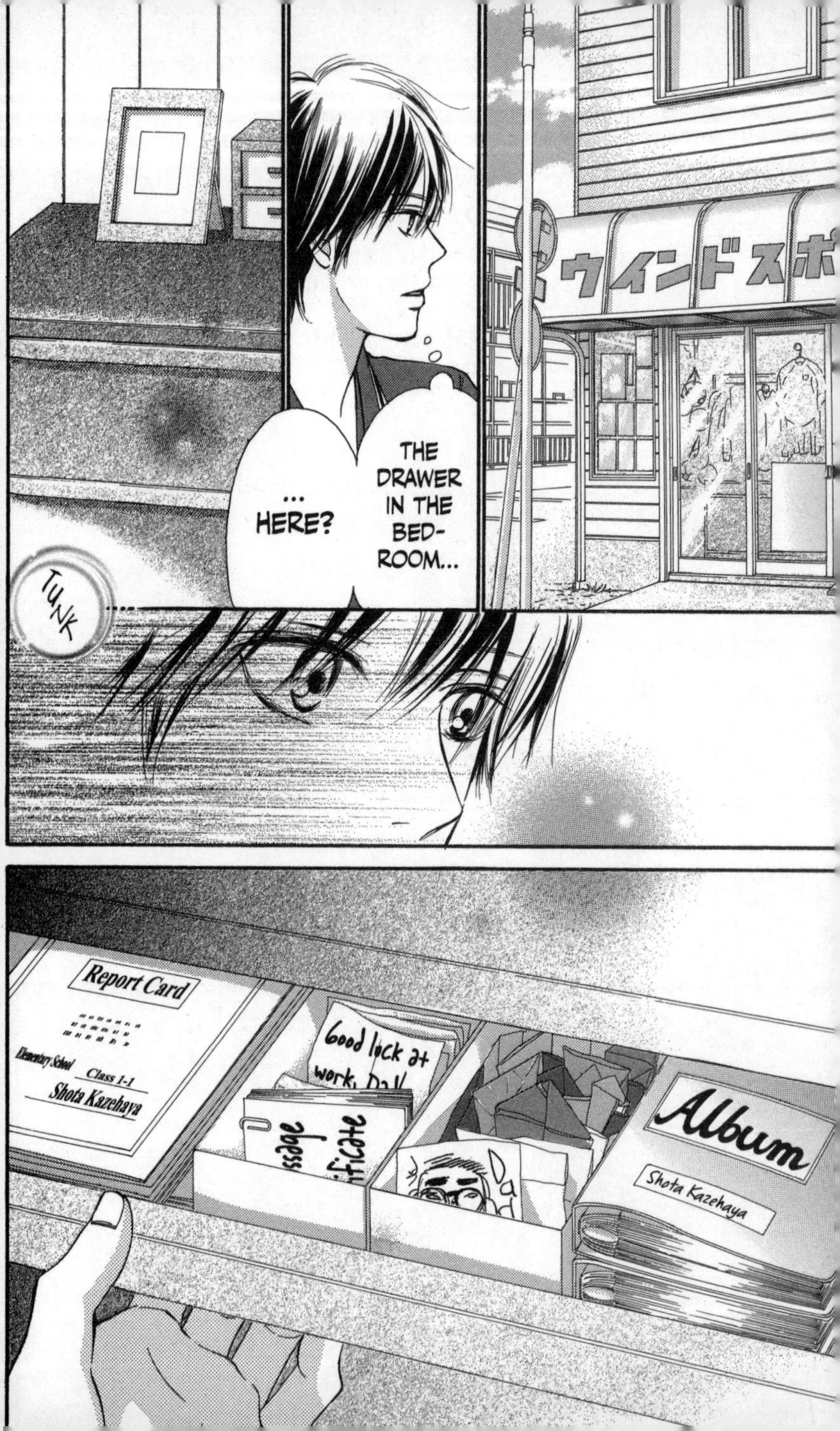
ウインドスポ
THE DRAWER IN THE BED-ROOM...
... HERE?
TUNK
Report Card
Elementary School
Class 1-1
Shota Kazehaya
Album
Shota Kazehaya

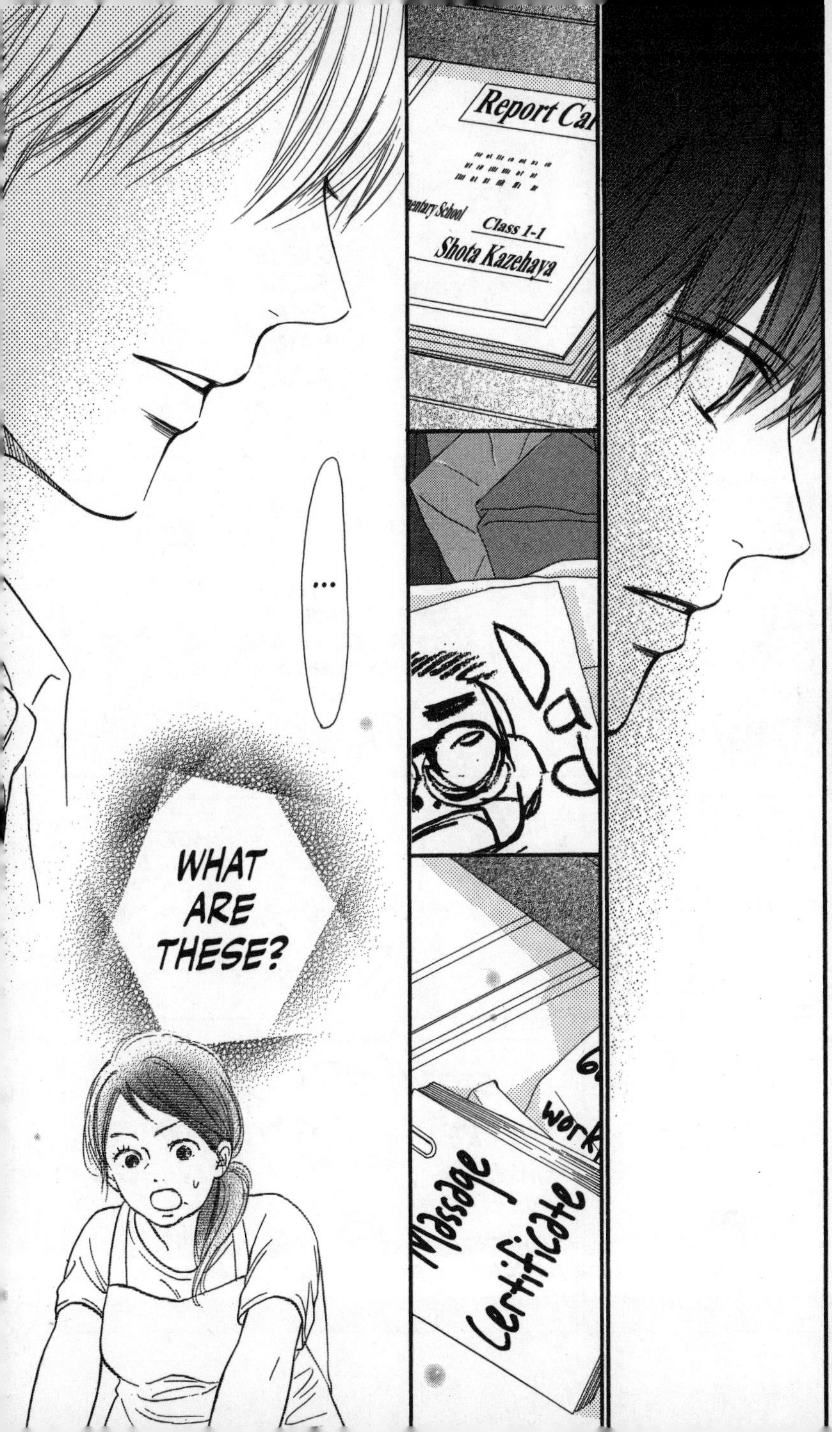
Class 1-1
Shota Kazehaya
DAD
Massage Certificate
...
WHAT ARE THESE?

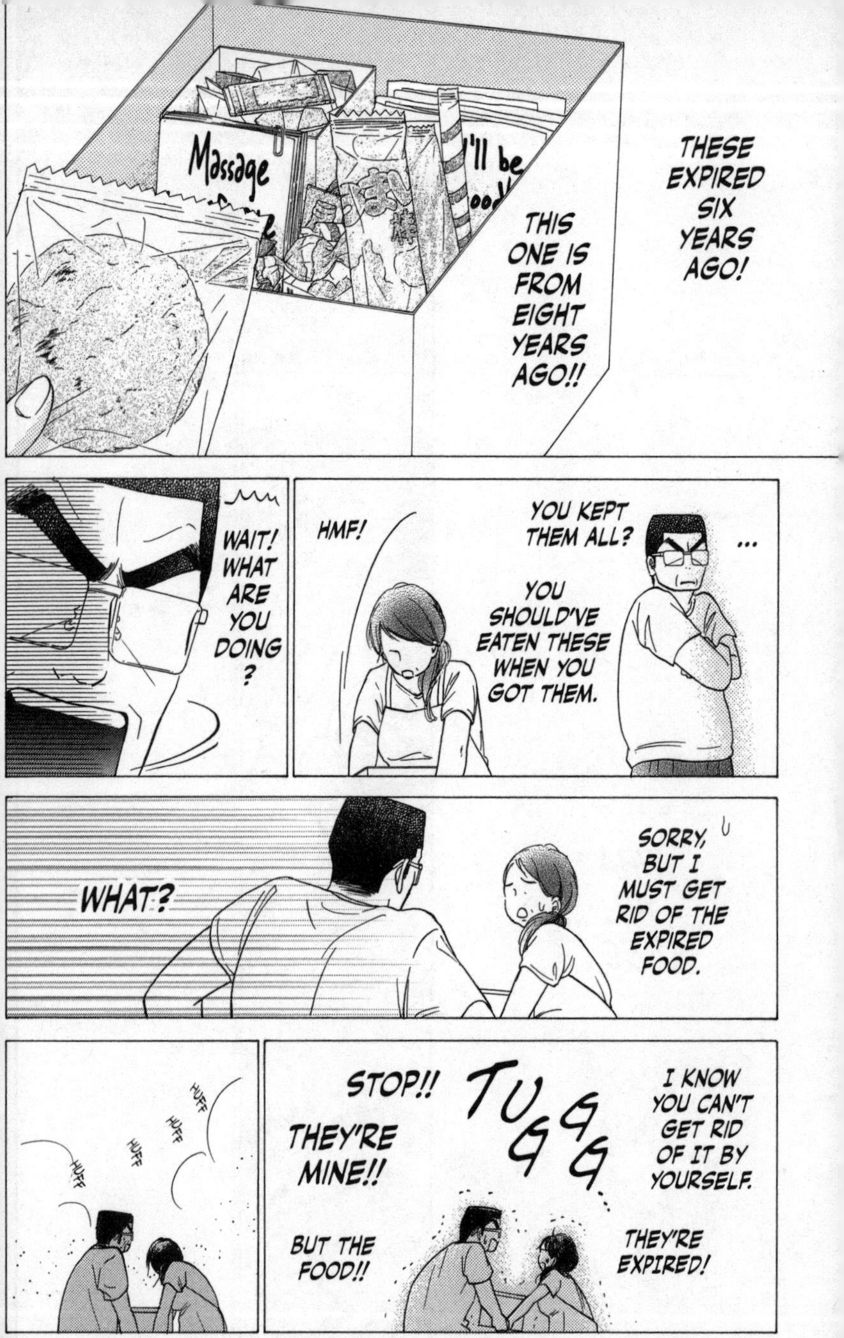
THESE EXPIRED SIX YEARS AGO!
THIS ONE IS FROM EIGHT YEARS AGO!!
Massage
YOU KEPT THEM ALL?
...
YOU SHOULD'VE EATEN THESE WHEN YOU GOT THEM.
HMF!
WAIT! WHAT ARE YOU DOING?
SORRY, BUT I MUST GET RID OF THE EXPIRED FOOD.
WHAT?
I KNOW YOU CAN'T GET RID OF IT BY YOURSELF.
TUGGG
STOP!!
THEY'RE EXPIRED!
THEY'RE MINE!!
BUT THE FOOD!!
HUFF
HUFF
HUFF
HUFF

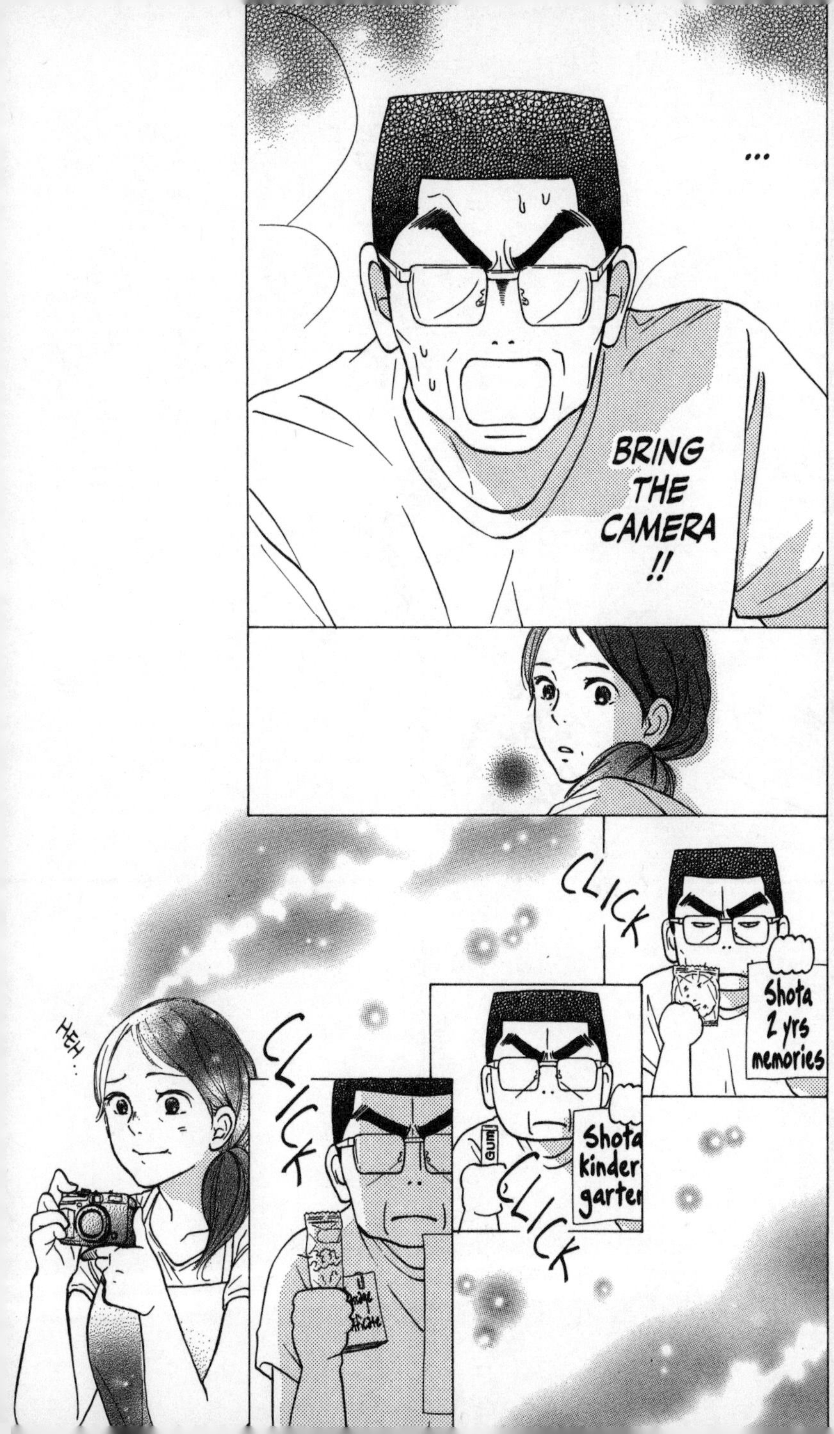
...
BRING THE CAMERA !!
CLICK
Shota 2 yrs memories
Shota kindergarten
GUMI
CLICK
CLICK
HEH...

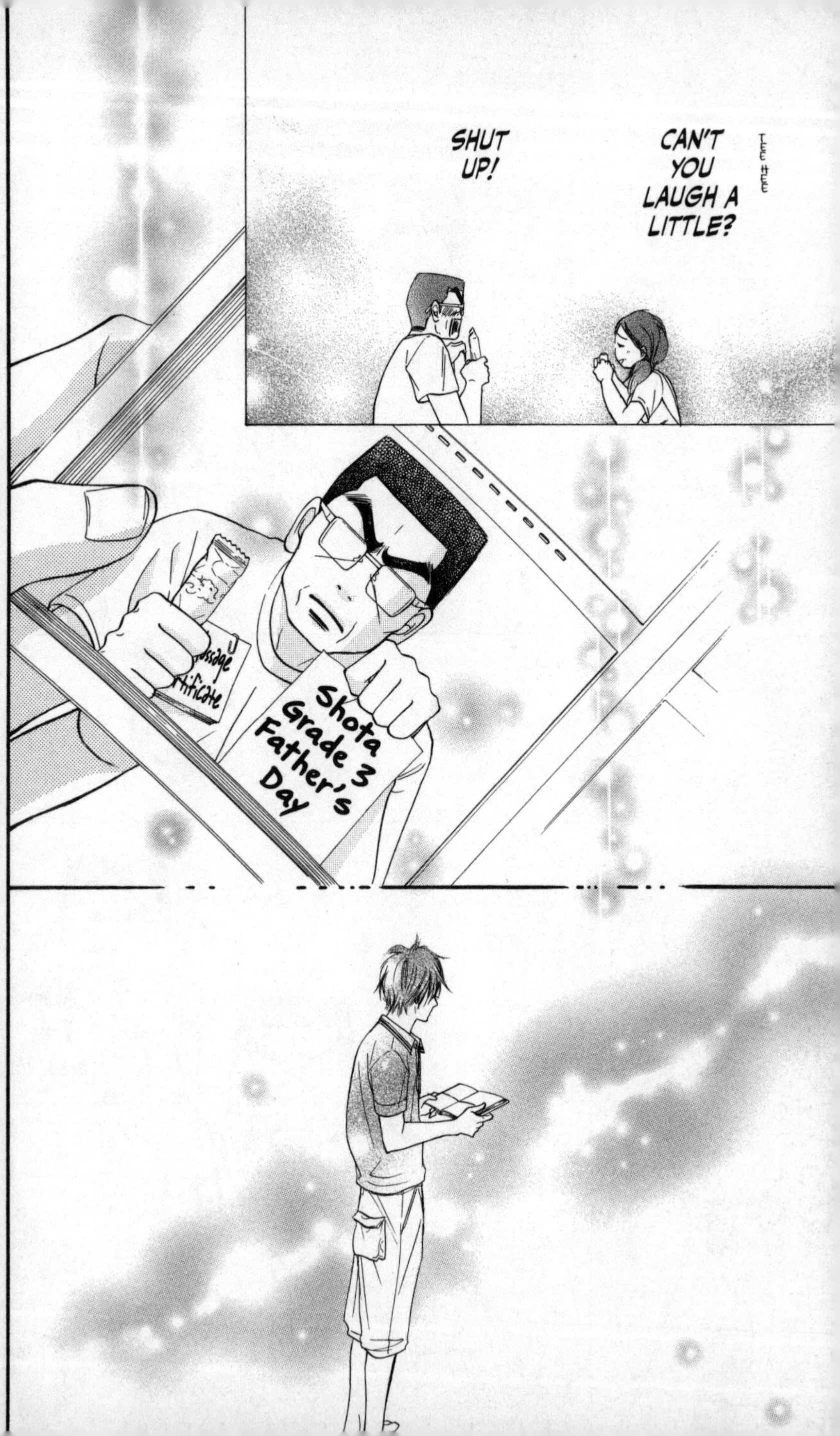
CAN'T YOU LAUGH A LITTLE?
TEE HEE
SHUT UP!
Shota
Grade 3
Father's Day

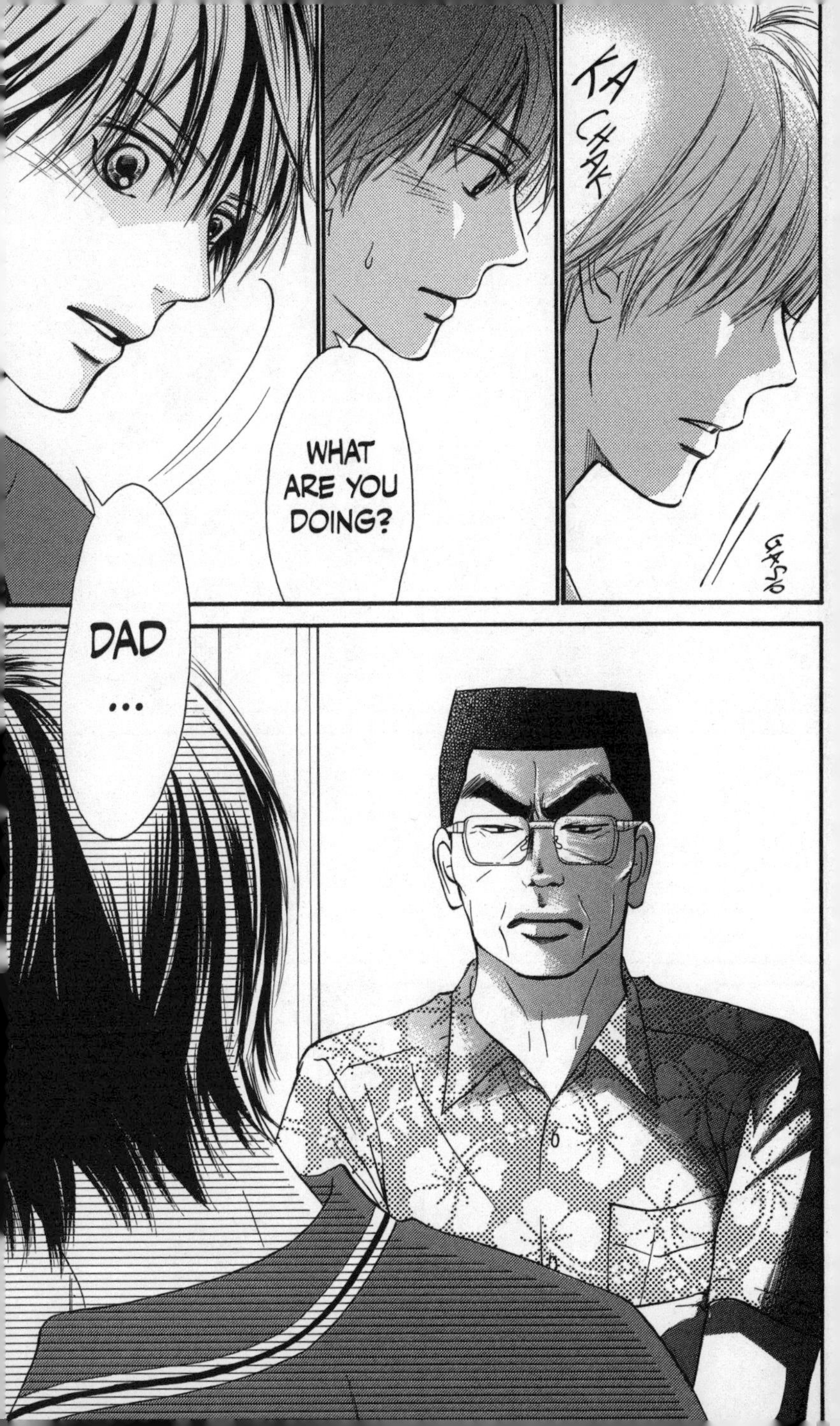
KA CHAK
GASA
WHAT ARE YOU DOING?
DAD ...

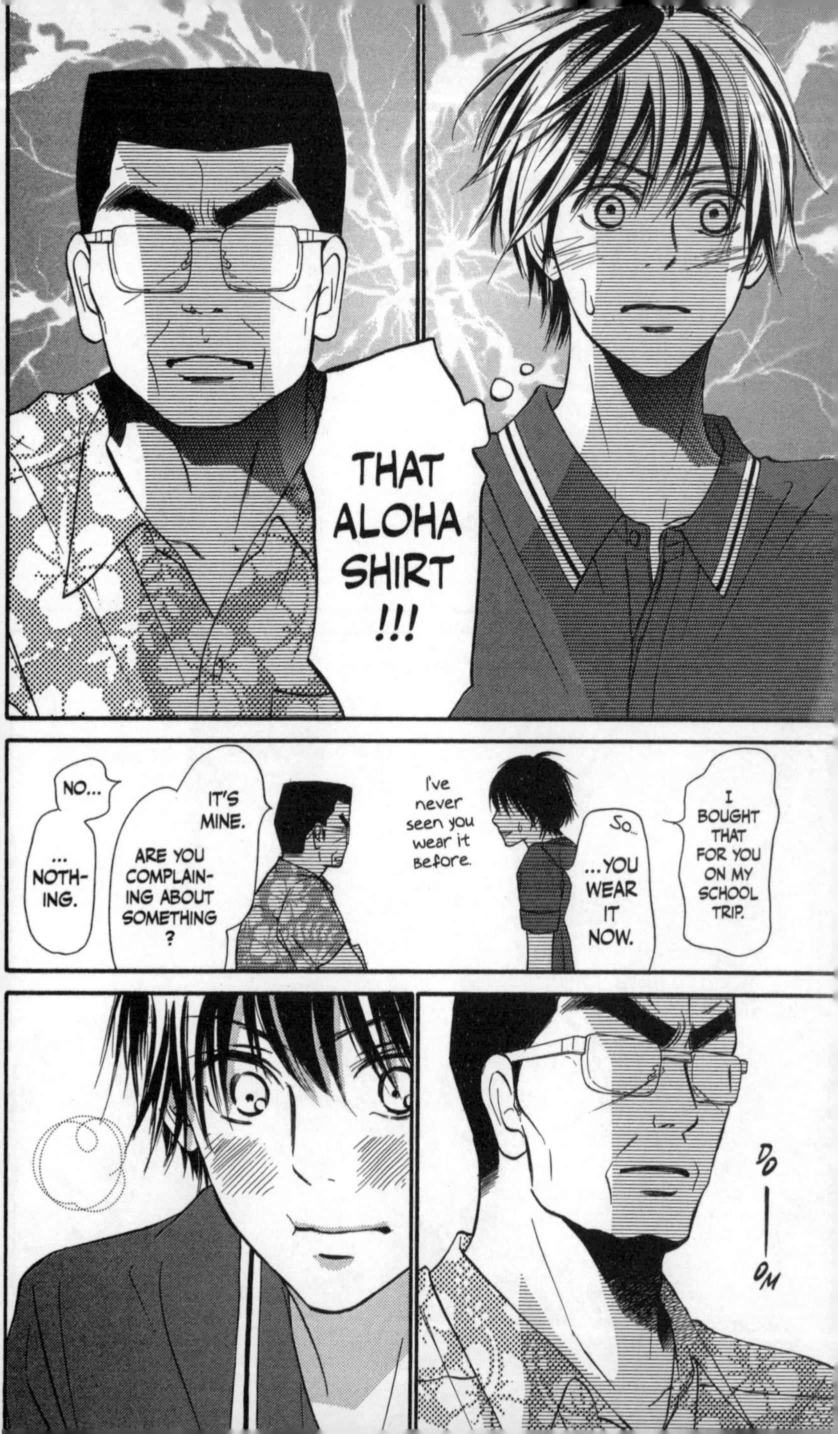
THAT ALOHA SHIRT!!!
I BOUGHT THAT FOR YOU ON MY SCHOOL TRIP.
So... ...YOU WEAR IT NOW.
I've never seen you wear it before.
IT'S MINE.
ARE YOU COMPLAINING ABOUT SOMETHING?
NO...
...NOTHING.
DO—OM

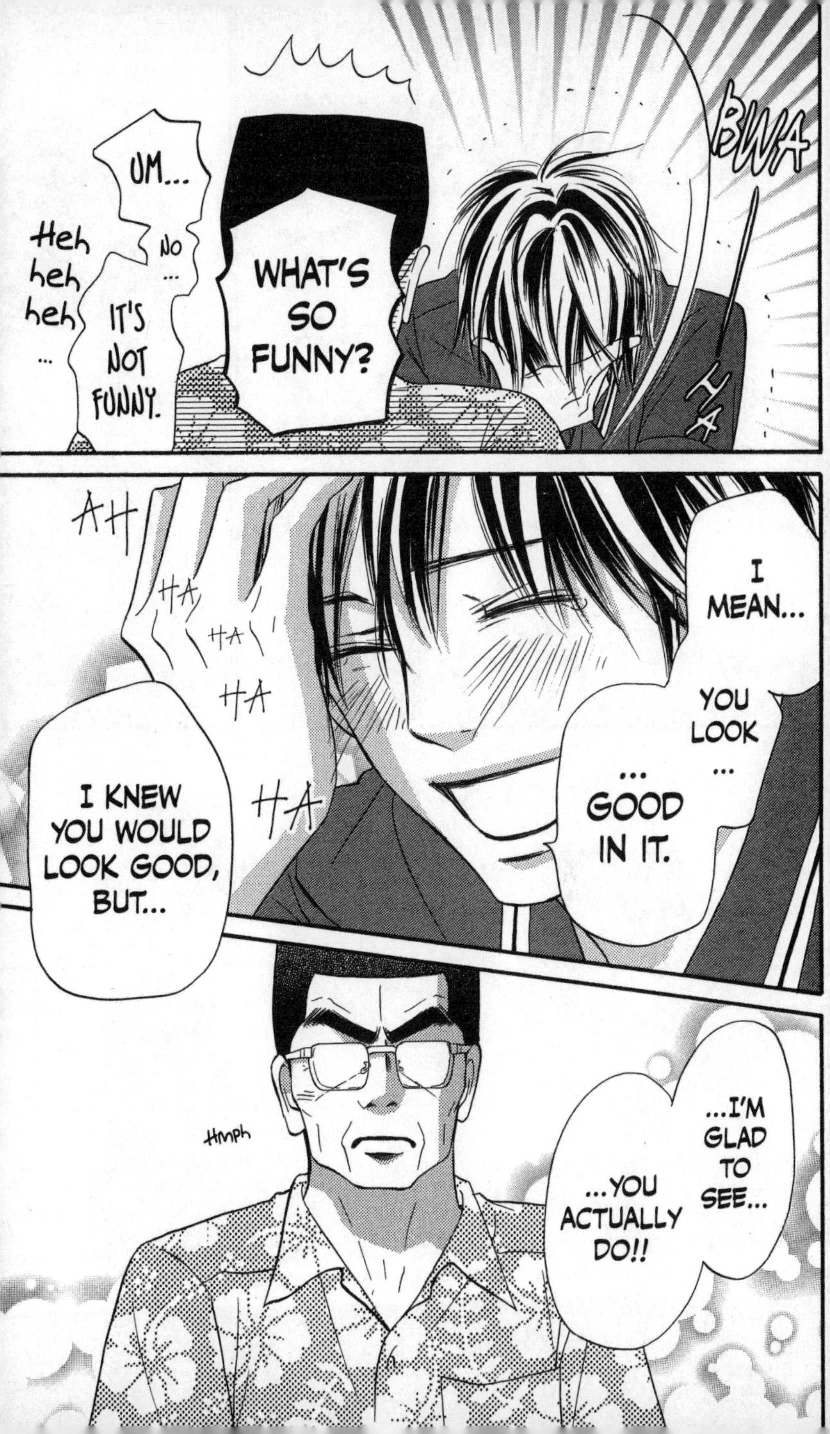
BWA HA
WHAT'S SO FUNNY?
UM...
NO... IT'S NOT FUNNY.
Heh heh heh...
I MEAN...
YOU LOOK...
...GOOD IN IT.
AH HA HA HA HA
I KNEW YOU WOULD LOOK GOOD, BUT...
...I'M GLAD TO SEE...
...YOU ACTUALLY DO!!
Hmph

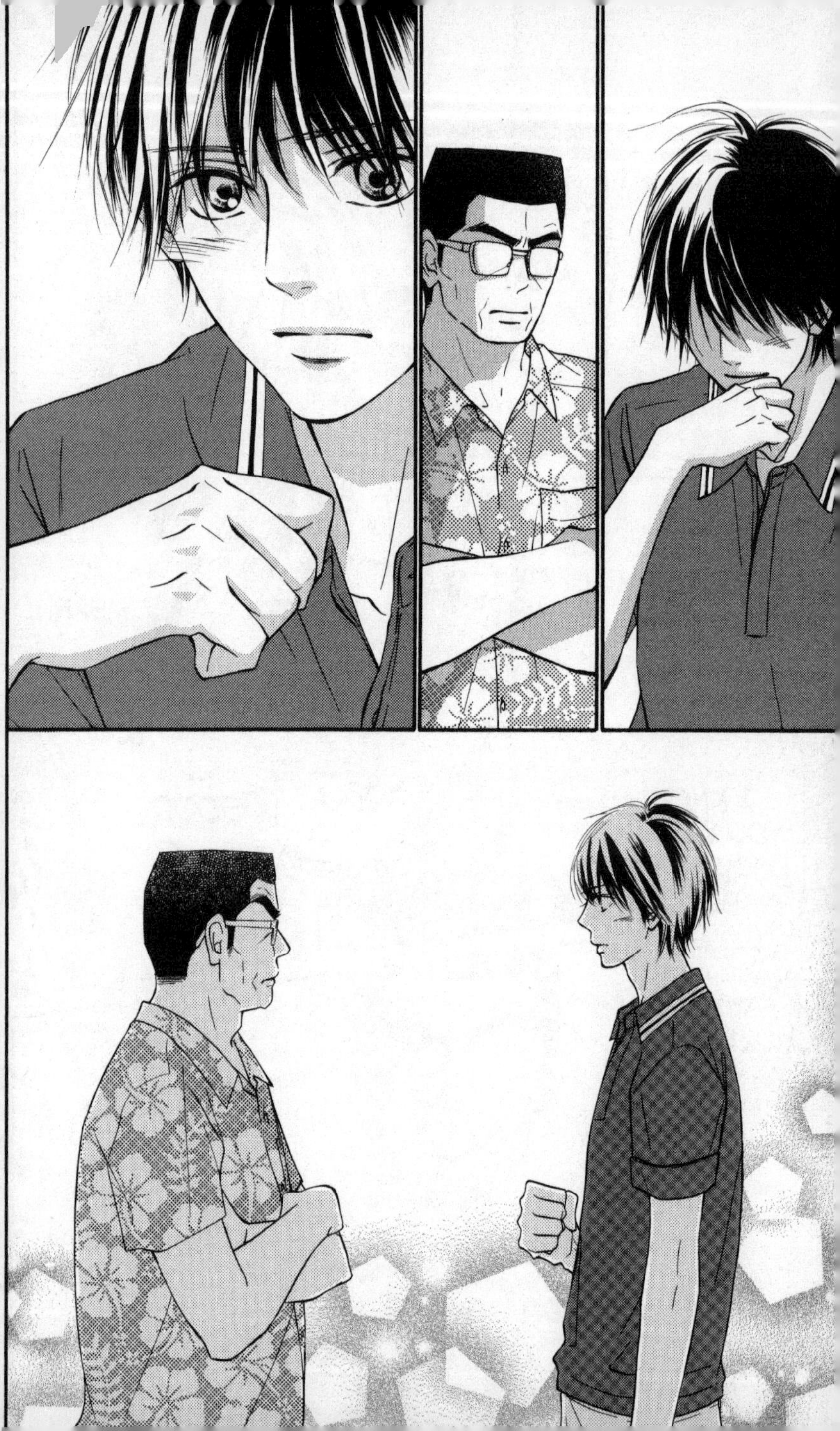

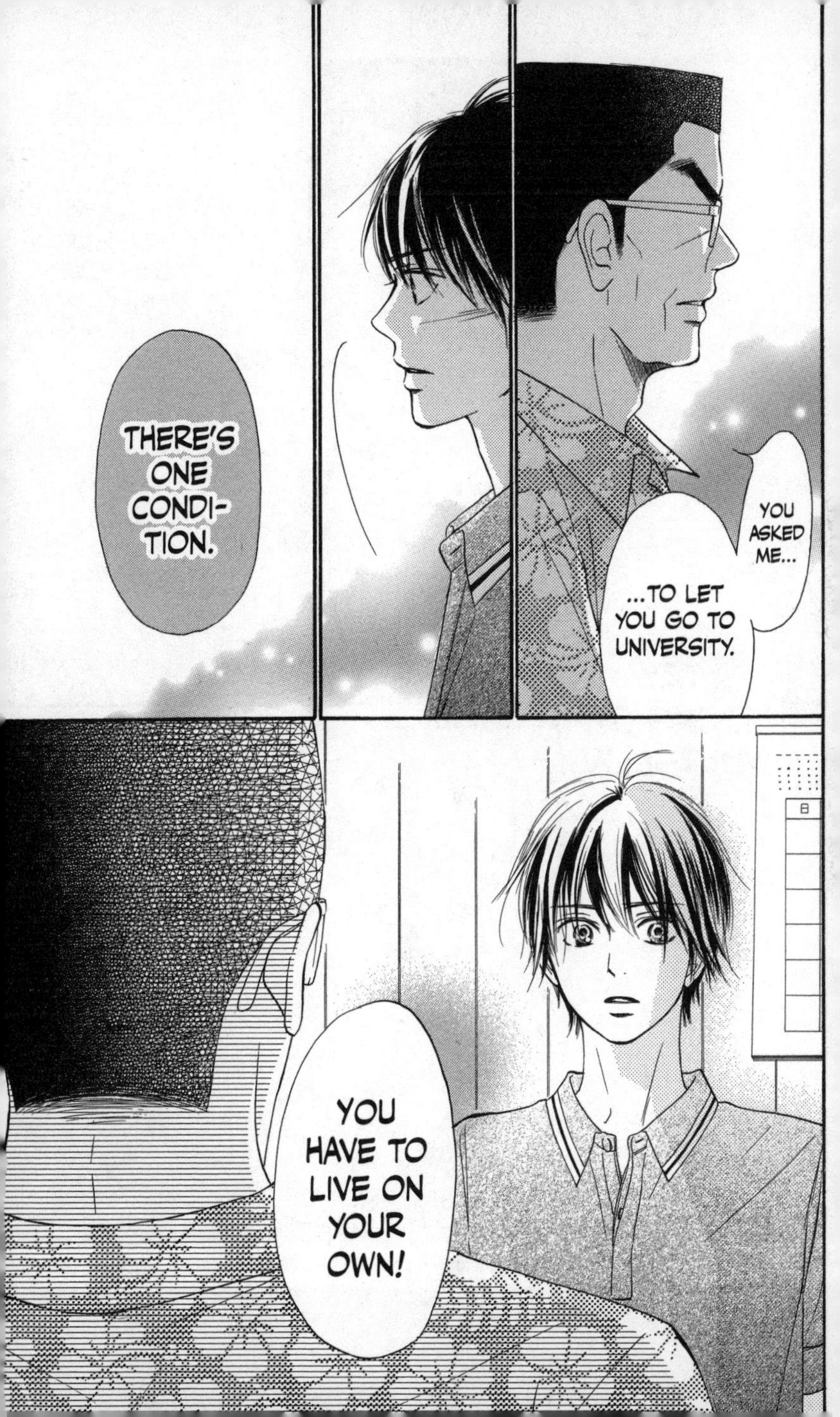
YOU ASKED ME...
...TO LET YOU GO TO UNIVERSITY.
THERE'S ONE CONDI- TION.
YOU HAVE TO LIVE ON YOUR OWN!

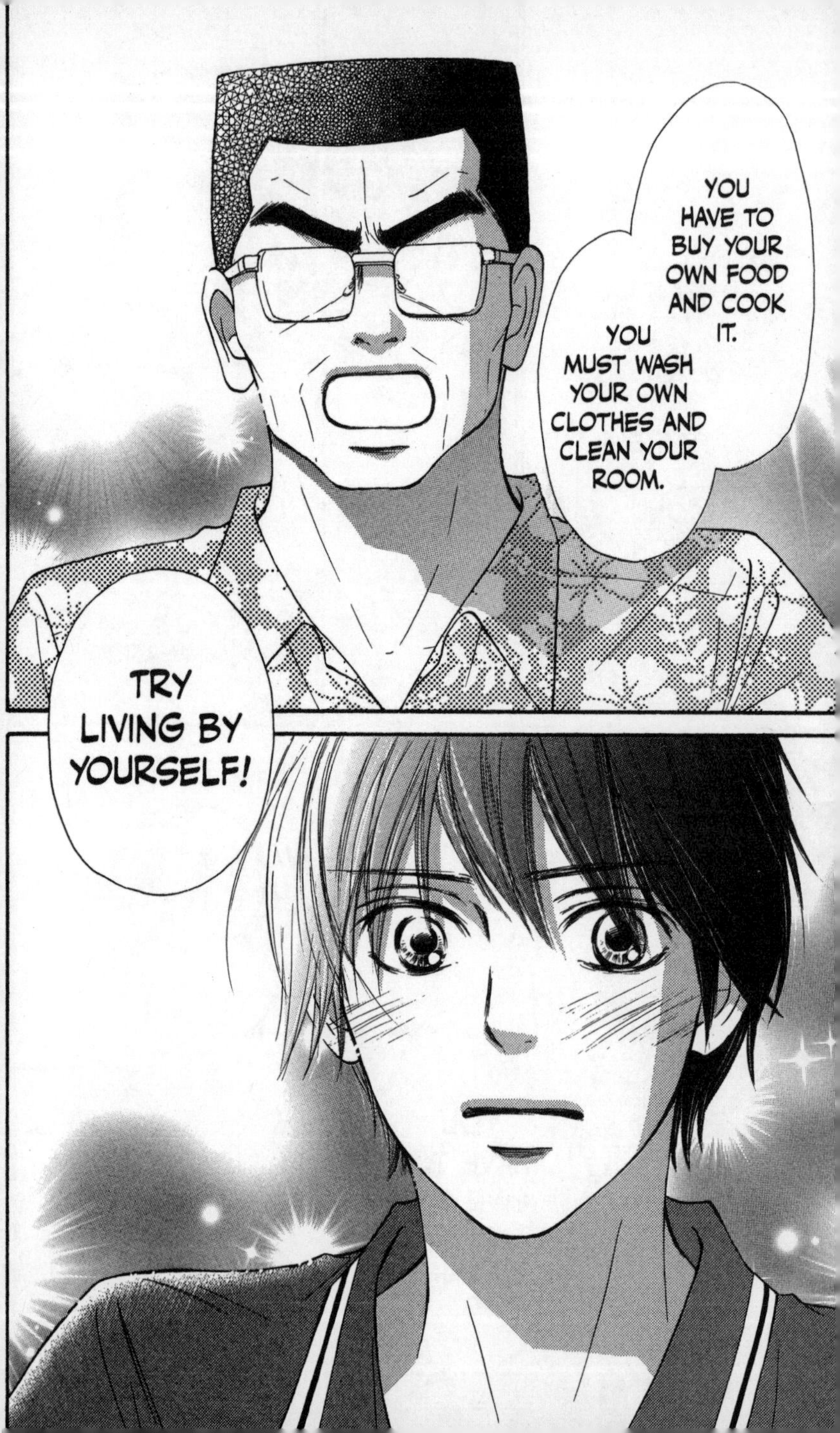
YOU HAVE TO BUY YOUR OWN FOOD AND COOK IT.
YOU MUST WASH YOUR OWN CLOTHES AND CLEAN YOUR ROOM.
TRY LIVING BY YOURSELF!

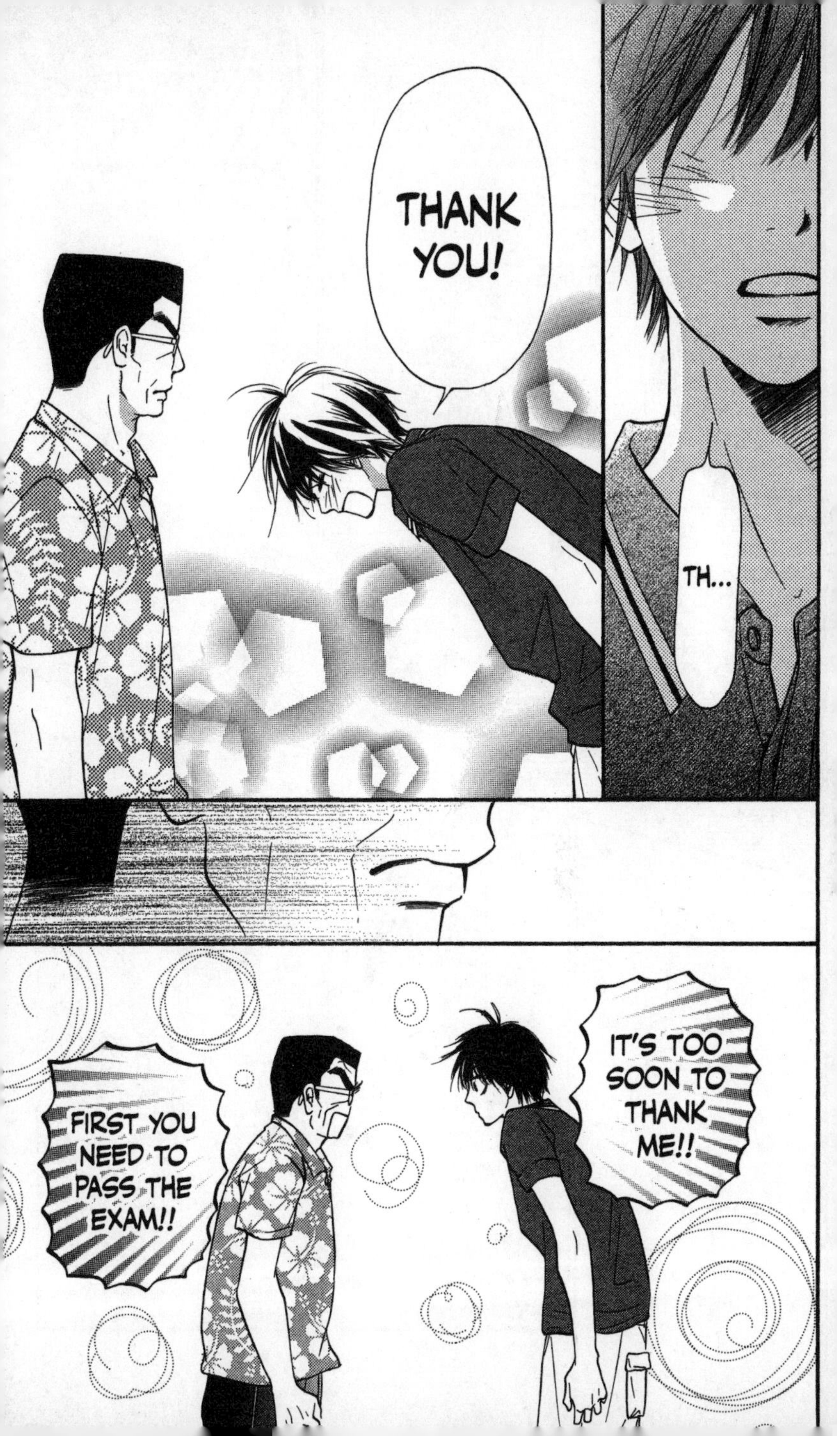
TH...
THANK YOU!
IT'S TOO SOON TO THANK ME!!
FIRST YOU NEED TO PASS THE EXAM!!

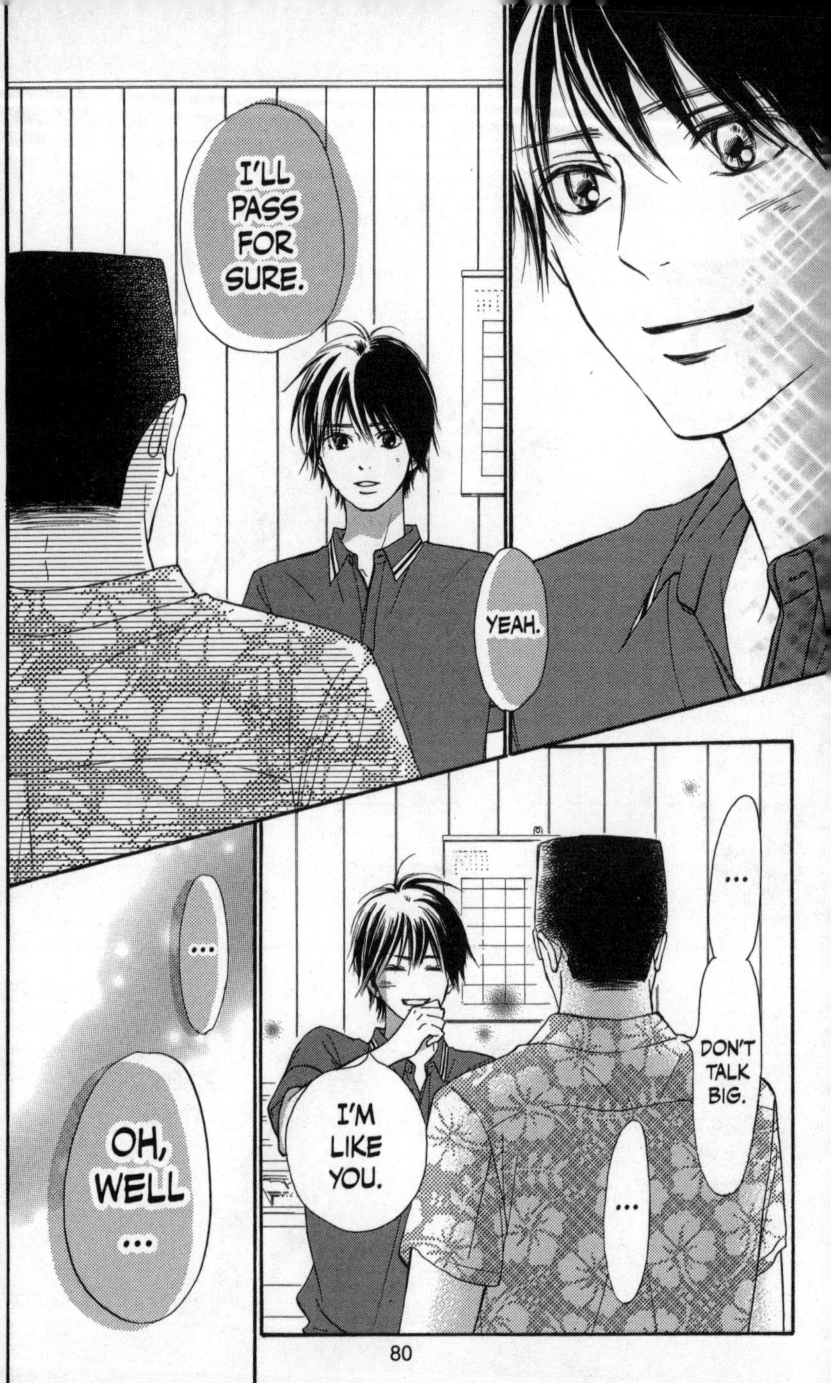
YEAH.
I'LL PASS FOR SURE.
...
DON'T TALK BIG.
...
I'M LIKE YOU.
...
OH, WELL ...

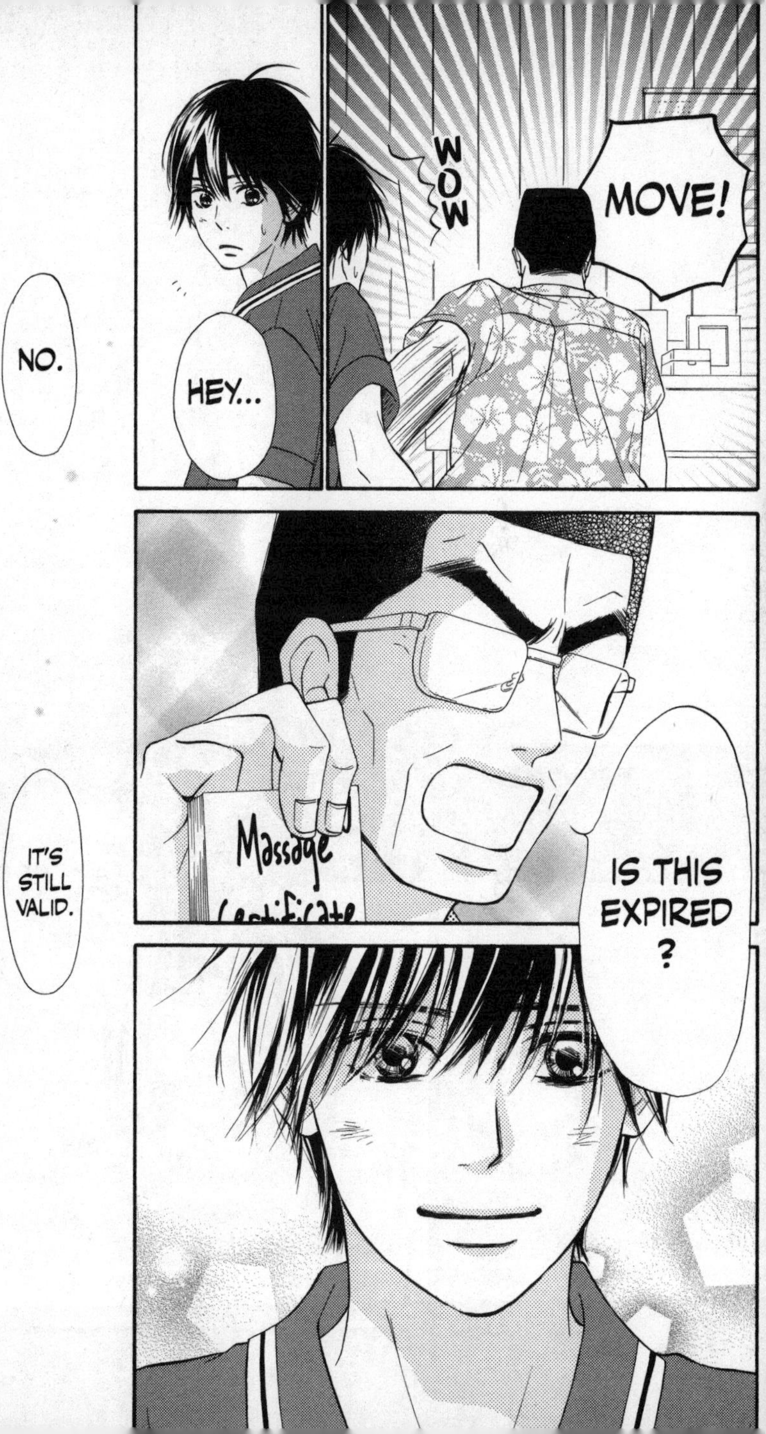
MOVE!
WOW
HEY...
NO.
IS THIS EXPIRED?
Massage Certificate
IT'S STILL VALID.

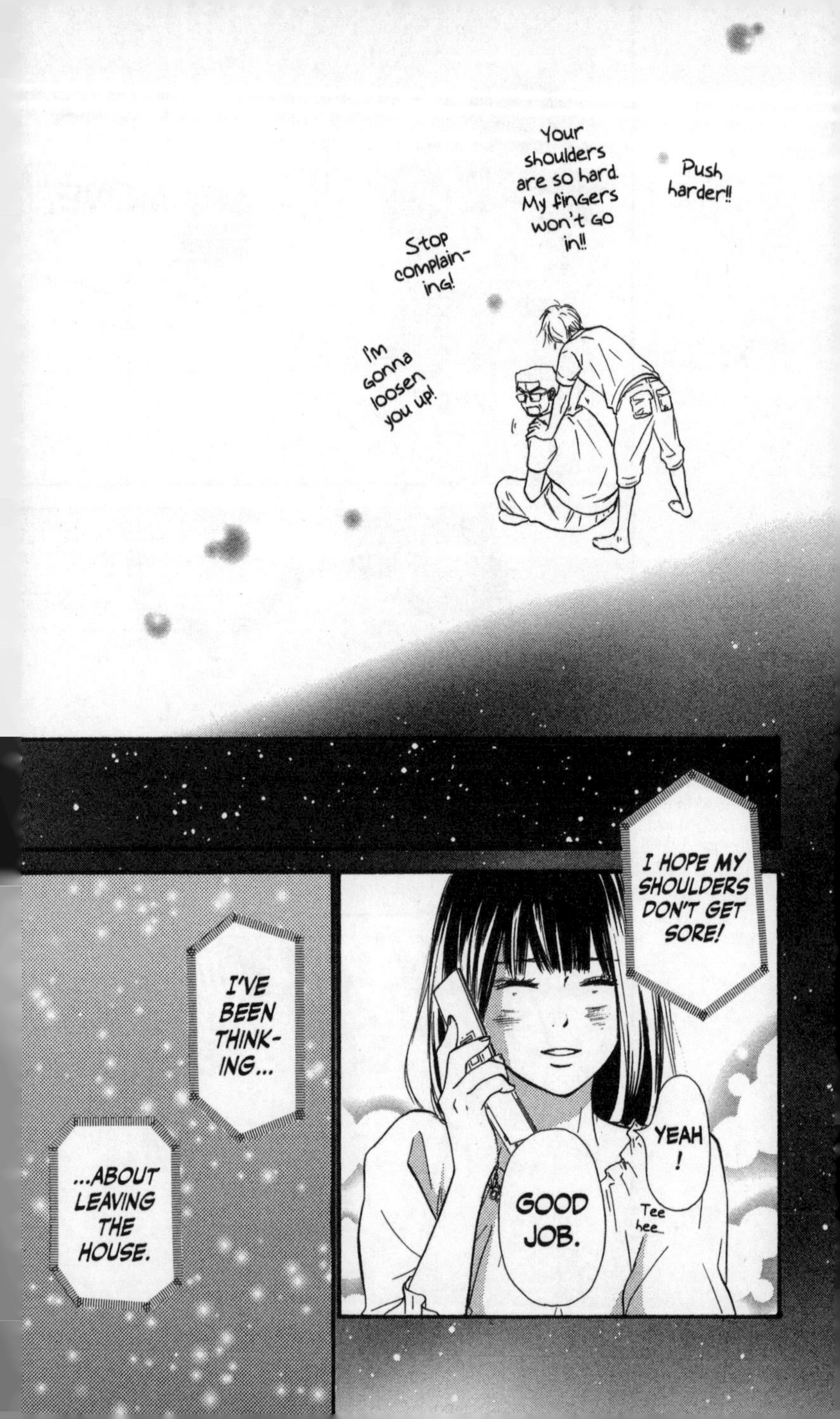
Push harder!!
Your shoulders are so hard. My fingers won't go in!!
Stop complaining!
I'm gonna loosen you up!
I HOPE MY SHOULDERS DON'T GET SORE!
YEAH!
Tee hee...
GOOD JOB.
I'VE BEEN THINKING...
...ABOUT LEAVING THE HOUSE.

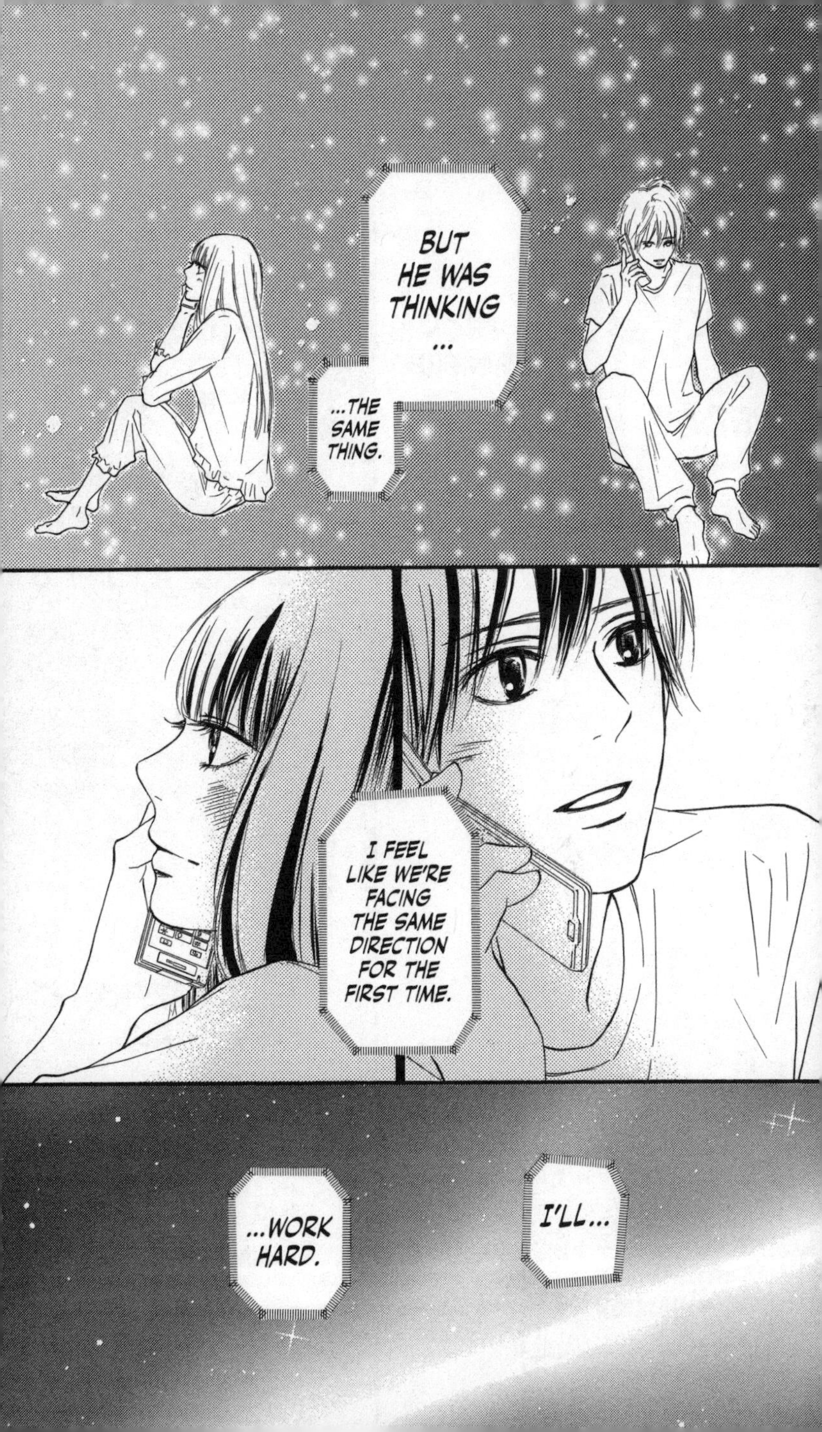
BUT HE WAS THINKING ...
...THE SAME THING.
I FEEL LIKE WE'RE FACING THE SAME DIRECTION FOR THE FIRST TIME.
I'LL...
...WORK HARD.

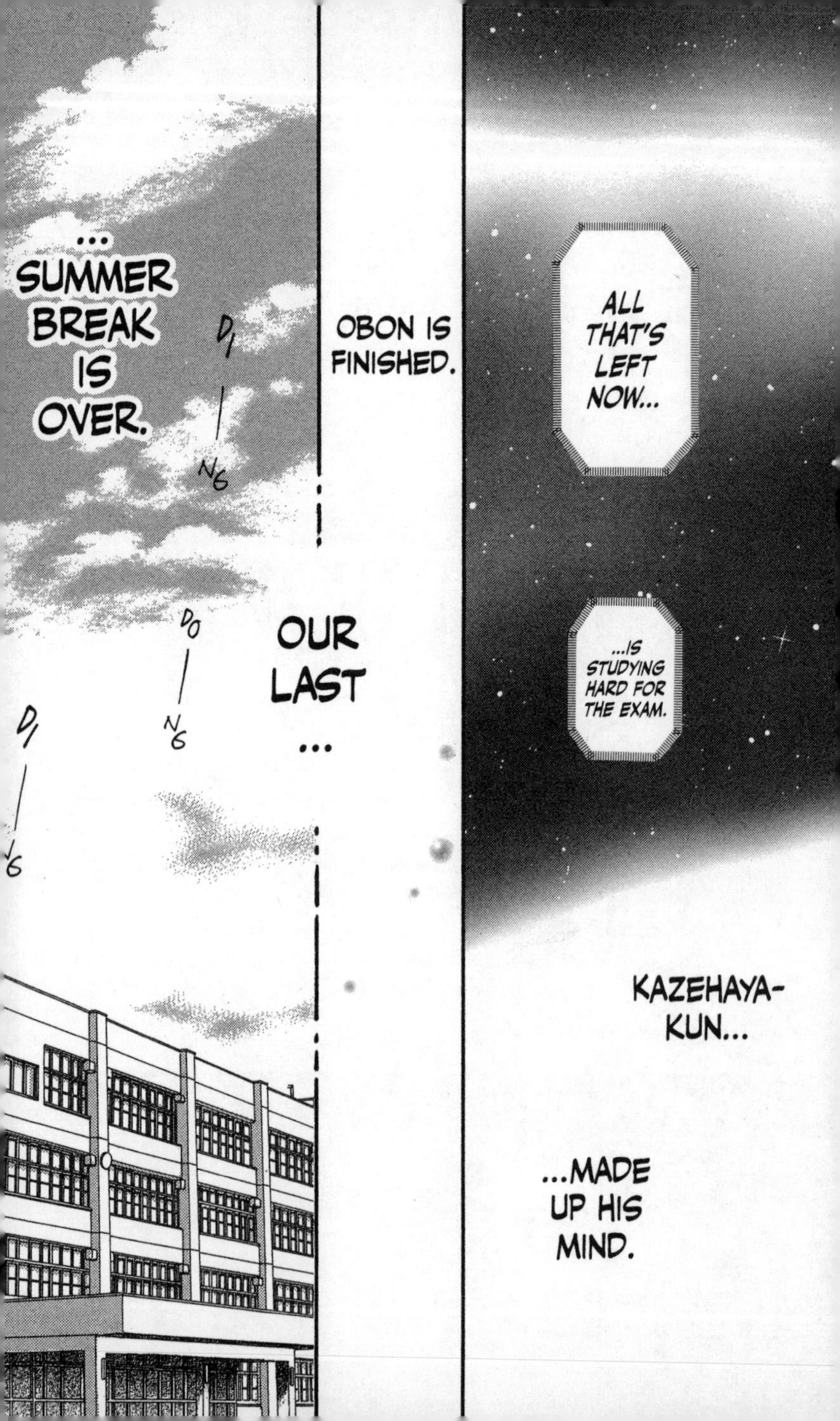
ALL THAT'S LEFT NOW...
...IS STUDYING HARD FOR THE EXAM.
KAZEHAYA-KUN...
...MADE UP HIS MIND.
OBON IS FINISHED.
OUR LAST ...
... SUMMER BREAK IS OVER.
DING
DONG
DING

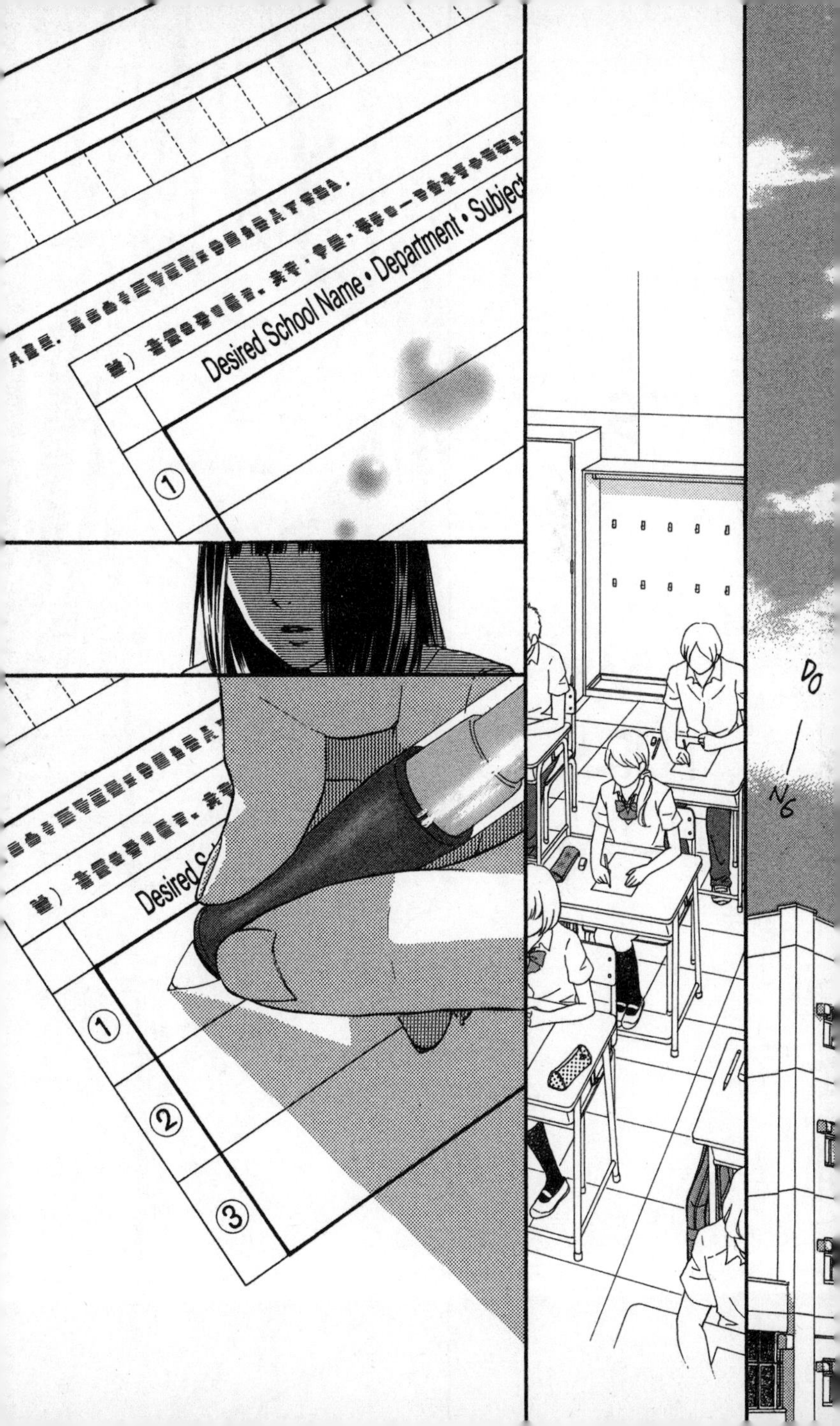
DO—NG
Desired School Name • Department • Subject
①
Desired
①
②
③

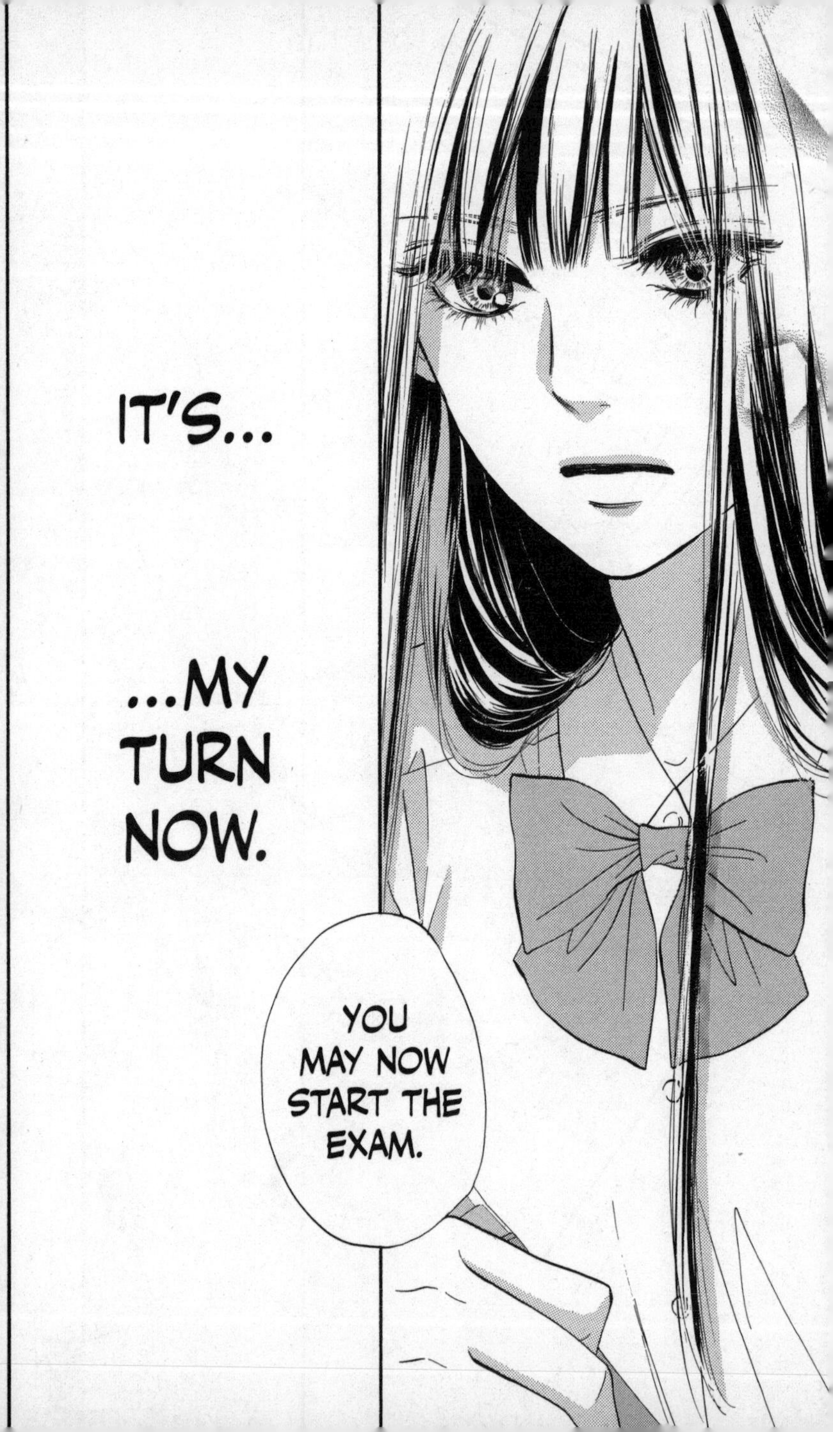
YOU MAY NOW START THE EXAM.
IT'S...
...MY TURN NOW.

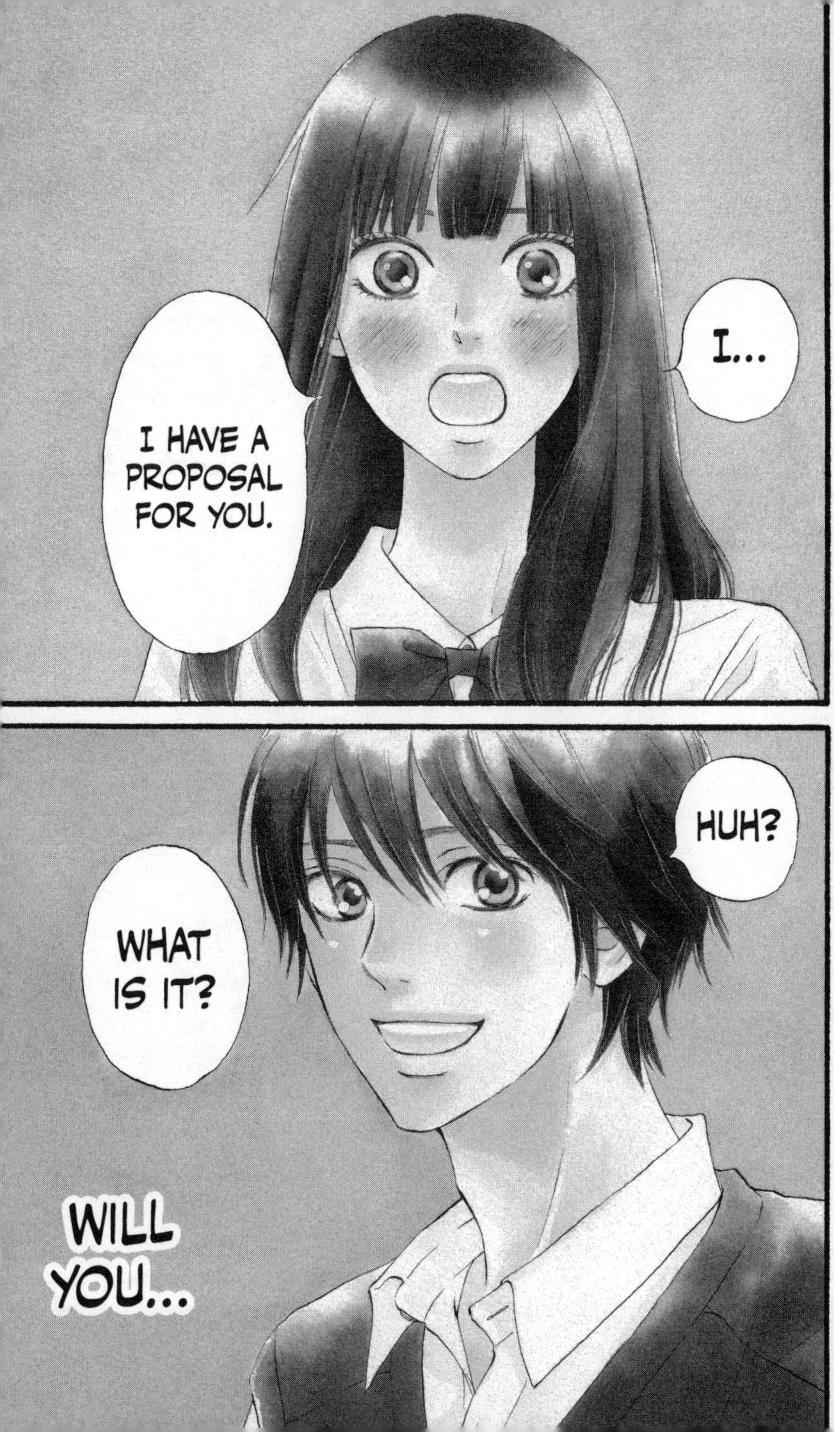
I...
I HAVE A PROPOSAL FOR YOU.
HUH?
WHAT IS IT?
WILL YOU...

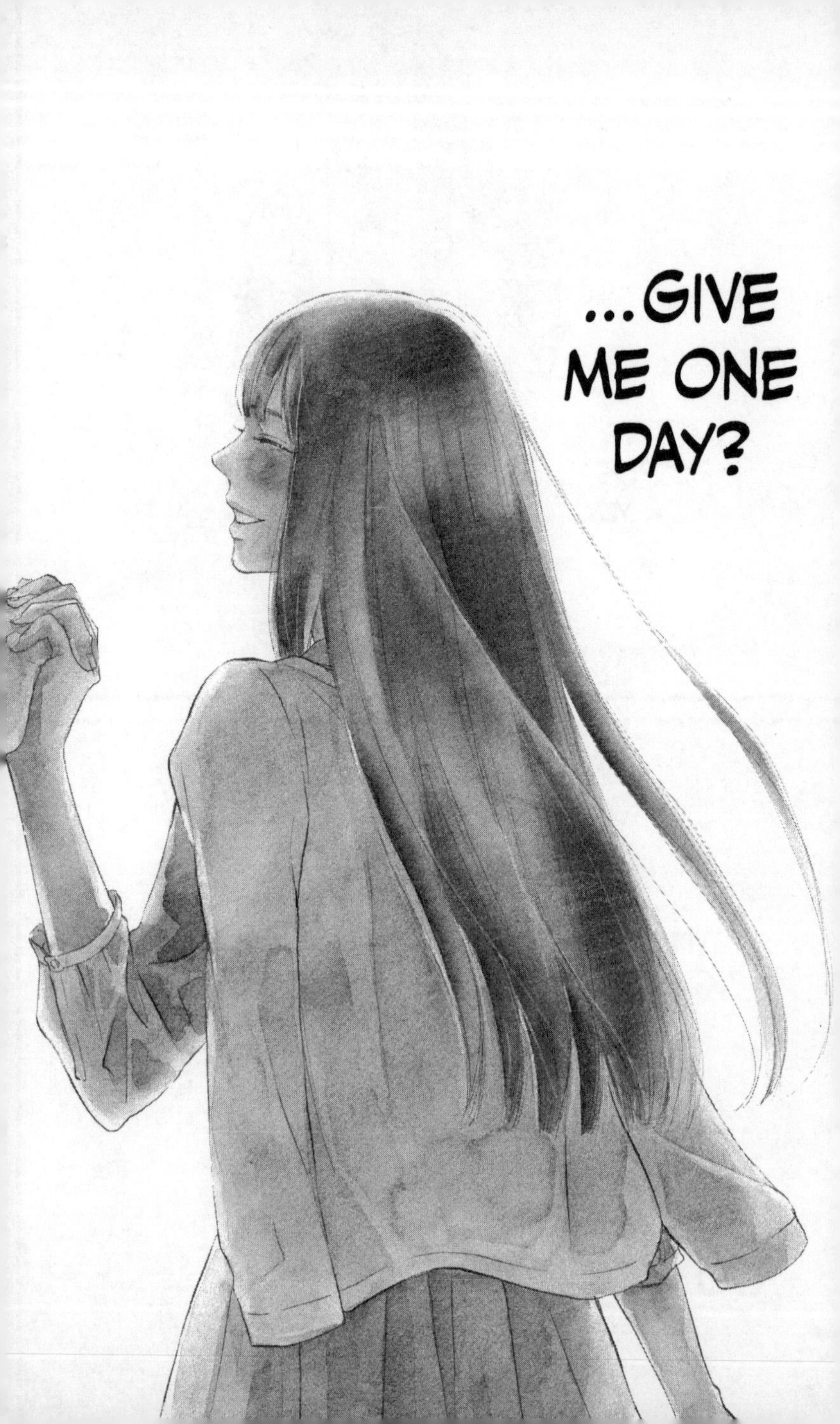
...GIVE ME ONE DAY?

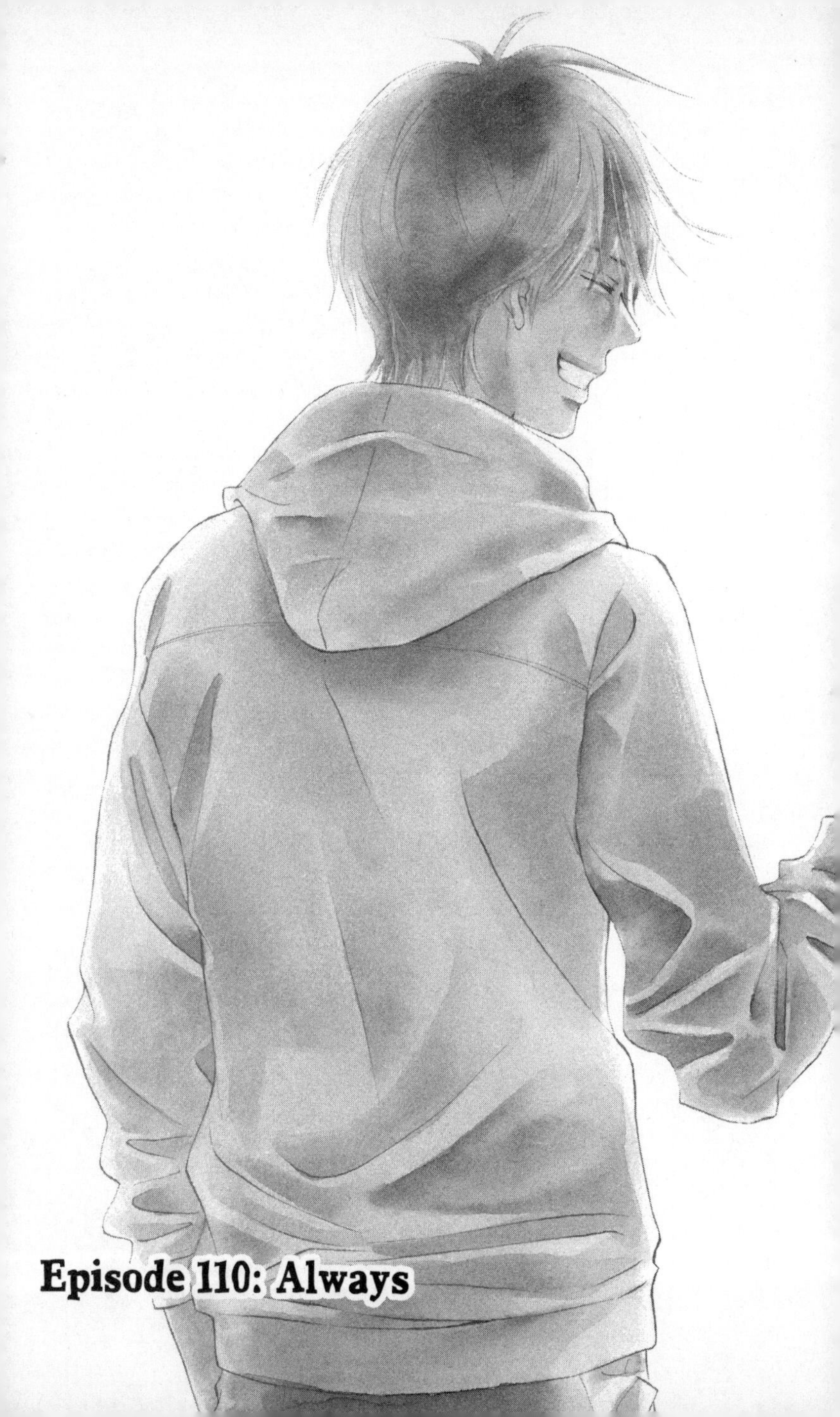

Episode 110: Always

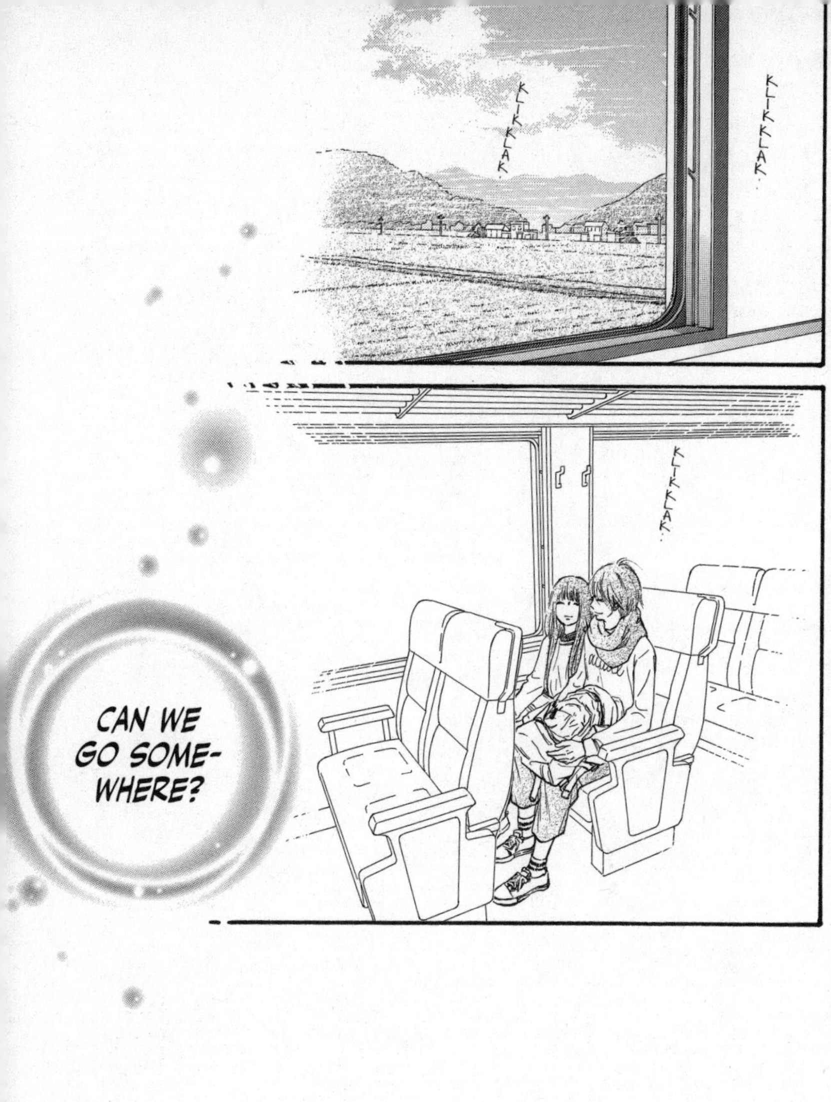
KLIKKLAK.
KLIKKLAK.
KLIKKLAK.
CAN WE GO SOME-WHERE?

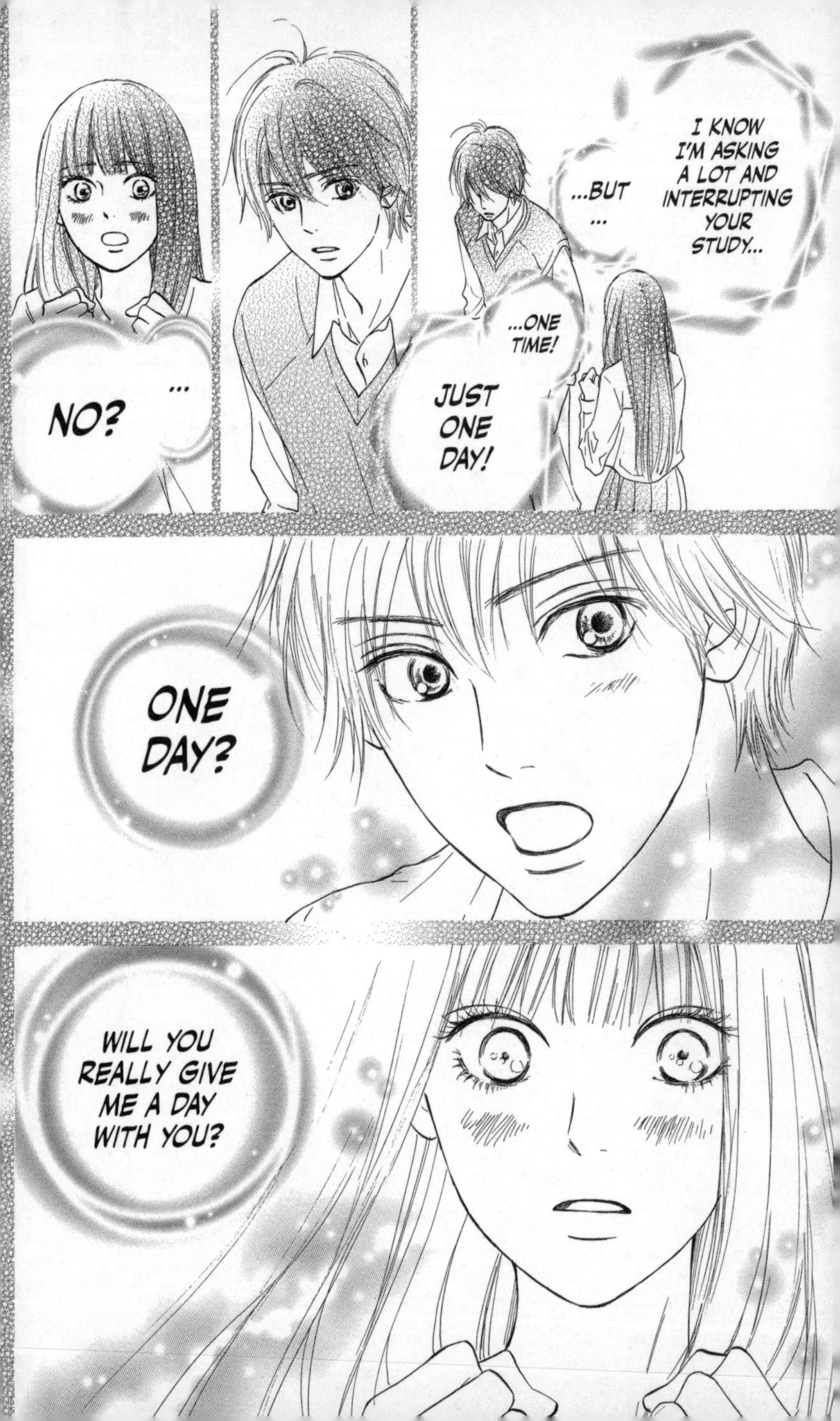
I KNOW I'M ASKING A LOT AND INTERRUPTING YOUR STUDY...
...BUT ...
...ONE TIME!
JUST ONE DAY!
...
NO?
ONE DAY?
WILL YOU REALLY GIVE ME A DAY WITH YOU?

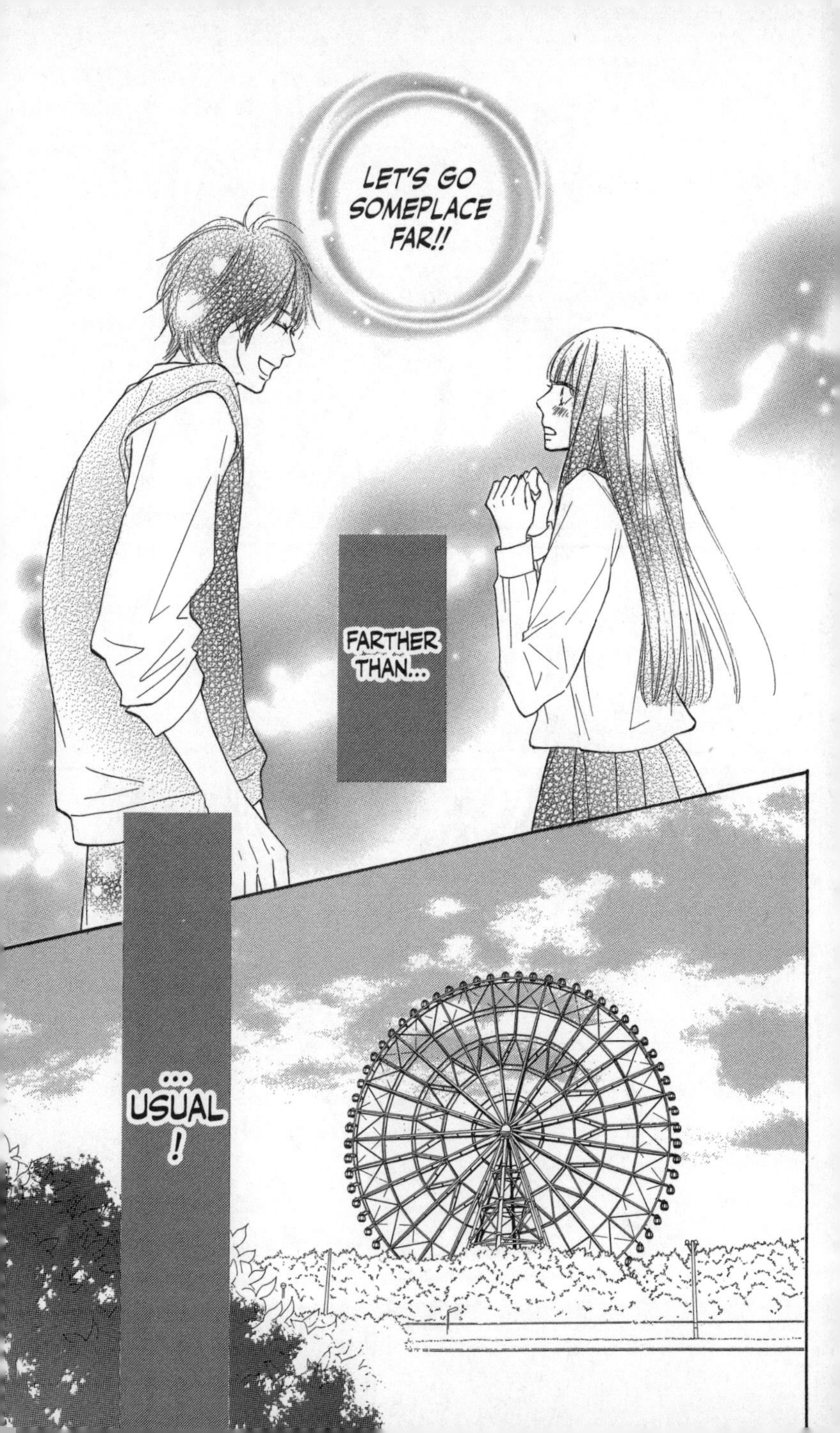
LET'S GO SOMEPLACE FAR!!
FARTHER THAN...
...USUAL!

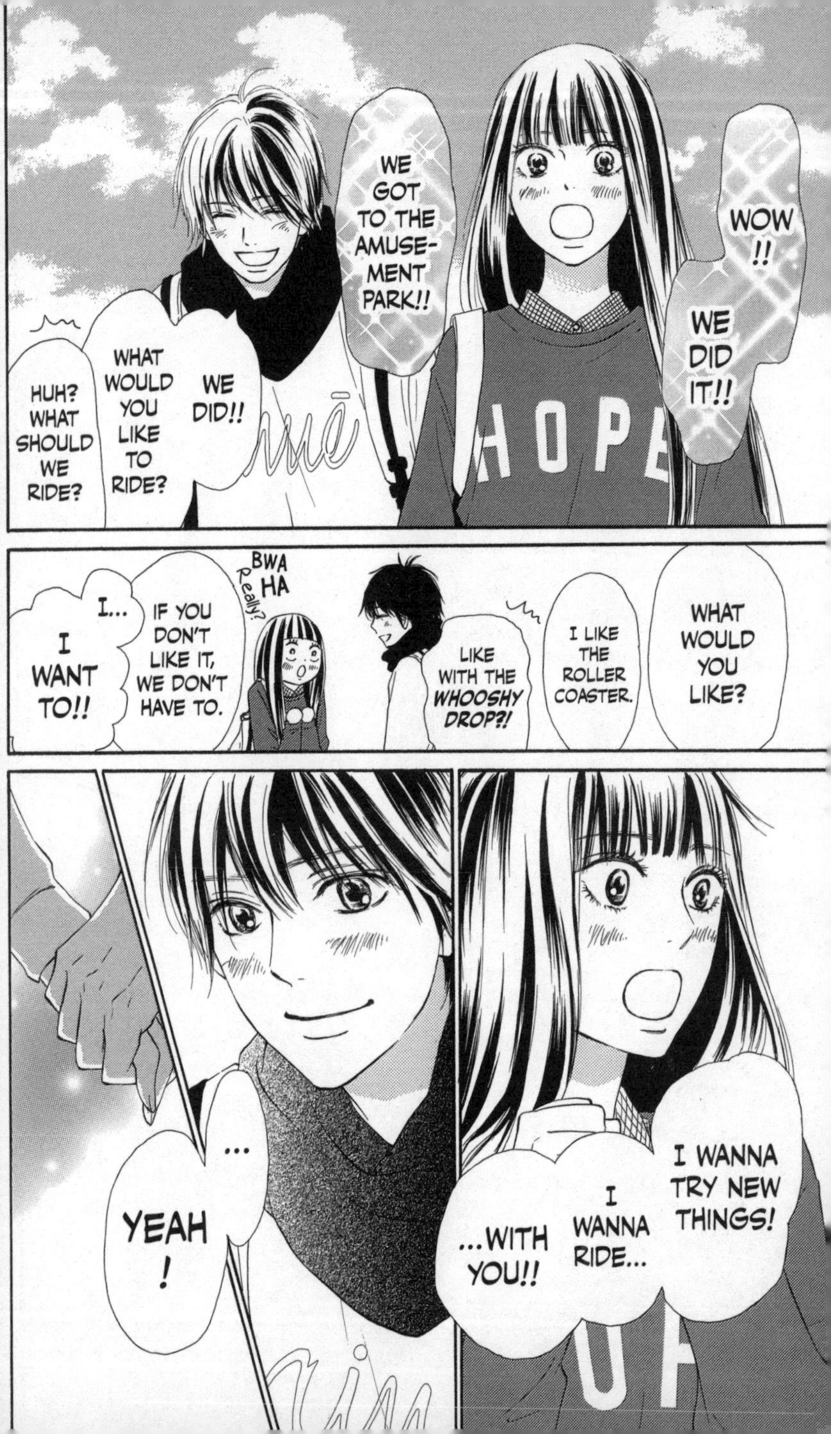
WOW!!
WE DID IT!!
WE GOT TO THE AMUSEMENT PARK!!
WE DID!!
WHAT WOULD YOU LIKE TO RIDE?
HUH? WHAT SHOULD WE RIDE?
WHAT WOULD YOU LIKE?
I LIKE THE ROLLER COASTER.
LIKE WITH THE WHOOSHY DROP?!
BWA HA
Really?
IF YOU DON'T LIKE IT, WE DON'T HAVE TO.
I...
I WANT TO!!
I WANNA TRY NEW THINGS!
I WANNA RIDE...
...WITH YOU!!
...
YEAH!

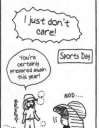

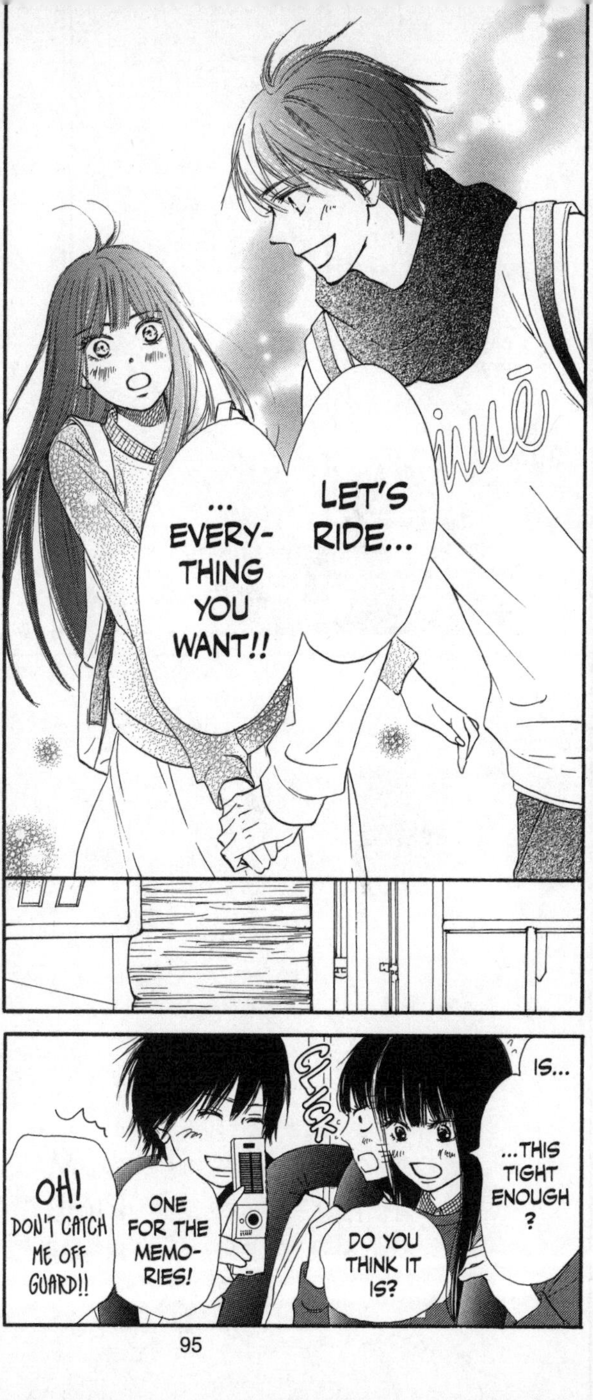
LET'S RIDE...
...EVERYTHING YOU WANT!!
IS... ...THIS TIGHT ENOUGH?
CLICK
DO YOU THINK IT IS?
ONE FOR THE MEMORIES!
OH! DON'T CATCH ME OFF GUARD!!

KARUPIN on JAPAN 2

I think I should walk more.

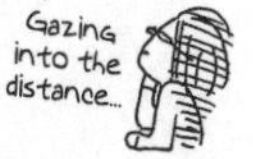
Gazing into the distance...

I should have a healthy lifestyle.

I have a skin allergy to sunlight, so I rarely go out in the summer.

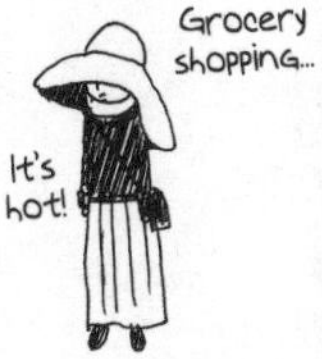
Grocery shopping...
It's hot!

Being fashionable or unfashionable or keeping my skin light...

...none of that matters.

I just don't care!

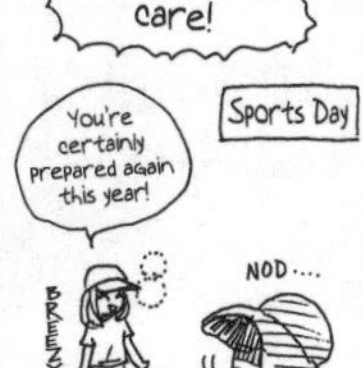
Sports Day
You're certainly prepared again this year!
NOD....
BREEZY

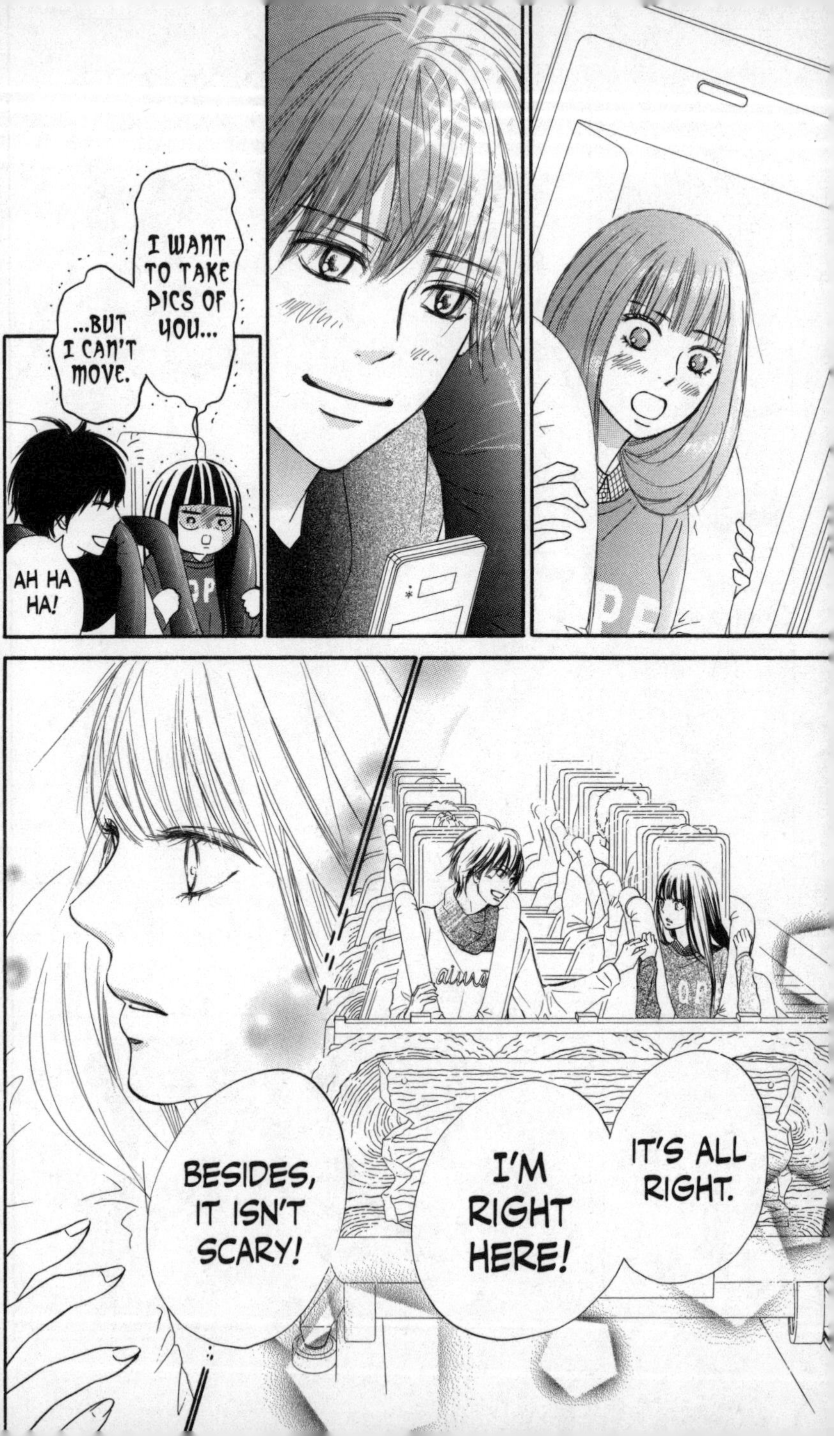
I WANT TO TAKE PICS OF YOU...
...BUT I CAN'T MOVE.
AH HA HA!
IT'S ALL RIGHT.
I'M RIGHT HERE!
BESIDES, IT ISN'T SCARY!

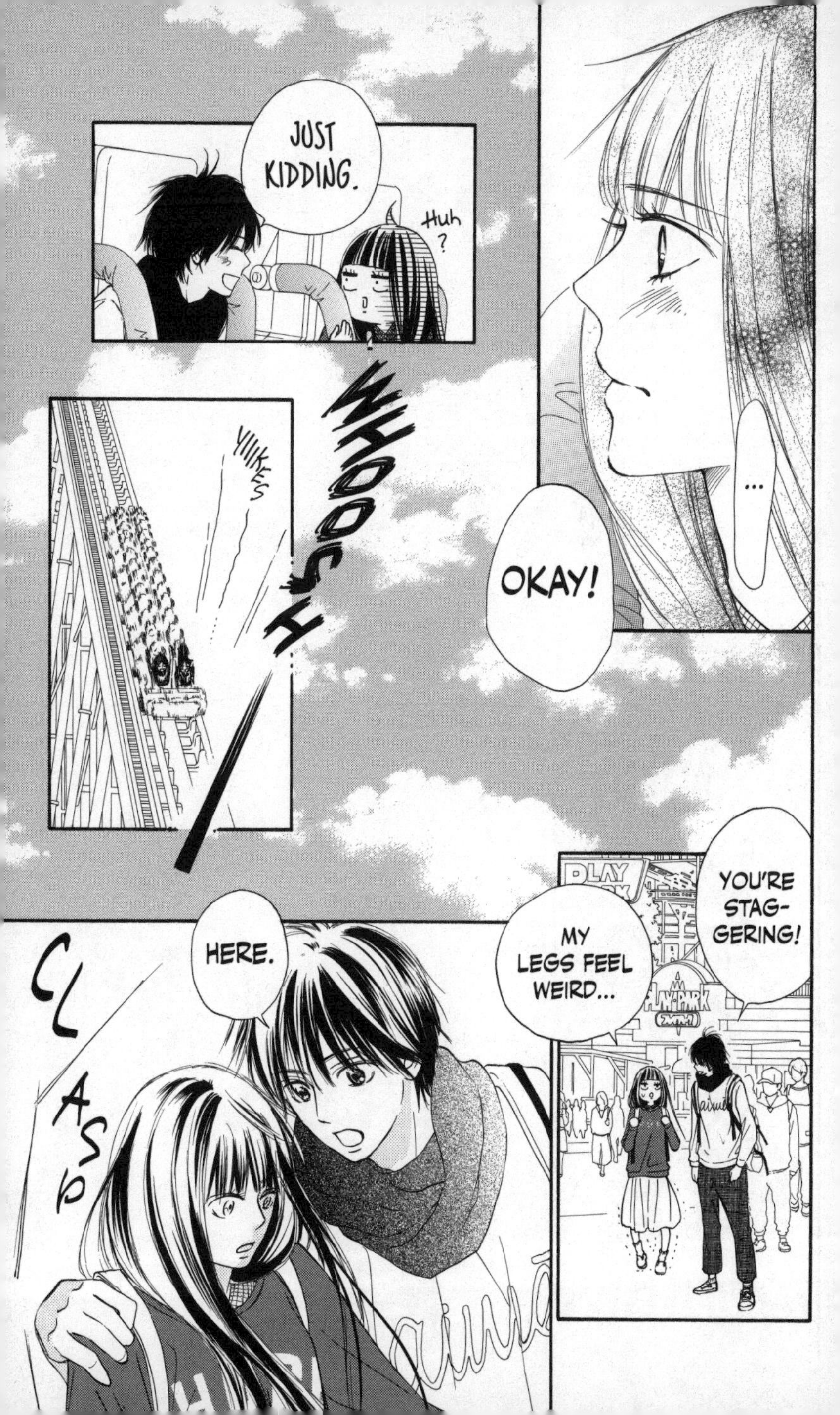
...
OKAY!
JUST KIDDING.
Huh ?
WHOOSH
YIIIKES
YOU'RE STAG-GERING!
MY LEGS FEEL WEIRD...
HERE.
CLASP

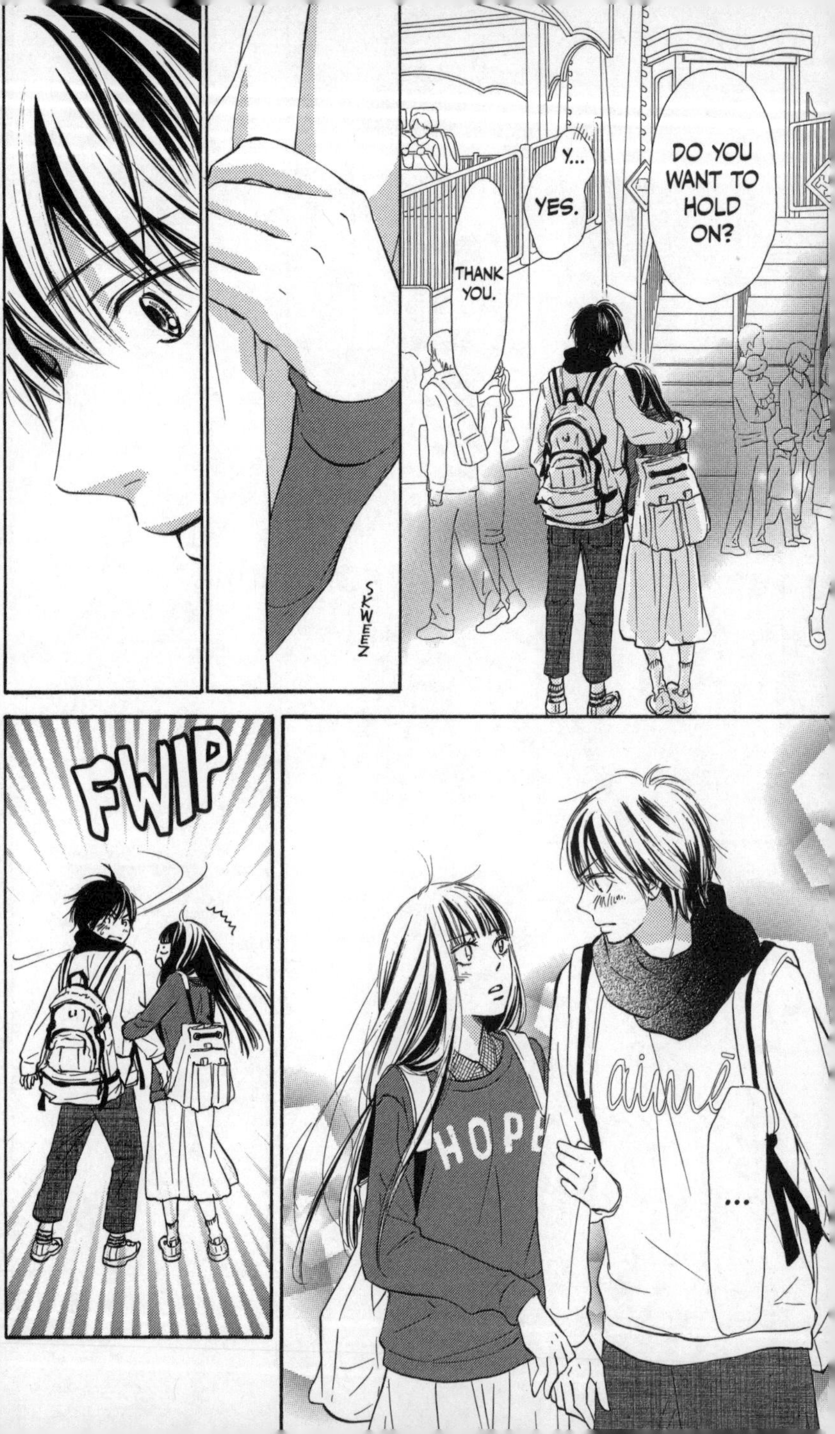
DO YOU WANT TO HOLD ON?
Y... YES.
THANK YOU.
SKWEEZ
...
FWIP

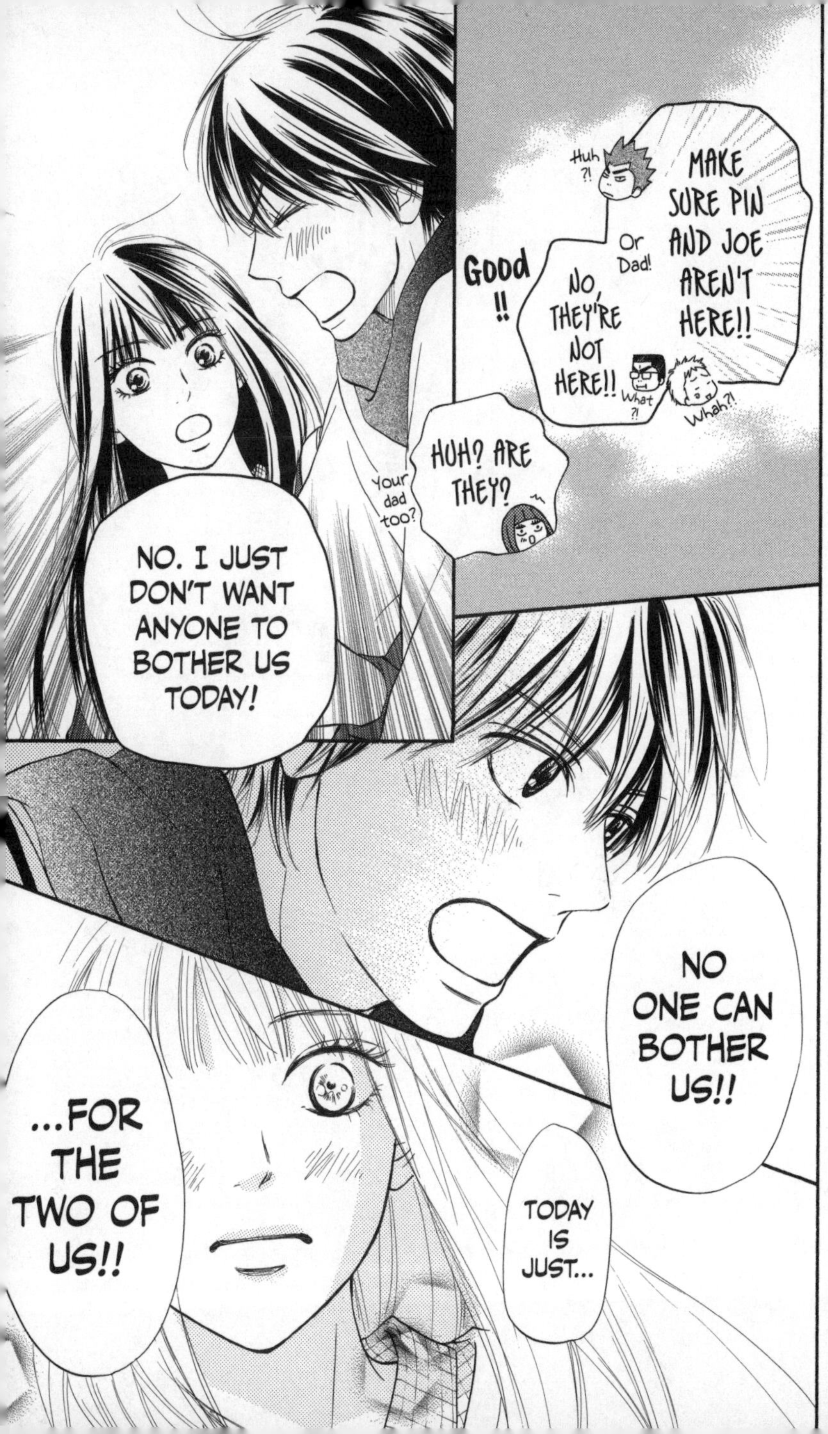
MAKE SURE PIN AND JOE AREN'T HERE!!
Huh ?!
Or Dad!
NO, THEY'RE NOT HERE!!
What ?!
Whah?!
Good !!
HUH? ARE THEY?
Your dad too?
NO. I JUST DON'T WANT ANYONE TO BOTHER US TODAY!
NO ONE CAN BOTHER US!!
TODAY IS JUST...
...FOR THE TWO OF US!!

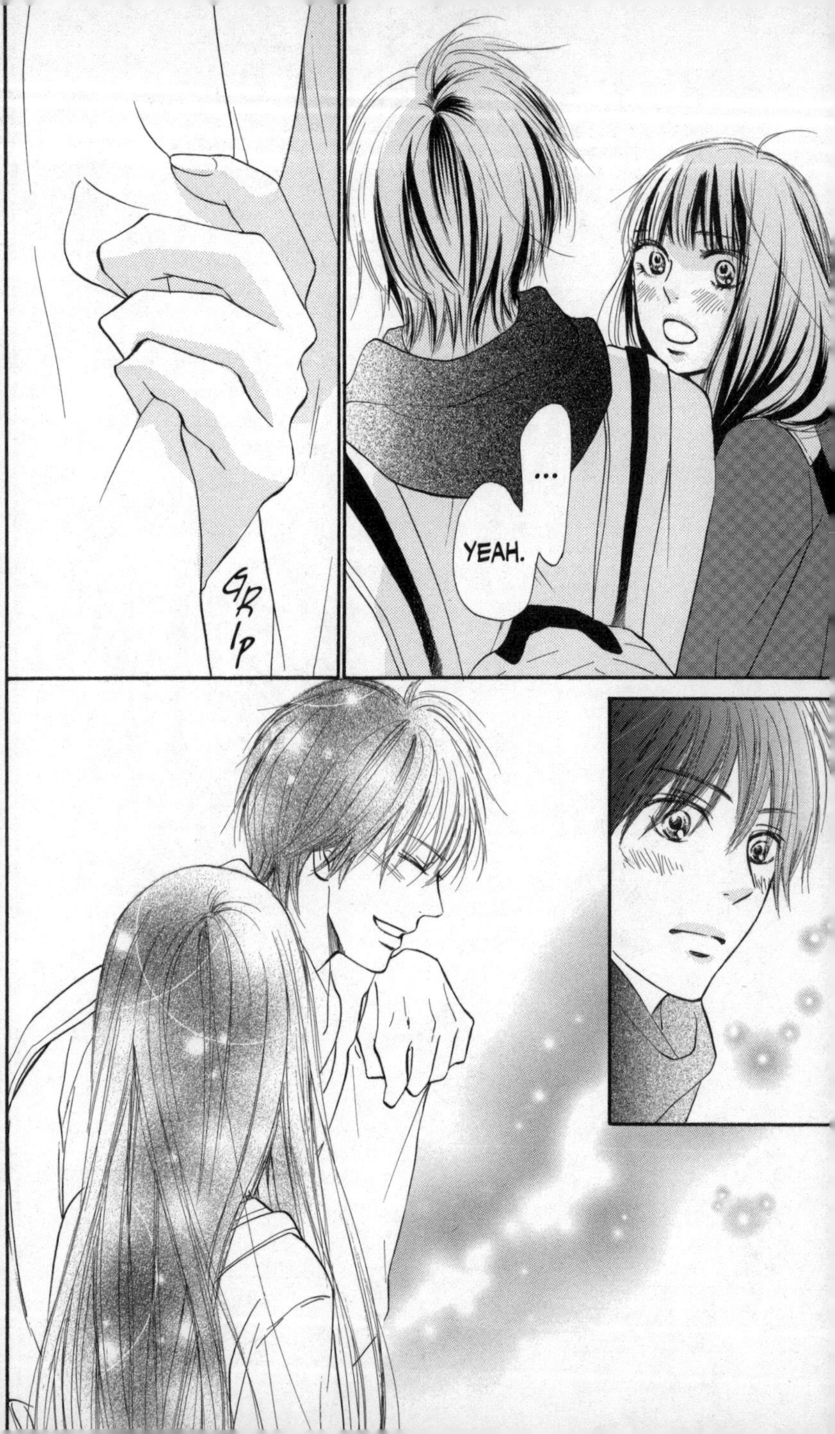
...
YEAH.
GRIP

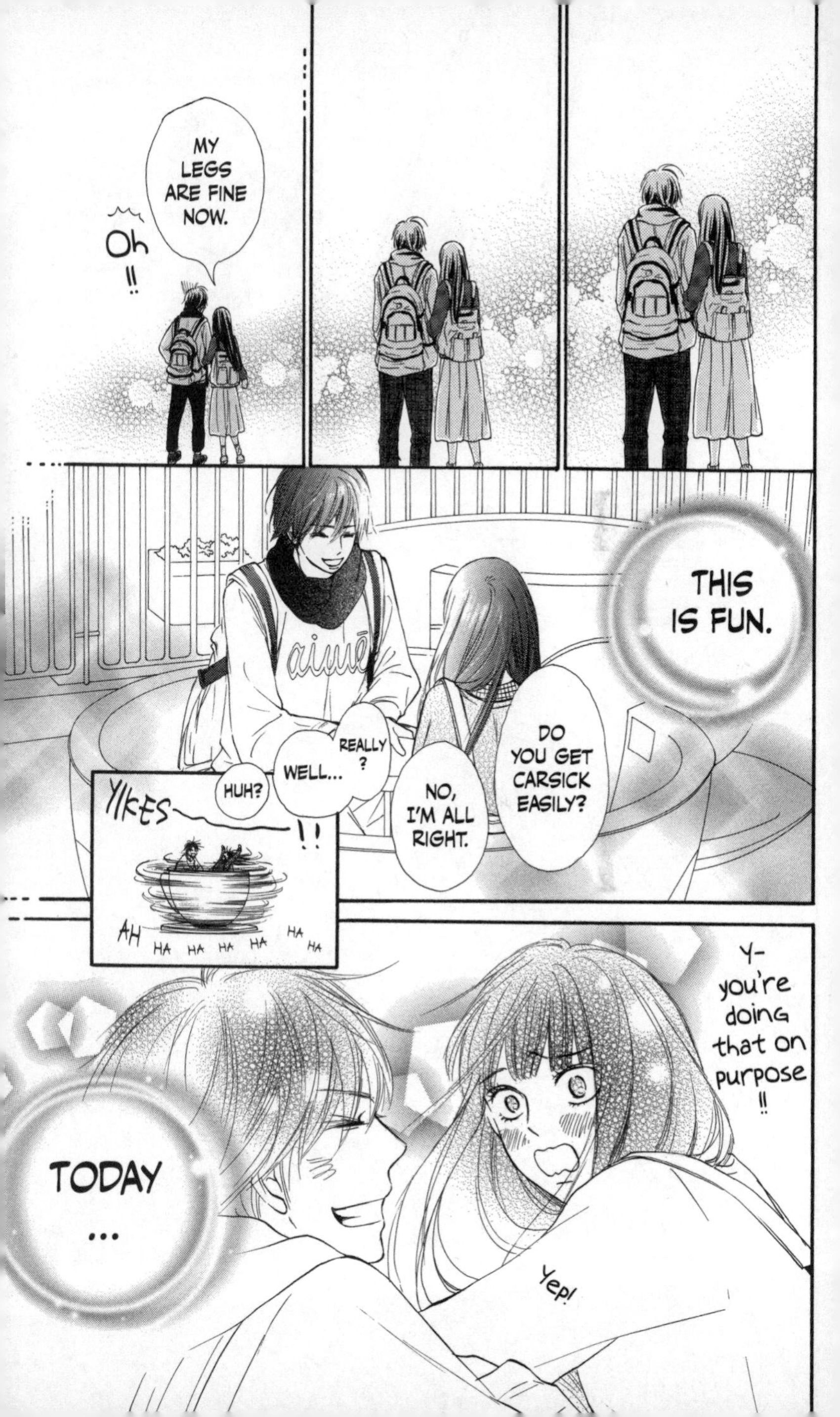
MY LEGS ARE FINE NOW.
Oh!!
THIS IS FUN.
DO YOU GET CARSICK EASILY?
NO, I'M ALL RIGHT.
REALLY?
WELL...
HUH?
YIKES!!
AH HA HA HA HA HA HA
Y-you're doing that on purpose!!
Yep!
TODAY...

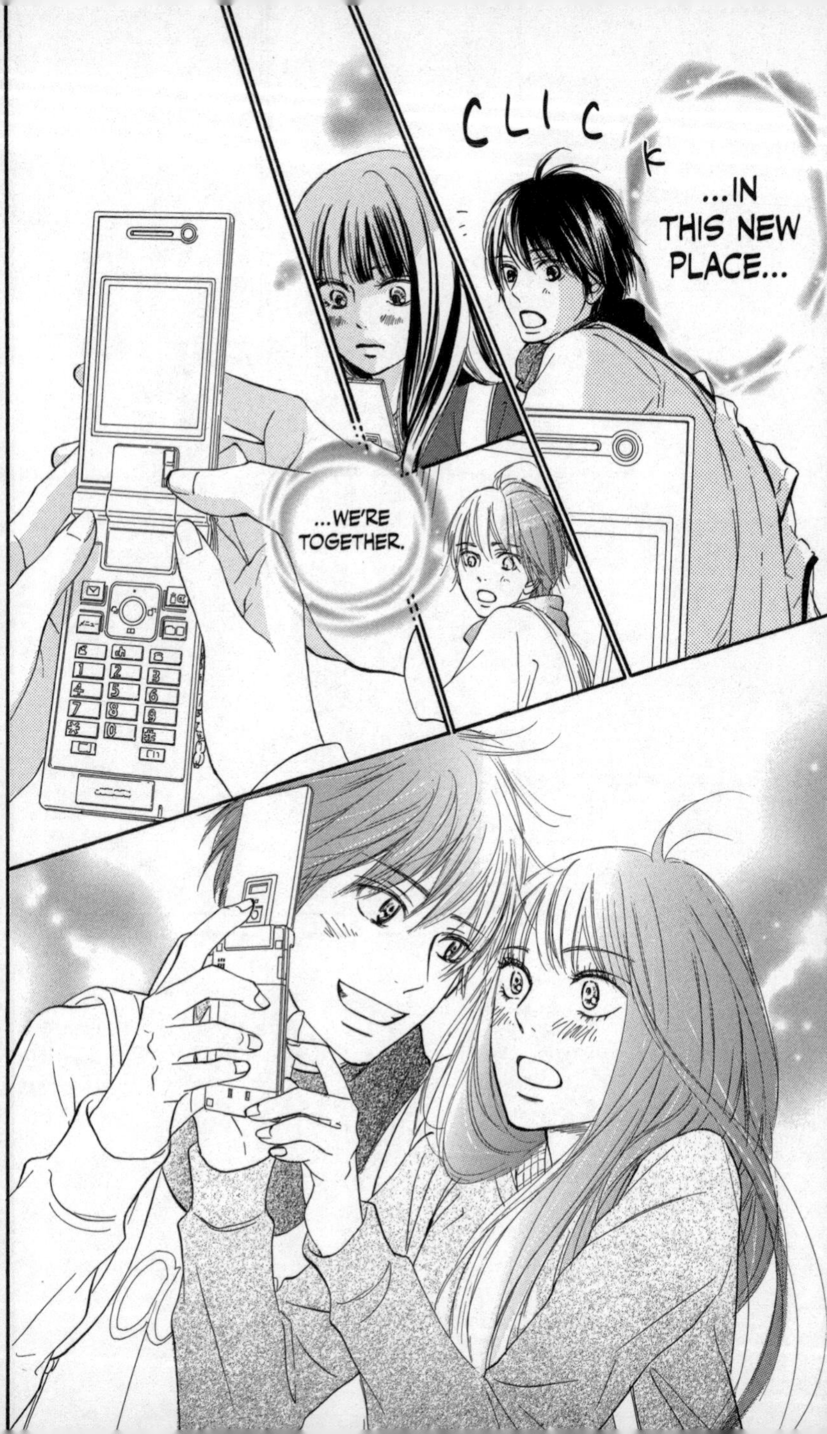
CLICK
...IN THIS NEW PLACE...
...WE'RE TOGETHER.

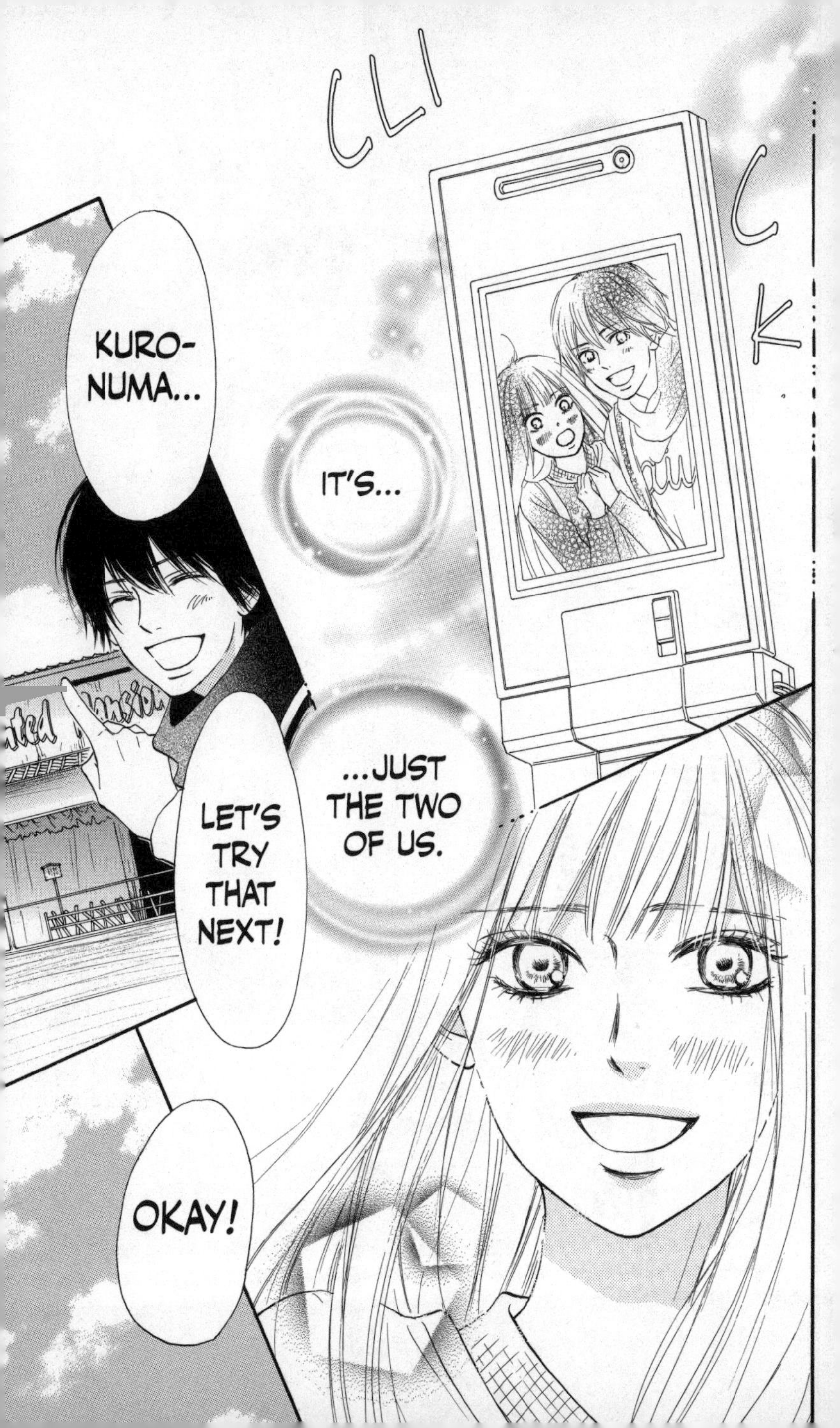
CLICK
KURO-NUMA...
IT'S...
...JUST THE TWO OF US.
LET'S TRY THAT NEXT!
OKAY!

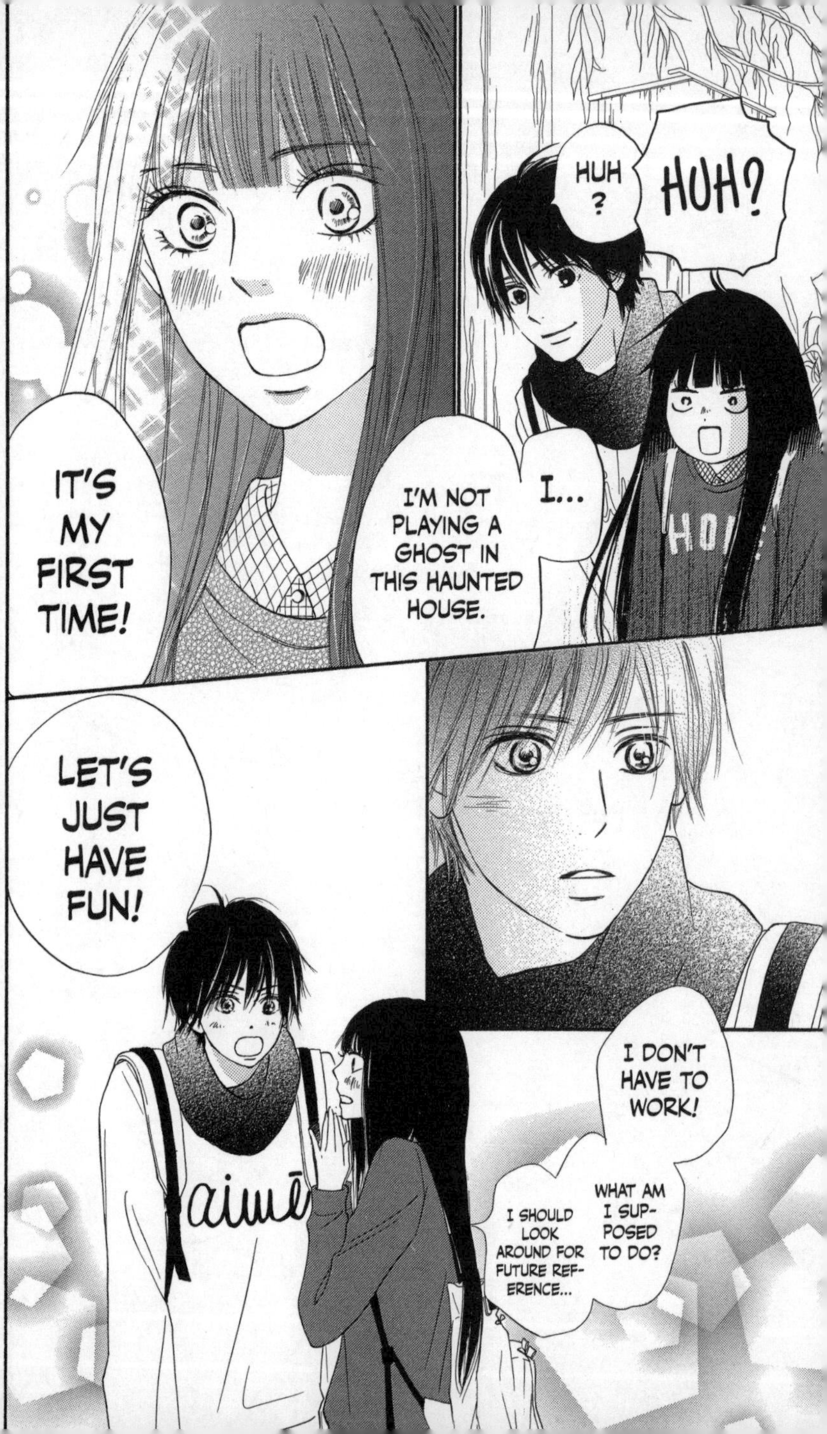
HUH ?
HUH?
I...
I'M NOT PLAYING A GHOST IN THIS HAUNTED HOUSE.
IT'S MY FIRST TIME!
I DON'T HAVE TO WORK!
WHAT AM I SUP-POSED TO DO?
I SHOULD LOOK AROUND FOR FUTURE REF-ERENCE...
LET'S JUST HAVE FUN!

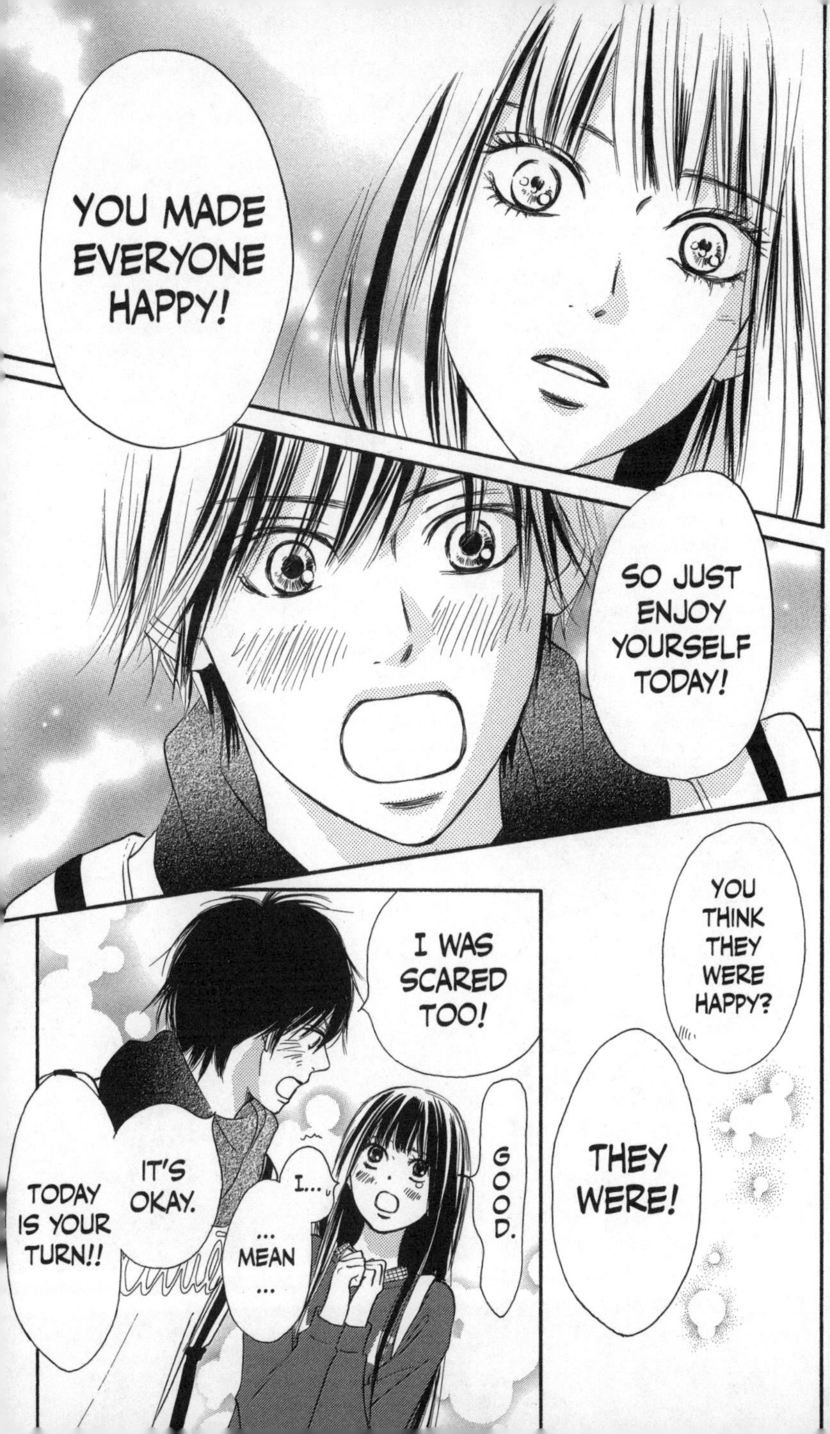
YOU MADE EVERYONE HAPPY!
SO JUST ENJOY YOURSELF TODAY!
YOU THINK THEY WERE HAPPY?
THEY WERE!
GOOD.
I WAS SCARED TOO!
I... ...MEAN...
IT'S OKAY.
TODAY IS YOUR TURN!!

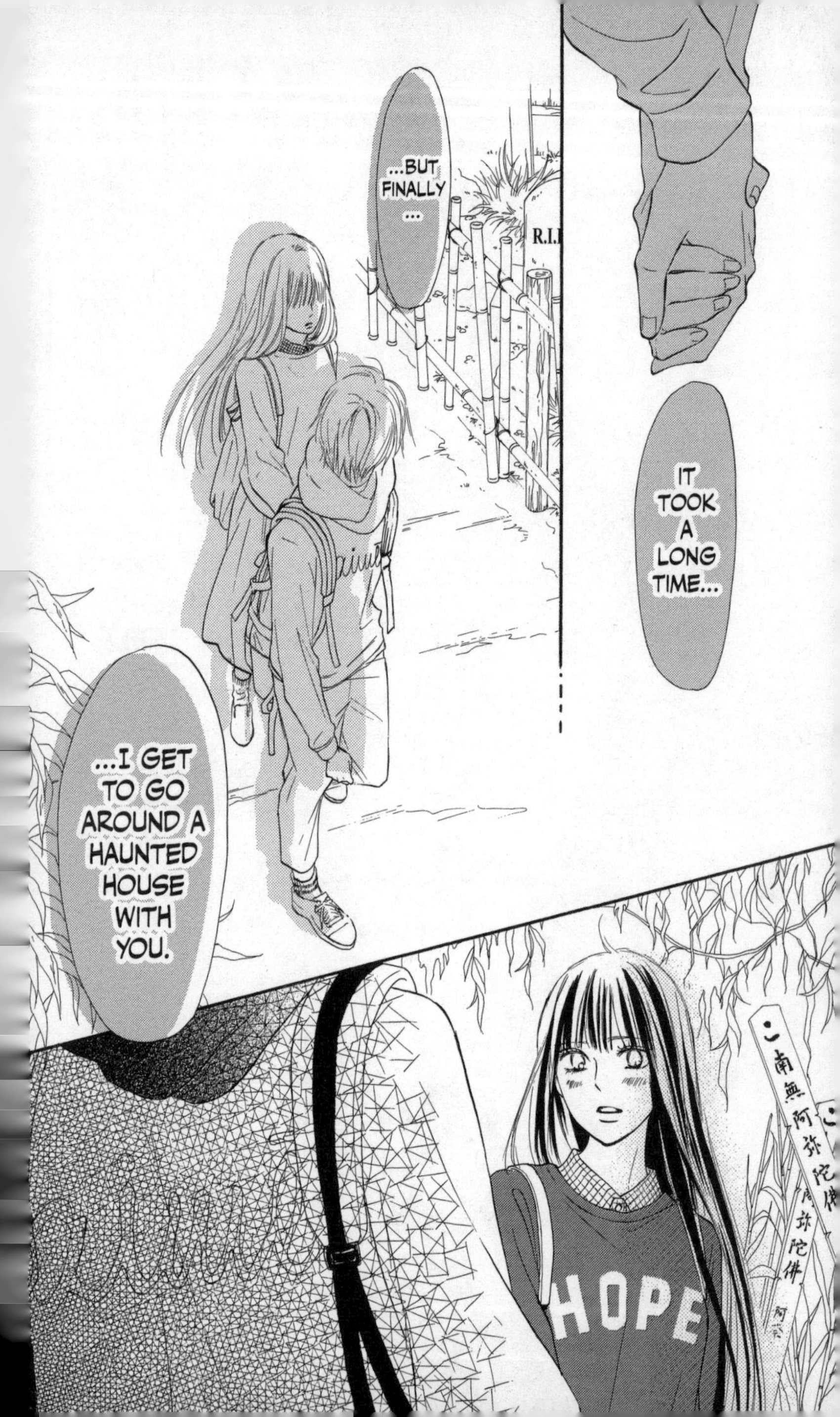
IT TOOK A LONG TIME...
...BUT FINALLY ...
...I GET TO GO AROUND A HAUNTED HOUSE WITH YOU.
HOPE

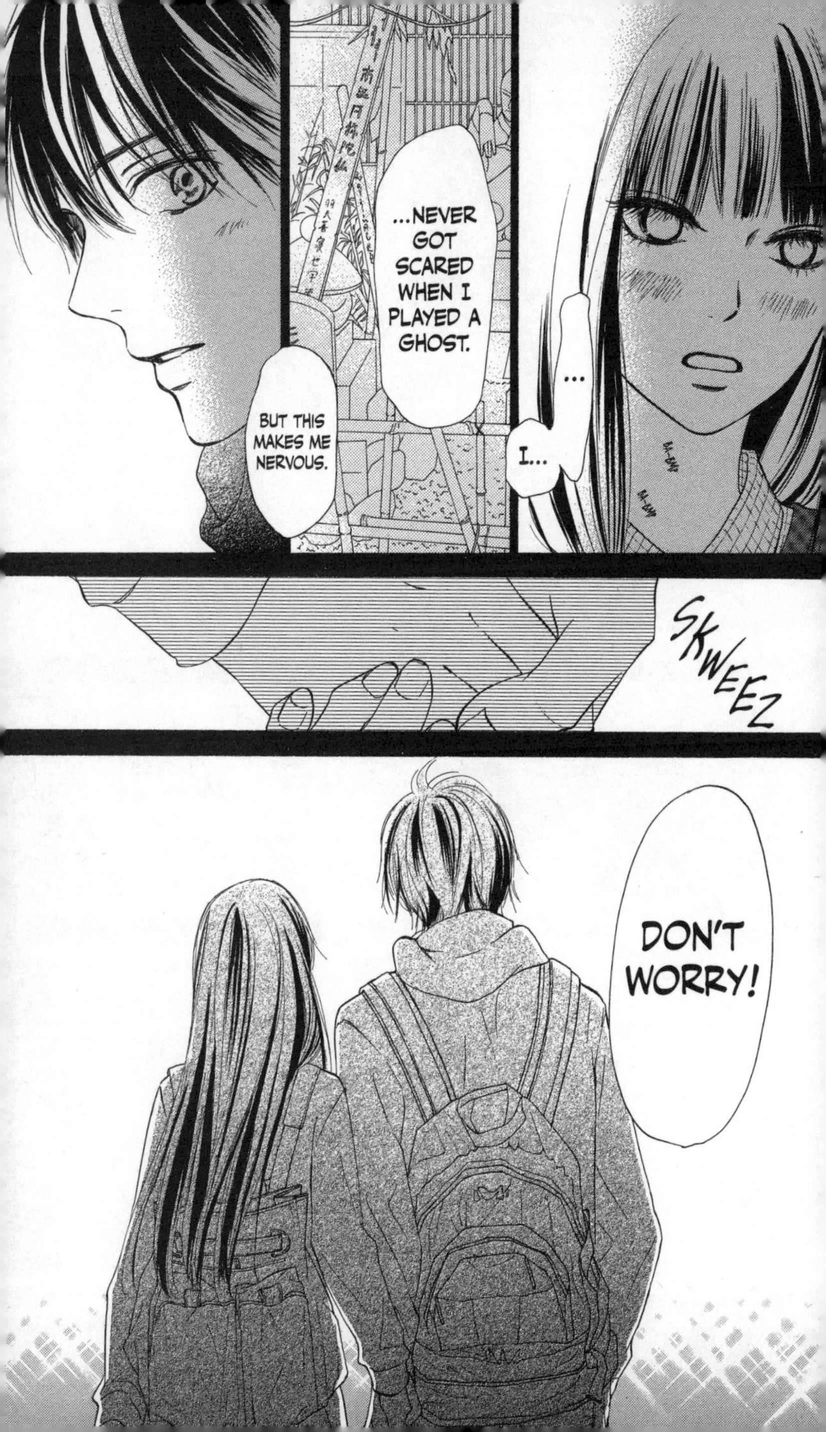
...
I...
...NEVER GOT SCARED WHEN I PLAYED A GHOST.
BUT THIS MAKES ME NERVOUS.
SKWEEZ
DON'T WORRY!

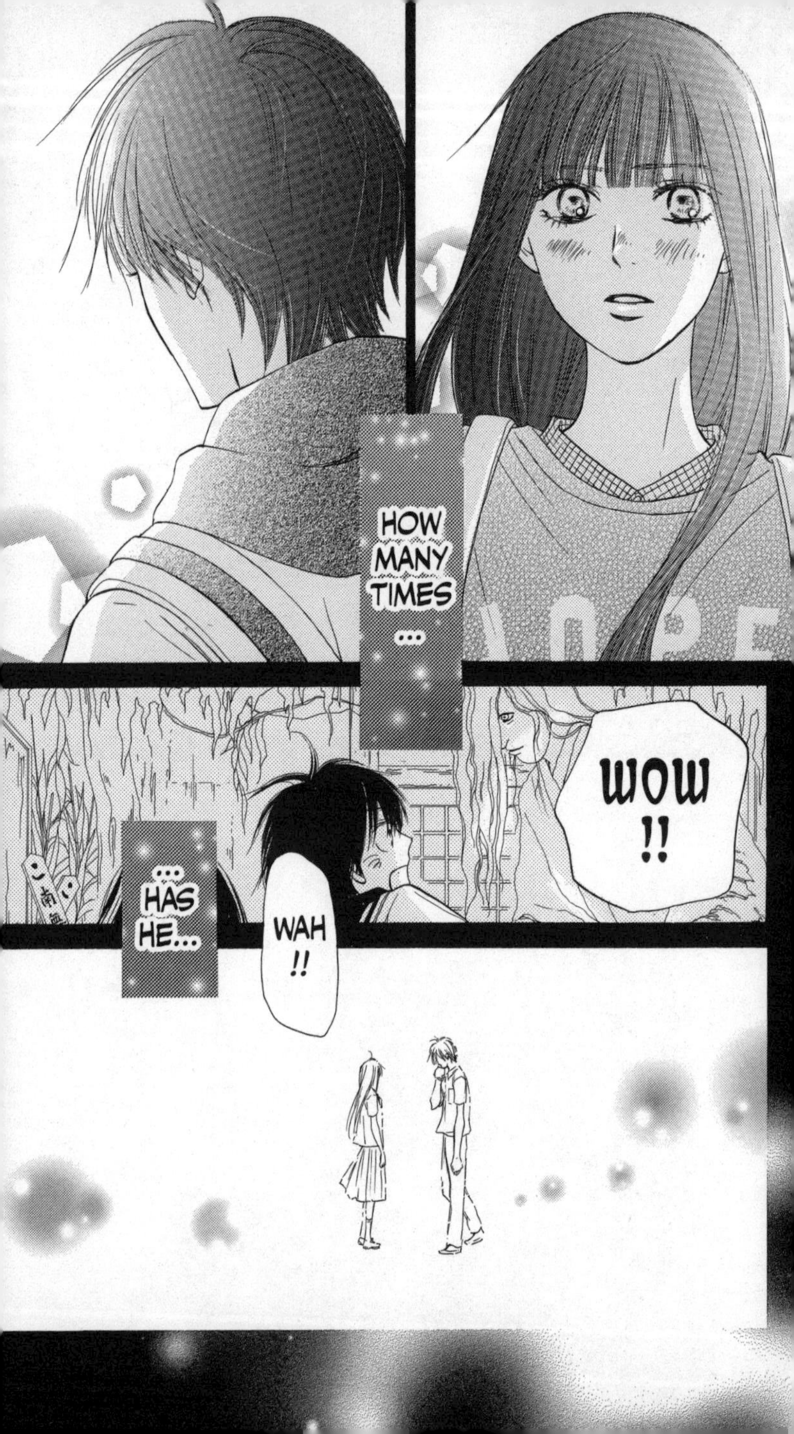
HOW MANY TIMES...
WOW !!
WAH !!
...HAS HE...

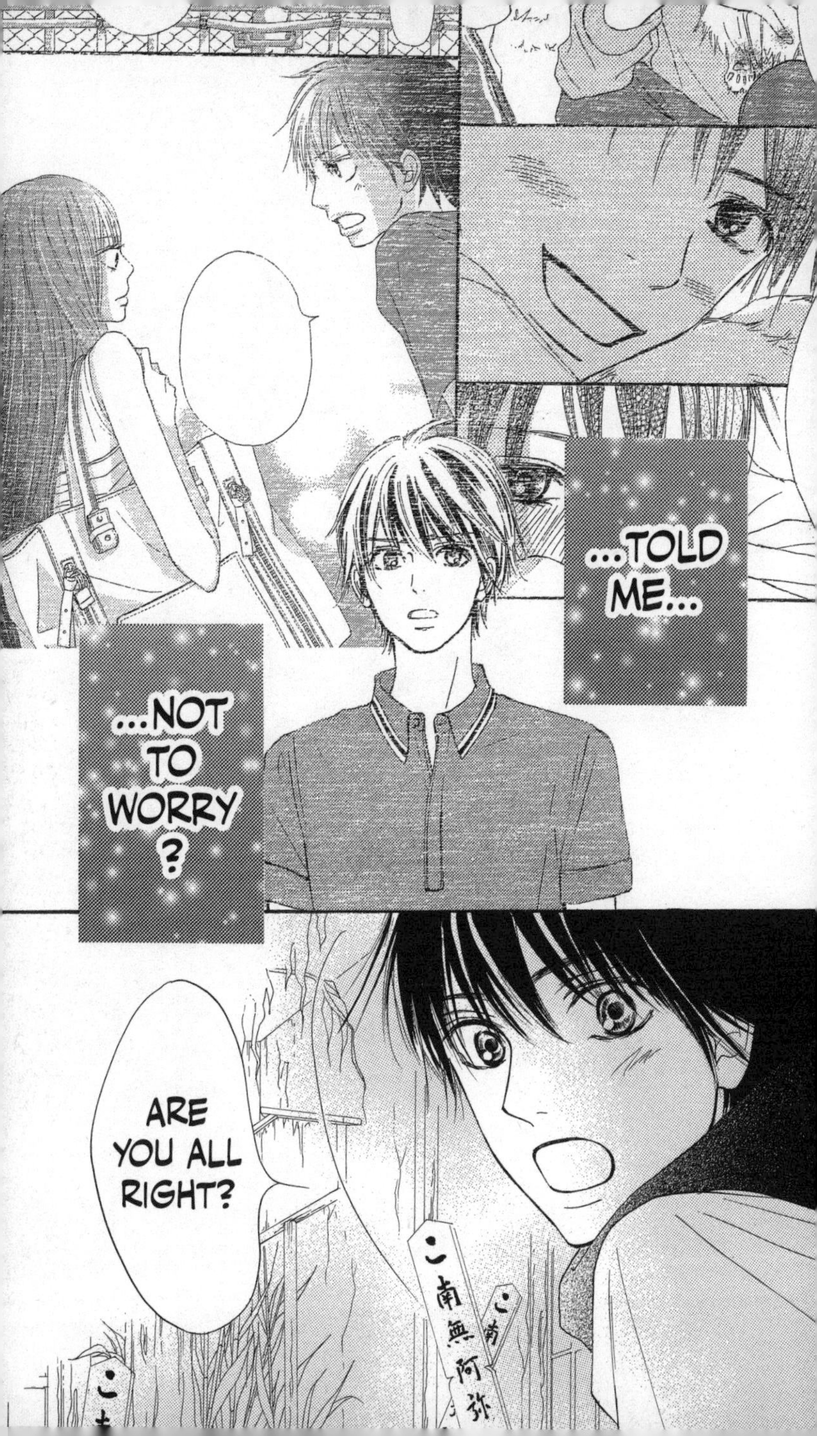
...TOLD ME...
...NOT TO WORRY?
ARE YOU ALL RIGHT?

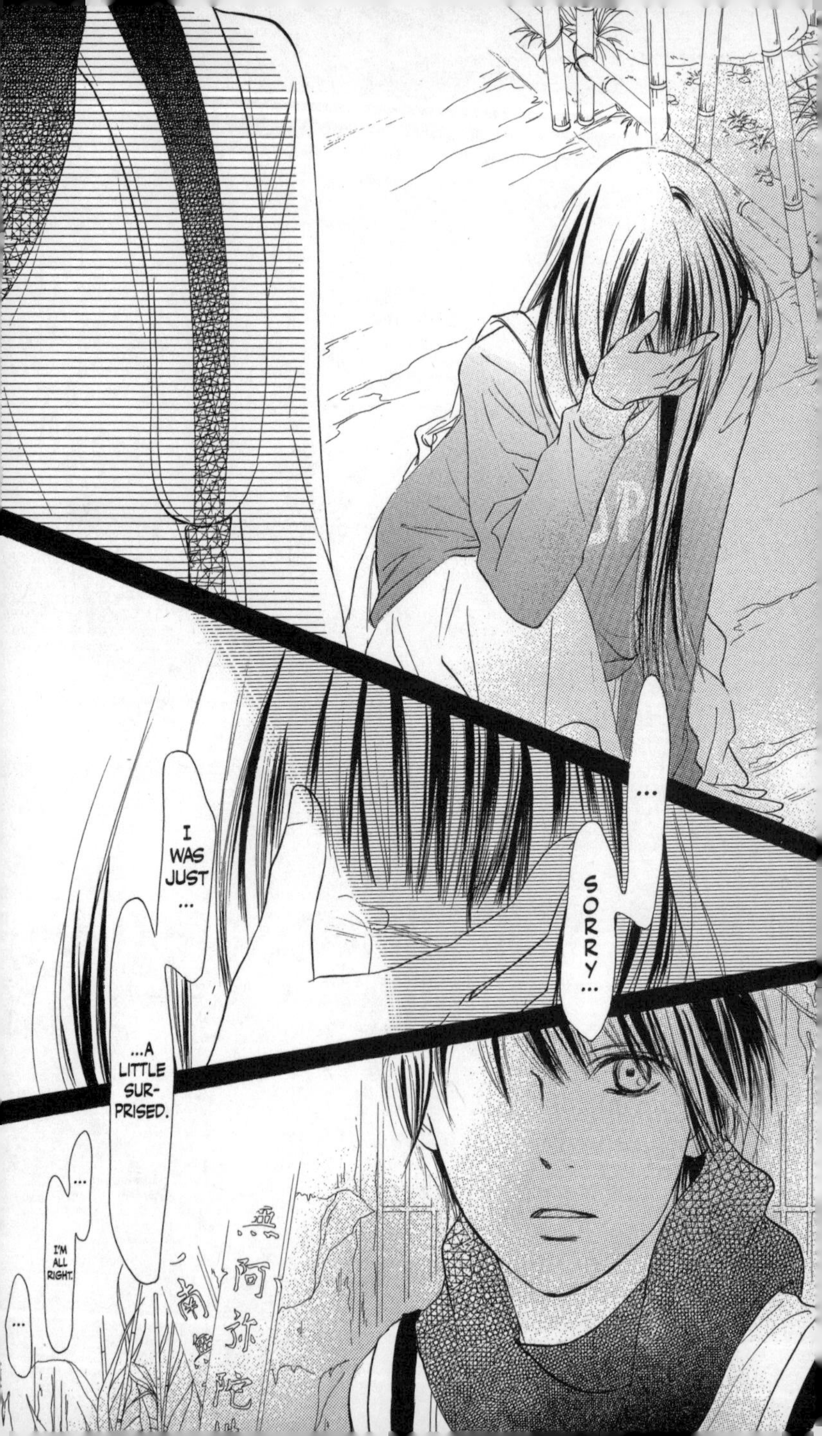
...
SORRY...
I WAS JUST...
...A LITTLE SURPRISED.
...
I'M ALL RIGHT.
...
南無阿弥陀仏

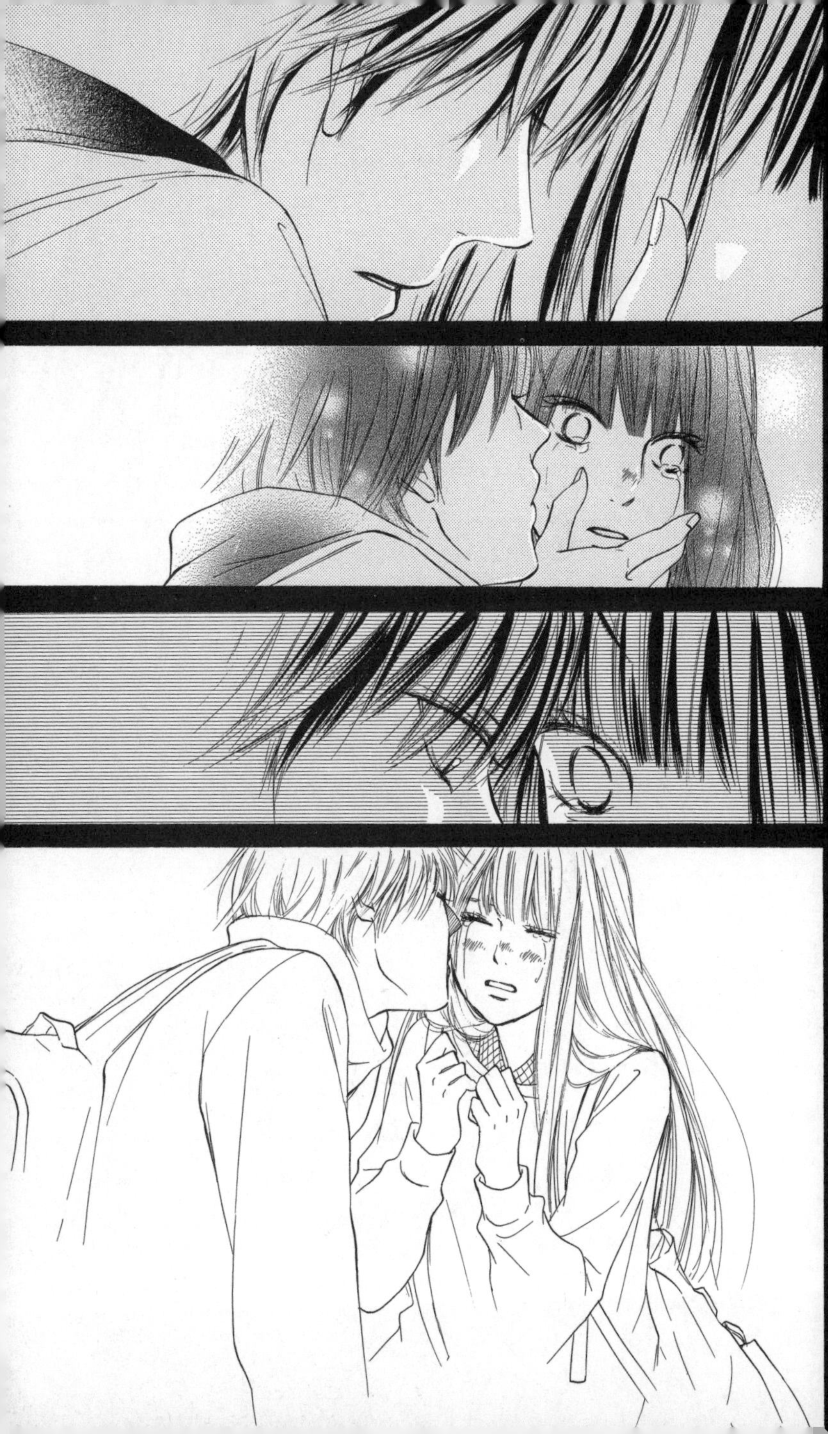

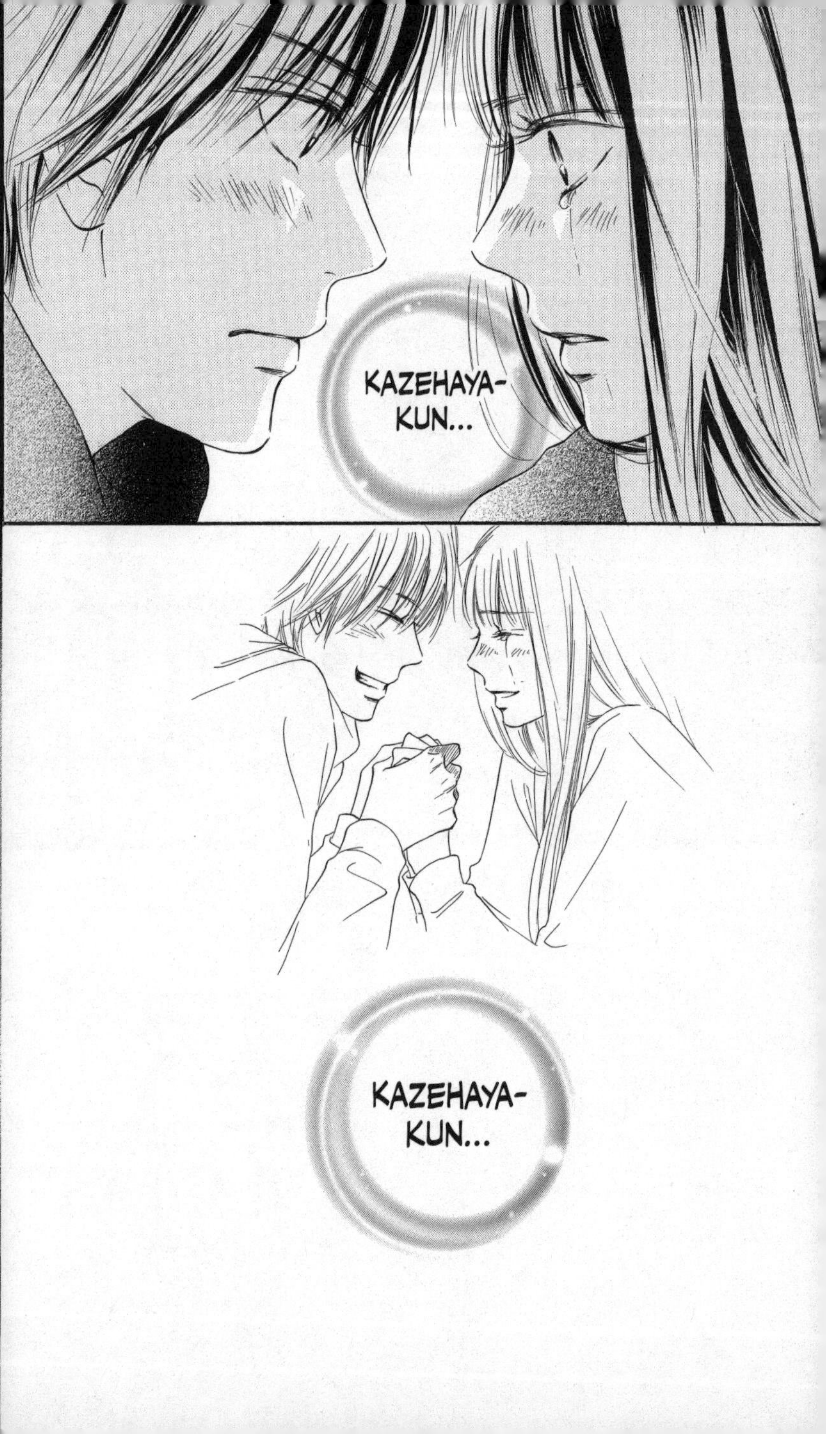
KAZEHAYA-KUN...
KAZEHAYA-KUN...

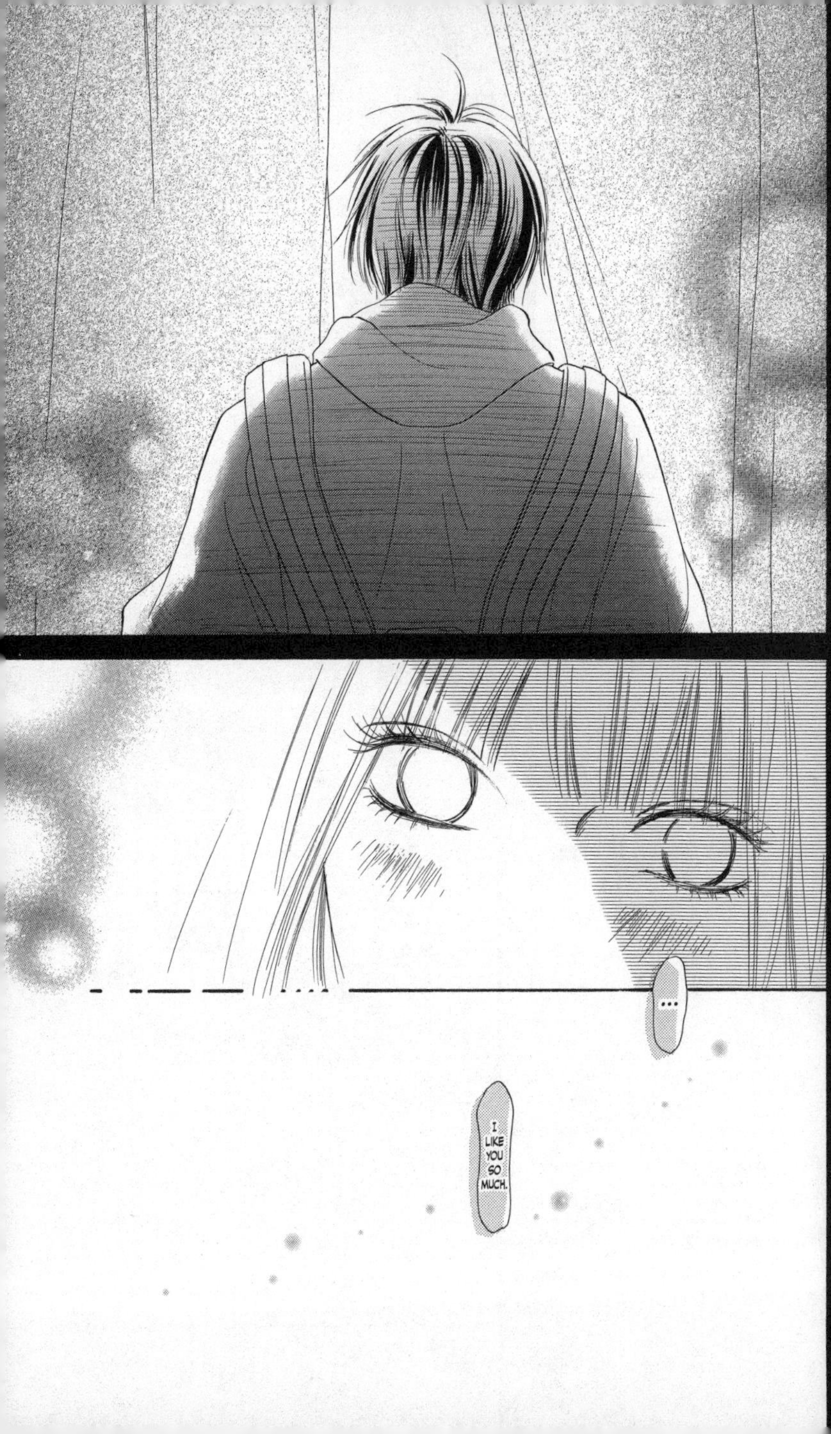
...
I LIKE YOU SO MUCH.

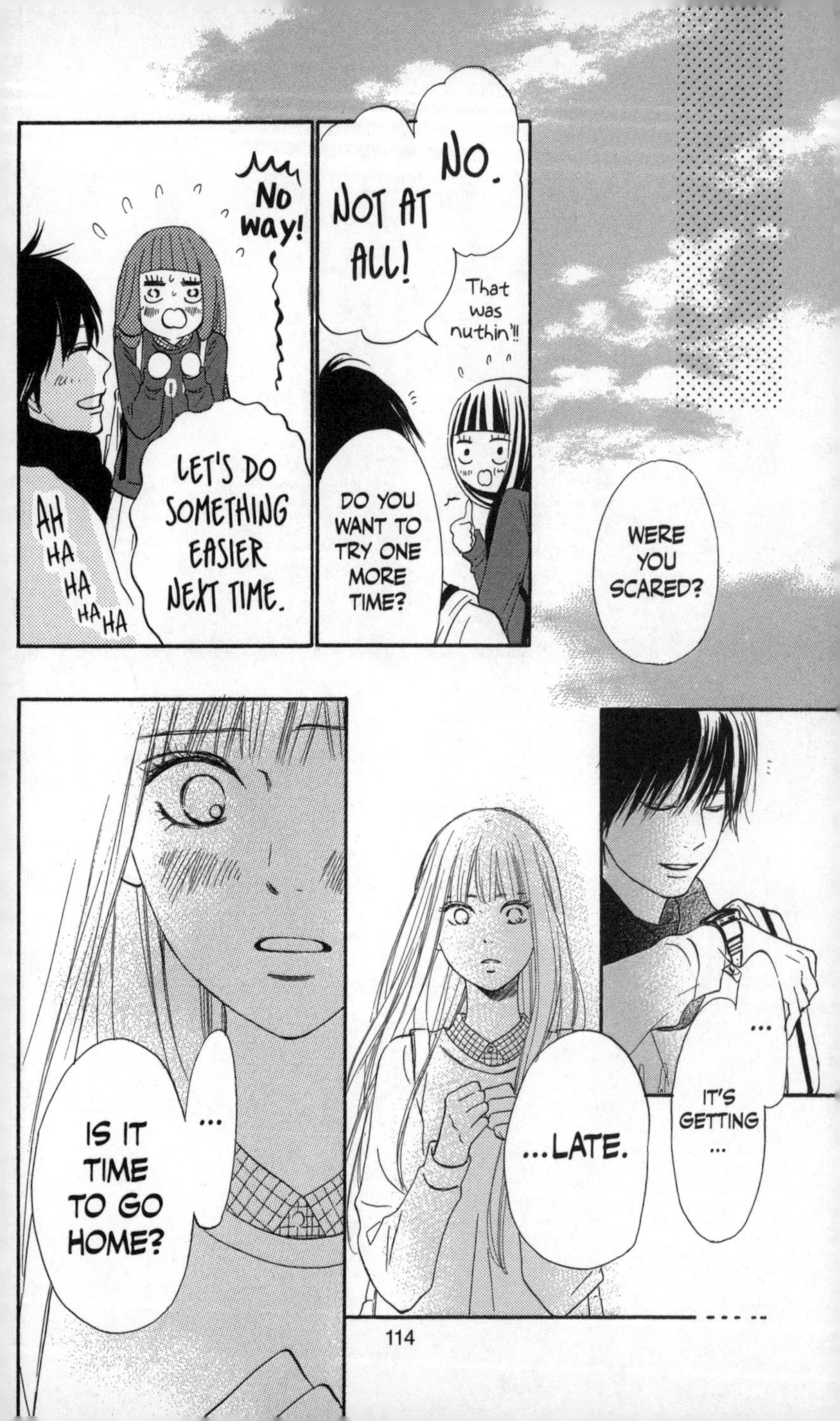
WERE YOU SCARED?
NO. NOT AT ALL!
That was nuthin'!!
DO YOU WANT TO TRY ONE MORE TIME?
No way!
LET'S DO SOMETHING EASIER NEXT TIME.
AH HA HA HA HA
...
IT'S GETTING ...
...LATE.
...
IS IT TIME TO GO HOME?

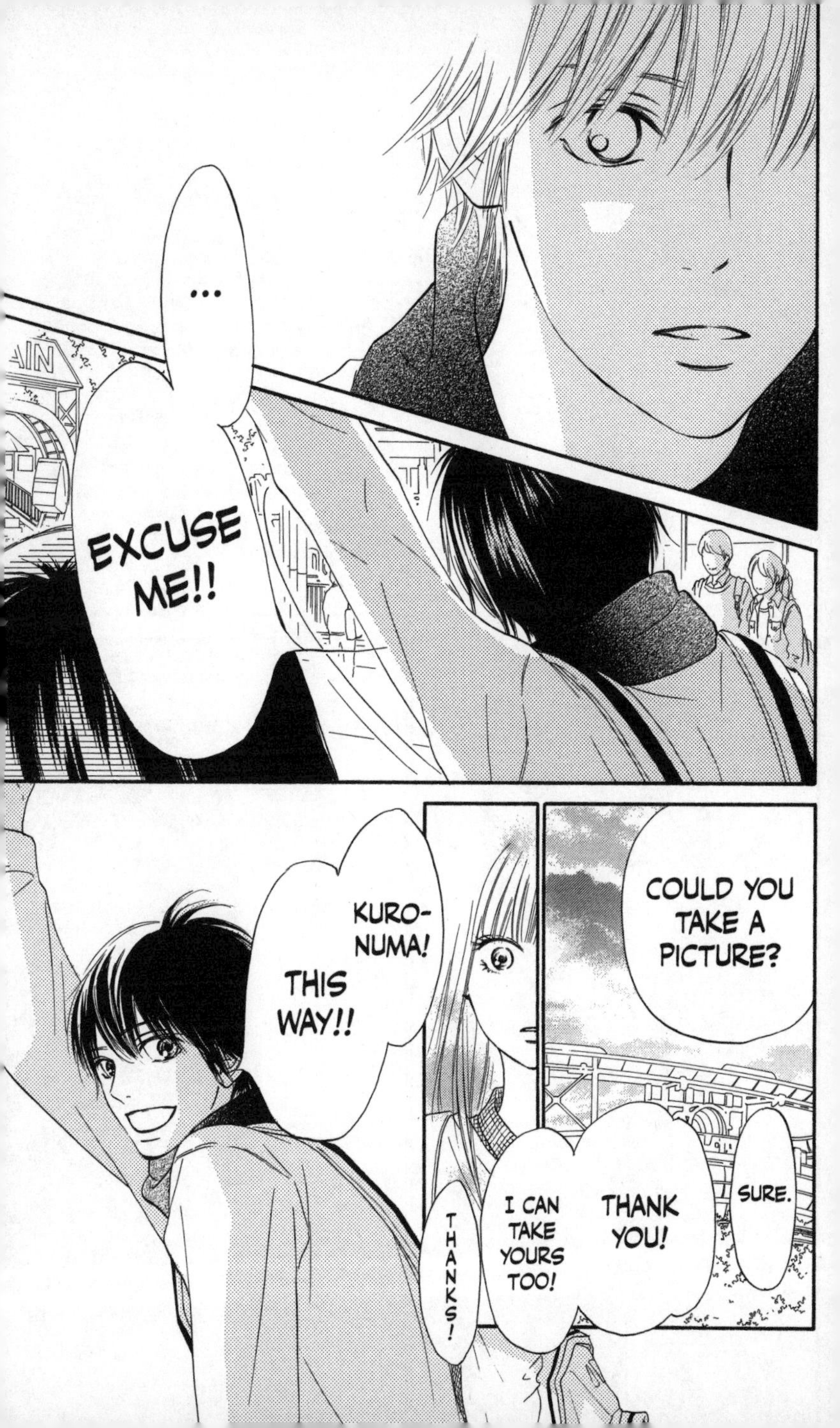
...
EXCUSE ME!!
COULD YOU TAKE A PICTURE?
SURE.
THANK YOU!
I CAN TAKE YOURS TOO!
THANKS!
KURO-NUMA! THIS WAY!!

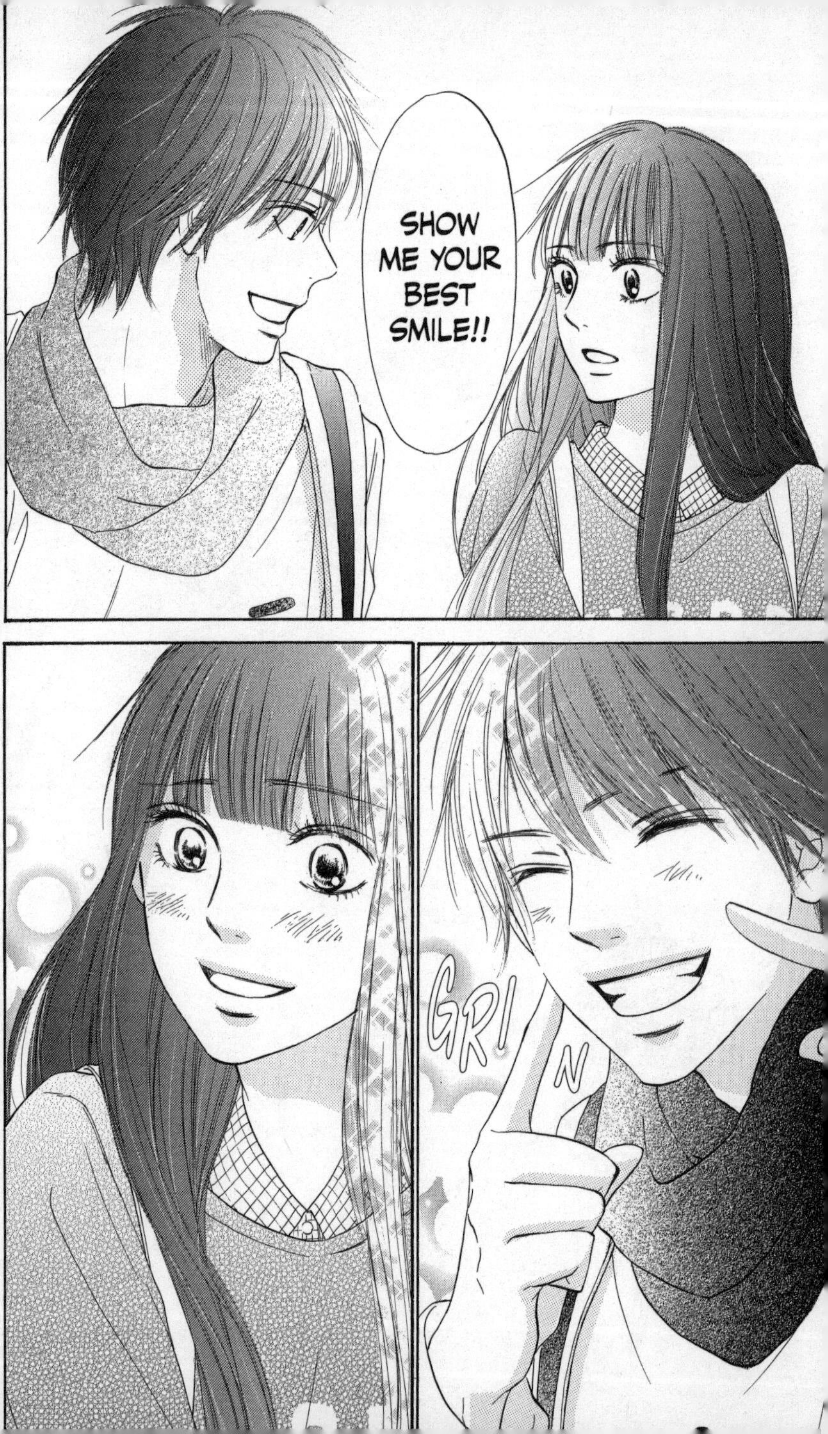
SHOW ME YOUR BEST SMILE!!
GRIN

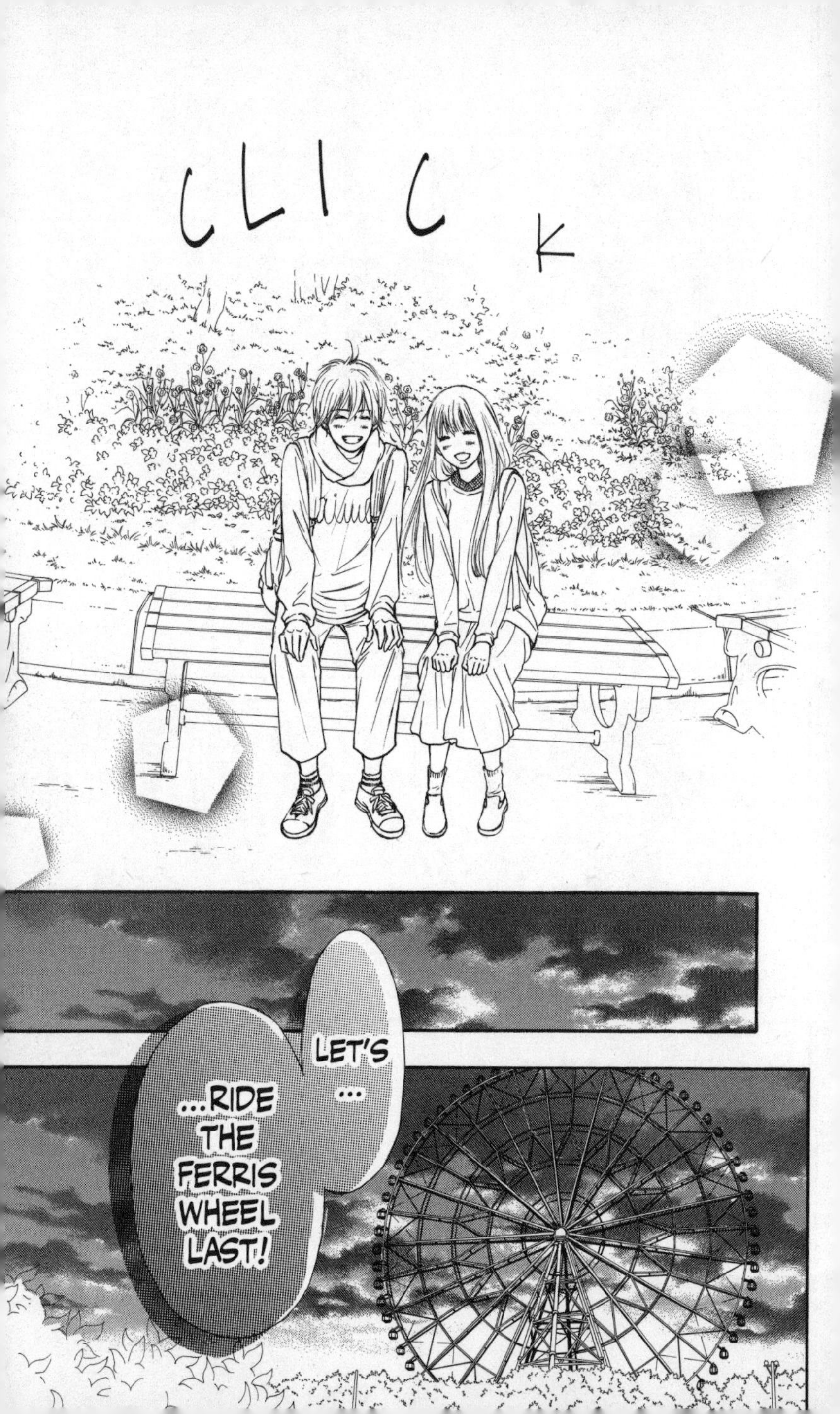
CLICK
LET'S ...
...RIDE THE FERRIS WHEEL LAST!

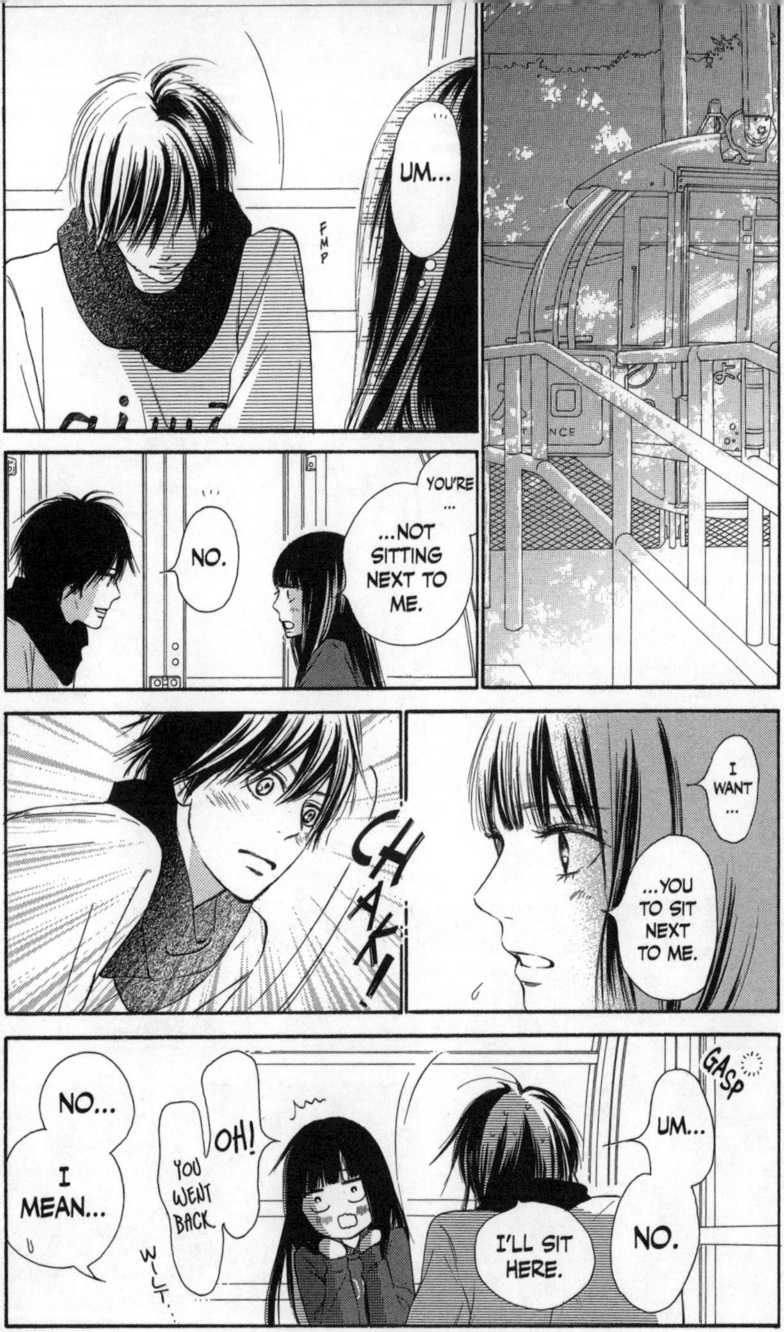
UM...
FMP
YOU'RE ...
...NOT SITTING NEXT TO ME.
NO.
I WANT ...
...YOU TO SIT NEXT TO ME.
CHAKI
GASP
UM...
NO.
I'LL SIT HERE.
OH!
YOU WENT BACK.
WILT...
NO...
I MEAN...

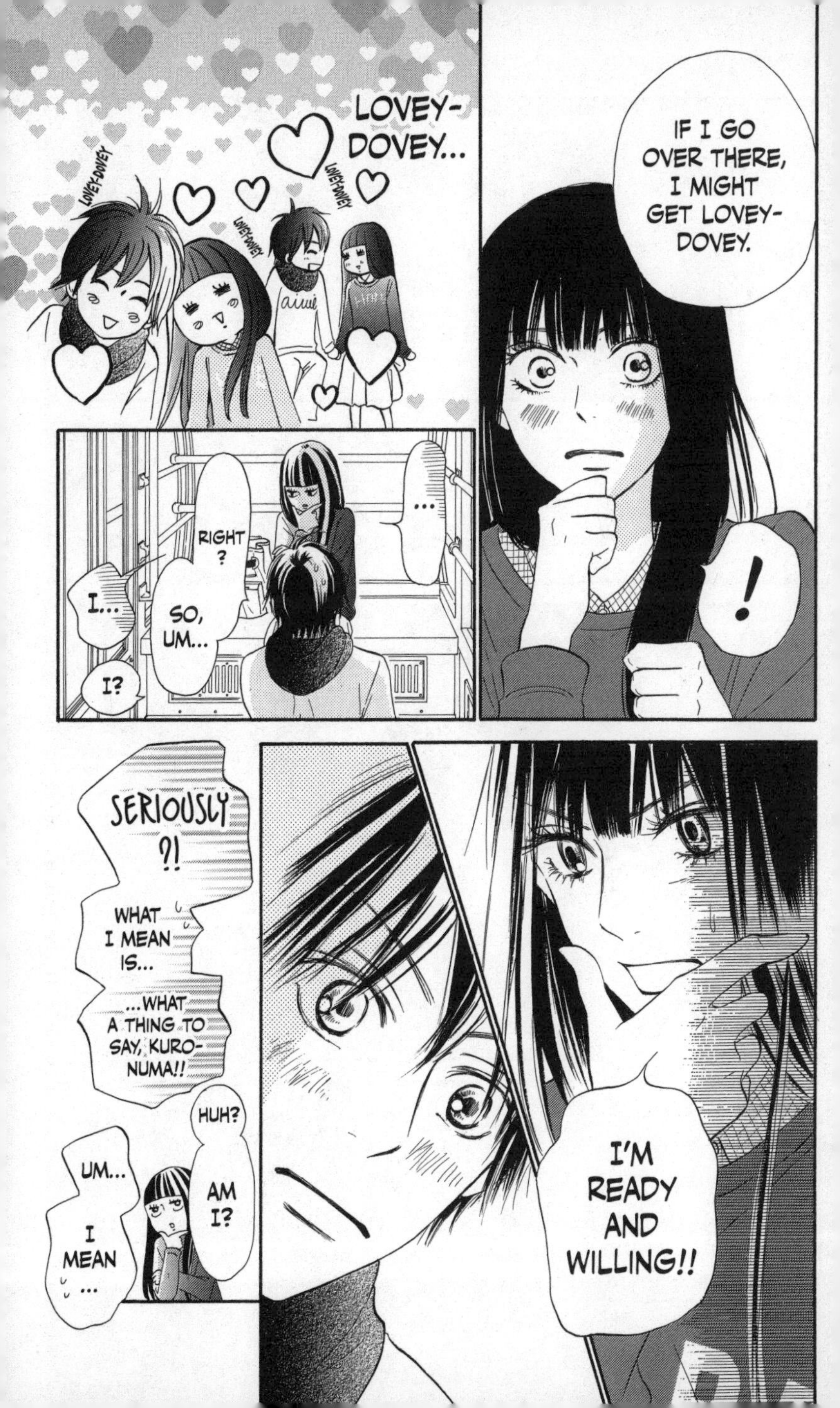
IF I GO OVER THERE, I MIGHT GET LOVEY-DOVEY.
!
LOVEY-DOVEY...
LOVEY-DOVEY
LOVEY-DOVEY
LOVEY-DOVEY
...
RIGHT?
SO, UM...
I...
I?
I'M READY AND WILLING!!
SERIOUSLY?!
WHAT I MEAN IS...
...WHAT A THING TO SAY, KURONUMA!!
HUH?
AM I?
UM...
I MEAN...

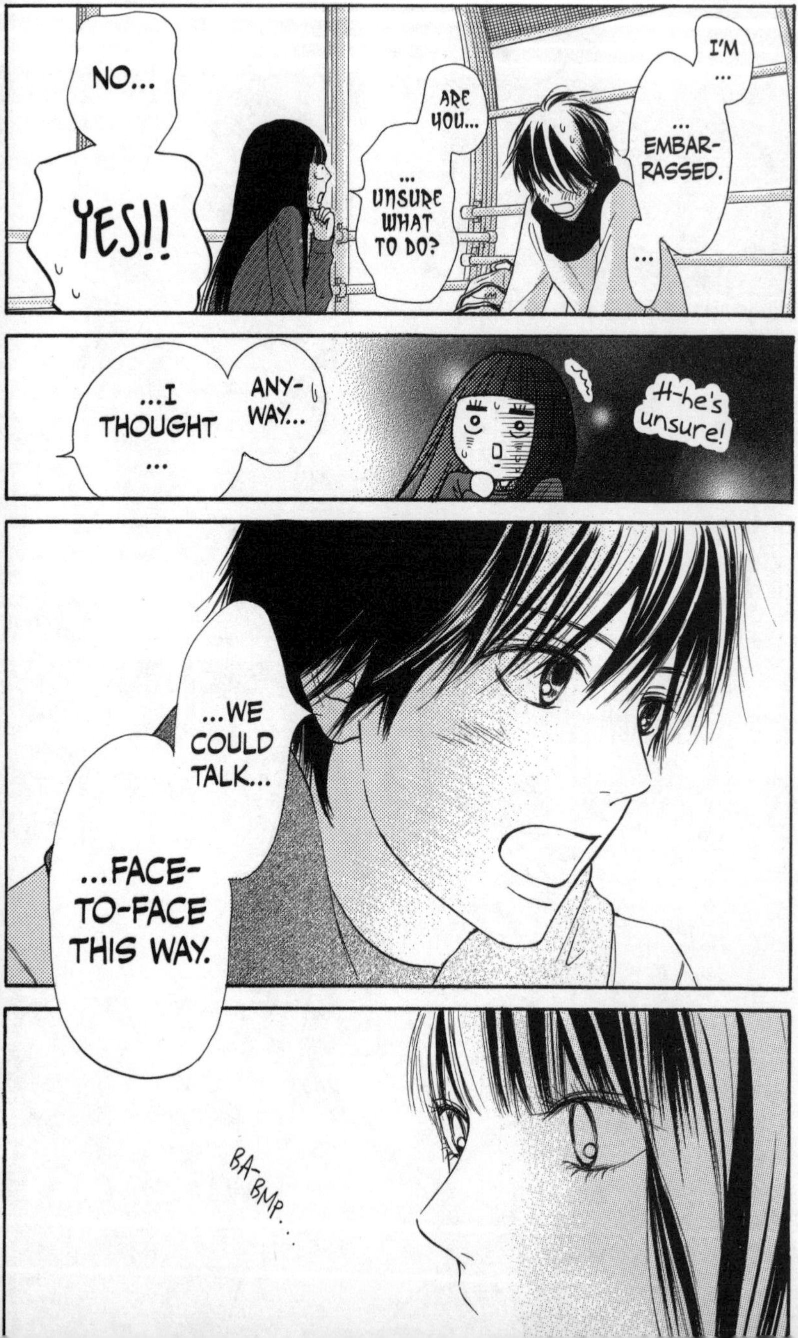
I'M ... ... EMBARRASSED. ...
ARE YOU... ... UNSURE WHAT TO DO?
NO... YES!!
H-he's unsure!
ANYWAY...
...I THOUGHT ...
...WE COULD TALK...
...FACE-TO-FACE THIS WAY.
BA-BMP...

OH...

HERE!

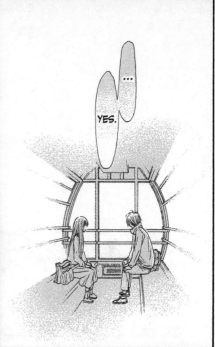

...

YES.

I TOOK THESE ...

... TODAY!

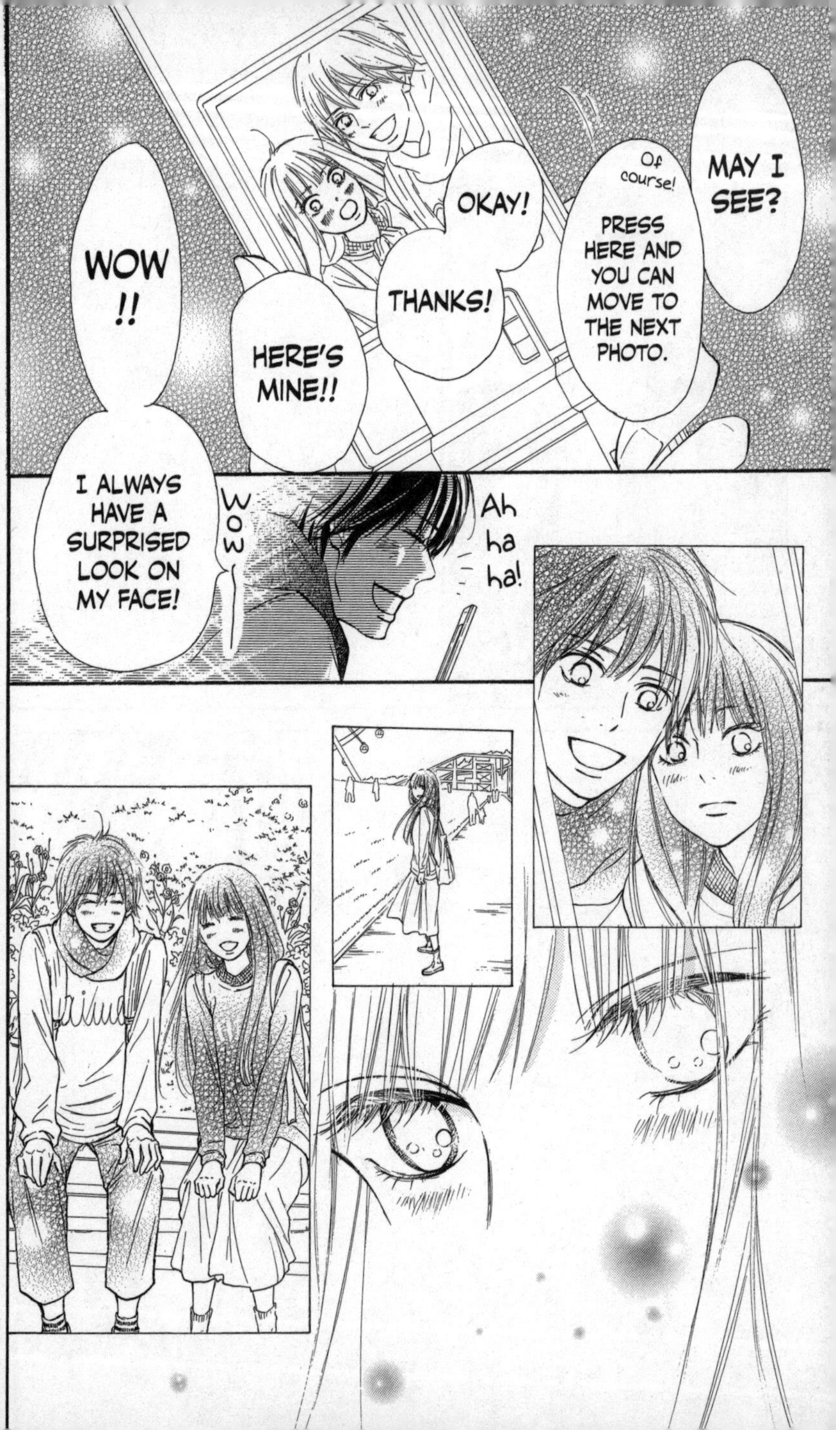
MAY I SEE?
Of course!
PRESS HERE AND YOU CAN MOVE TO THE NEXT PHOTO.
OKAY!
THANKS!
HERE'S MINE!!
WOW!!
I ALWAYS HAVE A SURPRISED LOOK ON MY FACE!
Ah ha ha!
Wow wow

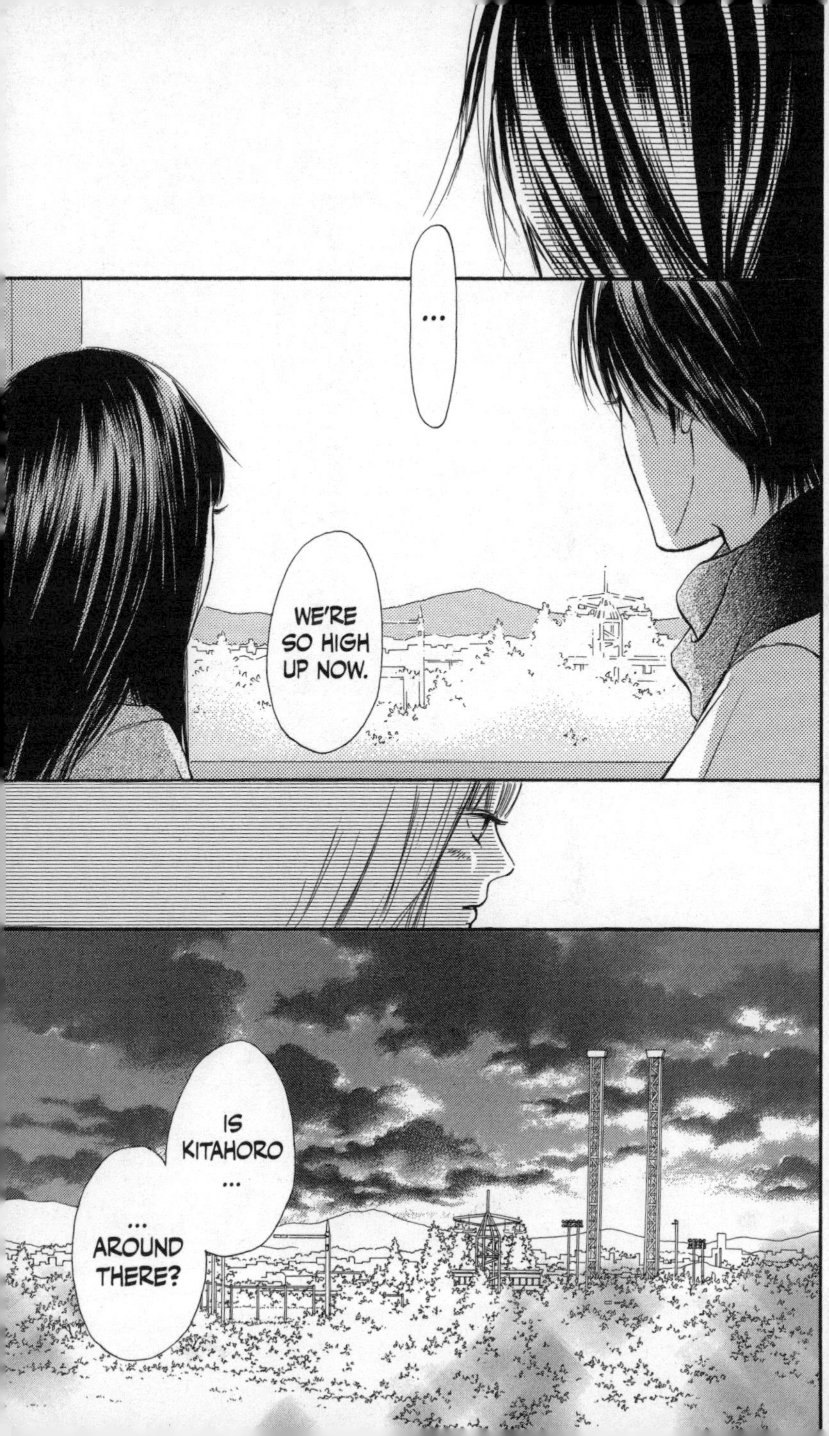
...
WE'RE SO HIGH UP NOW.
IS KITAHORO ...
... AROUND THERE?

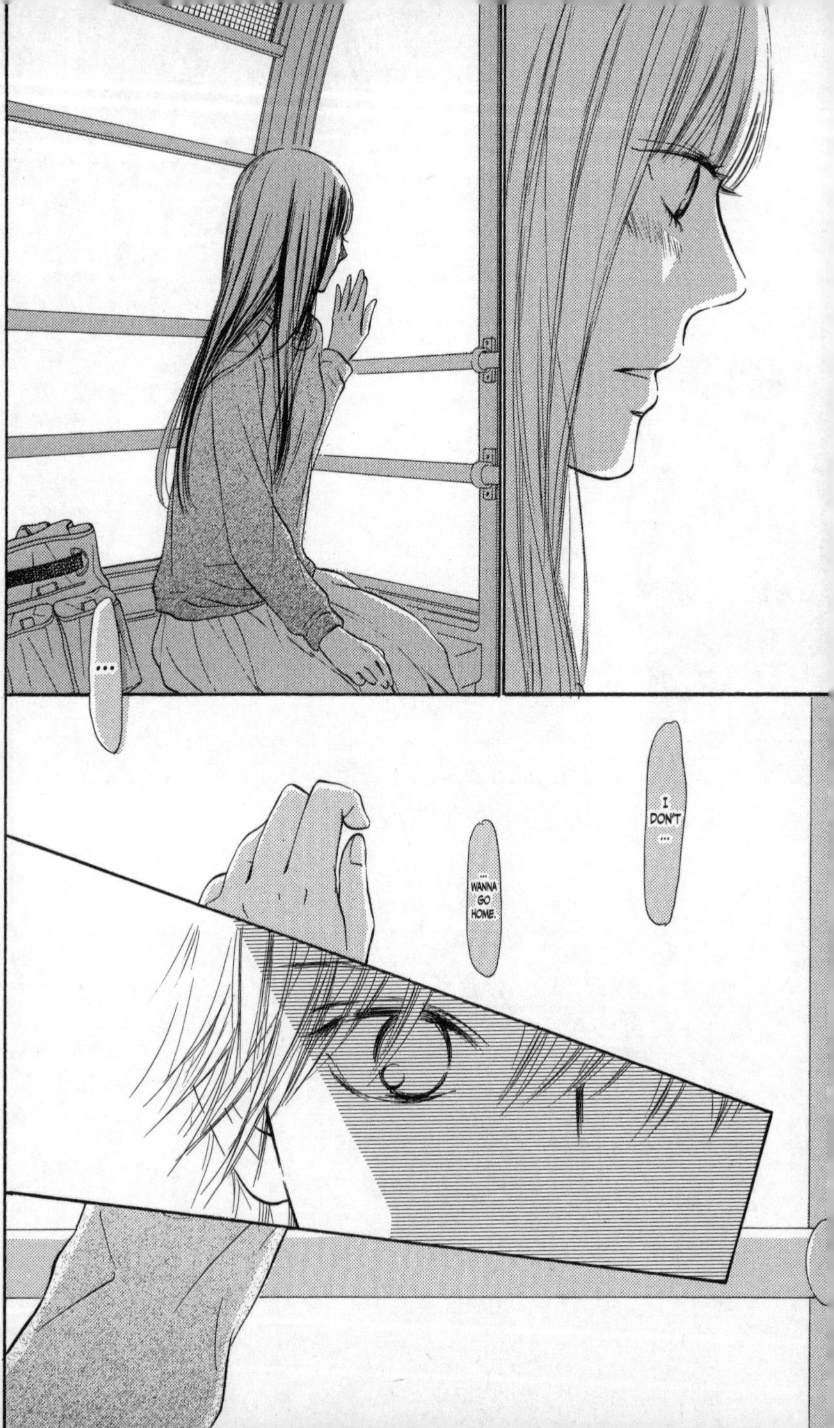
...
I DON'T ...
... WANNA GO HOME.

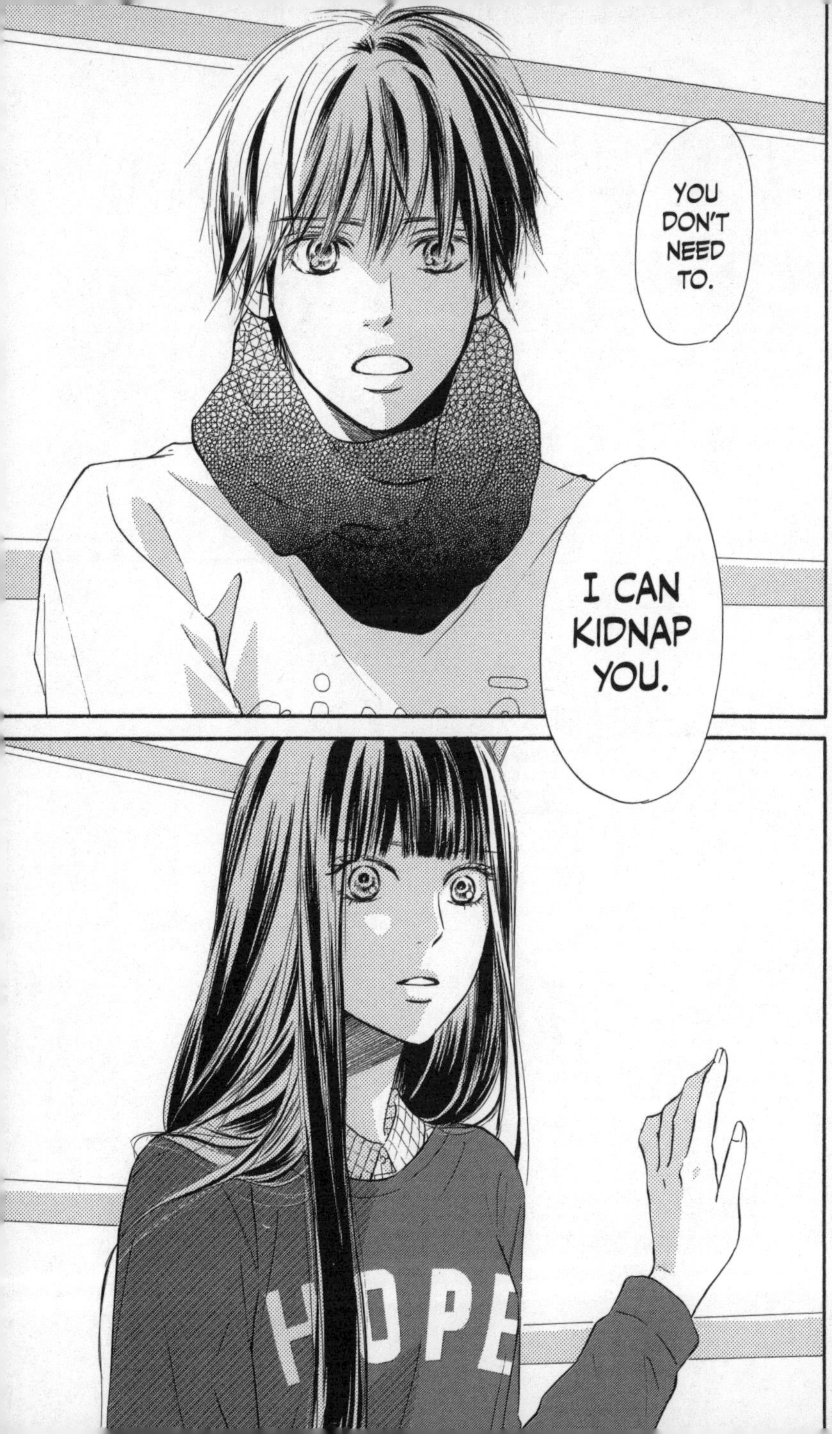
YOU DON'T NEED TO.
I CAN KIDNAP YOU.
HOPE

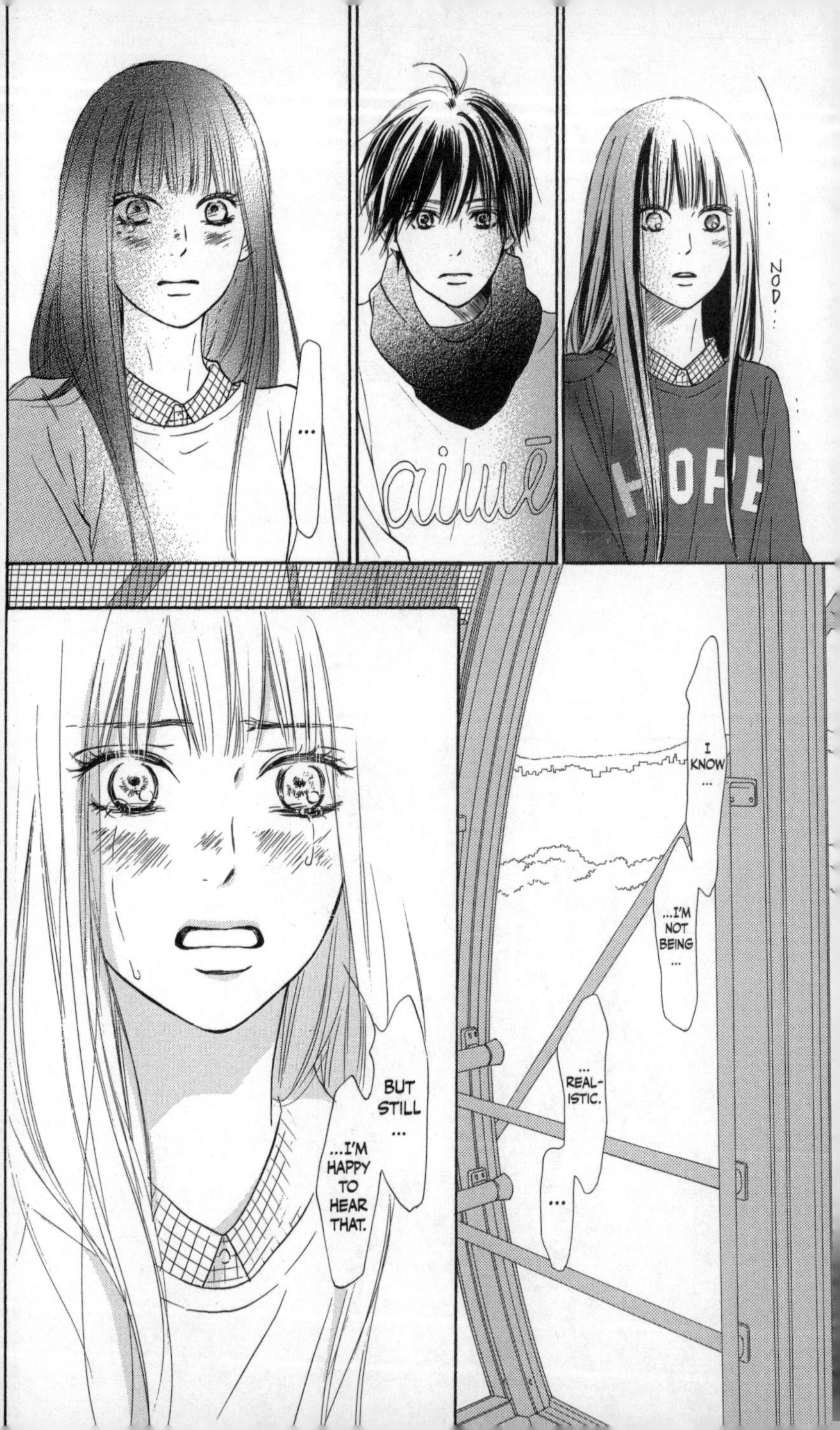
...
NOD...
...
I KNOW...
...I'M NOT BEING...
...REAL-ISTIC.
...
BUT STILL...
...I'M HAPPY TO HEAR THAT.

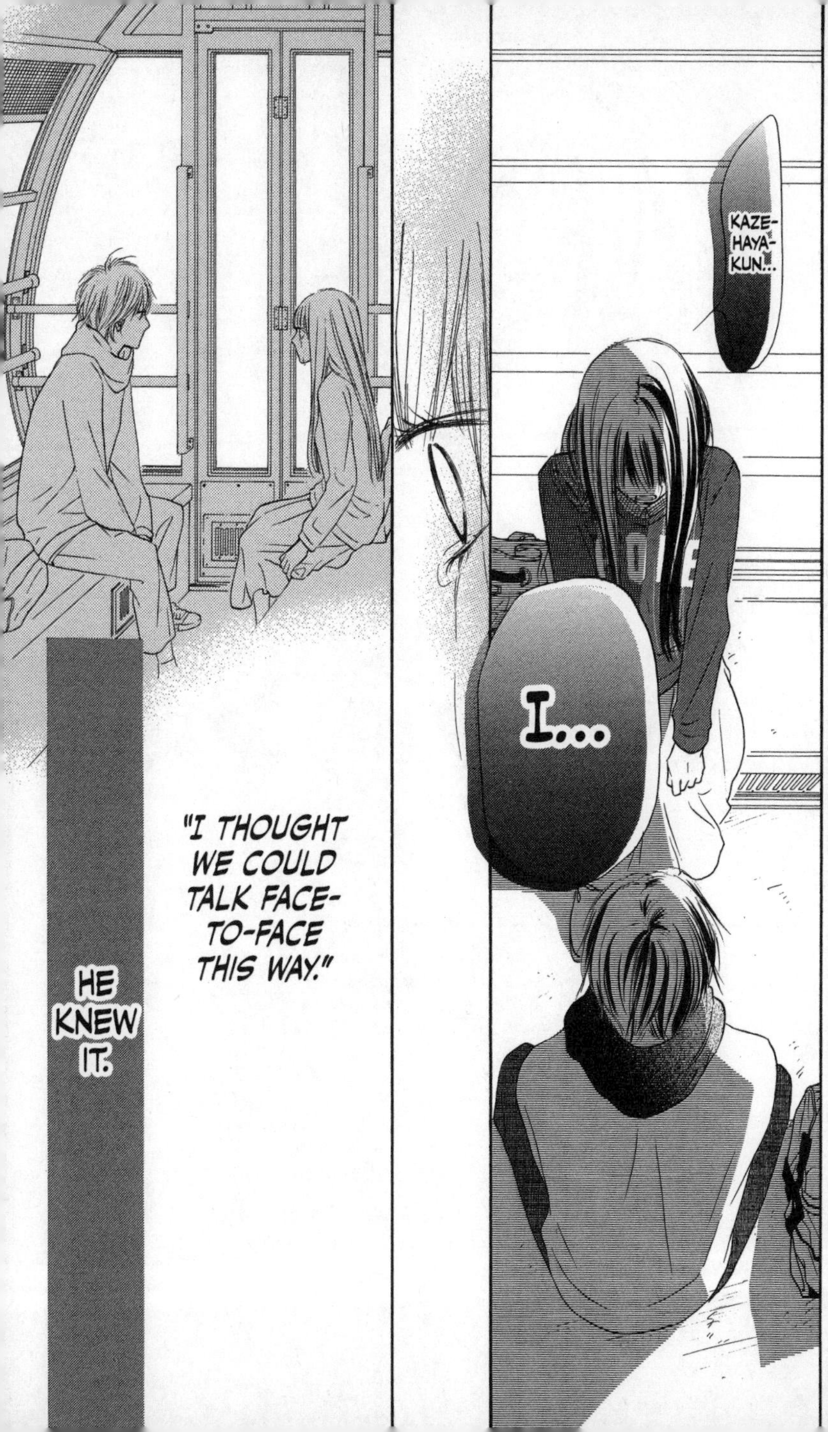
KAZE-HAYA-KUN...
I...
"I THOUGHT WE COULD TALK FACE-TO-FACE THIS WAY."
HE KNEW IT.

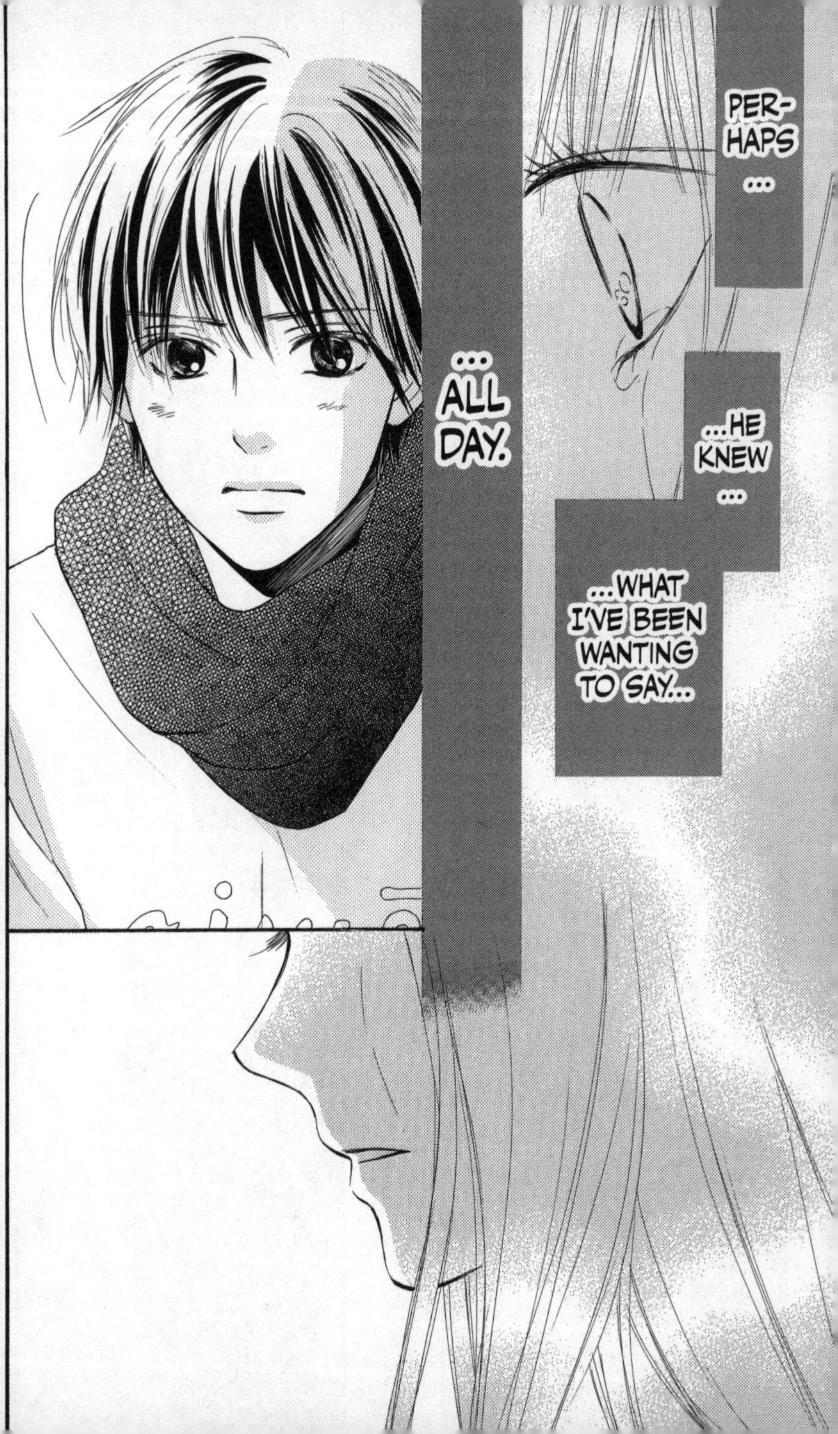
PER-HAPS ...
...HE KNEW ...
...WHAT I'VE BEEN WANTING TO SAY...
... ALL DAY.

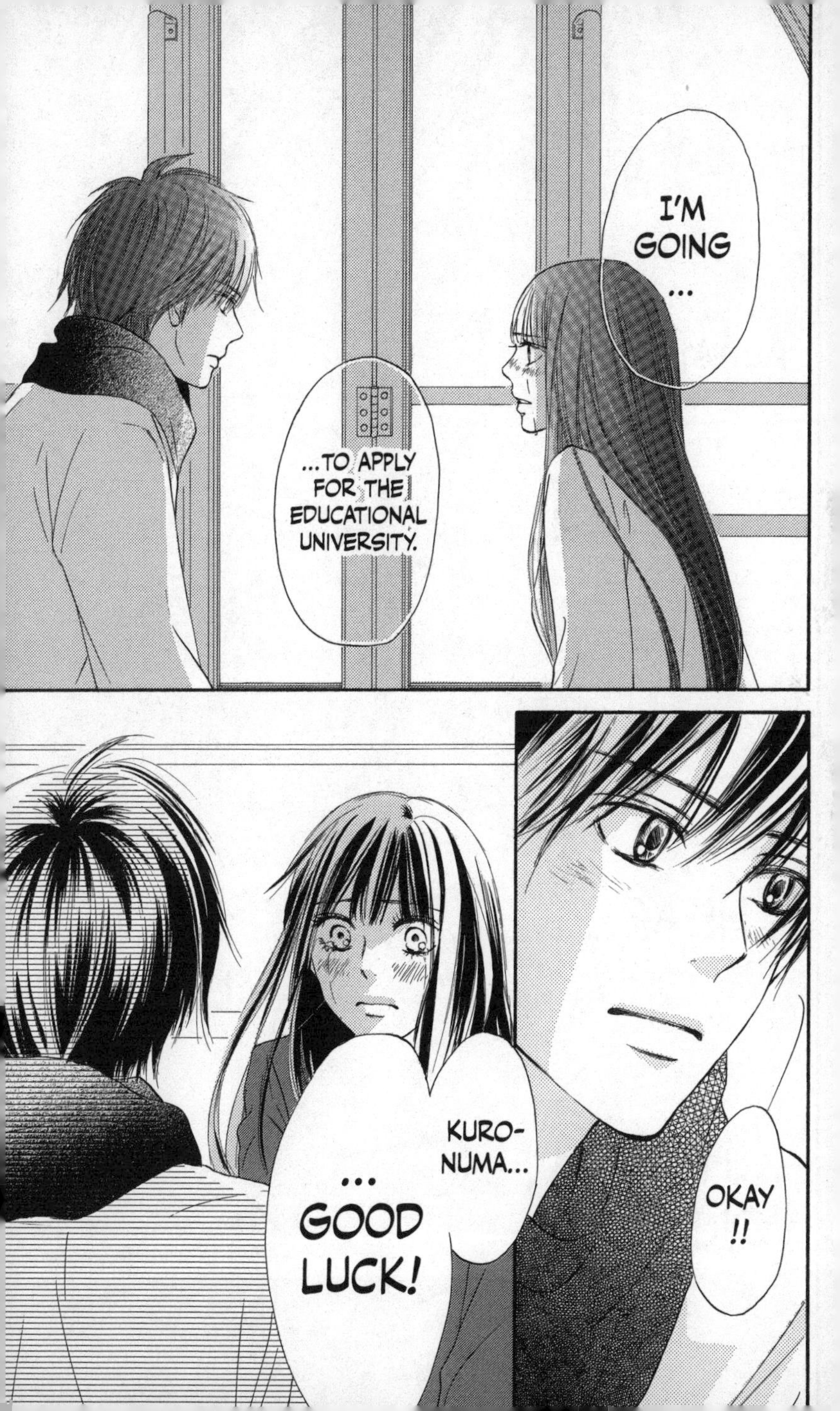
I'M GOING ...
...TO APPLY FOR THE EDUCATIONAL UNIVERSITY.
KURO-NUMA...
... GOOD LUCK!
OKAY !!

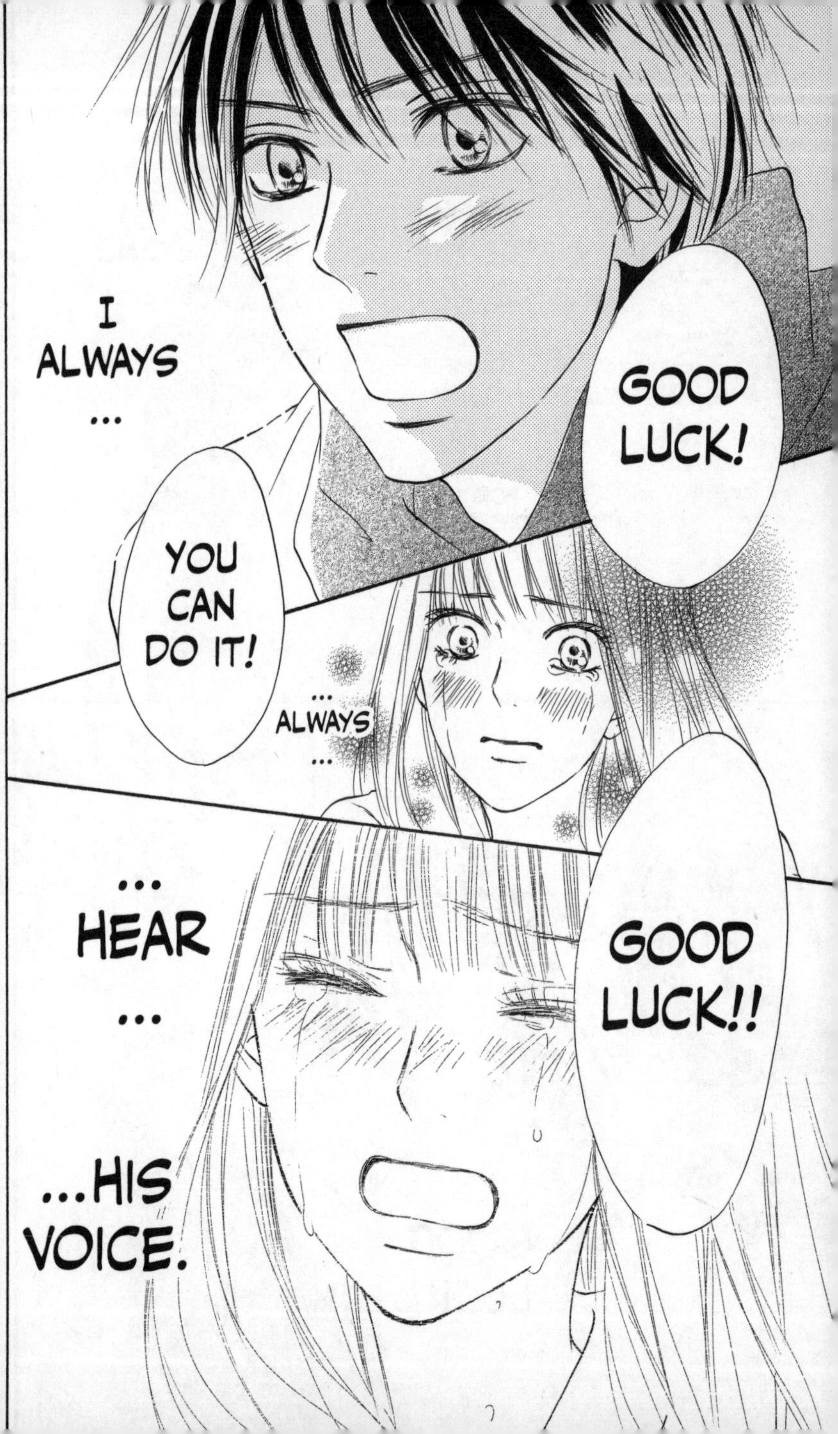
GOOD LUCK!
I ALWAYS ...
YOU CAN DO IT!
... ALWAYS ...
GOOD LUCK!!
... HEAR ...
...HIS VOICE.

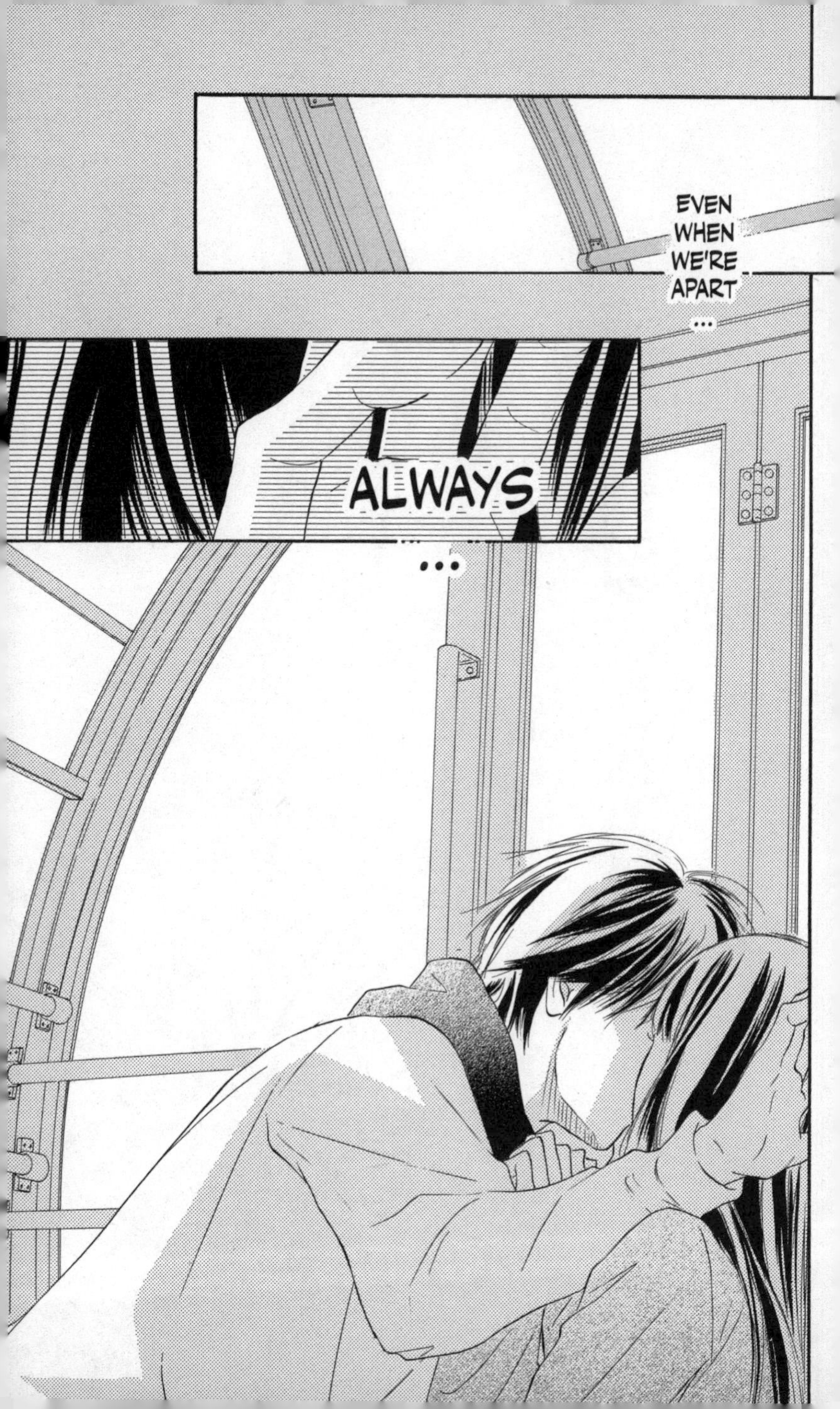
EVEN WHEN WE'RE APART ...
I ALWAYS ...

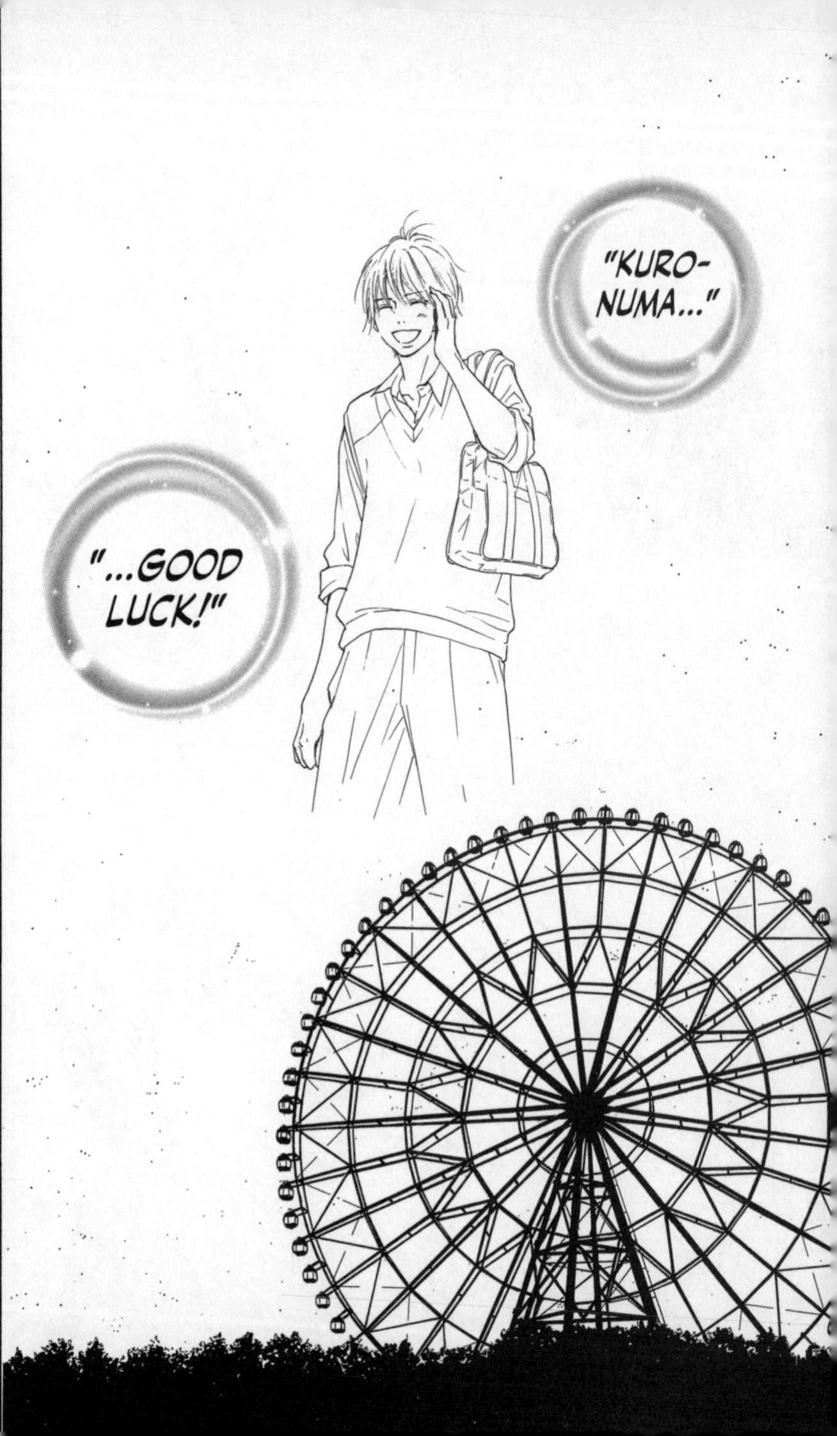
"KURO-NUMA..."
"...GOOD LUCK!"

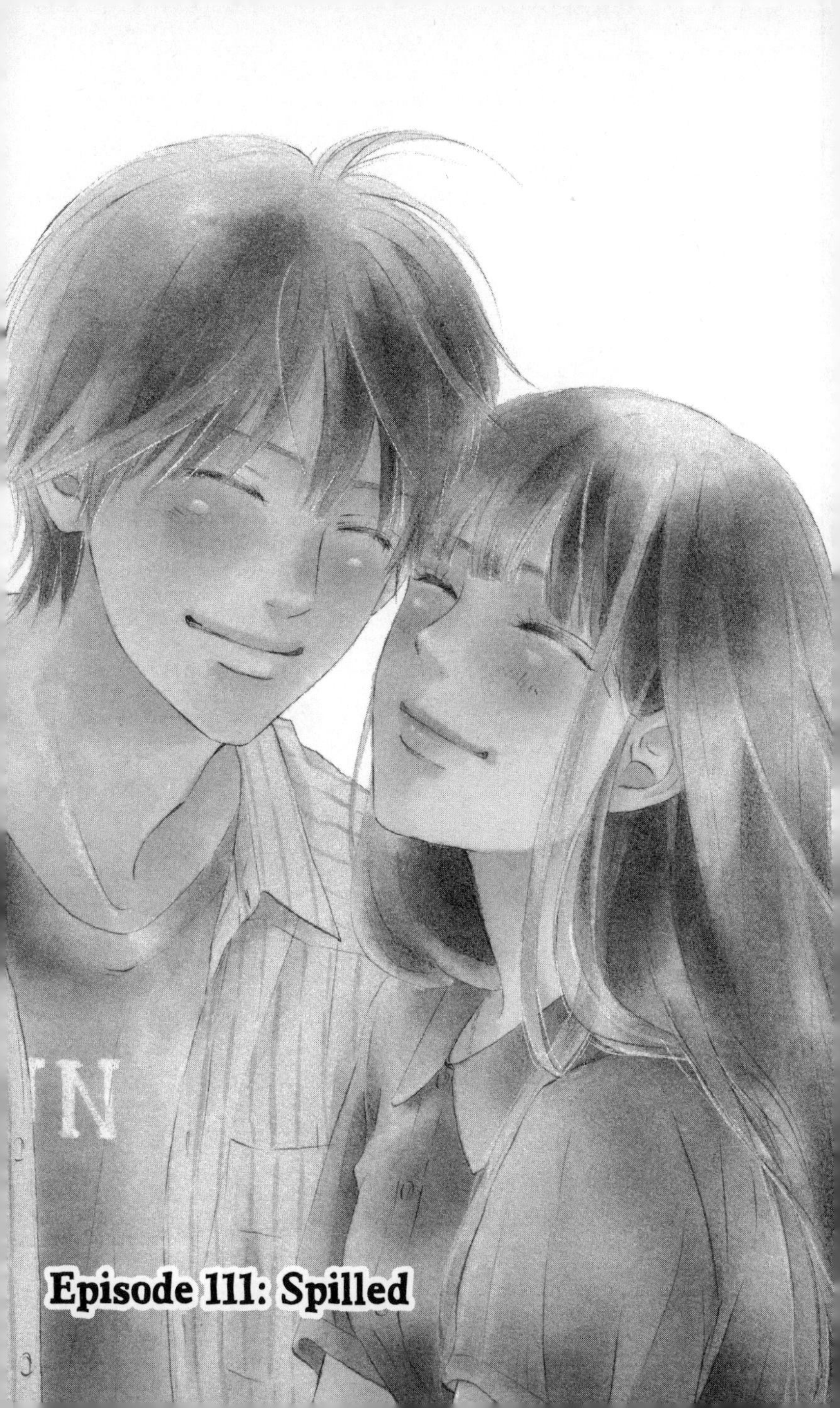

Episode 111: Spilled

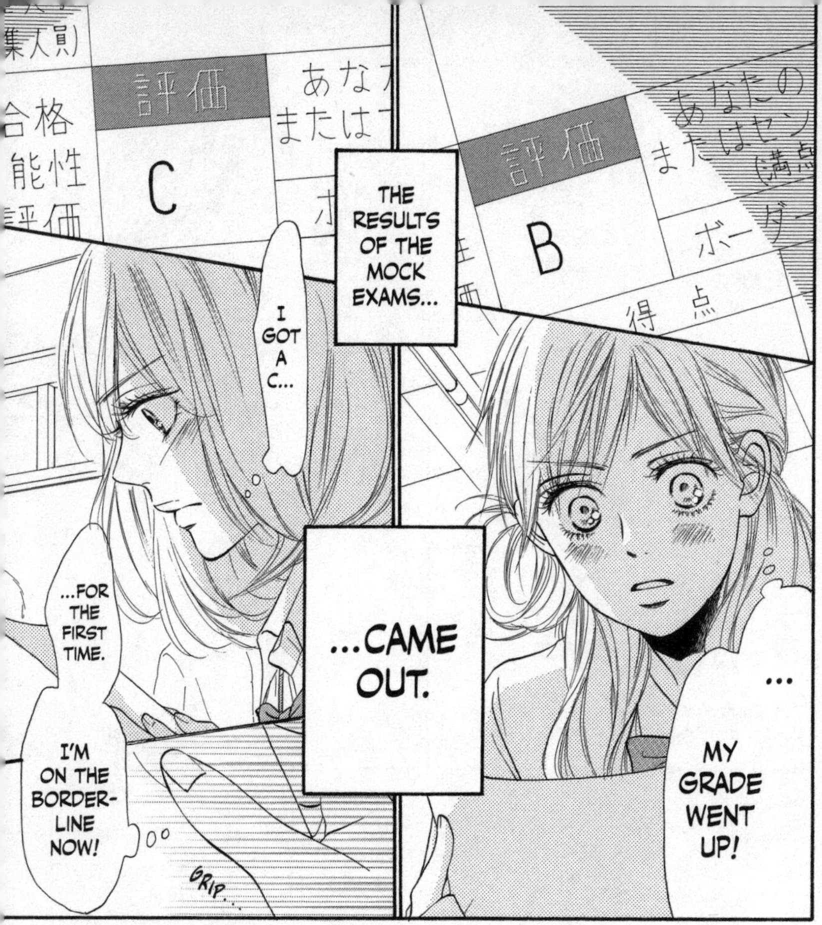
評価
B
得点
THE RESULTS OF THE MOCK EXAMS...
評価
C
...CAME OUT.
...
MY GRADE WENT UP!
I GOT A C...
...FOR THE FIRST TIME.
I'M ON THE BORDERLINE NOW!
GRIP...

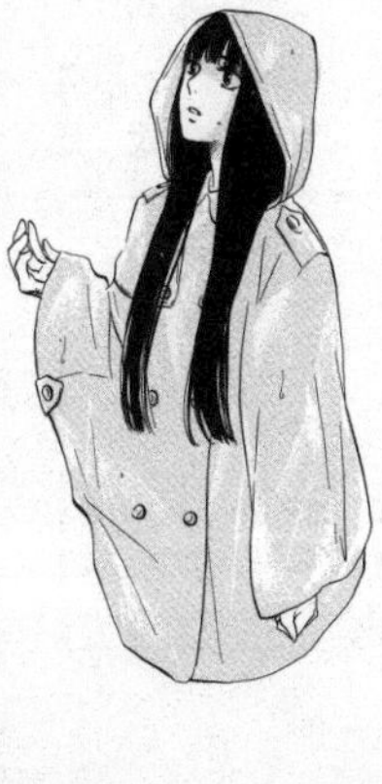

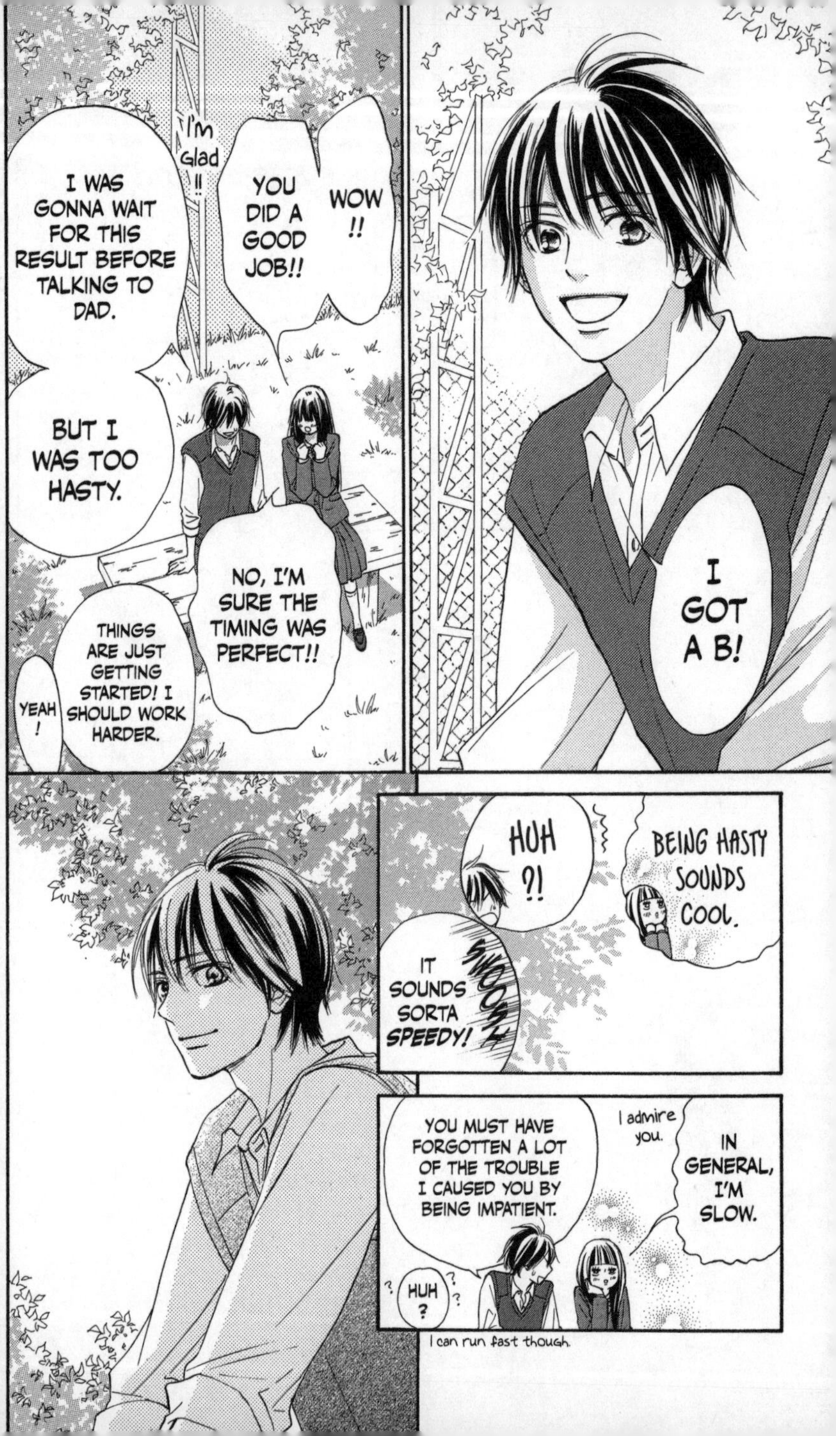
I GOT A B!
WOW!!
YOU DID A GOOD JOB!!
I'm Glad!!
I WAS GONNA WAIT FOR THIS RESULT BEFORE TALKING TO DAD.
BUT I WAS TOO HASTY.
NO, I'M SURE THE TIMING WAS PERFECT!!
THINGS ARE JUST GETTING STARTED! I SHOULD WORK HARDER.
YEAH!
BEING HASTY SOUNDS COOL.
HUH?!
IT SOUNDS SORTA SPEEDY!
SWOOOSH
IN GENERAL, I'M SLOW.
I admire you.
YOU MUST HAVE FORGOTTEN A LOT OF THE TROUBLE I CAUSED YOU BY BEING IMPATIENT.
HUH?
I can run fast though.

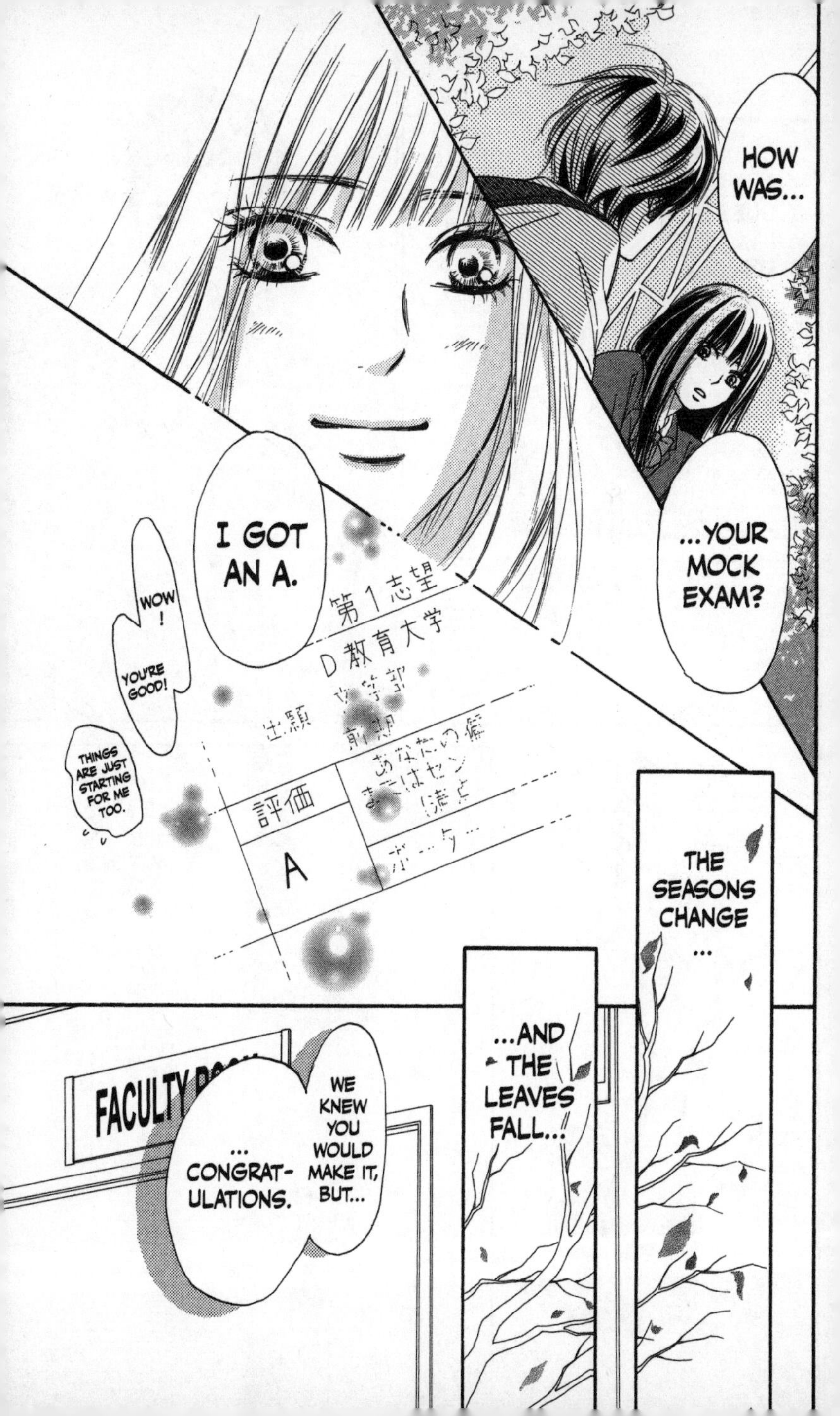
HOW WAS...
...YOUR MOCK EXAM?
I GOT AN A.
第1志望
D教育大学
評価
A
WOW! YOU'RE GOOD!
THINGS ARE JUST STARTING FOR ME TOO.
THE SEASONS CHANGE...
...AND THE LEAVES FALL...
WE KNEW YOU WOULD MAKE IT, BUT...
...CONGRAT-ULATIONS.
FACULTY

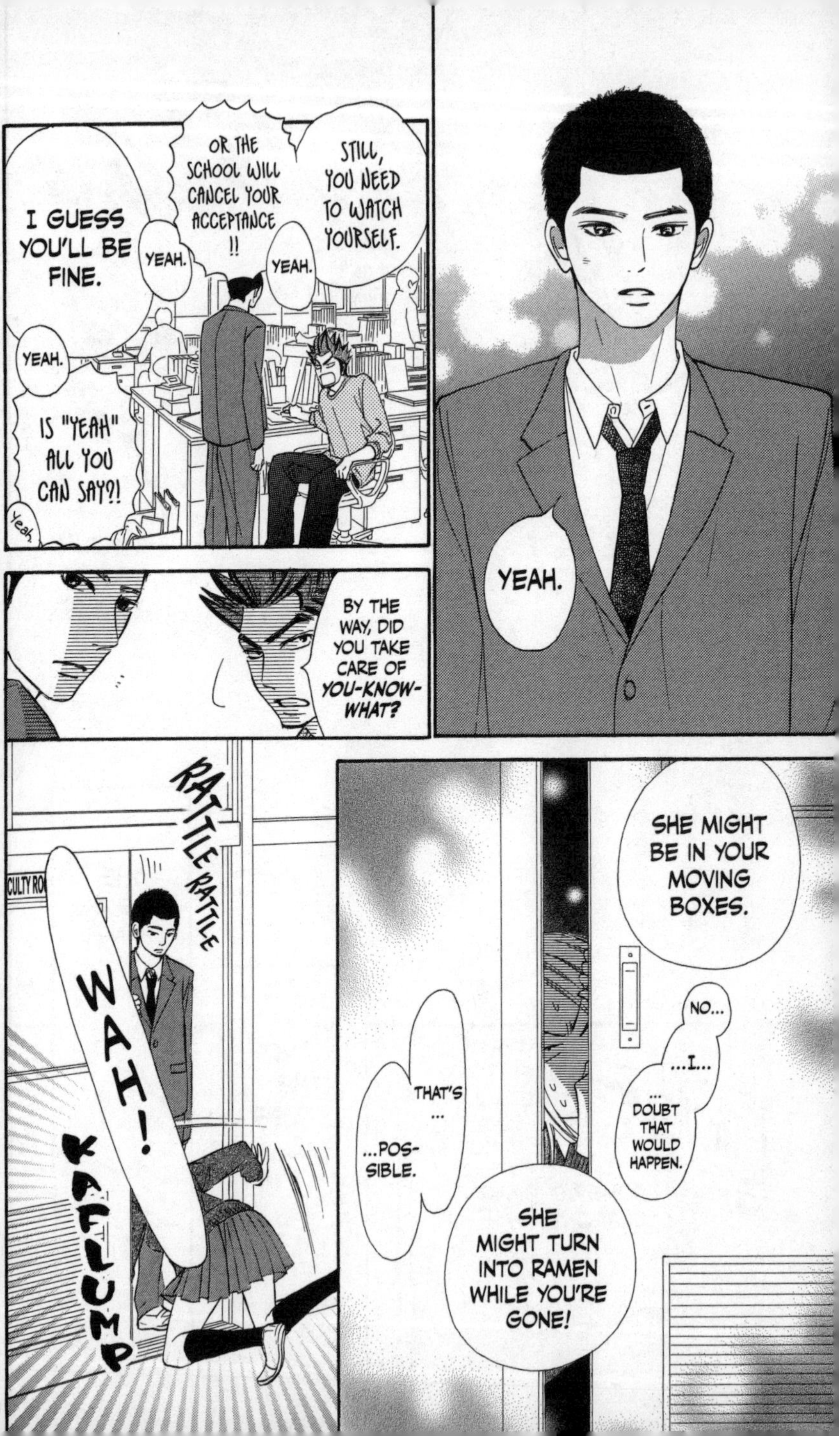
STILL, YOU NEED TO WATCH YOURSELF.
YEAH.
OR THE SCHOOL WILL CANCEL YOUR ACCEPTANCE !!
YEAH.
I GUESS YOU'LL BE FINE.
YEAH.
IS "YEAH" ALL YOU CAN SAY?!
Yeah
BY THE WAY, DID YOU TAKE CARE OF *YOU-KNOW-WHAT?*
...
YEAH.
SHE MIGHT BE IN YOUR MOVING BOXES.
NO...
...I...
... DOUBT THAT WOULD HAPPEN.
THAT'S ...
...POS-SIBLE.
SHE MIGHT TURN INTO RAMEN WHILE YOU'RE GONE!
RATTLE RATTLE
WAH!
KAFLUMP

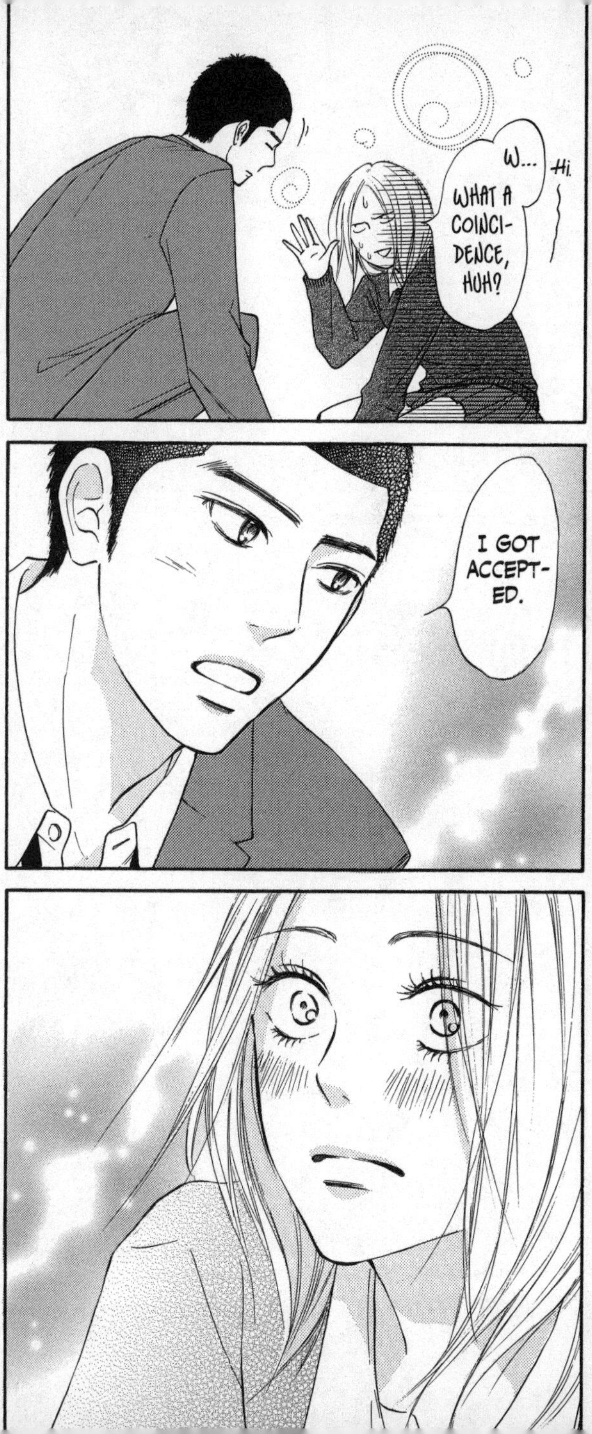
Hi.
W... WHAT A COINCIDENCE, HUH?
I GOT ACCEPTED.

KARUPIN on JAPAN 3

When this volume comes out it'll be autumn, but it's summer now.

I get a hankering for horror stuff around this time of the year.

I don't have any sort of sixth sense, so I'll probably never see a ghost. For that reason, I enjoy watching horror shows and reading horror stories.

When I see that opening warning...

...about watching responsibly and the risk of feeling ill...

...I'm already scared.

My child gets scared but also likes that stuff a little because she mentioned Kokkuri. (But we've never done that.)

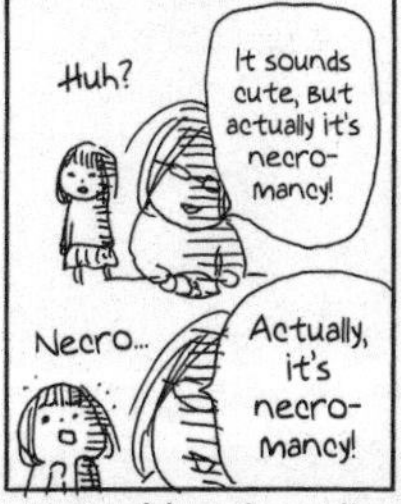
It sounds cute, but actually it's necromancy!
Huh?
Actually, it's necromancy!
Necro...

I scared her. See ya!!

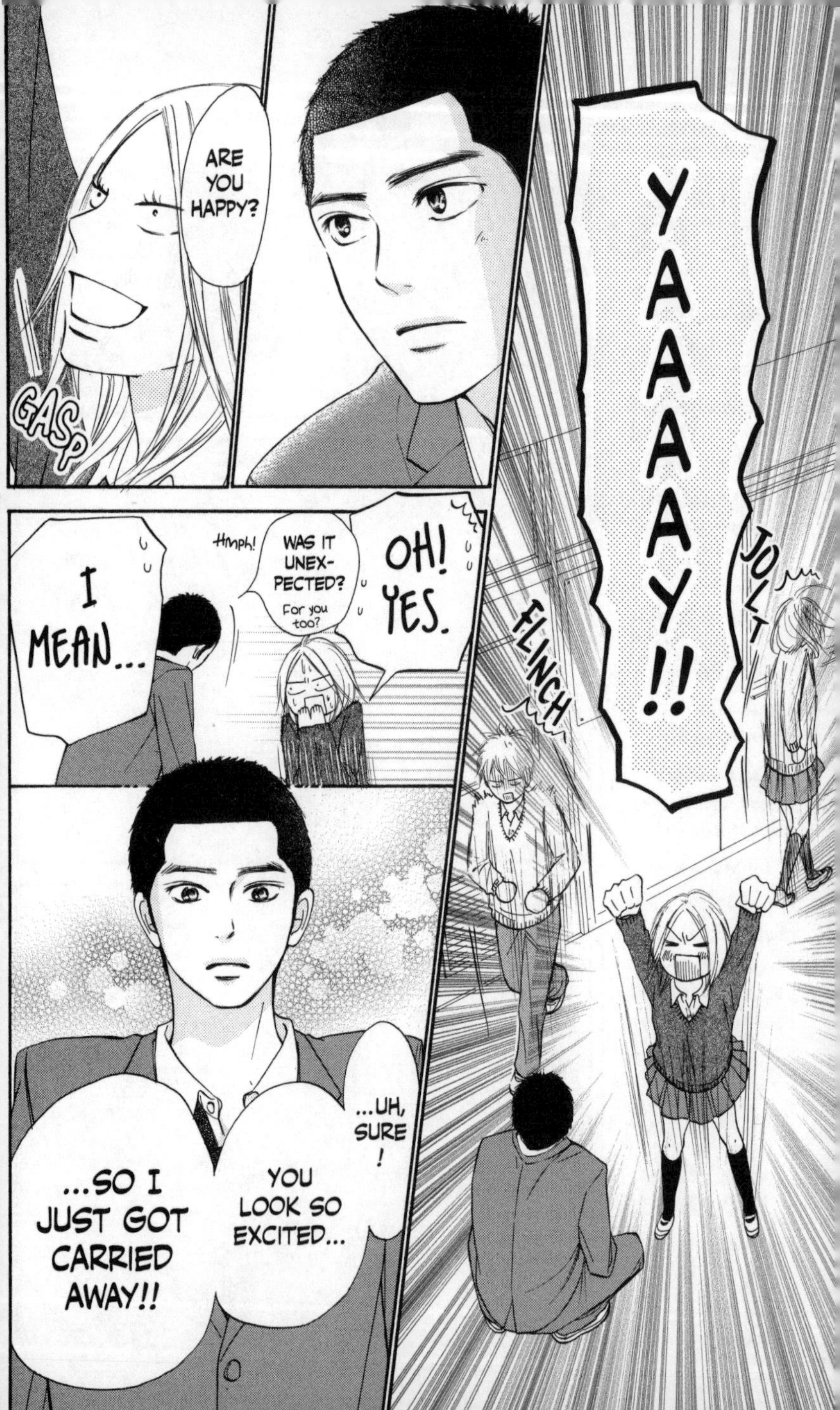
YAAAAY!!
JOLT
FLINCH
ARE YOU HAPPY?
GASP
OH! YES.
WAS IT UNEXPECTED?
For you too?
Hmph!
I MEAN...
...UH, SURE!
YOU LOOK SO EXCITED...
...SO I JUST GOT CARRIED AWAY!!

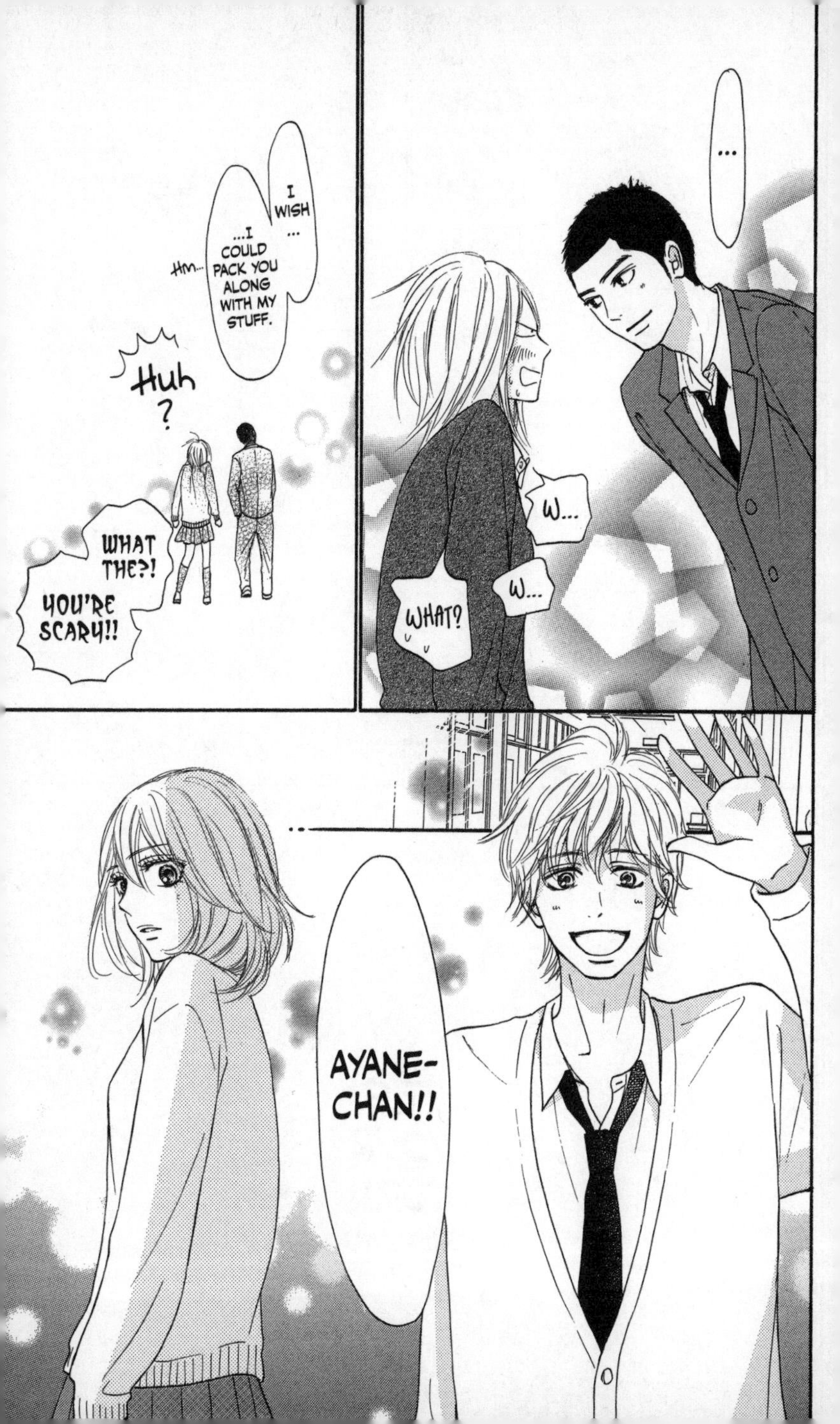
...
W...
W...
WHAT?
I WISH...
...I COULD PACK YOU ALONG WITH MY STUFF.
Hm...
Huh?
WHAT THE?!
YOU'RE SCARY!!
AYANE-CHAN!!
...

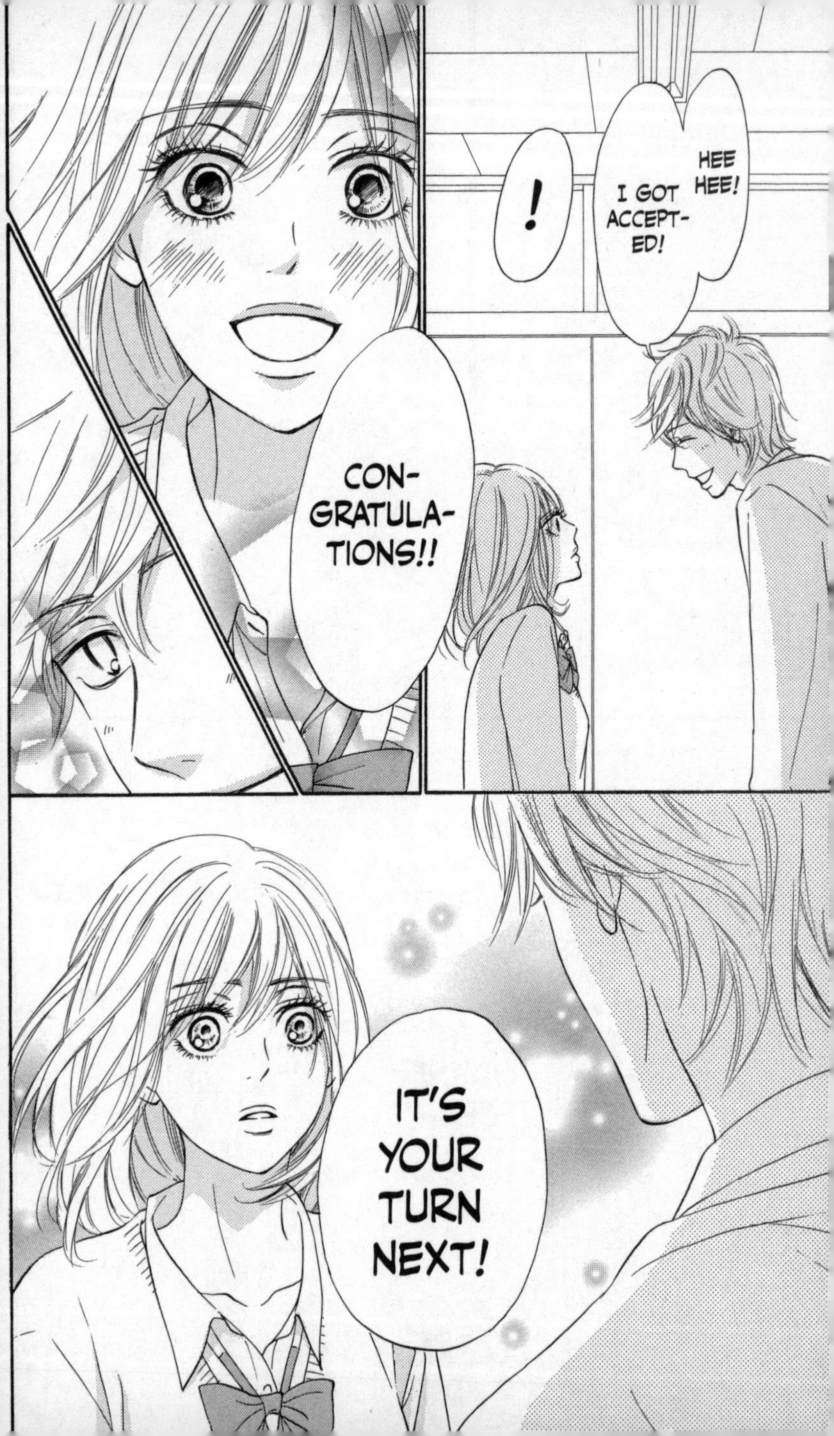
HEE HEE! I GOT ACCEPT-ED!
!
CON-GRATULA-TIONS!!
IT'S YOUR TURN NEXT!

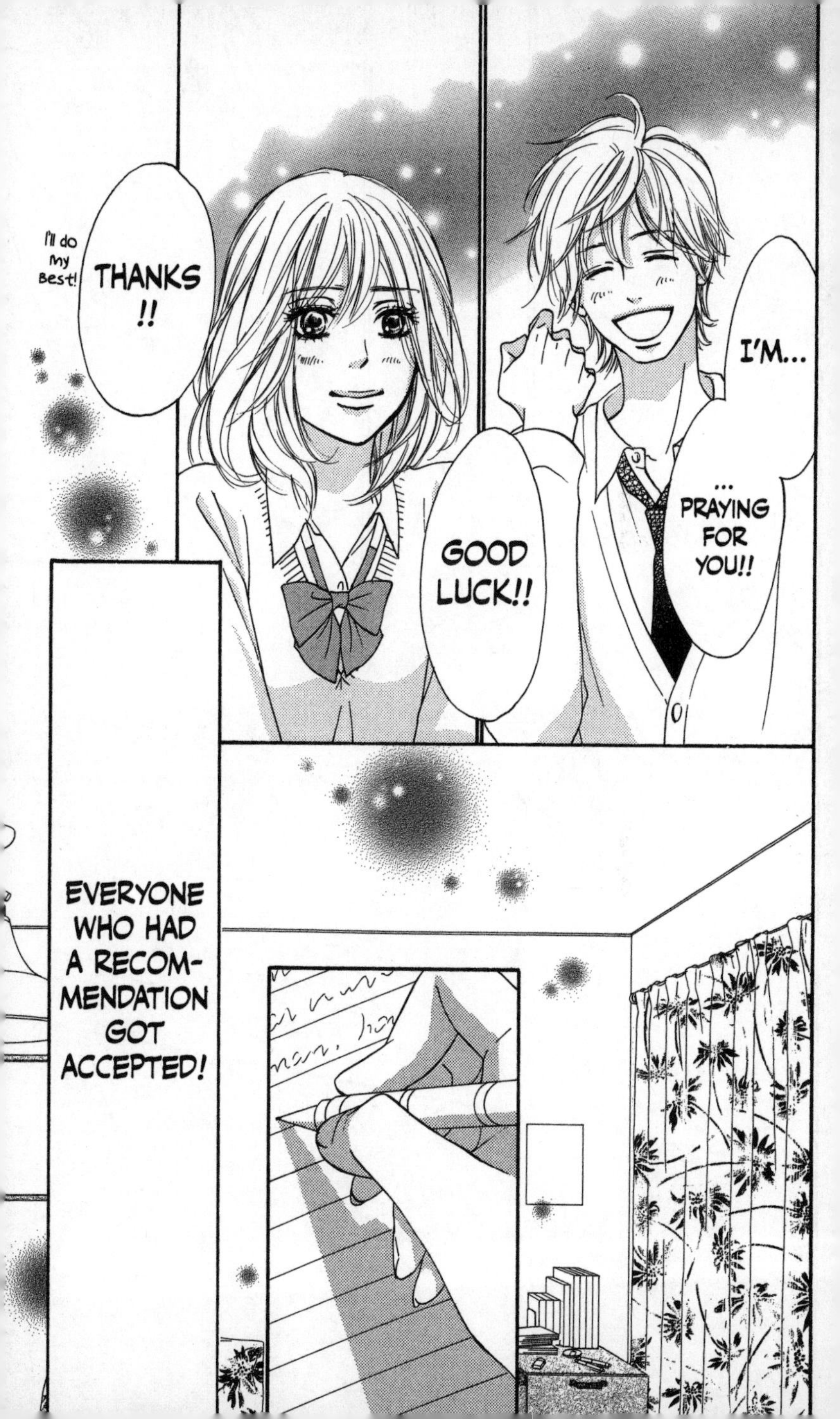
I'M...
...PRAYING FOR YOU!!
GOOD LUCK!!
THANKS!!
I'll do My Best!
EVERYONE WHO HAD A RECOMMENDATION GOT ACCEPTED!

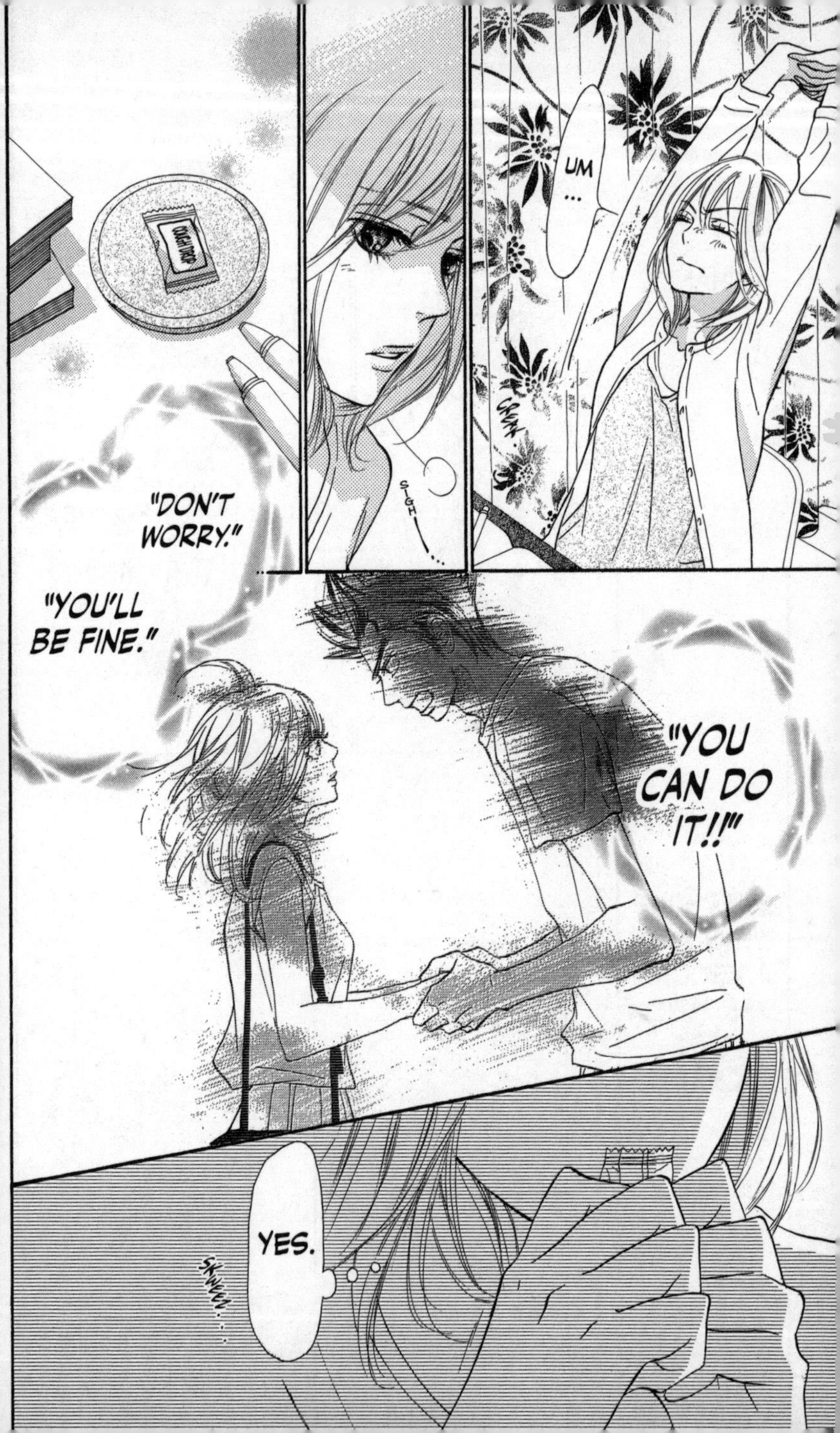
UM ...
CRUNK.
SIGH ...
COUGH DROP
"DON'T WORRY."
"YOU'LL BE FINE."
"YOU CAN DO IT!!"
YES.
SKWEEZ..

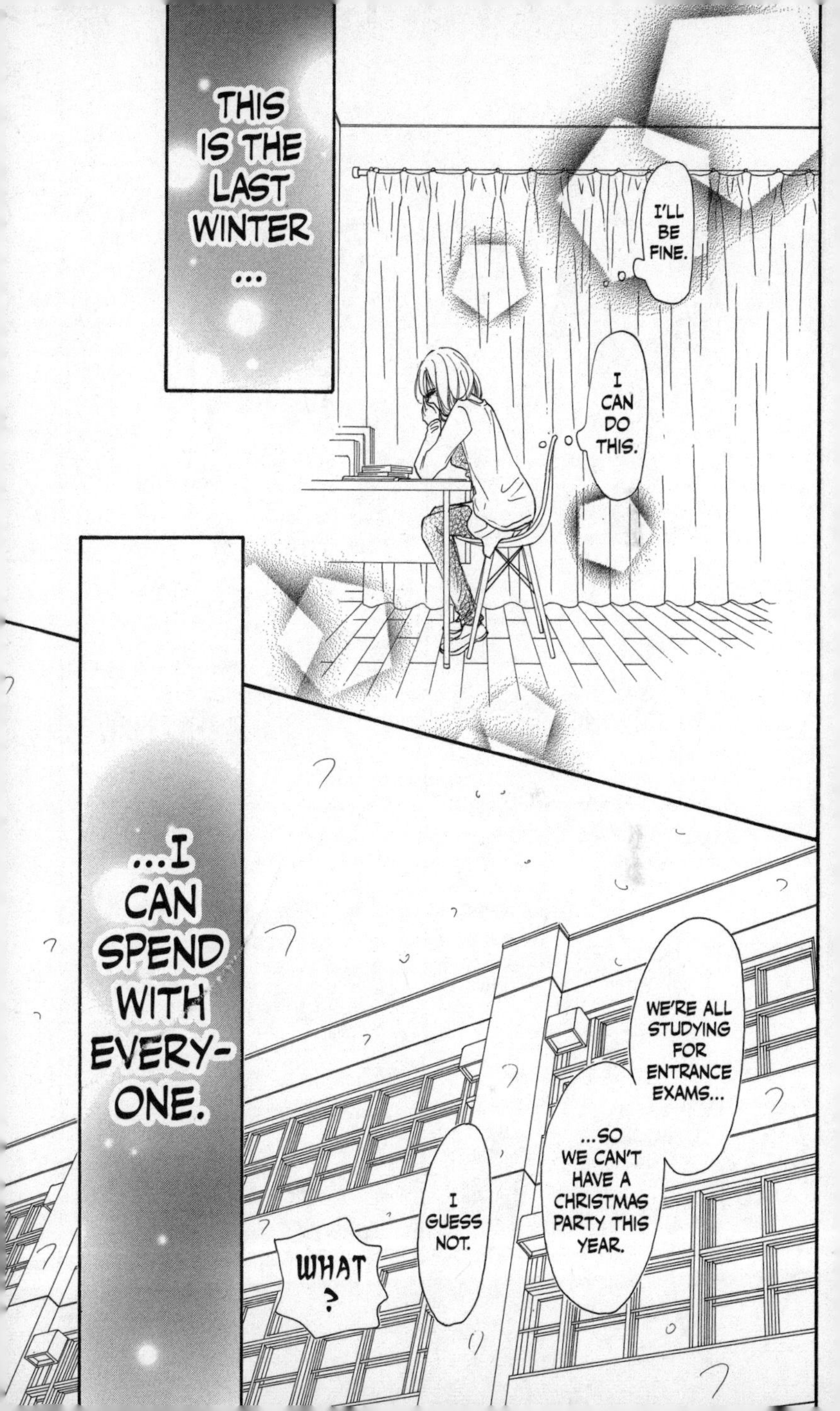
I'LL BE FINE.
I CAN DO THIS.
THIS IS THE LAST WINTER...
WE'RE ALL STUDYING FOR ENTRANCE EXAMS...
...SO WE CAN'T HAVE A CHRISTMAS PARTY THIS YEAR.
I GUESS NOT.
WHAT?
...I CAN SPEND WITH EVERY-ONE.

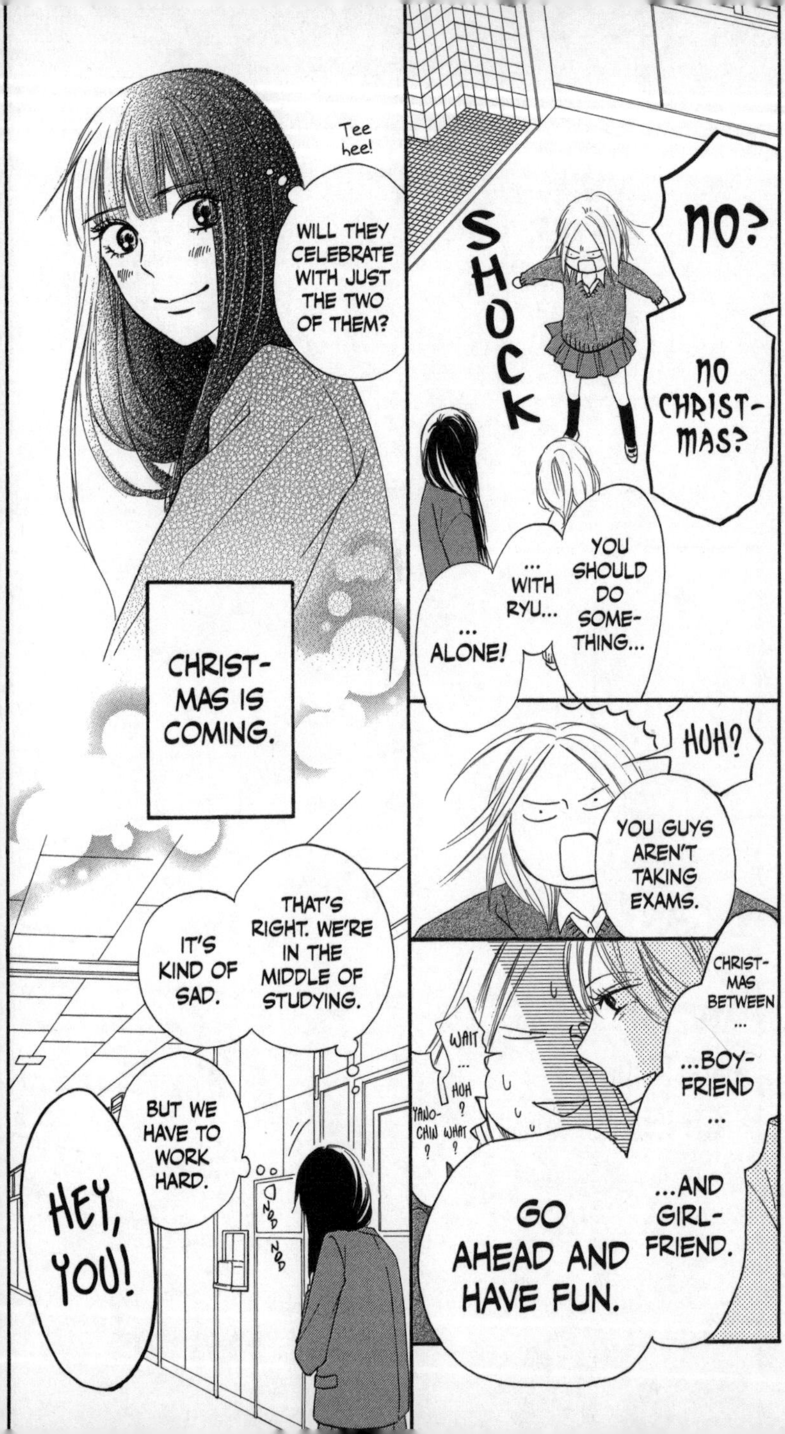
NO?
NO CHRISTMAS?
SHOCK
YOU SHOULD DO SOMETHING...
... WITH RYU...
... ALONE!
HUH?
YOU GUYS AREN'T TAKING EXAMS.
CHRISTMAS BETWEEN...
...BOYFRIEND...
...AND GIRLFRIEND.
GO AHEAD AND HAVE FUN.
WAIT... HUH? WHAT?
YANO-CHIN?
Tee hee!
WILL THEY CELEBRATE WITH JUST THE TWO OF THEM?
CHRISTMAS IS COMING.
THAT'S RIGHT. WE'RE IN THE MIDDLE OF STUDYING.
IT'S KIND OF SAD.
BUT WE HAVE TO WORK HARD.
NOD NOD
HEY, YOU!

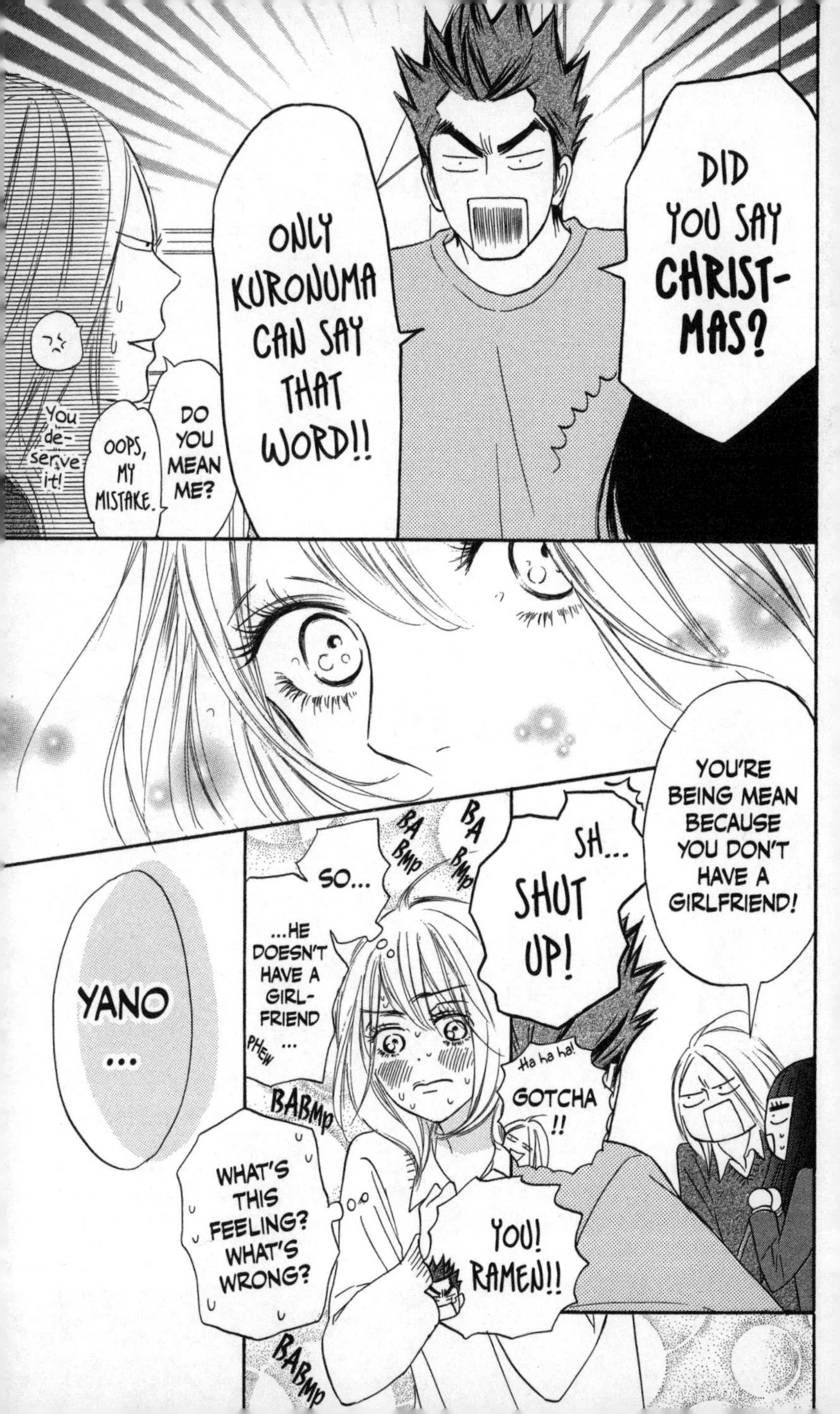
DID YOU SAY CHRISTMAS?
ONLY KURONUMA CAN SAY THAT WORD!!
DO YOU MEAN ME?
OOPS, MY MISTAKE.
You deserve it!
YOU'RE BEING MEAN BECAUSE YOU DON'T HAVE A GIRLFRIEND!
SH... SHUT UP!
BA BMP
BA BMP
SO...
...HE DOESN'T HAVE A GIRLFRIEND...
PHEW
Ha ha ha!
GOTCHA!!
BABMP
YOU! RAMEN!!
WHAT'S THIS FEELING? WHAT'S WRONG?
BABMP
YANO...

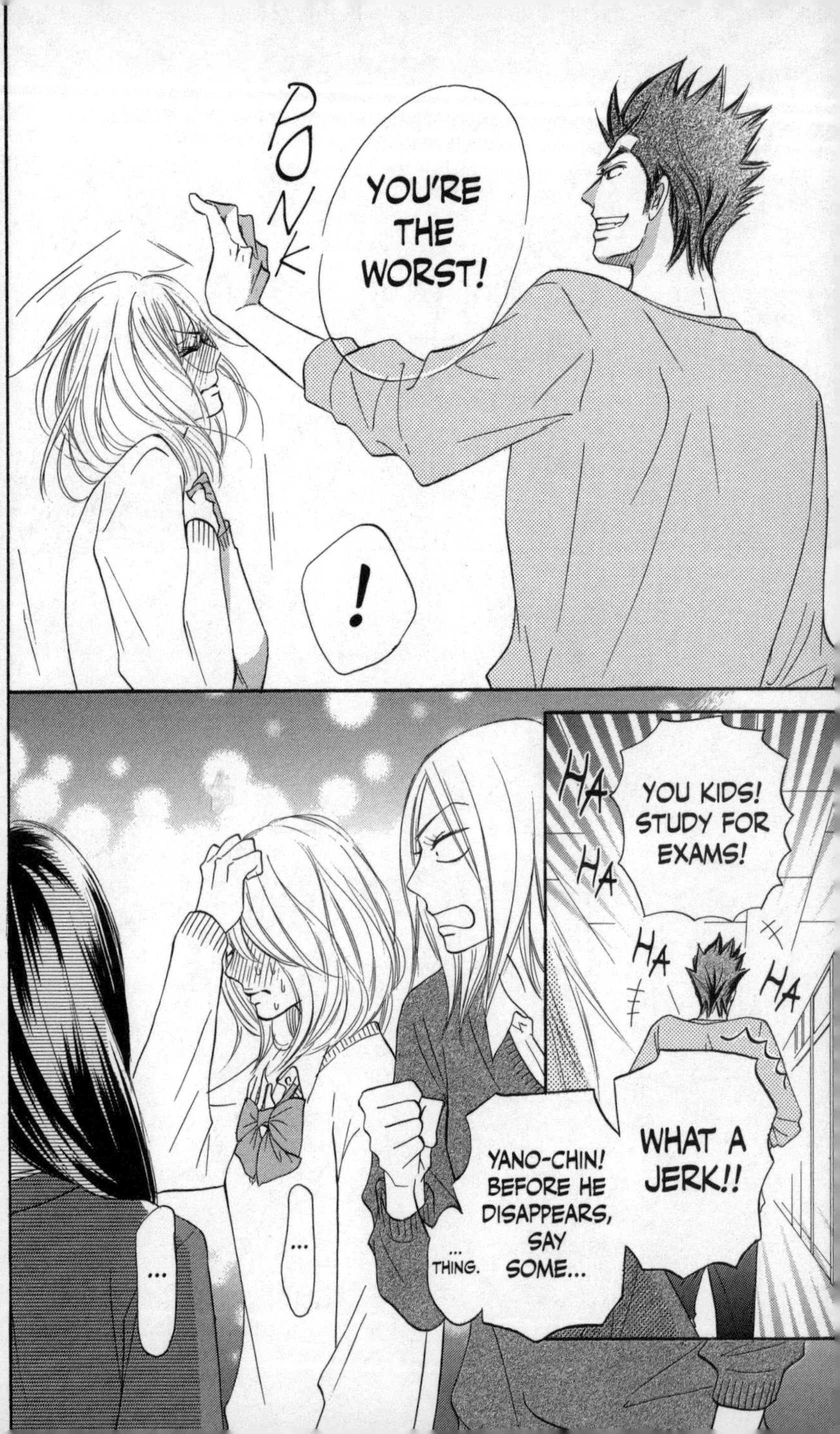
YOU'RE THE WORST!
PONK
!
YOU KIDS! STUDY FOR EXAMS!
HA HA HA HA
WHAT A JERK!!
YANO-CHIN! BEFORE HE DISAPPEARS, SAY SOME...
...THING.
...
...

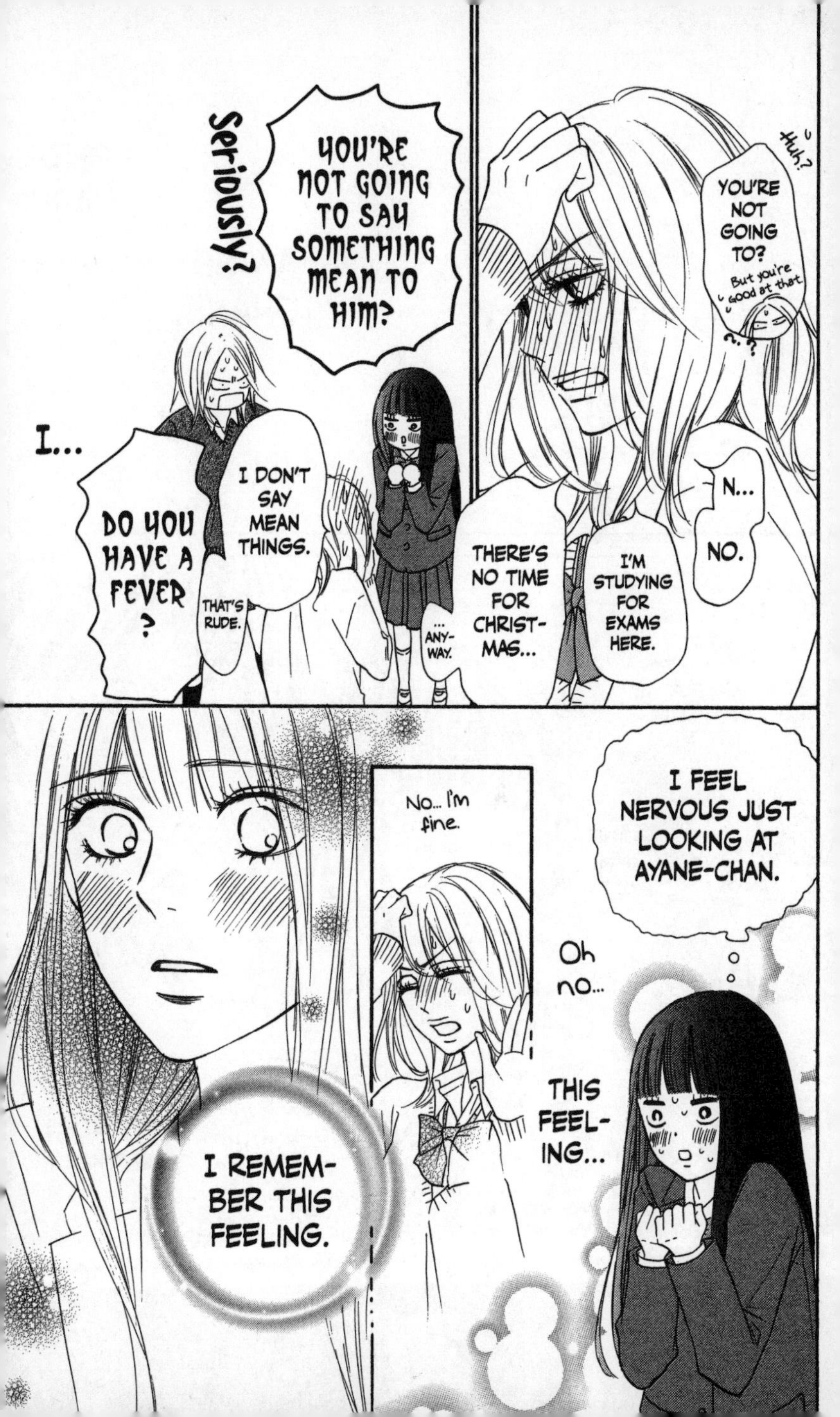
Huh?
YOU'RE NOT GOING TO?
But you're good at that.
N...
NO.
I'M STUDYING FOR EXAMS HERE.
THERE'S NO TIME FOR CHRIST-MAS...
... ANY-WAY.
YOU'RE NOT GOING TO SAY SOMETHING MEAN TO HIM?
Seriously?
I DON'T SAY MEAN THINGS.
THAT'S RUDE.
I...
DO YOU HAVE A FEVER?
I FEEL NERVOUS JUST LOOKING AT AYANE-CHAN.
Oh no...
THIS FEEL-ING...
No... I'm fine.
I REMEM-BER THIS FEELING.

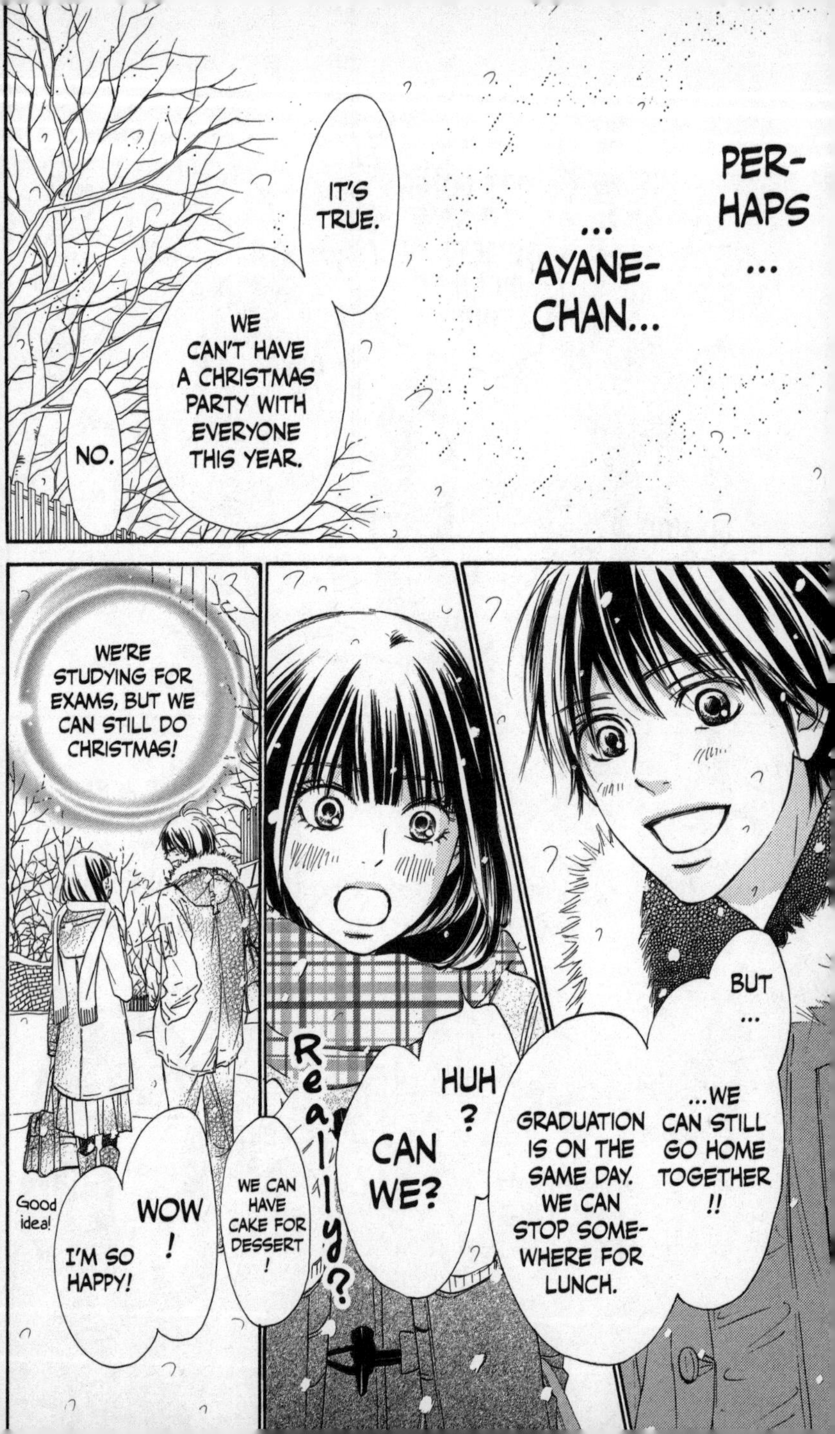
PER-
HAPS
...
...
AYANE-
CHAN...
IT'S TRUE.
WE CAN'T HAVE A CHRISTMAS PARTY WITH EVERYONE THIS YEAR.
NO.
BUT
...
...WE CAN STILL GO HOME TOGETHER!!
GRADUATION IS ON THE SAME DAY. WE CAN STOP SOME-WHERE FOR LUNCH.
HUH?
CAN WE?
Really?
WE'RE STUDYING FOR EXAMS, BUT WE CAN STILL DO CHRISTMAS!
WE CAN HAVE CAKE FOR DESSERT!
WOW!
I'M SO HAPPY!
Good idea!

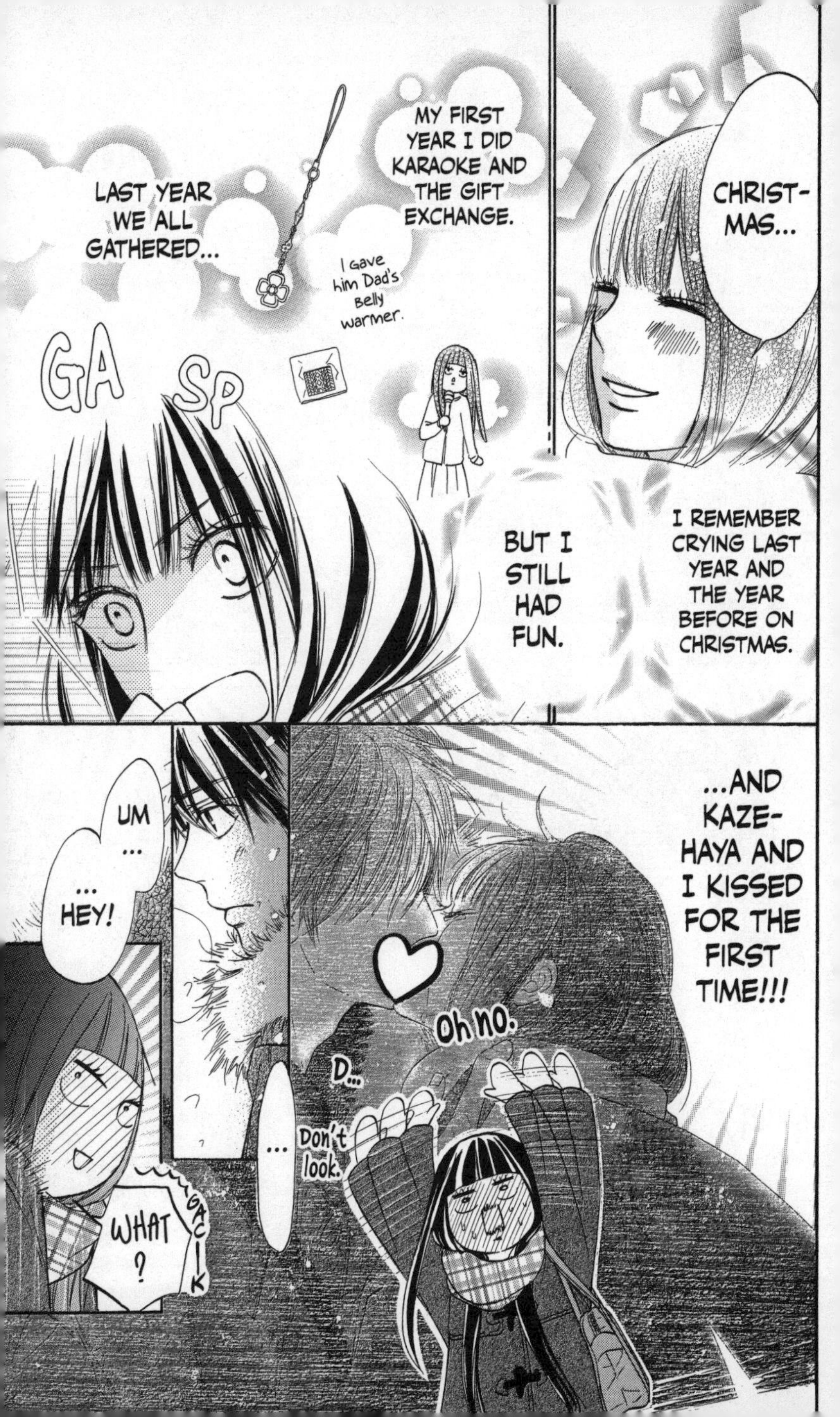
CHRIST-MAS...
I REMEMBER CRYING LAST YEAR AND THE YEAR BEFORE ON CHRISTMAS.
BUT I STILL HAD FUN.
MY FIRST YEAR I DID KARAOKE AND THE GIFT EXCHANGE.
LAST YEAR WE ALL GATHERED...
I gave him Dad's Belly warmer.
GASP
...AND KAZE-HAYA AND I KISSED FOR THE FIRST TIME!!!
Oh no.
D...
Don't look.
...
UM... ...HEY!
WHAT?
GACK

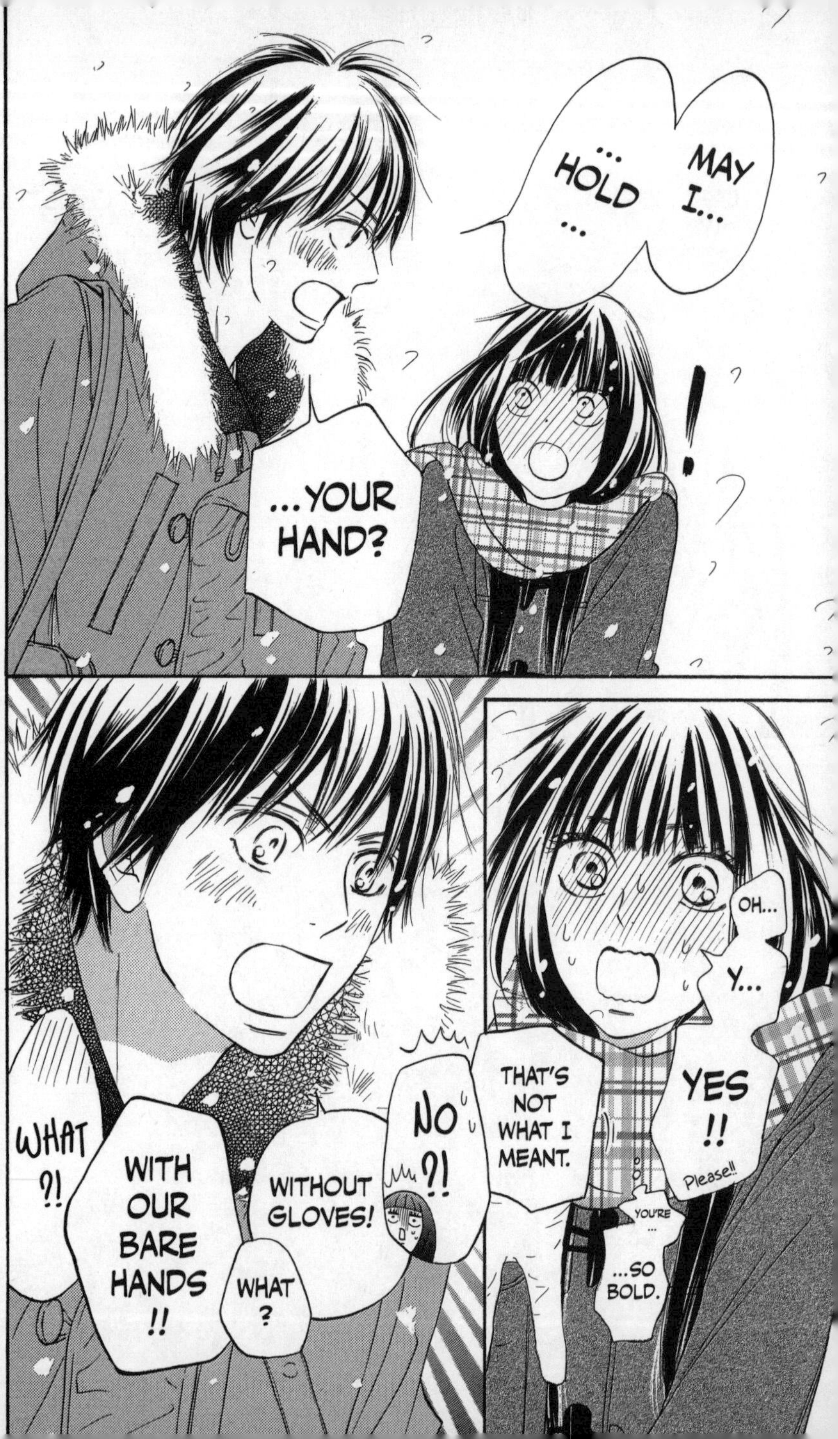
MAY I... ...HOLD ...
...YOUR HAND?
!
OH...
Y...
YES!!
Please!!
YOU'RE ...
...SO BOLD.
THAT'S NOT WHAT I MEANT.
NO ?!
WITHOUT GLOVES!
WHAT ?
WITH OUR BARE HANDS !!
WHAT ?!

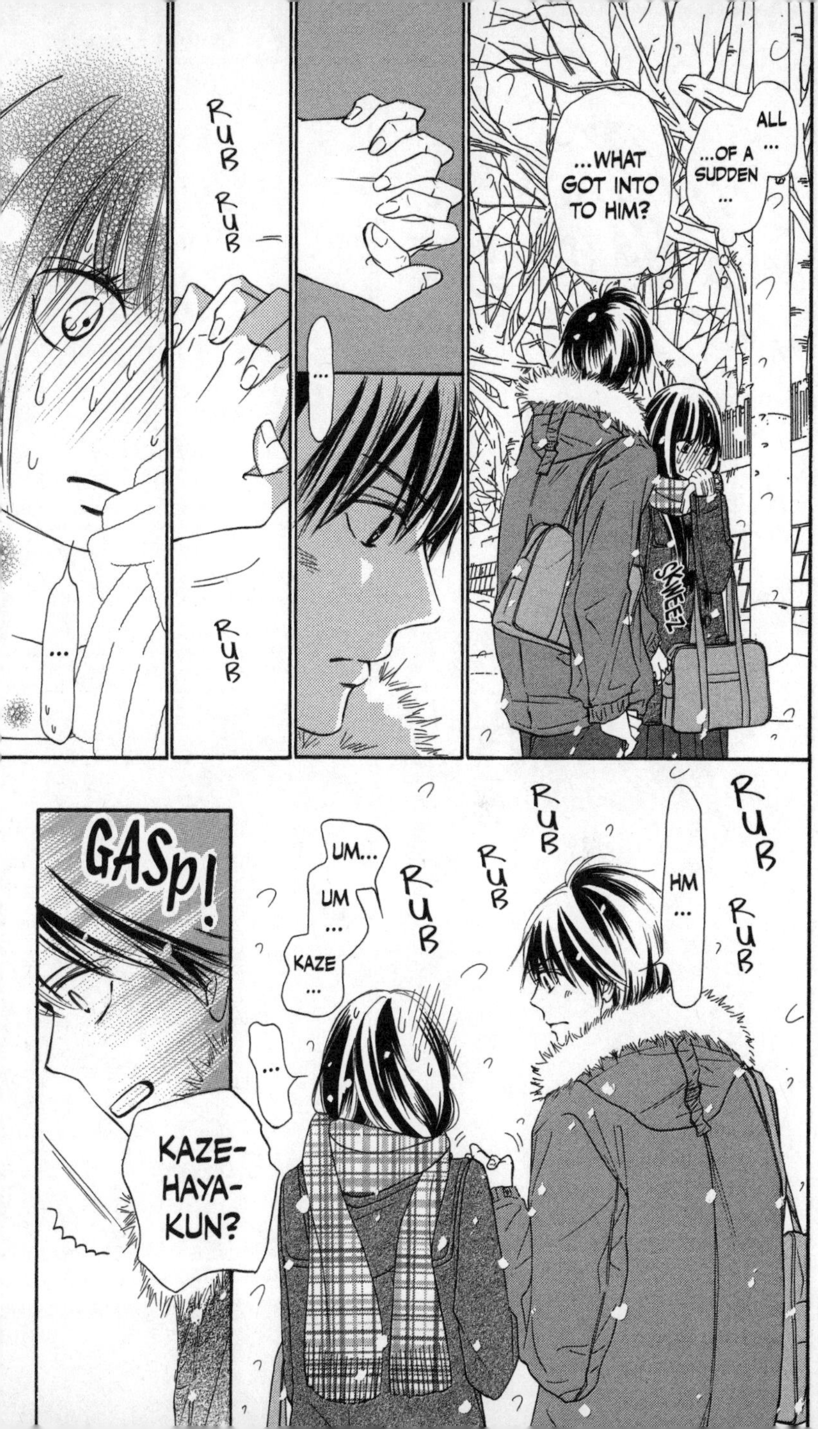
ALL... ...OF A SUDDEN...
...WHAT GOT INTO TO HIM?
SKWEEZ
...
RUB RUB
RUB
...
RUB RUB
HM...
RUB
RUB
RUB
UM... UM... KAZE...
...
GASp!
KAZE-HAYA-KUN?

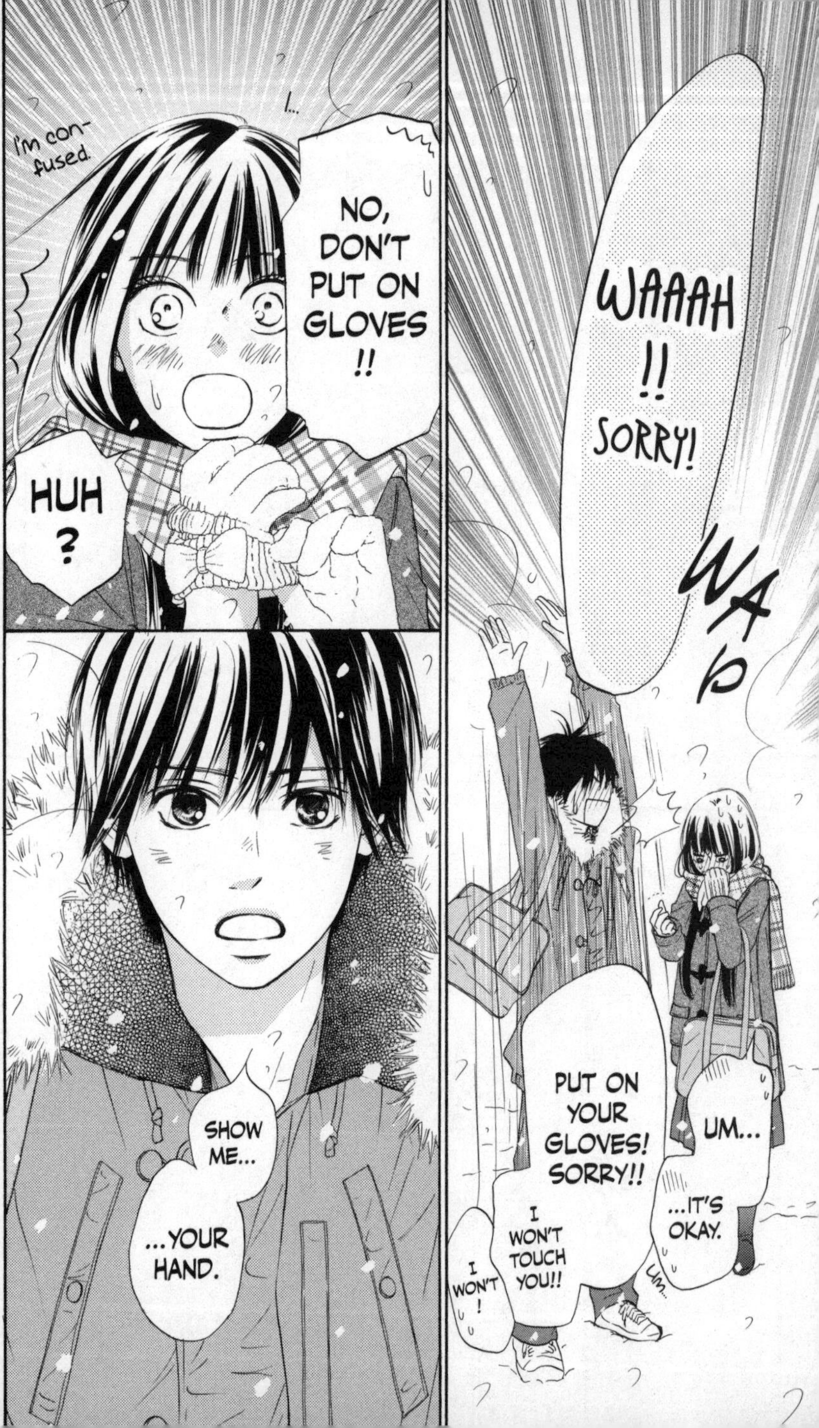
WAAAH !! SORRY!
WAP
UM...
...IT'S OKAY.
Um...
PUT ON YOUR GLOVES! SORRY!!
I WON'T TOUCH YOU!!
I WON'T!
I...
NO, DON'T PUT ON GLOVES !!
I'm confused.
HUH ?
SHOW ME...
...YOUR HAND.

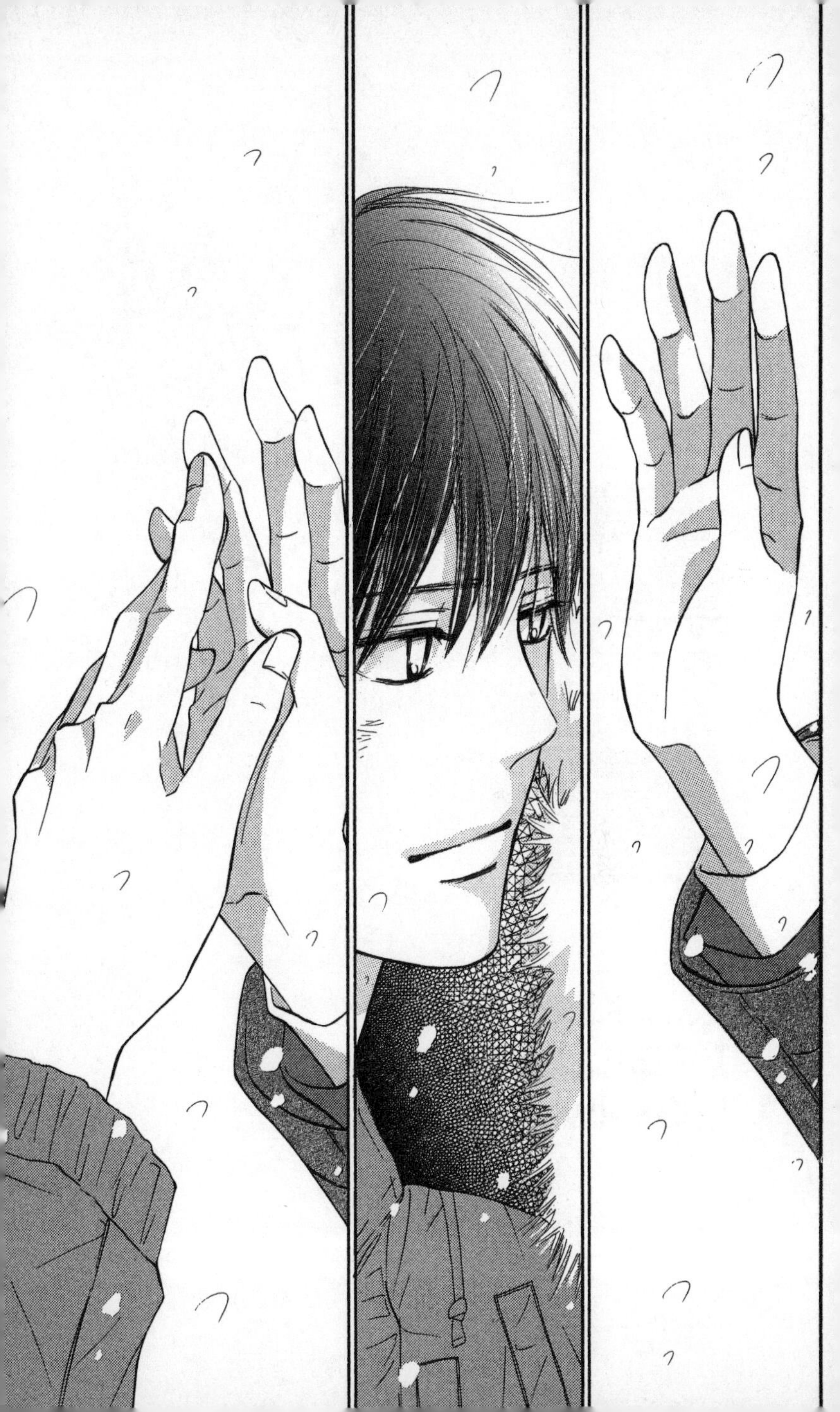

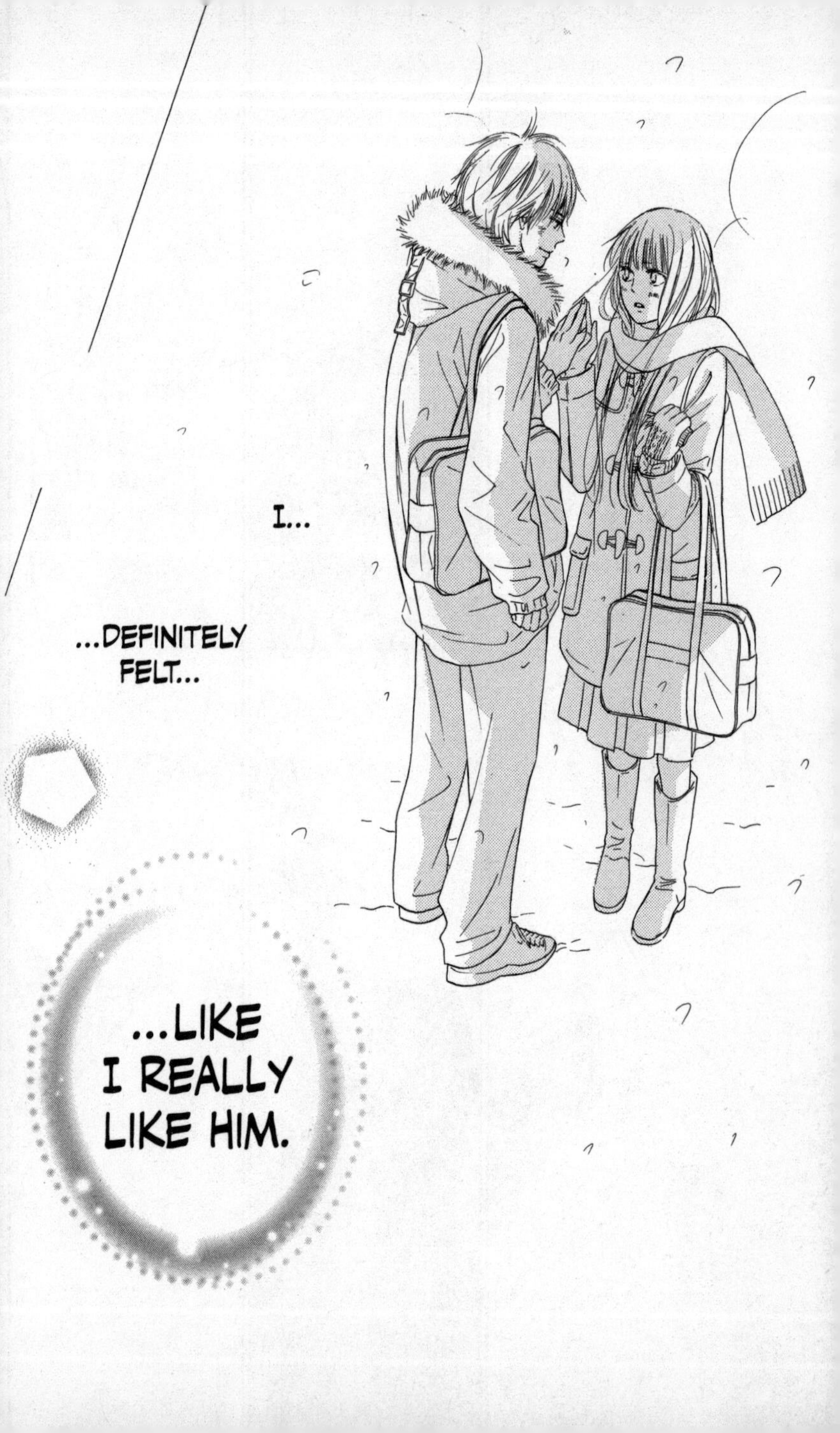
I...
...DEFINITELY FELT...
...LIKE I REALLY LIKE HIM.

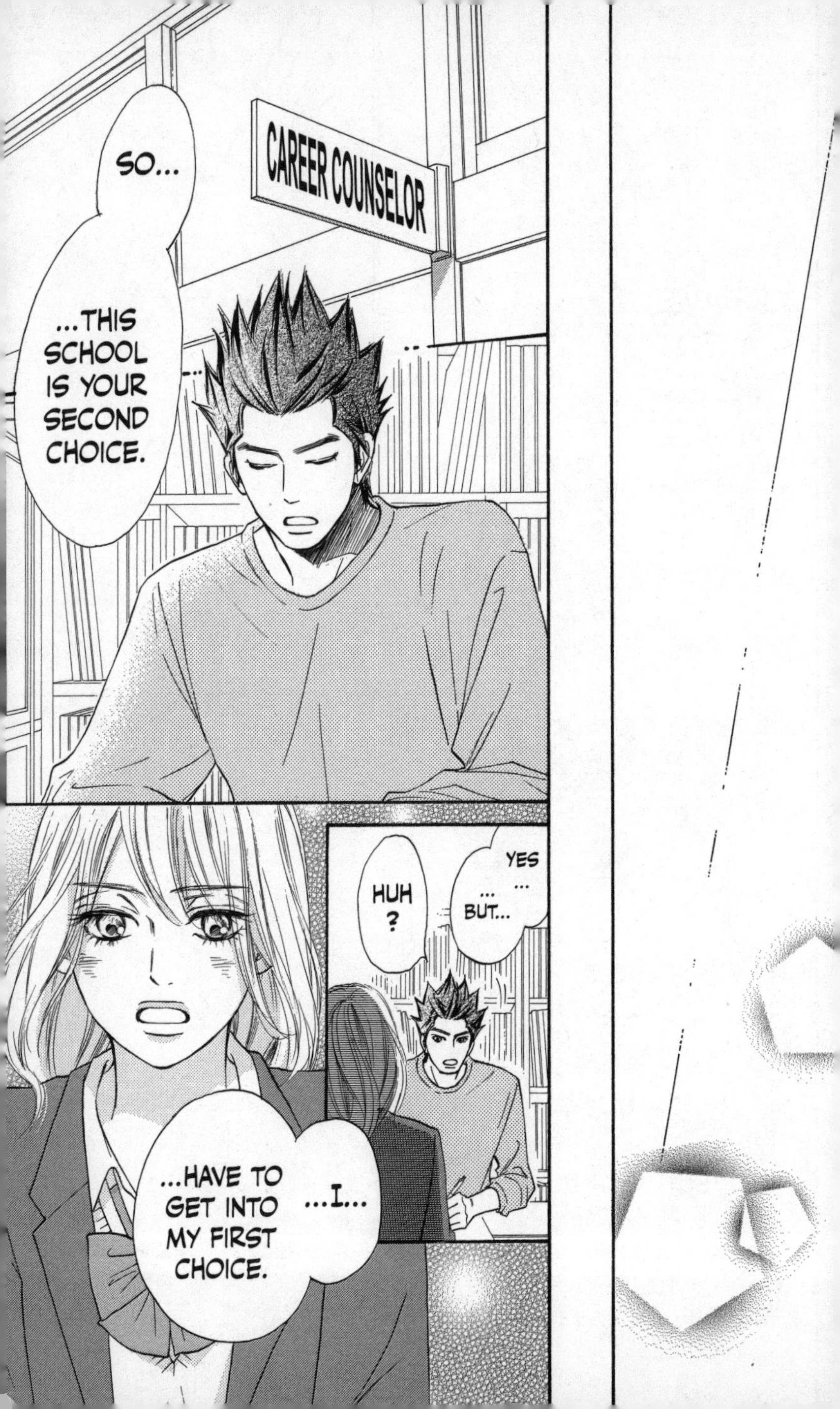
CAREER COUNSELOR
SO...
...THIS SCHOOL IS YOUR SECOND CHOICE.
YES ... ... BUT...
HUH ?
...I...
...HAVE TO GET INTO MY FIRST CHOICE.

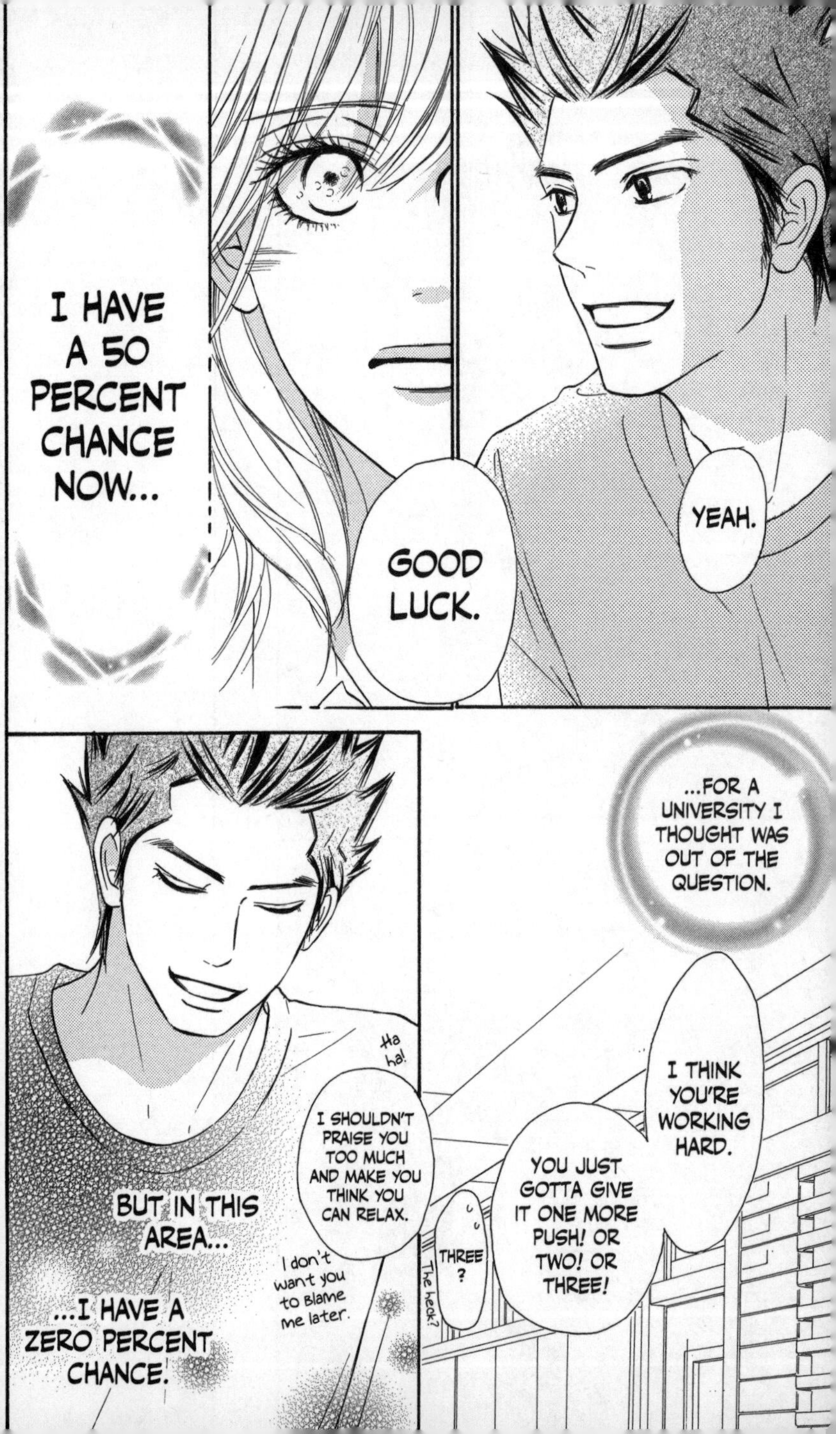
YEAH.
GOOD LUCK.
I HAVE A 50 PERCENT CHANCE NOW...
...FOR A UNIVERSITY I THOUGHT WAS OUT OF THE QUESTION.
I THINK YOU'RE WORKING HARD.
YOU JUST GOTTA GIVE IT ONE MORE PUSH! OR TWO! OR THREE!
THREE?
The heck?
Ha ha!
I SHOULDN'T PRAISE YOU TOO MUCH AND MAKE YOU THINK YOU CAN RELAX.
I don't want you to blame me later.
BUT IN THIS AREA...
...I HAVE A ZERO PERCENT CHANCE.

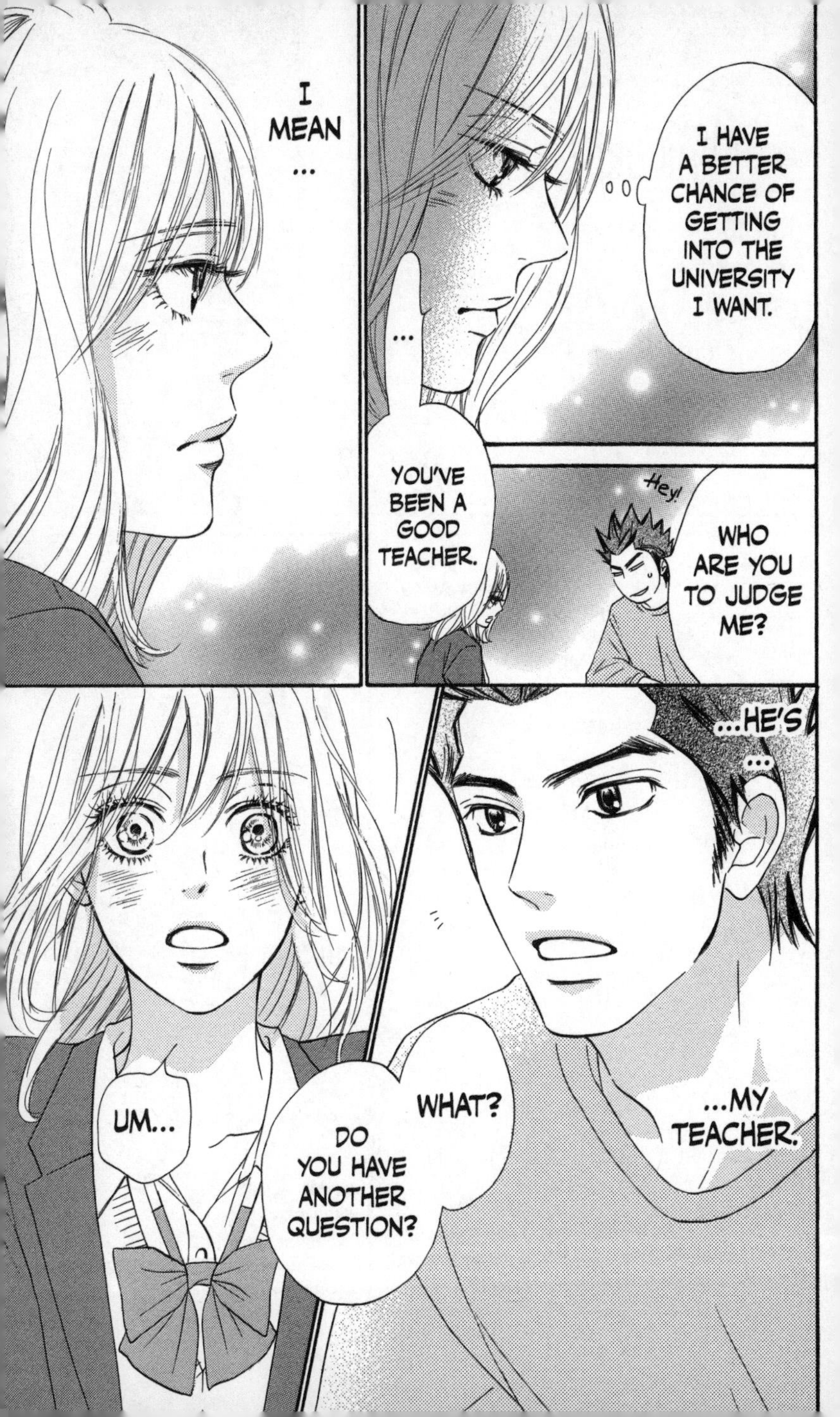
I HAVE A BETTER CHANCE OF GETTING INTO THE UNIVERSITY I WANT.
...
Hey!
WHO ARE YOU TO JUDGE ME?
YOU'VE BEEN A GOOD TEACHER.
I MEAN ...
...HE'S ...
...MY TEACHER.
WHAT?
DO YOU HAVE ANOTHER QUESTION?
UM...

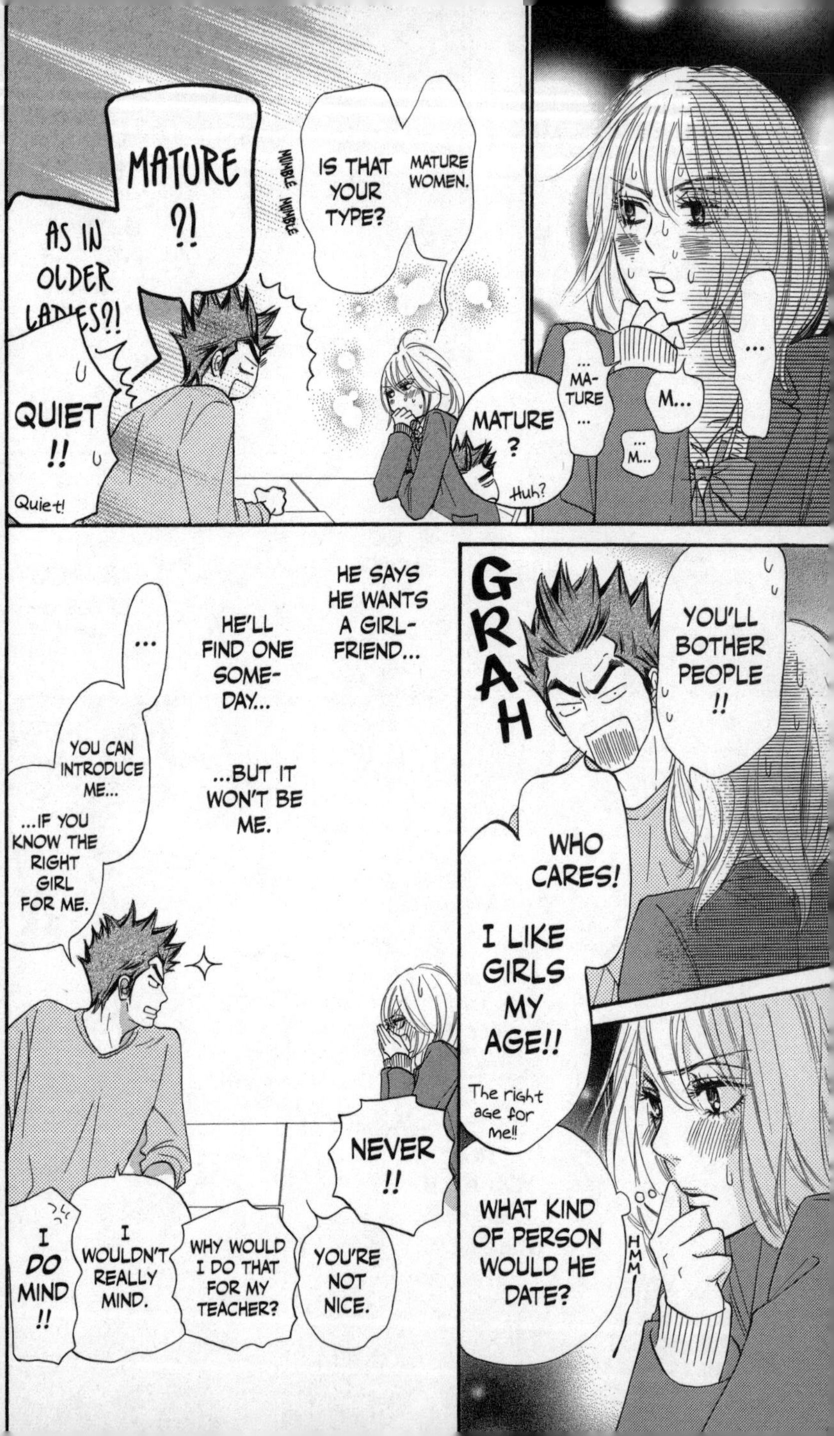
...
M...
...MA-TURE...
...M...
MATURE WOMEN.
IS THAT YOUR TYPE?
MUMBLE MUMBLE
MATURE ?!
AS IN OLDER LADIES?!
MATURE ?
Huh?
QUIET !!
Quiet!
GRAH
YOU'LL BOTHER PEOPLE !!
WHO CARES!
I LIKE GIRLS MY AGE!!
The right age for me!!
WHAT KIND OF PERSON WOULD HE DATE?
HMM
HE SAYS HE WANTS A GIRLFRIEND...
HE'LL FIND ONE SOMEDAY...
...BUT IT WON'T BE ME.
...
YOU CAN INTRODUCE ME...
...IF YOU KNOW THE RIGHT GIRL FOR ME.
NEVER !!
YOU'RE NOT NICE.
WHY WOULD I DO THAT FOR MY TEACHER?
I WOULDN'T REALLY MIND.
I *DO* MIND !!

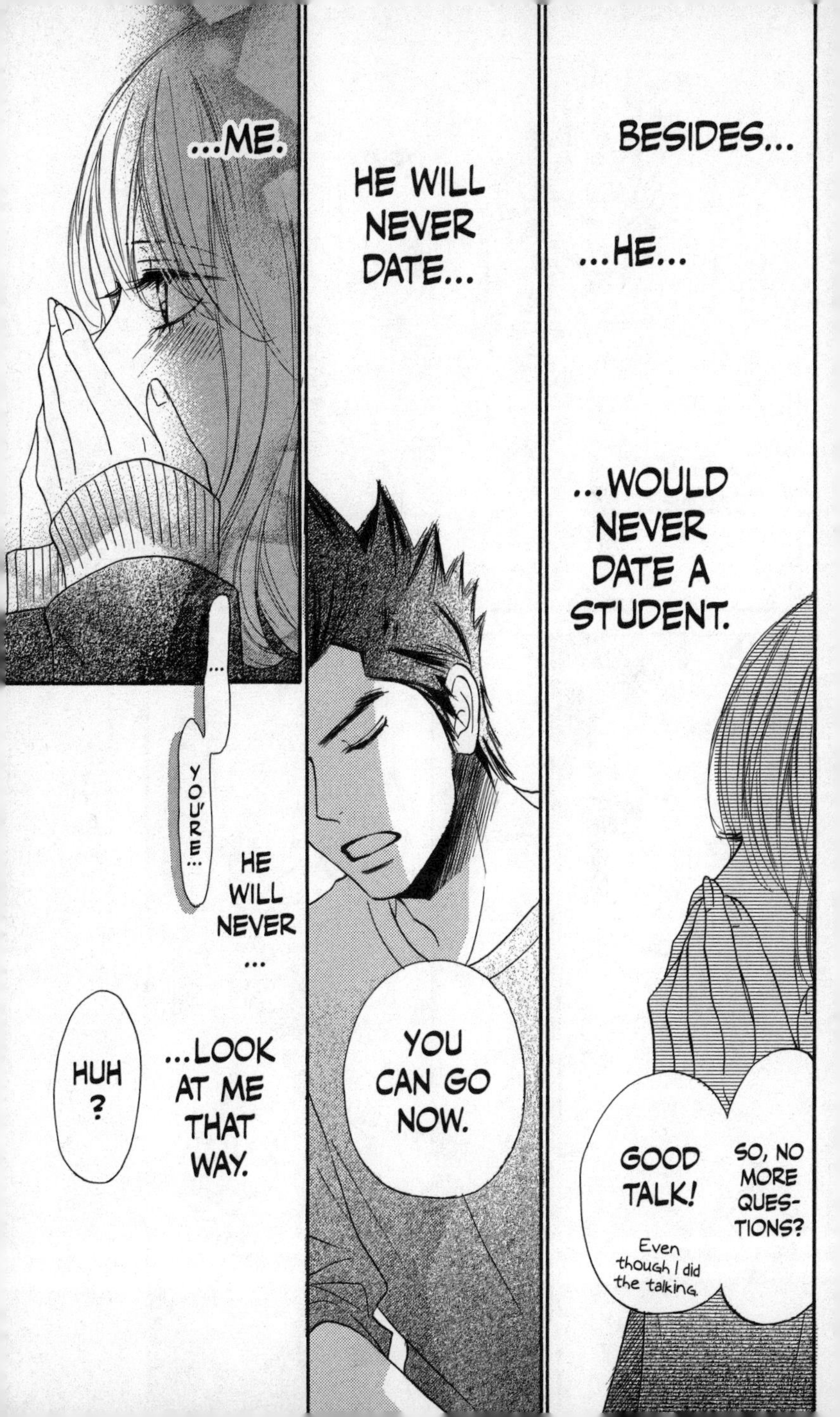
BESIDES...
...HE...
...WOULD NEVER DATE A STUDENT.
SO, NO MORE QUES-TIONS?
GOOD TALK!
Even though I did the talking.
HE WILL NEVER DATE...
YOU CAN GO NOW.
...ME.
...
YOU'RE...
HE WILL NEVER ...
...LOOK AT ME THAT WAY.
HUH?

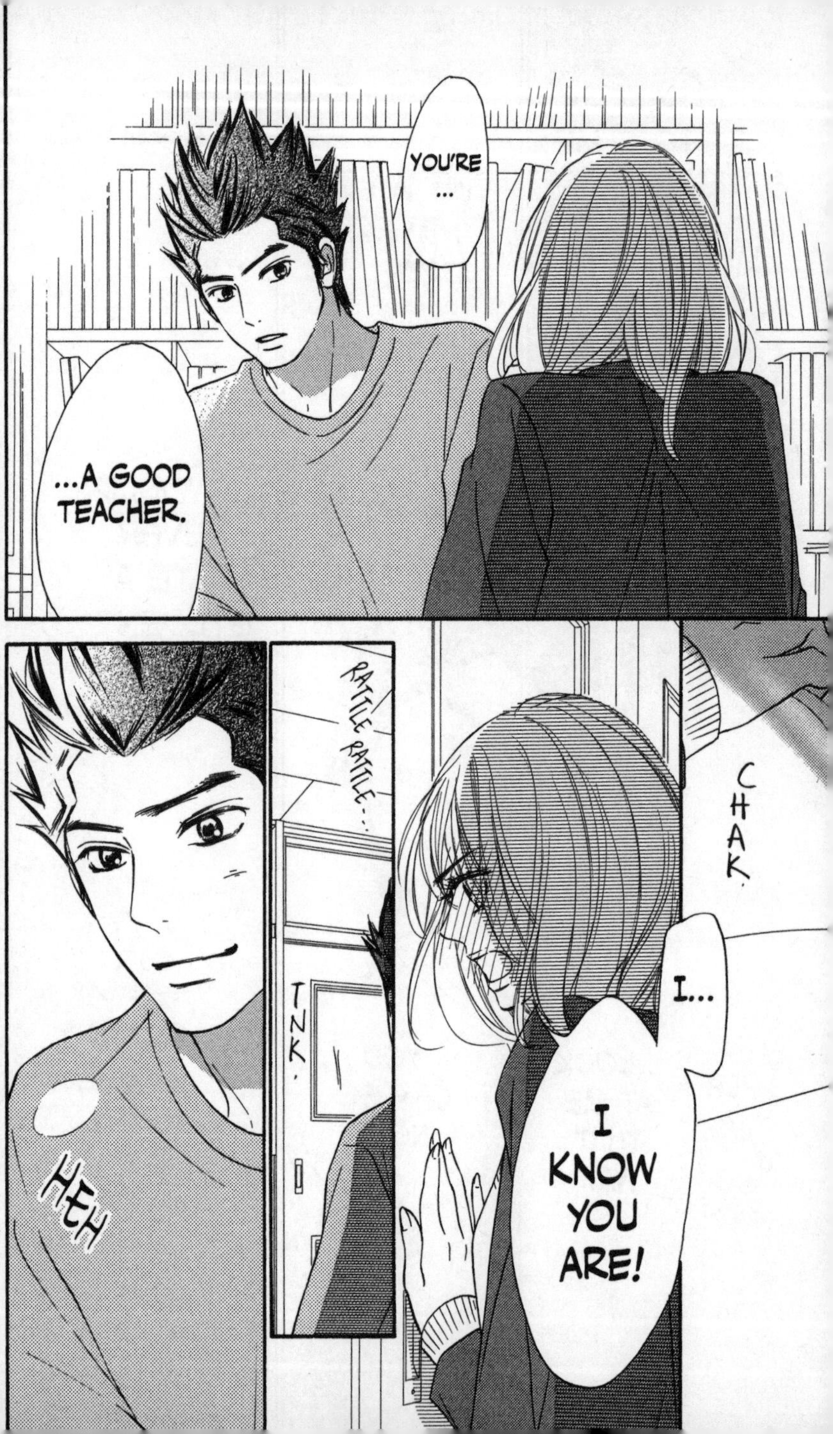
YOU'RE ...
...A GOOD TEACHER.
CHAK
I...
I KNOW YOU ARE!
RATTLE RATTLE...
TNK
HEH

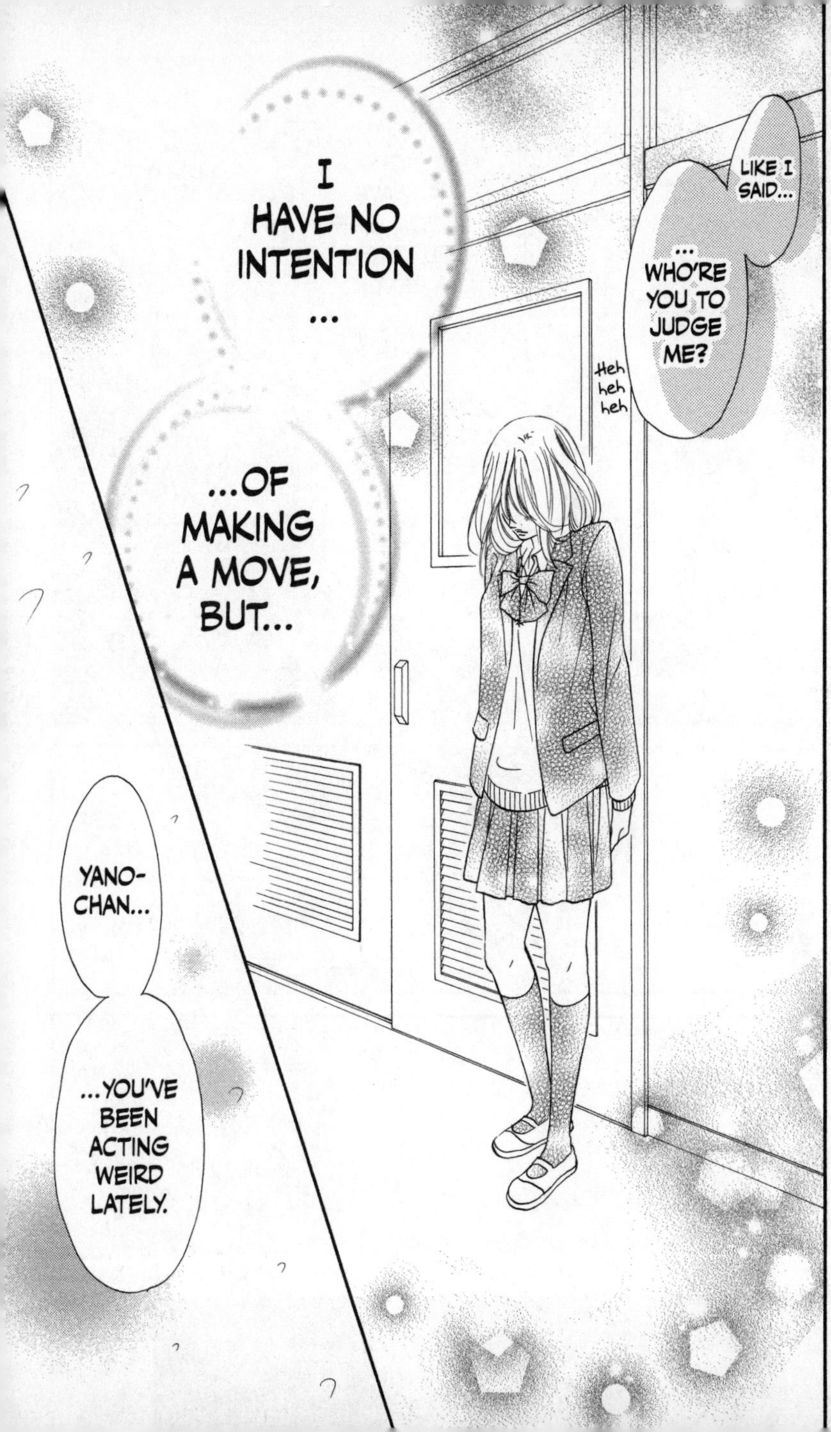
LIKE I SAID...
...WHO'RE YOU TO JUDGE ME?
Heh heh heh
I HAVE NO INTENTION ...
...OF MAKING A MOVE, BUT...
YANO-CHAN...
...YOU'VE BEEN ACTING WEIRD LATELY.

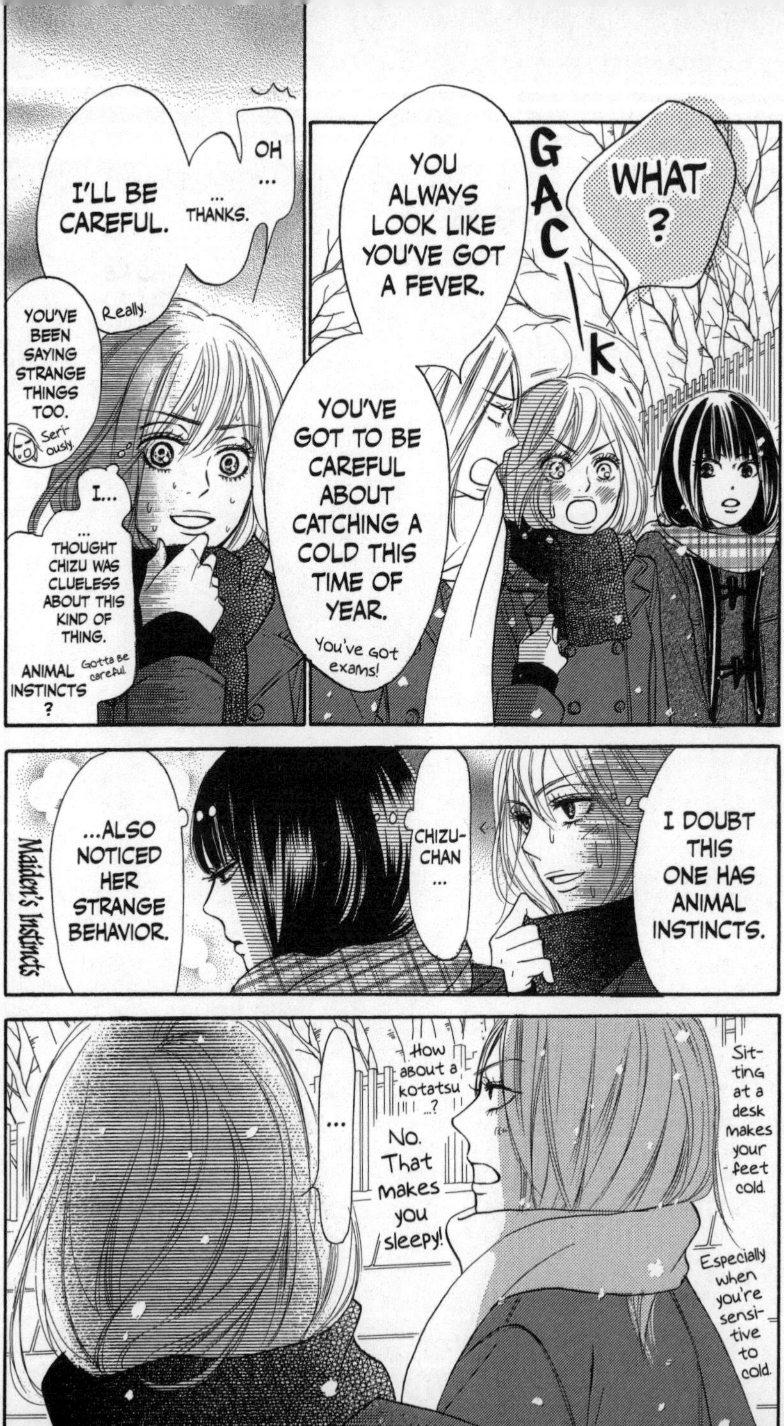
WHAT?
GACK
YOU ALWAYS LOOK LIKE YOU'VE GOT A FEVER.
YOU'VE GOT TO BE CAREFUL ABOUT CATCHING A COLD THIS TIME OF YEAR.
You've got exams!
OH ... THANKS.
I'LL BE CAREFUL.
Really.
YOU'VE BEEN SAYING STRANGE THINGS TOO.
Seriously.
I... ... THOUGHT CHIZU WAS CLUELESS ABOUT THIS KIND OF THING.
Gotta be careful.
ANIMAL INSTINCTS?
I DOUBT THIS ONE HAS ANIMAL INSTINCTS.
CHIZU-CHAN ...
...ALSO NOTICED HER STRANGE BEHAVIOR.
Maiden's Instincts
Sitting at a desk makes your feet cold.
Especially when you're sensitive to cold.
How about a kotatsu...?
No. That makes you sleepy!
...

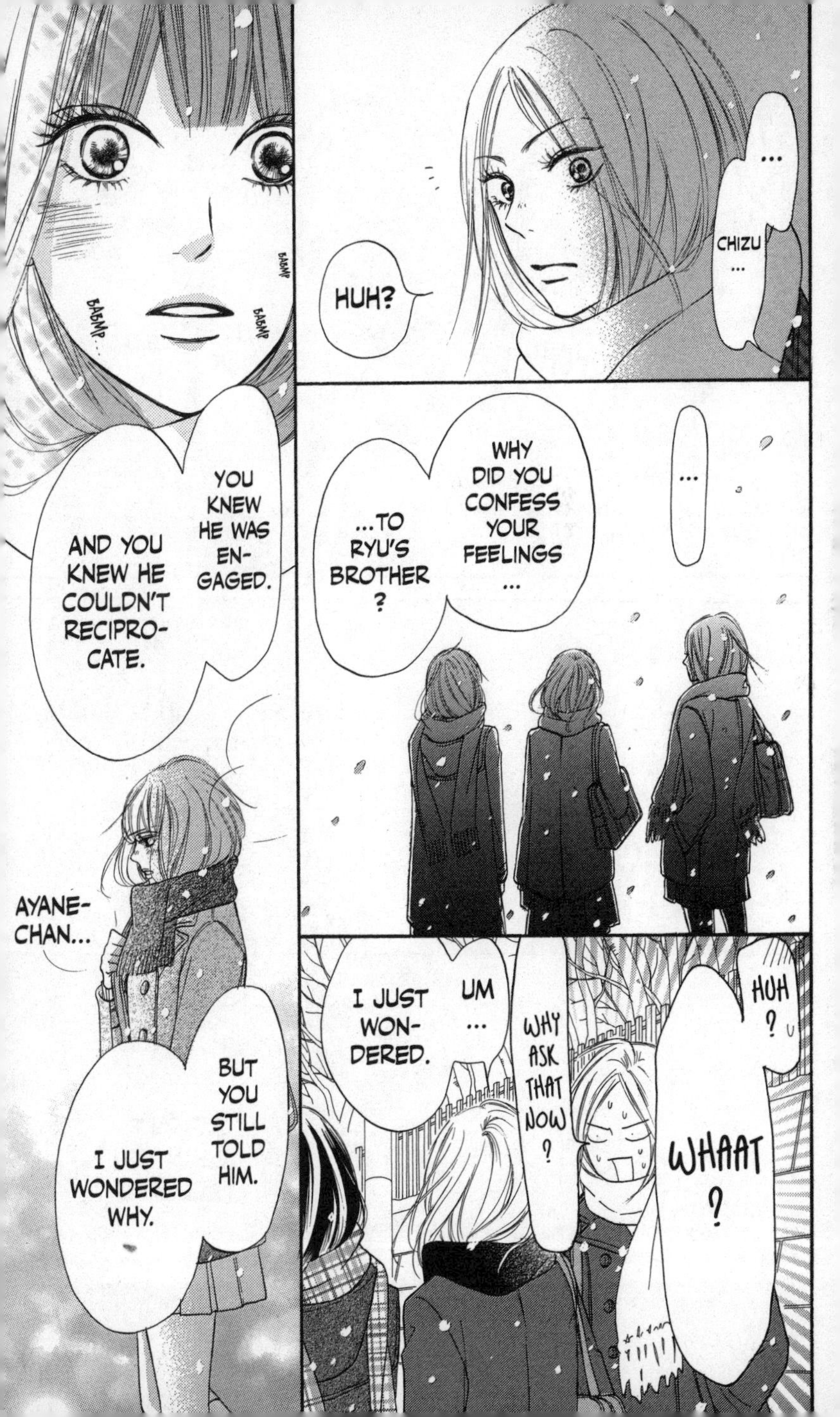
...
CHIZU ...
HUH?
...
WHY DID YOU CONFESS YOUR FEELINGS ...
...TO RYU'S BROTHER ?
HUH ?
WHAAT ?
WHY ASK THAT NOW ?
UM ...
I JUST WONDERED.
BADMP
BADMP
BADMP...
YOU KNEW HE WAS ENGAGED.
AND YOU KNEW HE COULDN'T RECIPROCATE.
AYANE-CHAN...
BUT YOU STILL TOLD HIM.
I JUST WONDERED WHY.

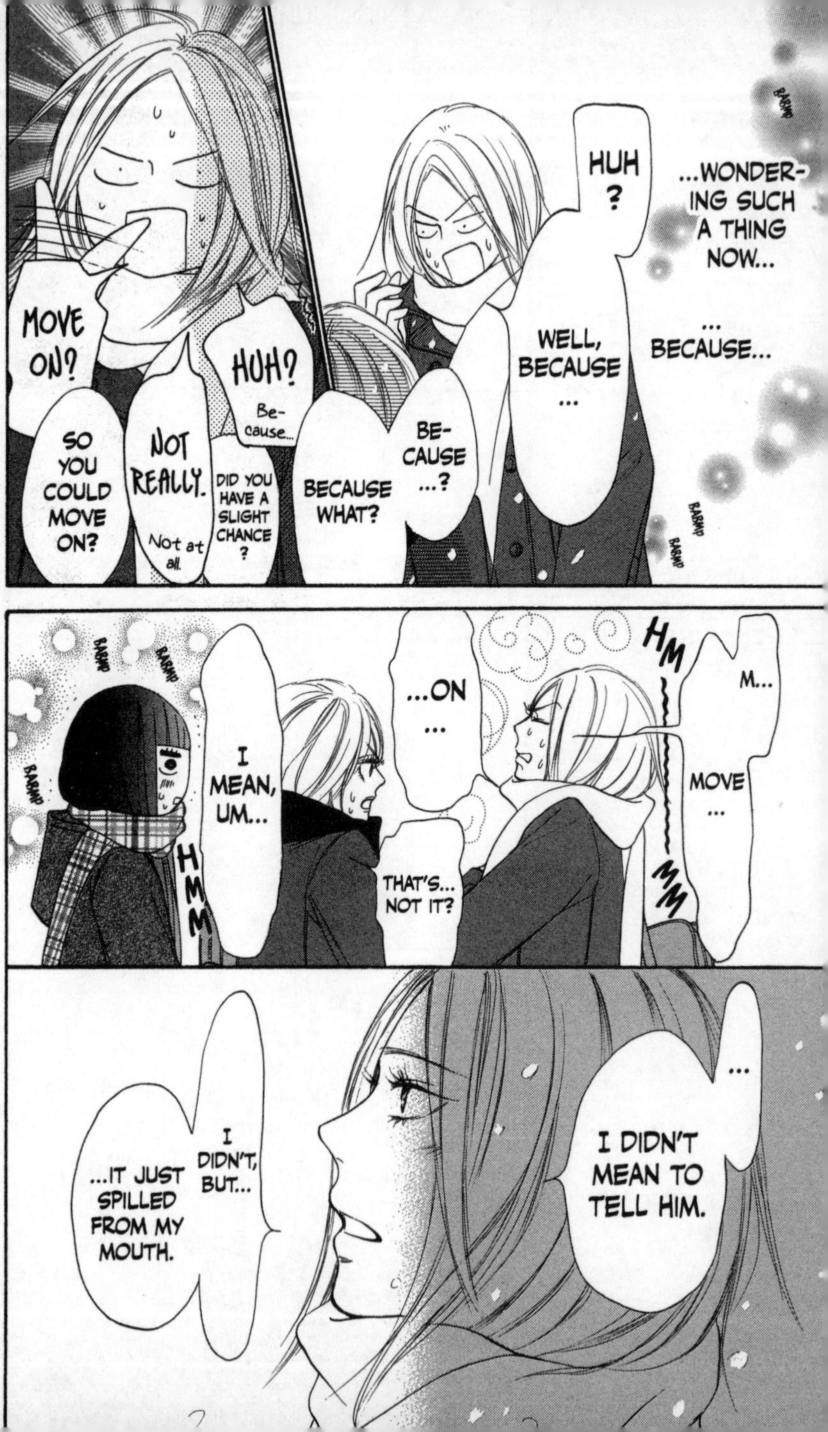
BABMP
...WONDERING SUCH A THING NOW...
... BECAUSE...
BABMP
BABMP
HUH ?
WELL, BECAUSE ...
BE-CAUSE ...?
BECAUSE WHAT?
HUH?
Be-cause...
DID YOU HAVE A SLIGHT CHANCE ?
MOVE ON?
NOT REALLY.
Not at all.
SO YOU COULD MOVE ON?
M... MOVE ...
HM~~~MM
...ON ...
THAT'S... NOT IT?
I MEAN, UM...
HMM
BABMP
BABMP
BABMP
... I DIDN'T MEAN TO TELL HIM.
I DIDN'T, BUT...
...IT JUST SPILLED FROM MY MOUTH.

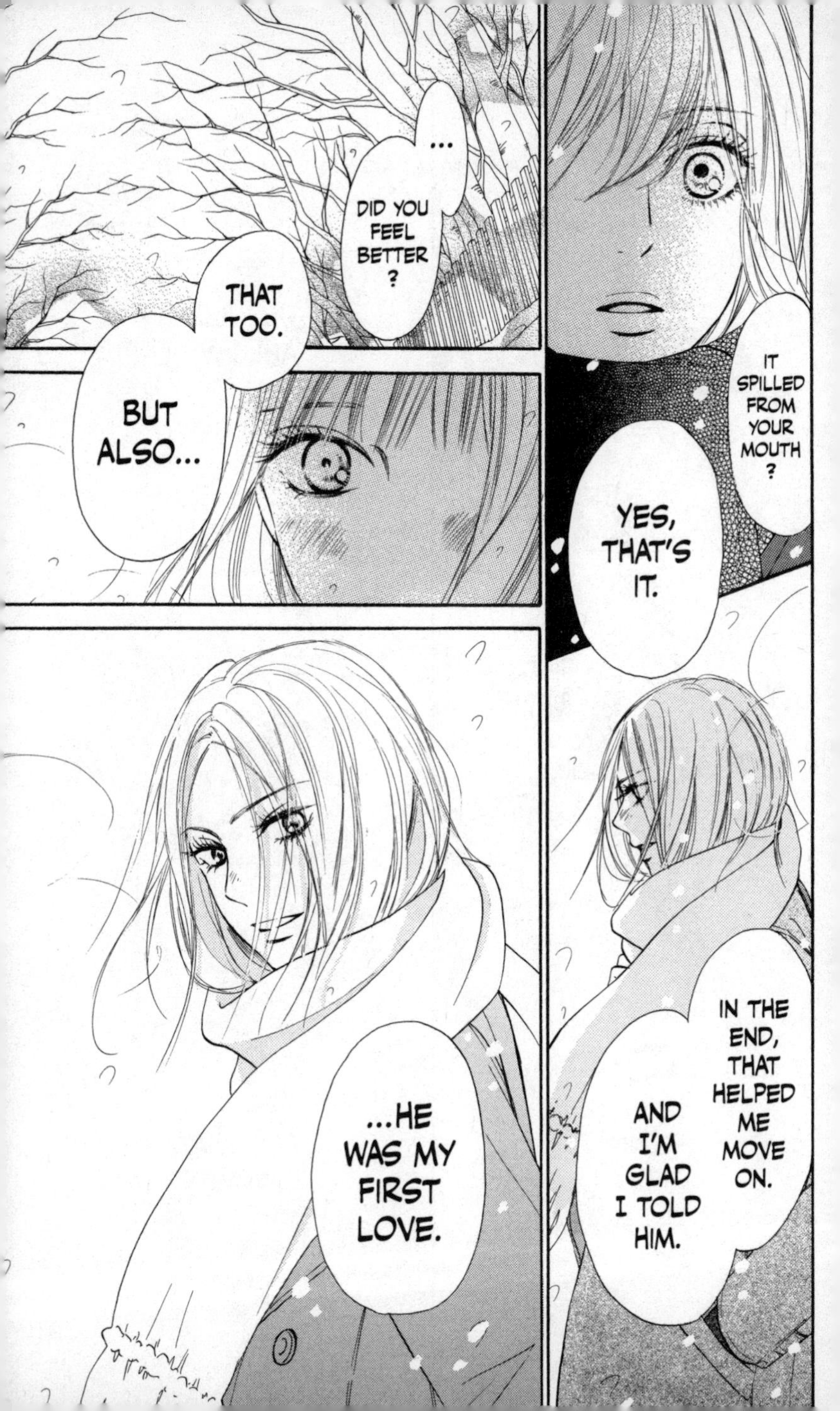
IT SPILLED FROM YOUR MOUTH?
YES, THAT'S IT.
IN THE END, THAT HELPED ME MOVE ON.
AND I'M GLAD I TOLD HIM.
...
DID YOU FEEL BETTER?
THAT TOO.
BUT ALSO...
...HE WAS MY FIRST LOVE.

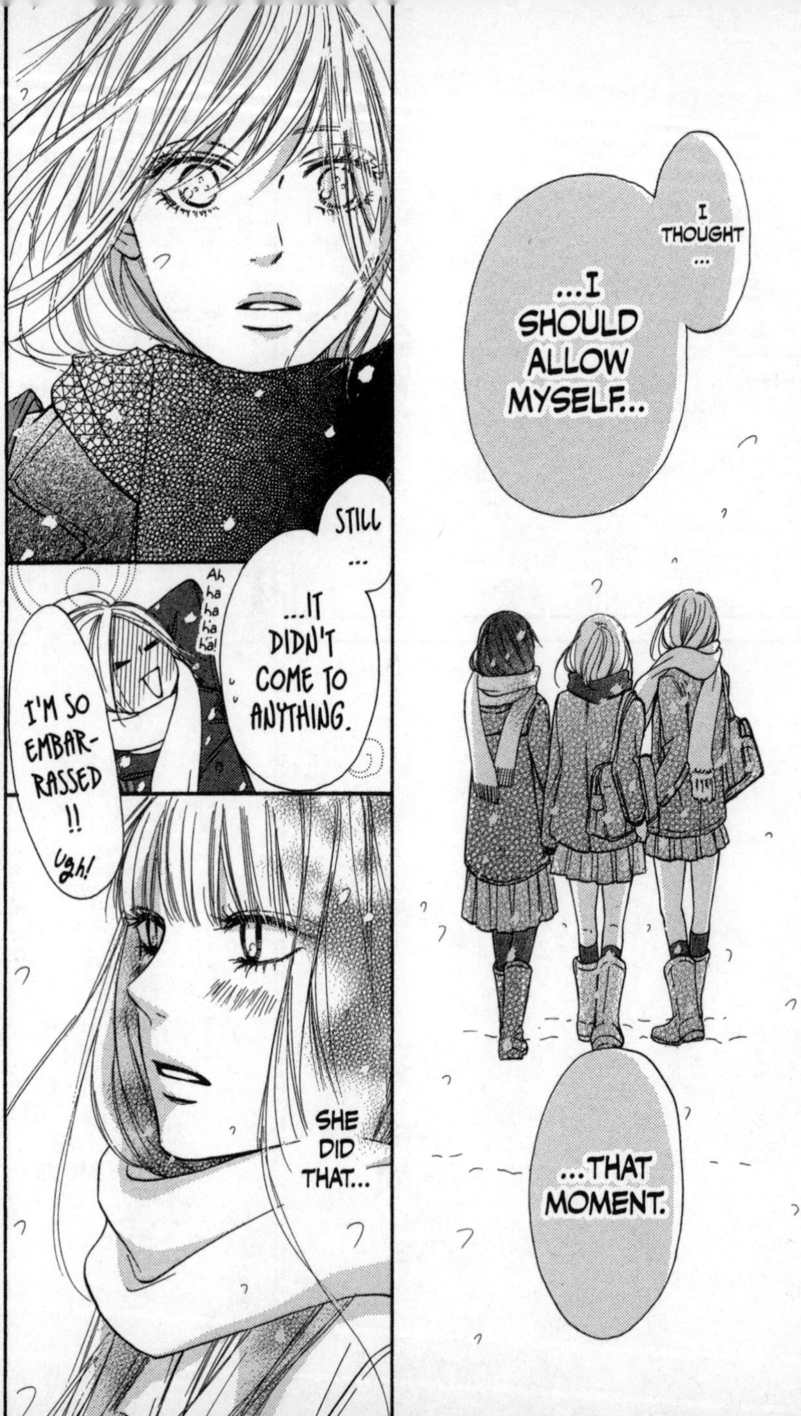

I THOUGHT...
...I SHOULD ALLOW MYSELF...
...THAT MOMENT.
STILL...
...IT DIDN'T COME TO ANYTHING.
Ah ha ha ha ha!
I'M SO EMBARRASSED!!
Ugh!
SHE DID THAT...

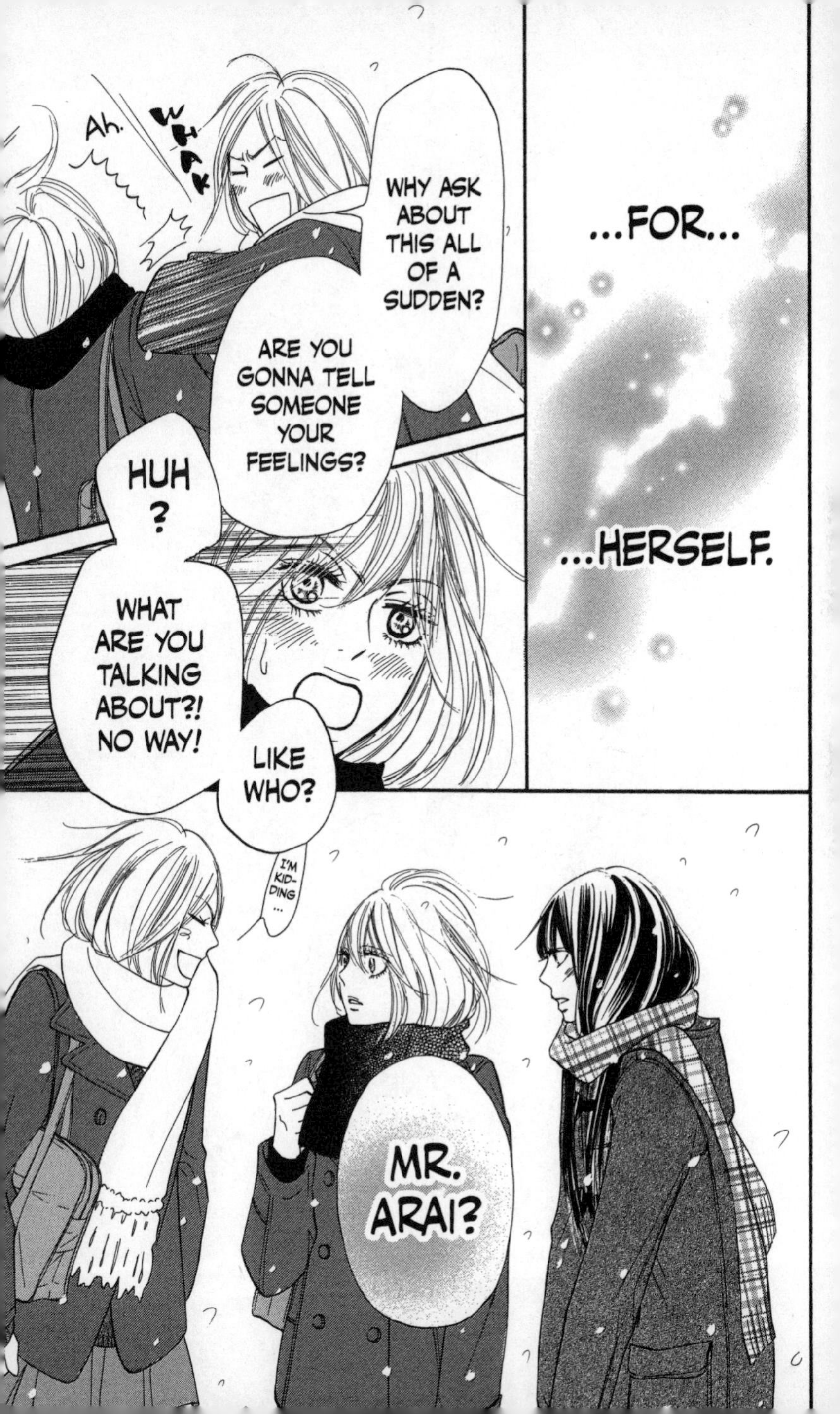
...FOR...
...HERSELF.
WHY ASK ABOUT THIS ALL OF A SUDDEN?
ARE YOU GONNA TELL SOMEONE YOUR FEELINGS?
WHAK
Ah.
HUH?
WHAT ARE YOU TALKING ABOUT?! NO WAY!
LIKE WHO?
I'M KID-DING...
MR. ARAI?

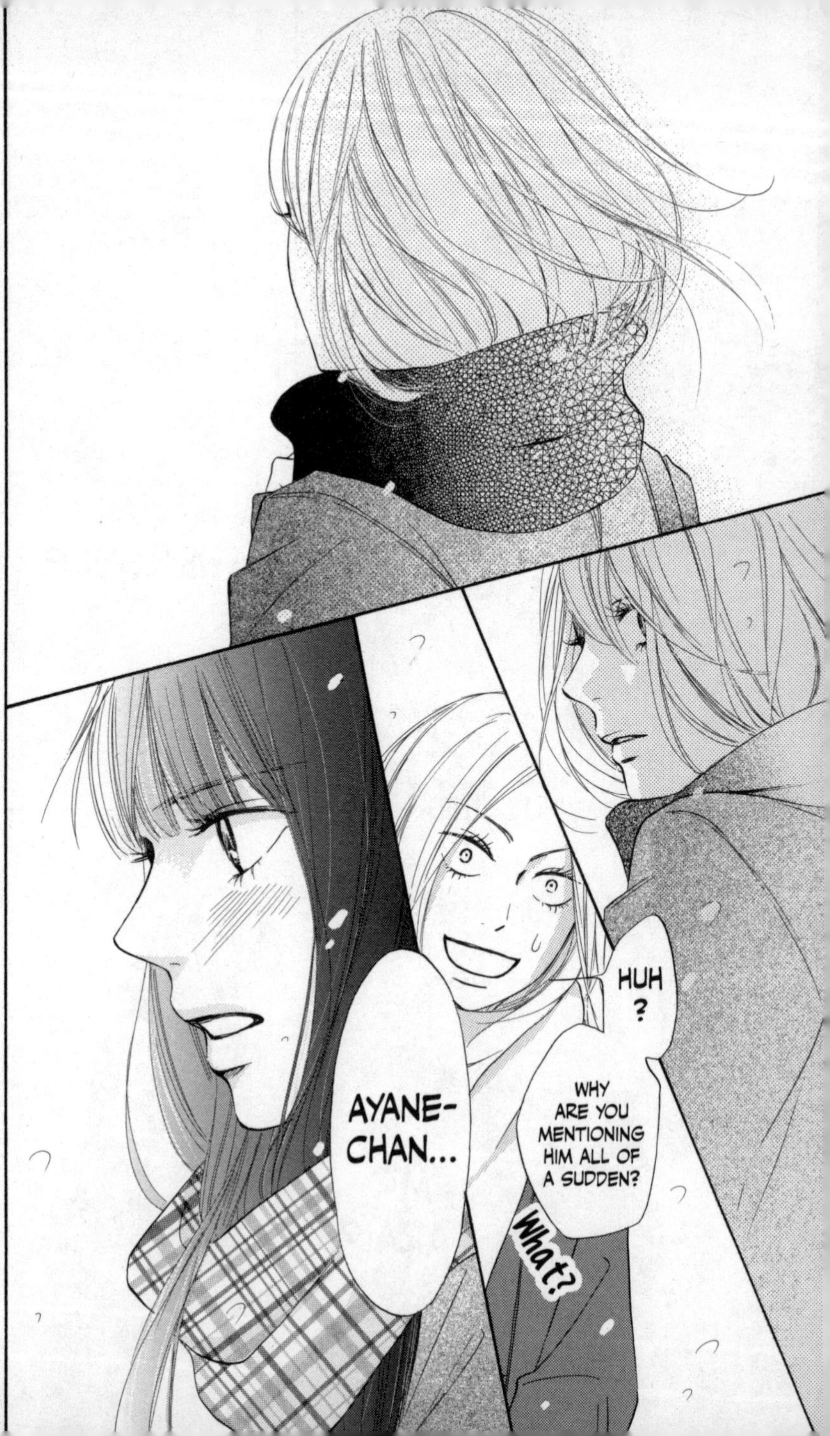
HUH?
WHY ARE YOU MENTIONING HIM ALL OF A SUDDEN?
What?
AYANE-CHAN...

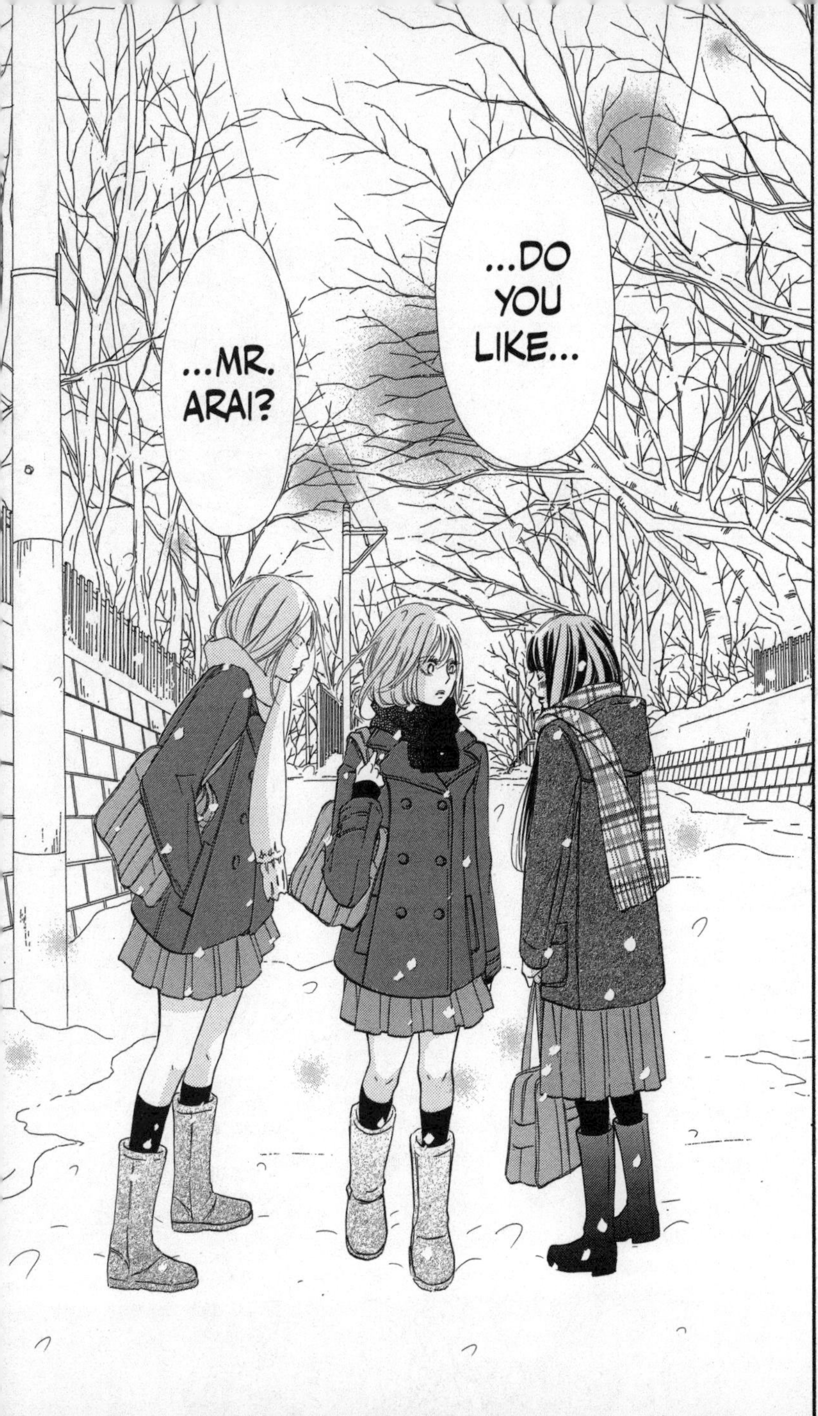
...DO YOU LIKE...
...MR. ARAI?

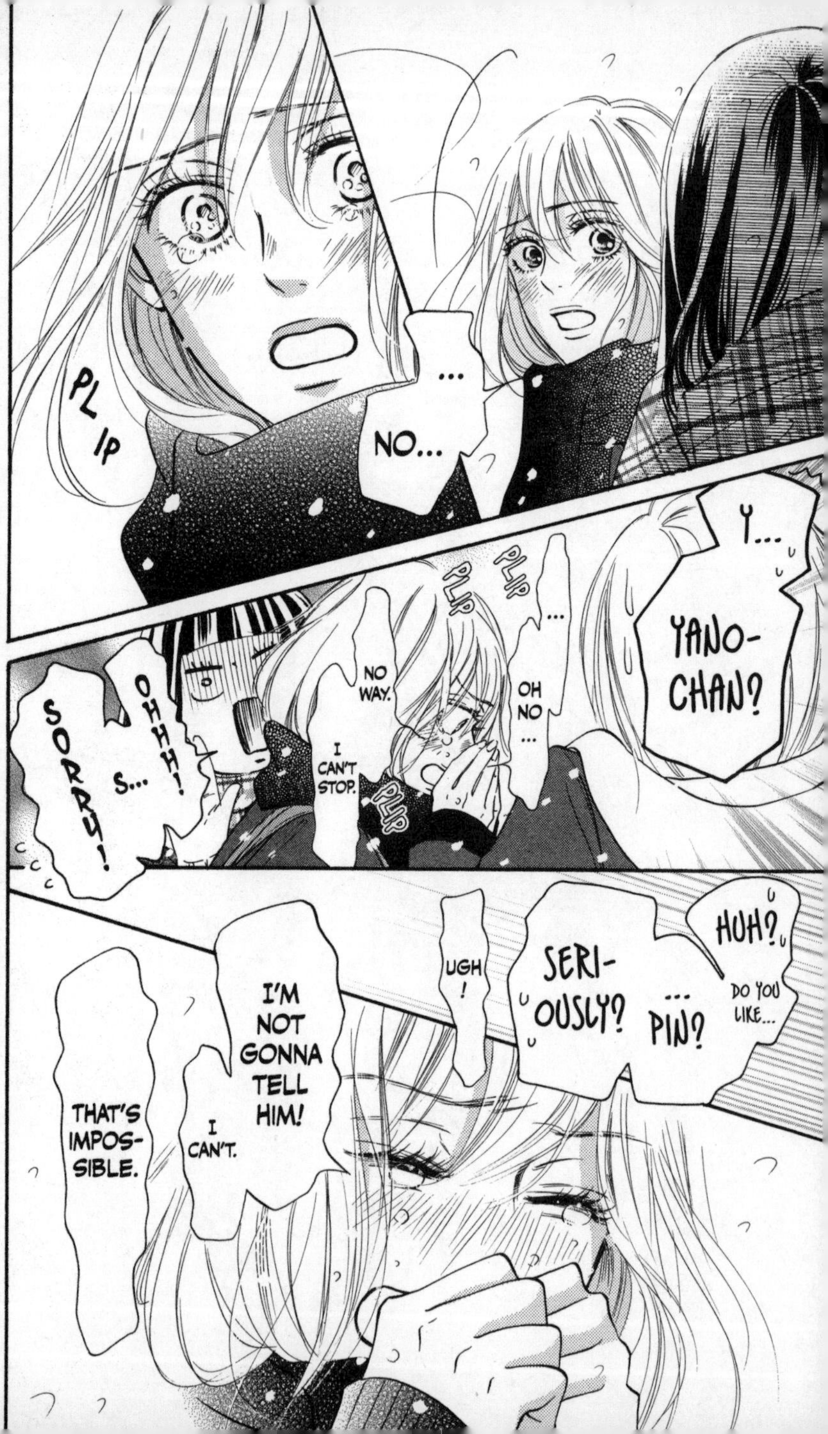
...
NO...
PLIP
Y...
YANO-CHAN?
...
OH NO...
PLIP PLIP
NO WAY.
I CAN'T STOP.
PLIP
OHHH!
S...
SORRY!
HUH?
DO YOU LIKE...
... PIN?
SERI-OUSLY?
UGH!
I'M NOT GONNA TELL HIM!
I CAN'T.
THAT'S IMPOS-SIBLE.

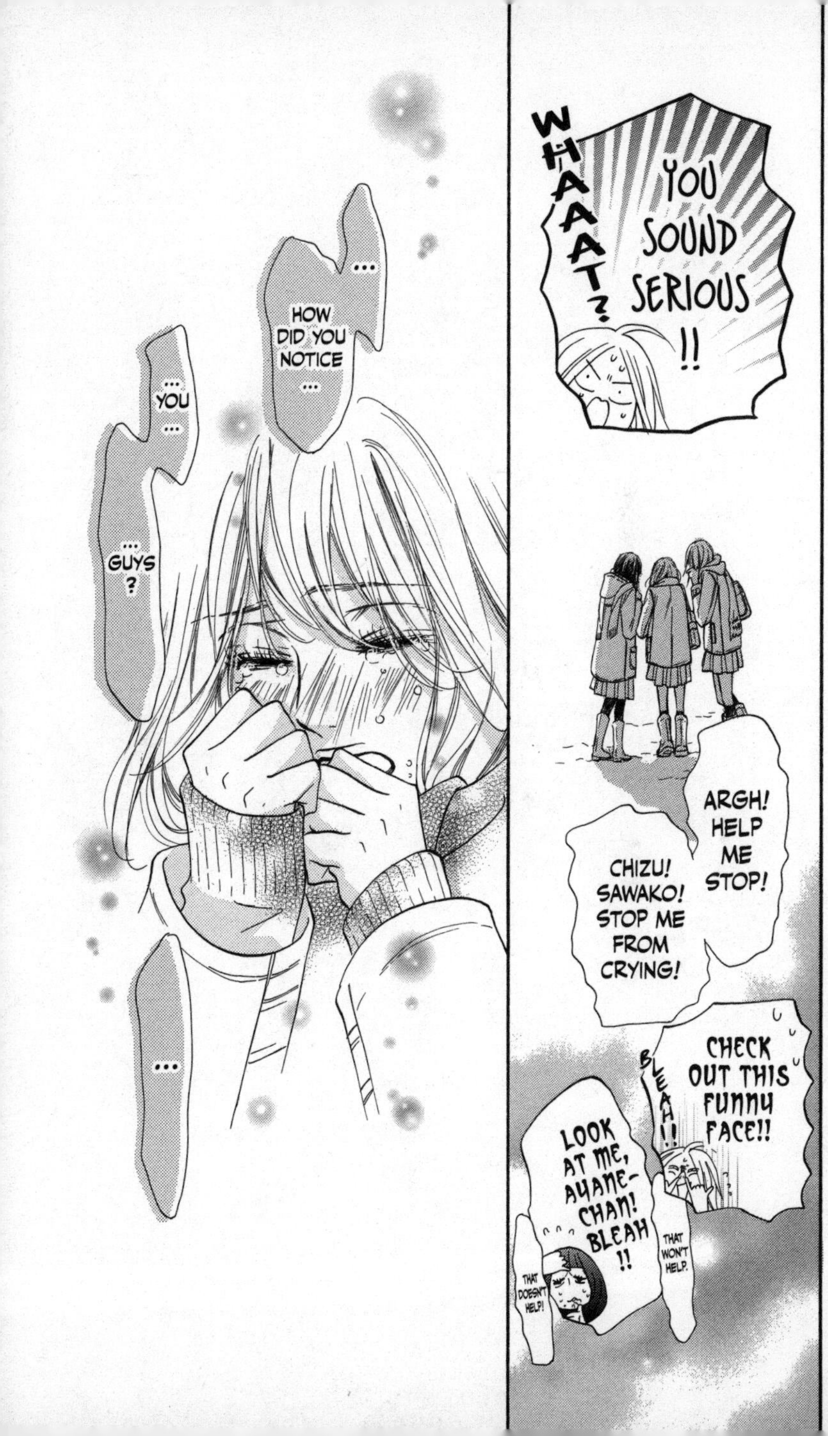
YOU SOUND SERIOUS!!
WHAAAT?
ARGH! HELP ME STOP!
CHIZU! SAWAKO! STOP ME FROM CRYING!
CHECK OUT THIS FUNNY FACE!!
BLEAH!!
LOOK AT ME, AYANE-CHAN! BLEAH!!
THAT WON'T HELP.
THAT DOESN'T HELP!
...
HOW DID YOU NOTICE...
...YOU...
...GUYS?
...

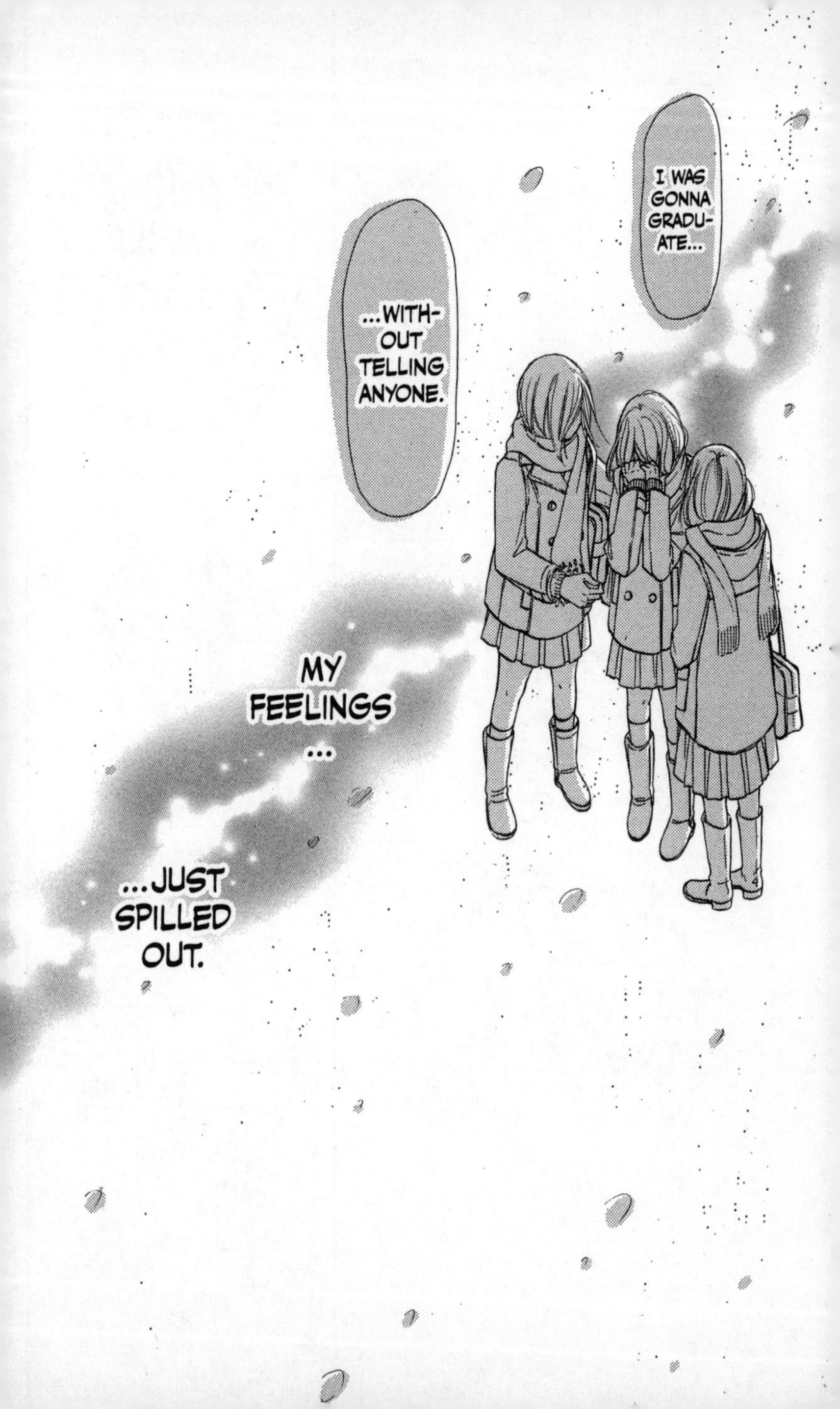
I WAS GONNA GRADU-ATE...
...WITH-OUT TELLING ANYONE.
MY FEELINGS...
...JUST SPILLED OUT.

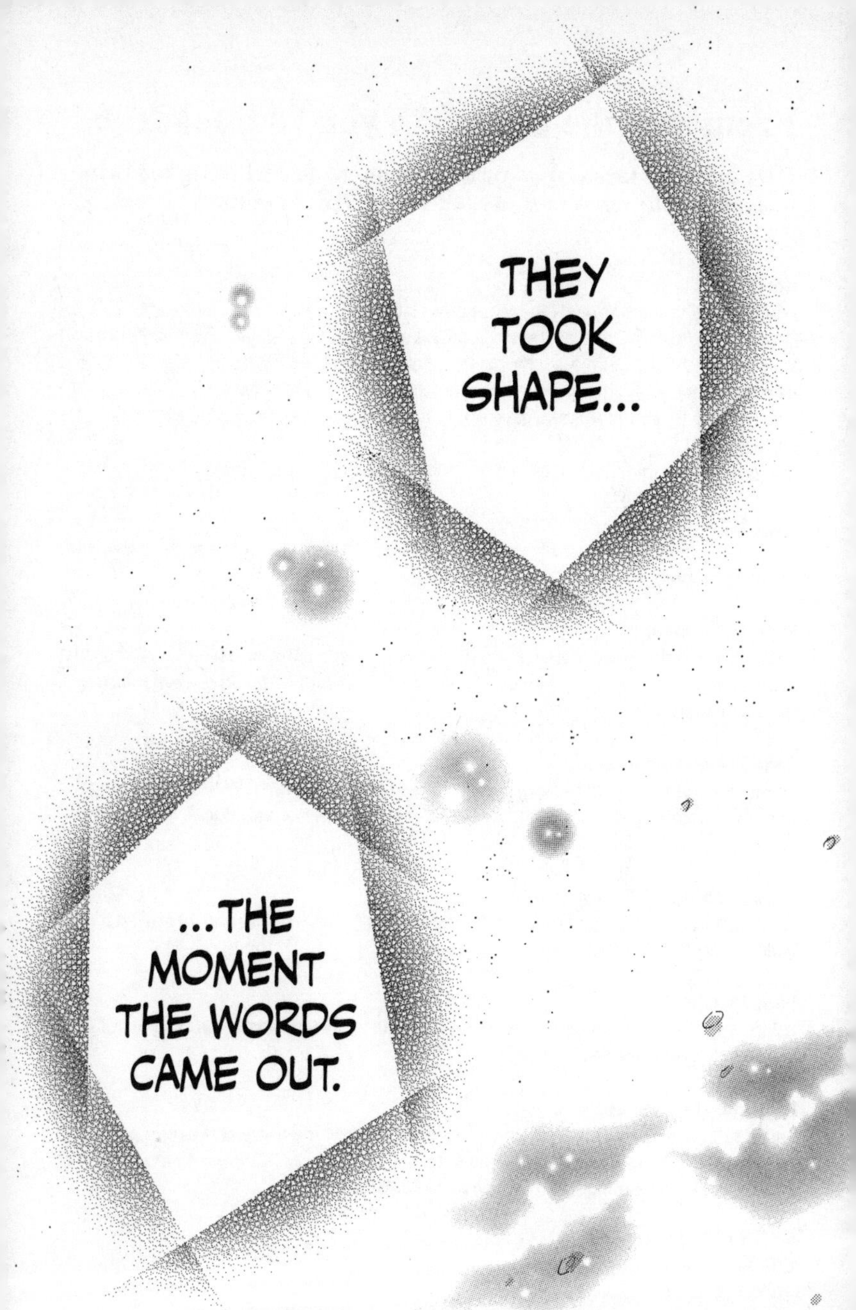
THEY TOOK SHAPE...
...THE MOMENT THE WORDS CAME OUT.

Vol. 27 End

From me (the editor) to you (the reader).

Here are some Japanese culture explanations that will help you better understand the references in the *Kimi ni Todoke* world.

Honorifics:
When saying someone's name in Japanese, a suffix is often attached to indicate how familiar the speaker is with the person. Some are more polite and respectful, while others are endearing. Calling someone by just their first name is the most informal.
-*kun* is used for young men or boys, usually someone you are familiar with.
-*chan* is used for young women, girls or young children and can be used as a term of endearment.
-*san* is used for someone you respect or are not close to, or to be polite.

Page 9, Onee-chan:
This literally means "older sister" and is an honorific suffix that can be used to address girls or young women.

Page 18, Ice Manju:
Manju is a traditional Japanese confection with an outer coating and sweet azuki bean filling. Manju comes in many forms in Japan. Kazehaya's father's favorite, Ice Manju, is served as a popsicle.

Page 22, *Taiko no Tatsujin*:
The title of a video game that translates to "Drum Master." Sawako doesn't understand that Tota is referring to a game and thinks he wants to practice traditional Japanese drums.

Page 60, "Shota Kazehaya" kanji:
Each version of "Shota" here uses a different kanji for "Sho." Far right: Sho = Fly (Kazehaya's spelling); Middle: Sho = Victory; Left: Sho = General.

Page 84, Obon:
A Japanese Buddhist festival that honors the spirits of one's ancestors. Obon generally takes place over three days in August.

Page 106–110, cemetery markers:
Called *sotoba,* these vertical wooden grave markers carry the name of the deceased along with a prayer. The haunted-house sotoba shown here read "*Namu Amida Butsu,*" a Buddhist prayer meaning "I entrust myself to Buddha."

Page 139, Kokkuri:
A Japanese spirit-summoning game resembling a Ouija board.

Page 164, kotatsu:
A low table, common in Japan, with an attached heater and blanket.

When the season in the story is different from the season in reality, it's a little hard to express the feeling of that season. I guess it's easy to forget a season once it passes! Or maybe other people don't forget? Am I the only forgetful one? Anyway... the real seasons usually catch up to the season in the story pretty quickly.
Ha ha ha...

--Karuho Shiina

Karuho Shiina was born and raised in Hokkaido, Japan. Though *Kimi ni Todoke* is only her second series following many one-shot stories, it has already racked up accolades from various "Best Manga of the Year" lists. Winner of the 2008 Kodansha Manga Award for the shojo category, *Kimi ni Todoke* also placed fifth in the first-ever Manga Taisho (Cartoon Grand Prize) contest in 2008. In Japan, an animated TV series debuted in October 2009, and a live-action film was released in 2010.

Kimi ni Todoke
VOL. 27

Shojo Beat Edition

STORY AND ART BY
KARUHO SHIINA

Translation/Ari Yasuda, HC Language Solutions, Inc.
Touch-up Art & Lettering/Vanessa Satone
Design/Nozomi Akashi
Editor/Megan Bates

KIMI NI TODOKE © 2005 by Karuho Shiina
All rights reserved. First published in Japan in 2005 by SHUEISHA Inc.,
Tokyo. English translation rights arranged by SHUEISHA Inc.

The stories, characters and incidents mentioned
in this publication are entirely fictional.

Printed in the U.S.A.

Published by VIZ Media, LLC
P.O. Box 77010
San Francisco, CA 94107

10 9 8 7 6 5 4 3 2 1
First printing, September 2017

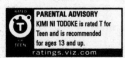

Honey
So Sweet

Story and Art by *Amu Meguro*

Little did Nao Kogure realize back in middle school that when she left an umbrella and a box of bandages in the rain for injured delinquent Taiga Onise that she would meet him again in high school. Nao wants nothing to do with the gruff and frightening Taiga, but he suddenly presents her with a huge bouquet of flowers and asks her to date him—with marriage in mind! Is Taiga really so scary, or is he a sweetheart in disguise?

RATED T FOR TEEN

ratings.viz.com

viz media

viz.com

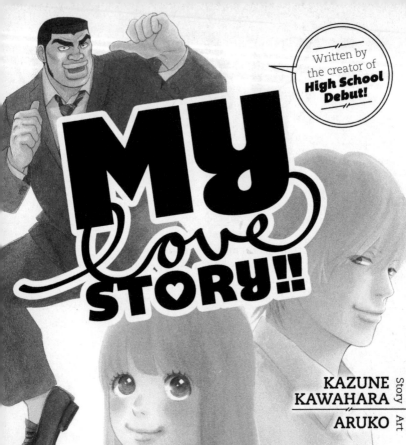

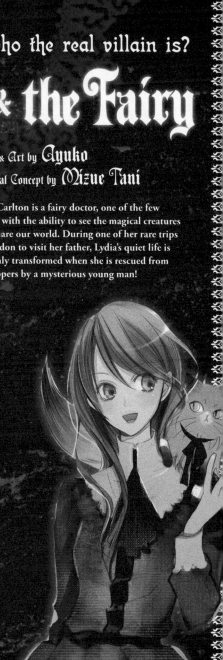

Surprise!

You may be reading the wrong way!

It's true: In keeping with the original Japanese comic format, this book reads from right to left—so action, sound effects, and word balloons are completely reversed. This preserves the orientation of the original artwork—plus, it's fun! Check out the diagram shown here to get the hang of things, and then turn to the other side of the book to get started!

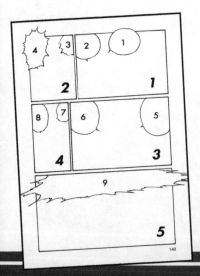